Pharmageddon

Pharmageddon

David Healy

UNIVERSITY OF CALIFORNIA PRESS
Berkeley · Los Angeles

University of California Press, one of the most
distinguished university presses in the United States,
enriches lives around the world by advancing
scholarship in the humanities, social sciences, and
natural sciences. Its activities are supported by the UC
Press Foundation and by philanthropic contributions
from individuals and institutions. For more
information, visit www.ucpress.edu.

University of California Press
Berkeley and Los Angeles, California

Library of Congress Cataloging-in-Publication Data

Healy, David, MRC Psych.
    Pharmageddon / David Healy.
        p. cm.
    Includes bibliographical references and index.
    ISBN 978–0-520–27098-5 (cloth : alk. paper)
    [DNLM: 1. Drug Industry.   2. Drug Utilization.   QV
736].   I. Title.
    LC-classification not assigned
    338.4′76153—dc23

                                          2011026063

Manufactured in the United States of America

20 19 18 17 16 15 14 13 12
10 9 8 7 6 5 4 3 2

In keeping with a commitment to support
environmentally responsible and sustainable printing
practices, UC Press has printed this book on Rolland
Enviro100, a 100% post-consumer fiber paper that
is FSC certified, deinked, processed chlorine-free,
and manufactured with renewable biogas energy.
It is acid-free and EcoLogo certified.

For over fifteen years I have been involved in cases linked to injuries on drug treatment. This book is for those who have survived to pass their stories on, for the families who have been left behind, and especially for those who have struggled to put things right.

When she was a child I read Exodus
To my daughter   'The children of Israel . . . '

Pillar of fire
Pillar of cloud

We stared at the end
Into each other's eyes   Where
She said hushed

Were the adults

—George Oppen, "Exodus"

The new wood as old as carpentry

Rounding the far buoy, wild
Steel fighting in the sea, carpenter,

Carpenter
Carpenter and other things, the monstrous welded seams

Plunge and drip in the seas, carpenter,
Carpenter, how wild the planet is.

—George Oppen, "Carpenter's Boat"

Contents

Acknowledgments

I have accumulated so many debts it would take an ocean-going liner to accommodate everyone who should be acknowledged. Some of those to whom I am most indebted have been critics, a number of whom over the last decade have held open a forum for debate in which I've been able to test and discard ideas. Ocean-going liners have luxuries like showers and bidets. Over the past year I've given lectures on the subject matter of this book in several North American settings under the informal title of "The Shower and Bidet Approach to Medical Care," as well as in Oslo, Uppsala, Bruxelles, Gent, and Milan, and I have Andy Scull, Joel Braslow, Ned Shorter, Cindy Hall, David Antonuccio, Masumi Minaguchi, Tom Ban, and others to thank for this, and much else. Joanna Le Noury, Margaret Harris, Stef Linden, Tony Roberts, and other colleagues in North Wales have helped supply the data for many of these talks.

It takes a lot to divert an ocean-going liner off course. Not so for a carpenter's boat like George Oppen's, where staying within the harbor walls seems advisable. There is a much smaller number of people to whom I owe particular debts who might fit on such a boat. These include Charles Medawar, Andrew Herxheimer, Vera Sharav, Annemarie Mol, Steve Lanes, Kal Applbaum, and Dee Mangin, who will see the beams they have contributed here but may feel they have been monstrously welded to the wrong seams, in which case they more than anyone are likely to turn green at the gills once the boat ventures out beyond the harbor mouth.

Far from getting outside the harbor, at one point it looked like the boat would never float, but Jonathan Cobb came to the rescue through wonderful editing. Rather magically he showed me how to write the book I thought I'd written. Bev Slopen, my agent, and Hannah Love, my editor, have also had to keep faith through some tricky moments. And finally Sarah, Helen, and Justin have had to put up with a lot, including "sibling" rivalry.

Introduction

My father smoked all his adult life. He had a number of physical disorders, including ulcerative colitis, ironically one of the few conditions for which smoking is beneficial. In 1974, when he was in hospital for colitis, a routine chest X-ray revealed a shadow on his lung. Dr. Neligan, the surgeon called in, advised my mother on the importance of an operation.

Our general practitioner at the time was Dr. Lapin, whom I remembered from childhood as being tall, silver-haired, and distinguished, often wearing a bow tie. He had spent time, I was told, as a doctor in the British army, a very unusual occurrence then in Ireland. To a child, Dr. Lapin had appeared effortlessly wise and seemed to transcend the boundaries of religion, politics, and division I saw elsewhere.

When my mother developed problems in the early 1960s after giving birth, Dr. Lapin had suggested she come to see him once a week, but at the time she felt the arrangement was too open-ended, and she could not afford it. She was seen instead by another doctor, diagnosed with an ulcer and ultimately received the standard operation of the day, which involved cutting the vagus nerve and partial removal of stomach. This left her with bowel problems for the rest of her life, and regrets for not having taken Dr. Lapin's offer of treatment for what she later regarded as postnatal depression.

When my mother consulted him about the wisdom of an operation for my father, Dr. Lapin was slow to comment. But when pressed, he pointed out that my father had a number of illnesses, any of which could kill him before the tumor would. Many people, he said, went to their graves with cancers, heart disease, or other problems, but these were not what killed them. An operation would take a heavy toll on him.

My mother relayed this perspective to my father and suggested that he take six months to build himself up and then have an operation if he felt stronger; he agreed. When this plan was mentioned to the surgeon, he responded, "That's fine, but have him out of the hospital within 48 hours." When my mother revealed that my father still didn't know he had a cancer, the surgeon went straight from the phone to tell him. Without an operation my father would be dead within months, Dr. Neligan indicated, but an operation offered the prospect of a cure. My father, alarmed, agreed and the operation took place two days later. Dr. Neligan afterwards said there was little they could do about my father's tumor when they opened him up. He died six months later, his life almost certainly shortened by the operation.

If there had been progress to speak of in the treatment of lung cancer in the years since my father's death, his medical care might be viewed as one of those sacrifices that at least ultimately benefits others. But there has been little progress, even though advances on almost all medical fronts are trumpeted daily. Genuine progress has been made in some areas, but far less in most areas than many people have been led to believe. More importantly, when it comes to pharmaceuticals in particular, many of these apparent advances underpin and contribute to what in recent decades has become a relentless degradation in medical *care,* a replacement of Lapins with Neligans, a quickening march toward Pharmageddon. While drugs played no part in what happened to my father, they have played a huge role in fostering a surgical attitude to medical care, a kind of fast healthcare.

My father's illness came just as I entered medicine, seventy years after a momentous change in Western clinical practice. Around 1900, a series of new diagnostic measures, some based on blood tests, others linked to X-rays, and yet others involving the culture of sputum or urine samples for bacteria, enabled physicians to distinguish among many diseases and find remedies for some of them. Before this, the diagnosis patients got was based on how they looked and what they said about themselves when they walked through the door of a doctor's office—if they were weak and tired, they had "debility"; if they were wasting, they had "consumption." If they were diagnosed with a tumor, it was because it was visible or could be felt; if they had diabetes, it was because their urine had a distinctive smell. With the development of new tests, however, the diagnosis only came after a blood test or X-ray confirmed what was wrong, perhaps weeks after the visit to a doctor's office or admission to hospital. And the tests revealed new conditions such as heart attacks and duodenal ulcers. Among the states of consumption, it became clear some stemmed from tuberculosis, while others did not.

A new breed of physician and hospital emerged. In Boston, Richard Cabot was celebrated for his diagnostic acumen, and the reputation of Massachusetts General Hospital in the early decades of the twentieth century began to soar on the abilities of its physicians, aided by their new technologies, to get the diagnosis right, which, it was presumed, would lead to better medical care. But others were concerned. Alfred Worcester, a professor of hygiene and prominent Massachusetts physician, who was later lauded as a father of both modern geriatrics[1] and palliative care,[2] lamented that "the demands of modern diagnosis diverted doctors away from developing and exercising their traditional knowledge of human nature." Worcester was troubled that the new testing requirements for making a diagnosis would alter a doctor's interactions with his patients. Absorbed in the new technologies, doctors would lose their ability to have an ongoing therapeutic influence over their patients.[3]

Good medical care, we might imagine, should manage to embrace the visions of both Cabot and Worcester. The new techniques after all made a great difference in our ability to help patients, and while humane medical care is wonderful, most people would regard a cure as excellent care even if they don't much like the doctor. Patients in the early twentieth century voted with their feet and sought out the new generation of specialists. But as my father's case illustrates all too vividly, there is a balance to be sought between caring and attempts at curing, and this balance is particularly important in the many instances where cures aren't possible.

Early concerns that medicine might lose its caring soul in exchange for earthly cures were sidelined in the 1940s and 1950s when a host of new life-saving treatments came onstream. While there were also great surgical advances, culminating in the dramas of the first kidney and heart transplants, the key breakthroughs occurred in the pharmaceutical domain. In addition to offering cures in their own right, new drugs like the immunosuppressants and antibiotics laid a basis for developments in surgery and other areas of medicine.

Despite these wonderful breakthroughs–indeed, some critics thought in part because of them–concerns about medical specialism reemerged in the 1960s framed in terms of medicalization. Concerned observers argued that we were ceding too much power to a medical establishment engaged in pathologizing huge swathes of daily life and not equipped to take it upon themselves to define what it meant to be human. The most powerful critique of medicalization came from the Austrian philosopher, Ivan Illich, in his book *Medical Nemesis*,[4] published in 1975, the year my father died.

In retrospect, the mid-1970s can be seen as close to the acme of medicine's ascendancy. The pharmaceutical industry was still at this point a junior partner to the medical establishment. But as roles have shifted and the power of drug companies has become more apparent, references to medicalization since the mid-2000s have begun to be replaced by references to pharmaceuticalization, which increasingly sees our identities as a series of behaviors to be managed by drug use.

Then in 2007, Charles Medawar, Great Britain's leading healthcare consumer advocate, raised the prospect of something beyond pharmaceuticalization: "I fear that we are heading blindly in the direction of Pharmageddon. Pharmageddon is a gold-standard paradox: individually we benefit from some wonderful medicines while, collectively, we are losing sight and sense of health. By analogy, think of the relationship between a car journey and climate change—they are inextricably linked, but probably not remotely connected in the driver's mind. Just as climate change seems inconceivable as a journey outcome, so the notion of Pharmageddon is flatly contradicted by most personal experience of medicines."[5]

By "Pharmageddon," what Medawar and colleagues (myself included) had in mind was something quite different than a simple pharmaceuticalization, where we talk about our neurotransmitters rather than our moods, a biological reduction of secularism.[6] Pharmageddon refers not to a change in the language of medicine or a change from religious to biological language, but to a process that was deployed in the first instance in the belief that it would better enable us to care for each other, though now it is a process that seems set to eliminate our abilities to care—a fate that beckons in spite of what everyone wants. At the heart of this process is the turn toward quantification in the middle years of the twentieth century. While genuinely helpful, this turn gave healthcare a set of scientific appearances that a handful of shrewd advisors and marketers have been able to manipulate to infect our abilities to care as if with a clinical immuno-deficiency virus (CIV). As a result the defense reactions that we might expect from prestigious journals and professional bodies just don't happen. Indeed the virus seems to have been able to subvert these bodies to its own purposes, so that when critical comments are raised they have reacted almost as though it was their programmed duty to shield a few fragile companies from the malignant attentions of a pharmaco-vigilante.

PHARMAGEDDON UNFOLDING

Since the 1970s, a profound change has been occurring both in the nature of the drugs marketed and in the practice of medicine. New drugs, like the statins, have continued to appear as have new diagnostic tests to measure, for instance, our cholesterol levels, apparently in the tradition of testing that led to so many medical advances in the early twentieth century. But where previous drugs and tests were geared toward the diagnosis and cure of diseases that posed an imminent risk to life, now medical practice is increasingly geared to chronic disease management with drugs that modify risk and lifestyle factors rather than save lives. This is a post-Worcester and post-Cabot world, in which pharmaceutical companies sell diseases rather than cures.

On the surface medical practice appears the same but underneath it's not. For instance, a small number of people have a genetic disorder that leads to excessively high cholesterol levels and for them drugs like the statins can save lives, almost in the way that antibiotics or insulin saved lives half a century ago. The statins can also save lives among people who have had strokes or heart attacks and who also smoke or are overweight, but in this case hundreds of people have to be persuaded to take them for the rest of their lives in order for a handful among them to be saved. For the most part, however, the statins are instead given to healthy people who have mild elevations of their cholesterol levels. Similarly, treatments for asthma or osteoporosis are now given to many people who would never have been diagnosed and treated before. Treatment happens now in response to results on a series of tests that have emerged in recent years—but these new tests don't help make a diagnosis that will lift a threat to our lives. Instead they effectively make a diagnosis of some drug deficiency disorder, and they often enter medical practice as part of the marketing strategy for a new drug.

These new diseases and their treatments have gained a purchase on us because they are presumed to represent the latest advances in a story of progress that runs through insulin and the antibiotics and will hopefully lead someday to cures for cancer. These are the drugs that, had they been available, some presume might have saved many of my father's generation. But far from saving either their lives or ours, clinical trials show that the indiscriminate use of drugs to lower lipids or blood sugars, to relieve respiratory wheeze, or to block stress hormones may even increase the risk of loss of life,[7] and appear to be doing so in the United States, the country that makes the greatest use of the latest pharmaceuticals, where since the mid-1970s life expectancy has been falling progressively further behind other developed countries.[8]

If you looked around a restaurant, cinema, or office thirty or forty years ago that had a hundred or more people in it, you could predict that 5 to 10 percent of them might have a medical condition—sometimes unbeknownst to themselves—and a trained doctor would have been able to spot many of them just by looking. If you look around the same restaurant or office now at the apparently healthy people, those a doctor can't readily spot as ill, chances are that 80 to 90 percent of them could be diagnosed with one of these new "disorders." Almost all will have cholesterol, blood sugar, blood pressure, bone density, or asthma numbers or one of an ever growing number of "mental health disorders" for which a pill will be suggested. Unlike being diagnosed with a traditional medical illness, these people won't be diagnosed because they are suffering and take themselves to a doctor. They will be diagnosed because an apparatus will come to them, perhaps coincidentally when they are at their doctor's for something else, or perhaps soon to a supermarket near them, an apparatus that will show them that their "numbers" are not quite right. It is only then that they will begin to suffer, either because of their discomfort and fear following a diagnosis or by virtue of the very real side effects triggered by the new pill they have been put on, a pill which has been marketed as an answer for any of us whose numbers aren't quite right.

Recent books have attempted to diagnose what lies at the heart of our growing disquiet at what is happening to medical care.[9] These critical studies almost universally blame the pharmaceutical companies, who are now among the most profitable corporations on the planet and who, due to grossly inflated estimates of drug development costs and the emergence of blockbusters—drugs that gross at least a billion dollars per year—are supposedly making too much money. This money lets them buy lobbyists and influence, do a variety of things to turn the heads of doctors, as well as sponsor patient groups to lobby against attempts to limit in any way access to the latest high-cost treatments.

While making many excellent points and calling for action to tackle the problems the pharmaceutical industry poses, these concerned critics, largely from the medical profession, typically portray medicine itself as fundamentally healthy. The serenity of these physicians stems from their perception that, in contrast to an earlier time, medicine is now secure behind the ramparts of science. This science is not the laboratory science that emerged at the turn of the century with doctors like Richard Cabot but rather a science of randomized controlled trials (RCTs) that stems from the 1950s. In these trials new drugs are pitted against dummy pills, or placebos, and it is only if the new drug "wins" that it is allowed into use.

These trials have laid the basis for what has come to be called "evidence-based medicine." The results of RCT trials are also incorporated into evidence-based guidelines for the treatment of different diseases, and these guidelines, when embraced by particular agencies, constrain the prescriptions doctors can write. Many professionals involved in healthcare see such guidelines as keeping doctors within a straight and narrow path of therapeutic virtue, whatever the blandishments of pharmaceutical or medical equipment companies. Few suspect, as I will argue in chapters 5 and 6, that these guidelines in fact hand medicine over to the drug industry. Insofar as evidence-based medicine means that doctors stick to treatments that "work" and eliminate those that don't, many professionals involved in healthcare see it as offering the only possible basis for a universal healthcare system, if such a system were wanted. But as currently practiced, evidence-based medicine tolls a death-knell for the possibility of universal healthcare in the United States or its continued existence elsewhere.

Aware that something is wrong, we cast around for a villain and often settle on the insurance companies or other third party payers for our current woes. While many grievances against insurance companies are legitimate, they too have a diminishing grip on the healthcare agenda. Because only the drugs and the style of care that goes with them have been proven to work, insurance companies are trapped into reimbursing for these treatments and in the case of hospital stays often only for periods of time that permit little more than the institution of a drug treatment regimen. In doing this they are just following the guidelines drawn up on the basis of the best evidence by medical academics with no links to industry, guidelines that typically endorse the latest high-cost treatments over more effective, cheaper, and more humane forms of care.

The medical establishment, aware of problems in their interface with the pharmaceutical industry but not sure of the source of those problems, increasingly concedes there are senior figures and other opinion leaders in the field who have overly close links with the pharmaceutical industry or other conflicts of interest. But these academics are seen simply as the rotten apples that can be found in any barrel and the assumption is that their behavior will soon be put right by new rules on disclosure of links to pharmaceutical companies.

There is also an acknowledgment that pretty well all the trials that a new drug has to go through for approval are designed, and implemented, by pharmaceutical companies, and a growing awareness that rather than being written up in journals by the academics whose names appear on their authorship line, these papers have commonly been "ghostwritten." But for most commentators these are simply more reasons to rein in the pharmaceutical industry, rather than reasons to consider the need for more far-reaching changes such as the nature of our current patents on drugs or the prescription-only status of many drugs, or for a close look at how these ghostwriting and other practices, as laid out in chapters 4 and 5, compromise clinical care itself.

Criticizing success is not a winning formula. In a market economy what company is going to try to be less successful? The door is left wide open for pharmaceutical companies to argue that the reason there are so many medical care problems is that the rest of the healthcare economy has not fully embraced the market.[10] The argument is so seductive that even left-leaning commentators, whether in the United States or Europe, concede some validity to proposals that the way forward in health must involve some embrace of the market.[11]

For the pharmaceutical industry, attacks from the medical community have turned into a version of rope-a-dope. Muhammad Ali-like, they let the medical George Foremans punch themselves out on issues like conflict of interest, the sponsoring of patient groups, and ghostwriting. Industry is happy to settle back on the ropes and take the punishment.

I will argue that the problems that give rise to attacks from the medical community and other commentators stem from three sources not acknowledged elsewhere. First, at the start of the modern era of medical practice, in the 1950s, the basis on which drugs are patented was changed, allowing companies to have monopolies on drugs in a way they hadn't had before. This permitted the development of blockbuster drugs, laying the basis for the marketing of drugs we now see. Second, also in the 1950s these drugs were made available on a prescription-only basis, putting a relatively small group of people with no training in or awareness of marketing techniques—doctors—in the gun sights of the most sophisticated marketing machinery on the planet. Third, having been under siege by industry for a century, in the 1960s we in medicine woke up to find a horse outside the gates of Troy in the shape of controlled trials and hauled it inside, not realizing that industry-designed trials provide wonderful evidence about the benefits of drugs but very little evidence of what might be best for patients.

Against this background, discussions of conflict of interest and ghostwriting, while important, only scratch the surface. We need to ask whether faith in controlled trials when we are not allowed to see the data from those trials can protect us against the biases introduced by commerce. Whether making drugs available on prescription-only status is appropriate in an age of blockbuster drugs. Whether the basis on which we now permit drugs to be patented is delivering the benefits to society that patents were originally designed to provide. As I will argue, every assault on industry paradoxically has instead reinforced the apparent need for controlled trials, prescription-only privileges, product patents, and further regulatory arrangements, and together these have bound the medical profession and government ever tighter to the pharmaceutical industry. These are the changes that among them laid the basis for companies to create blockbusters, and as long as these changes remain unquestioned industry is happy to settle back on the ropes and take a pounding.

At times of change, there is a temptation to extol the virtues of some former golden age. But while the dogs may bark, the caravan invariably moves on. Generations of us have put our faith and the lives of those we love in the hands of doctors offering the latest in medical developments. Progress may be slow in many areas, but when it comes to life, death, and disability most of us—like my father—will opt for those who offer us hope however slender the odds may be. Up till now, we have been correct to do so. Is there a reason to think an author raising the prospect of Pharmageddon should detain us any more than concerned critics from Alfred Worcester to Ivan Illich have done in the past? Can the best critique do anything other than ask us to give up hope?

Worcester, Illich, and others talked about losing our humanity and our ability to care. In part these critiques failed, even though no one wants to lose their humanity or ability to care, because there were no specifics about what it means to care nor how to recognize the moment at which our humanity is threatened. In part they failed because until recently, whatever the drawbacks to developments, there was little doubt that life expectancies were increasing. All this is now changing. We are in a world where increasingly we need protection from the latest miracle cure to ensure we do not die prematurely.

It would never be good care to withhold a cure. But traditional medical wisdom as practiced by Worcester to my father's doctor, Dr. Lapin, stressed the quintessential importance of being able to recognize when a treatment might make things worse rather than better. This philosophy was best expressed two hundred years ago by Philippe Pinel, a doctor looking after the mentally ill in Paris in the midst of the French Revolution: "It is an art of no little importance to administer medicines properly," he said, "but it is an art of much greater and more difficult acquisition to know when to suspend or altogether to omit them."[12]

Cures almost by definition should lead to a fall in drug consumption, and good medical care as defined by Pinel should too. But instead we have seen an astonishing and relentless increase in the sale of supposed panaceas that do little or nothing to save lives or significantly improve their quality. The consumption of blockbuster drugs has grown from 6 percent of the pharmaceutical market in 1991 to 45 percent in 2006,[13] with the top ten drugs accounting for $60 billion in annual sales.[14] Where once the pharmaceutical industry made its money from drugs that cured, the big money now lies in marketing chronic diseases for which the current best-selling drugs in medicine offer little benefit. We are quite literally taking pills to save the lives of companies who have a greater interest in the vitality of the diseases they market drugs for than in our well-being. The only historical parallel we have here is the flourishing of patent or proprietary medicines in the late nineteenth and early twentieth centuries.

In 2010 the global market for pharmaceuticals was worth over $900 billion, more than the government bailout of the US economy following the 2008 financial crisis. Half of this came from sales within the United States and almost all came from treatments for chronic disease management rather than for life-saving treatments. Aside from treatments for cancer, in the global market for pharmaceuticals that year the best sellers were the antidepressants, mood stabilizers, and other central nervous system drugs ($50 billion), followed by the cholesterol-lowering statins ($34 billion), which along with other drugs for cardiovascular disorders were part of a $105 billion market, proton-pump inhibitors for acid reflux ($26 billion), the blood-sugar-lowering hypoglycemics ($24 billion), treatments for asthma like Advair (alone worth close to

$8 billion), treatments for osteoporosis, and drugs like Viagra for sexual functioning.[15]

These celebrity or blockbuster drugs have been showing growth in sales of 10 to 20 percent per annum worldwide; they grew even during the financial crisis. Once the markets in China and India come fully into play the profits can only grow larger, likely doubling. The markup on these drugs is on the order of several thousand percent, so they are now worth more than their weight in gold. There simply are no other goods in any other part of the economy that produce returns like these, and the profit margins of the companies that produce them far outstrip those of any other companies.

If this outlay of money saved our lives or restored productivity it would be readily justifiable, but in most cases when doctors talk about lowering our cholesterol levels with a statin they are not treating a disease, they are talking about risk management. They are not talking about saving our life but giving us a treatment for life. The statin prescribed for us may lower our cholesterol levels, but of even greater importance is the marketing by pharmaceutical companies that has changed both the doctors' and our perceptions so that lowering cholesterol has come to seem as important as treating a disease like tuberculosis.

This marketing is moving us steadily from what was the practice of medicine to a healthcare products limited market, and indeed not just a market but the creation of a new healthcare universe—a universe where the focus has shifted from medicine, in which progress occurred slowly but patients benefited, to a healthcare products market in which science and progress have become marketing terms and where benefits accrue to companies even while patients suffer harm.

It is easy to say that in the process we are poisoning our abilities to care. But what is care and where is the evidence that it is being poisoned? Care is what doctors bring to patients afflicted by something that threatens to take their life or leave them disabled. The ideal care will involve a cure. But what if the threat of disability and death comes from a treatment? Drug-induced injuries are now the fourth leading cause of death in hospital settings. They are possibly the greatest single source of disability in the developed world. The cost of drugs is often picked out in debates about the rising cost of healthcare, but healthcare providers spend more on remedying treatment-induced health problems than they do on drugs without any apparent effort to staunch this hemorrhage of lives or money. Why should this be? If we turn to the evidence base to care for and ideally cure this new disorder afflicting us, we find there is none—no guidelines, no studies, but instead close to a blanket dismissal of any evidence that things could be going wrong.

When it comes to care, the billions of dollars wrapped up in pharmaceutical sales only tell part of the story. Until recently in medicine there was vigorous debate on the appropriateness of various approaches to tackling disease and caring for patients, and medical meetings were filled with academics passionately arguing quite different points of view in discussions that often hinged on managing the risks of a treatment. But the money put into the marketing of pharmaceutical blockbusters is steadily silencing debate about differing therapeutic options and any discussion of the hazards that blockbusters pose. This is not just a problem in the United States—the silence is now being extended worldwide.

Fifty years ago many European countries put universal healthcare in place. Today, at a critical juncture in the history of healthcare, the United States is seeking to expand healthcare coverage. Fifty years ago it made sense to use taxpayer dollars to treat real diseases such as pneumonias and tuberculosis, for example, raising people from their deathbeds and putting them back to work, or taking them off disability lists and restoring them to productivity. This is an investment. If we can cure life-threatening or disability-producing diseases, the use of taxpayer dollars pays for itself—it would make the United States, for example, wealthier and better enable it to compete with China, Japan, and Europe. But treating raised cholesterol levels and other "number disorders" in an ever greater proportion of the population when medical necessity doesn't call for it is more likely to lead to a decrease in American productivity by increasing health anxieties and giving patients unpleasant side effects, if it doesn't actually kill them prematurely—and such pill dispensing is exactly what Americans do more than any other country on earth. This is an expense rather than an investment. Moreover, this is an expense that is crippling American industry, given that virtually everyone now has some set of numbers that pharmaceutical companies portray as needing "treatment."

The Obama administration and others have suggested that the only rational way forward is to embrace evidence-based medicine. But just as the insurance companies have found, anyone turning to this source will be faced by controlled trials which demonstrate that the most recent drug treatments work and supposedly save money. They will encounter guidelines drawn up by the most distinguished and independent figures in the field, advocating the use of the latest drugs. They will be told the biggest problem lies in doctors failing to adhere to evidence-based guidelines. A new generation of web-based companies is even offering to build devices into electronic medical records to ensure adherence to the latest guidelines in a way that would make it impossible for doctors to exercise discretion.

In a world where corporations can market bottled water to us, it appears to have occurred to virtually no one to ask how such marketing power might be applied to drug therapies. If the goal of medical marketing is to find out what doctors want in order to get the doctors to sell the product to themselves—and it is—and if doctors say they are influenced by the evidence above all else—and they do—it should not come as a surprise that industry might set about ensuring the evidence points in the right direction. The availability of drugs on a prescription-only basis in these circumstances makes the job of company marketers a great deal easier than it might otherwise be by enabling them to zero in on a small number of consumers who, when it comes to marketing, are often more naïve than the average adolescent.

We have an extraordinary paradox that attracts absolutely no comment. On the one hand the medical establishment portrays evidence-based medicine as our best means of reining in the pharmaceutical industry, while on the other hand pharmaceutical companies are now among the most vigorous advocates of evidence-based medicine. And it is just this kind of evidence that administrations in both the United States and Europe seem to think will help control health costs. If catch 22 hadn't existed we would now have to invent it.

AVOIDING PHARMAGEDDON

While ghostwriting by pharmaceutical companies has begun to make the news, there is little awareness of the extent to which medicine's major journals have been complicit in the practice and how, faced with articles on treatment hazards, our journals self-censor for fear of legal actions. There is no analysis to explain how treatment guidelines drawn up by academic bodies that are independent of the pharmaceutical industry invariably endorse the latest company products.

All the while doctors and patients complain about the profound changes in their clinical encounters. Where once we consulted our doctors because we had a problem and met a doctor who could spot differences in us from one visit to the next, someone who might have spotted a treatment-induced problem, we are now likely to meet a different face each time we go to the clinic. The main task of many doctors has changed from monitoring us for evidence of life-threatening diseases or the adverse effects of treatment to monitoring the results on computer screens from the latest tests of our risk factors, and managing those numbers on the basis of guidelines. Not unreasonably, the managers who increasingly run health systems from the United States to Europe assume that if the job involves looking at numbers on a computer screen and then following guidelines for what to do next, doctors should be interchangeable.

The engagement of a doctor with the person in front of him or her now means increasingly that on the basis of targets linked to guidelines the role of the doctor is to "educate," to cajole or coerce us into treatment for conditions we never knew we had, with treatments that in some instances are more likely to injure or kill us than improve our well-being. This is what caring has become.

Doctors complain about all this, but without an analysis of the forces pushing them to one side and unless they can offer an alternate model of care, such complaints are idle. Blaming the pharmaceutical industry without pinpointing anything they do other than make more profits than some might like is just scapegoating. Are the scapegoaters, we might ask, doing anything other than complaining? By the end of chapter 2 it will be clear that current patent law and prescription-only arrangements for drugs may in fact give rise to many of our more superficial difficulties—but are there any doctors or others seeking to change these arrangements? By the end of chapter 4, it will be clear that blockages to our access of the data from clinical trials constitute a serious breach of scientific norms, but it will be far less clear that there are any doctors taking a stand against this breach.

All of these issues come to a focus in chapter 7 in a description of a patient injured by treatment. Here we see at its clearest the divide between what medicine at its best once was and what it risks becoming. On the basis of the "evidence"—the published reports of controlled trials—our doctor may appear to have little rational option but to deny that the prescribed treatment could have caused us any problems. There is no evidence-based approach to determining whether treatments have injured a patient or what to do when it happens. Why ever not?

Avoiding Pharmageddon is not primarily a matter of containing the escalating costs of healthcare—although this is important. It is a matter of restoring the conditions in which doctors can diagnose what is afflicting us and can offer the appropriate care. This kind of care is not something intangible nor something that looks like current efforts to get health professionals to smile more and encourage their patients to have a nice day or other efforts to deliver a "good service." When it comes to treatment-induced injuries it will increasingly require those whom we entrust with our care to have the "right stuff."

While on the surface physicians and others in healthcare are now encouraged to become our partners, in fact the impulse to nurture us when we are afflicted so that we can realize our potential to its fullest extent is being thwarted by processes that render treatment-induced problems invisible. As a result, a vast reservoir of idealism and goodwill that those working in healthcare bring to their work daily is being squandered. And insofar as the essential wealth of a nation is people functioning at their best, rather than oil or other resources in the ground, our countries and economies are being correspondingly impoverished.

There is a climate change taking place in modern medicine that is quite different than the loss of perspective bemoaned by Worcester and generations of doctors since. Coming to grips with the factors driving this shift in climate may involve changes to things like patent law, prescription-only status for drugs, and access to the data from clinical trials, but it also needs doctors and patients as individuals to take action. In the face of global warming, actions on an individual scale can seem futile, but in medicine as in climate change, adding one to another can make a difference. *Pharmageddon* is part of that effort. It is written in the belief that almost every doctor in practice and every person who visits them will, once the issues are examined, be alerted to the growing chill in clinical care and that between us we can make a difference.

1

They Used to Call It Medicine

The careers of Alfred Worcester (1855–1951) and Richard Cabot (1868–1939) in Boston spanned the formative years of modern medicine. Worcester's medical training in the late nineteenth century included repeated visits to the homes of the sick and dying as a doctor's apprentice, whereas students of Cabot in the early twentieth century were trained in the new sciences basic to medicine, like bacteriology, and rarely got to meet the same patient more than once. Second-year medical students of 1912 knew more about diseases than the doctors of his generation ever did, Worcester conceded, but he argued that at the end of the day an exquisite knowledge of disease mechanisms was more likely to tell a doctor what his patients had died from rather than how to help them live or die. Older doctors, while not ignoring what they understood of disease processes, knew vastly more than their younger colleagues about human helplessness and were comfortable managing it. "It is when dealing with the mysteries of life that science fails the modern doctor," Worcester said.[1]

Bemoaning a recent shift in Harvard that saw pharmacology now taught by someone who had never engaged in medical practice, Worcester noted that "in the modern medical schools science is enthroned. Carried away by the brilliance of etiological discoveries, the whole strength of the school is devoted to the study of disease. The art of medical practice is not taught; even its existence is hardly recognized."[2] "Little wonder is it," he went on, that people "turn to the Christian

Scientists, or other charlatans who, either in their absurd denial of the existence of disease or for mercenary reasons, at least leave some hope in the sick room."

Worcester's words have an uncomfortable ring of truth. But while we undoubtedly hope our doctor will be "old school," few if any of us are prepared to give up the benefits science has brought to medicine over the past century. Aware of the hazards of a narrowly "medical" approach, many medical schools, Harvard in particular, attempt to ensure that students realize an illness is but an episode in their patient's lives.[3] But despite these efforts, clinical practice still seems to be degenerating.

Patients treated by Worcester might have seen him with an apprentice in tow or when they went to see Cabot at Massachusetts General they could well have encountered medical students sitting in on the visit. But now the pharmaceutical industry has been able to persuade doctors to allow trainee drug reps to sit in on clinics—recently illustrated in the movie *Love and Other Drugs*. For example, as part of her training as a sales representative, Jeanette got to sit in with Dr. N on a "medication management clinic." Dr. N is the fictional name for a real doctor—a high-volume prescriber of drugs—who is the subject of a research project looking at modern clinical practice.[4] Jeanette was struck by the amount of paperwork he had to fill out on each patient—charts tracking both the doctor's and patient's perceptions of whether a drug was working and whether any side effects were apparent. He was so busy filling out the forms that he barely looked up during his 10- to 15-minute sessions with patients.

One day, a middle-aged man came in, and while Dr. N completed the paperwork for the previous patient, Jeanette engaged him. He seemed to be in a good mood considering he was in a wheelchair and recently had had both legs amputated because of vascular problems. Dr. N began to ask the usual questions, ticking boxes as he went.

Finally, the patient interrupted: "Look at me, Dr. Do you notice anything different about me?" He repeated this several times until Dr. N looked up and focused directly on the man, while pushing his glasses up with his thumb. He stared at the patient for several seconds and finally said, "No, I don't notice anything different, what's up?" The patient smiled and said excitedly, "I got my legs cut off since that last time you saw me!" Dr. N steered the conversation back to the patient's medication, and the session ended a few minutes later.

While this neglect may have been extreme even for the fictional Dr. N, many of us face something similar when we visit our doctors today; even the best seem to spend an increasing proportion of their time looking at computer screens rather than at us. While Cabot was more committed to the latest science than Worcester, there is little doubt that he would have been as appalled at this as Worcester might have been. There is moreover no reason to believe that an embrace of science should lead to such degradation of medical practice. The case of Dr. N, comically extreme as it is, puts in stark relief a type of medical practice encouraged by the dominant forces in healthcare today.

This book sets out to explain how we have come to a situation where a Dr. N can not just exist but may become something of the norm in the near future. As a first step we need to outline two histories, one a relatively traditional history of medicine's relation to drugs culminating with the emergence of a set of truly effective magic-bullet treatments in the middle years of the twentieth century and the other a history of marketing that starts in the late nineteenth century. These two histories initially have little in common but in recent years, as we shall show, medicine seems to have become the home of the most sophisticated marketing on earth. The transformation is undeniable but if we wish to change things it is not sufficient to simply assert there has been a transformation—we need to pinpoint the mechanisms driving the change.

FROM MEDICINE TO MARKETING

In a 1951 ad featuring American soldiers at war, the pharmaceutical company Eli Lilly outlined the contribution it and other companies were making to the United States:

> A record of American Achievement. Thousands of Americans and of our allies too, are alive today because of the lifesaving gains made in World War II. The mortality rate of our own wounded dropped to the lowest level in the history of any army in the world. This was accomplished through better methods and techniques of medical care and especially through the use of new and improved pharmaceuticals. Tremendous quantities of penicillin, anesthetic agents, sulfonamides and processed blood were quickly supplied by such manufacturers as Eli Lilly and Company. The rewards of free enterprise had built an American industry large enough to do the job.[5]

Ironically, most of the treatments mentioned in this ad were produced not through free enterprise but through government funding or by the prewar German pharmaceutical industry cartel IG Farben. During the 1950s and 1960s, Czechoslovakia, then part of the Soviet bloc, produced more new drugs per capita than any other country. Nevertheless, capitalism and free markets at some level "work." Everyone now recognizes this. And, given a choice between a system that produces the best hi-tech healthcare in the world and contributes to the development of breakthrough drugs but is run as a business or a system that isn't run as a business, puts a premium more on caring than on breakthrough drugs, and takes social factors into account in considering appropriate care, the average person will opt for breakthroughs every day of the week.

The problem with this free market view of the world, nowhere more so than in the pharmaceutical industry, is that the free markets that supposedly lead to better mousetraps were cannibalized in the twentieth century by what became a few large firms, one of them being Eli Lilly, that were then in a position to favor marketing over innovation as the ultimate key to their profits. Where the research and development budgets of large pharmaceutical companies like Lilly and Pfizer were once much greater than their marketing budgets, the reverse is now true. The pharmaceutical industry, for example, now spends $30 billion annually on marketing in the United States alone. In 2002, Pfizer devoted roughly $1.2 billion to marketing the statin Lipitor as a treatment for raised cholesterol levels, an amount equivalent to the US National Institutes of Health budget for research on Alzheimer's disease, arthritis, autism, epilepsy, influenza, multiple sclerosis, sickle cell disease, and spinal cord injury combined.[6] Given that Lipitor was only one of six statins on the market at the time, anyone trying to get out a competing medical message—that statins have a very limited role in healthcare or that there are alternate ways to lower cholesterol through diet and other approaches—faces a daunting challenge. With money like this behind them, twenty-first-century corporate marketers are supremely confident they can sell anything. Bottled water, oxygen, and with the right packaging, even inferior mousetraps. And if they can do this, why not homeopathic or relatively worthless medicines?

Pharmaceutical companies have perhaps done more to undermine traditional markets than any other industrial companies. Not coincidentally, from Lilly's 1951 ad to a 2005 book by Hank McKinnell,[7] then CEO of Pfizer, they are also the corporations most active in spreading the message that there is no alternative to a free enterprise system. But while in fact many industrial corporations came to the conclusion a century ago that the capitalism of cutthroat competition and free markets didn't work as well as it might—at least not for them—no other branch of industry has been able to pursue this agenda in quite the way pharmaceutical companies have.

To begin to see how pharmaceutical companies have engineered what they have, we need to return to the mid-nineteenth century when the first science-based companies began producing goods made possible by the new physical and chemical sciences. These sciences formed the basis of electrical manufacturing as well as the chemical and metal industries, leading to a string of new goods from automobiles to plastics, explosives, dyes, rubber products, artificial fibers, and, later, pharmaceuticals. In all these cases, competition between companies should in theory drive prices down in an open market, especially when increasing automation reduced the cost of production. Faced with the risk of falling profits, the new manufacturing companies commonly banded together in cartels to keep prices artificially high. A cartel presents the world with apparent competition between companies when in fact the companies have agreed among themselves to coordinate prices and market arrangements, allowing them to enjoy the advantages of de facto monopolies.[8] But government resistance to cartels mounted in the United States and Europe at the end of the nineteenth century.

Companies needed to find another way to maintain or increase their profits. It was this that led to a turn to marketing. For manufacturers the problem was that as the genuine need for automobiles, plastics, dyes, nuts and bolts as well as mousetraps were increasingly met with capacity to spare, ever more production could only drive prices down. If prices could not be rigged by cartels, could demand be maintained or increased by tapping into what people might be persuaded they wanted or needed?[9]

An appreciation of the opportunities that marketing opened up led to the emergence of marketing departments within companies and the first university courses on marketing in the 1920s.[10] In a supreme irony, much of the raw material for these courses came from a brilliant set of ad hoc developments that underpinned the marketing of proprietary, over-the-counter medicines in the nineteenth century. The early exponents of the new science of marketing realized that the true experts on understanding what people might be persuaded they needed were quacks pushing worthless medical remedies. It was these who more than anyone else created advertising and shaped modern marketing.[11]

One of the first lessons that proprietary medicines taught later marketers came in the 1830s, when a war broke out in the newspapers between Samuel Lee, Jr. of Connecticut who produced "Bilious Pills" and another Samuel Lee from Connecticut who also produced a Bilious Pills remedy. Far from leading to market collapse, this dispute spurred demand for Bilious Pills, and soon other proprietors across the country were joining in with their own preparations. In contrast to the producers of dyes and metal goods, these businessmen found competition among producers led to increase in sales for their commodities, without prices falling. In the drug domain this phenomenon has been demonstrated again and again from the marketing of Aspirin as a brand name product in the nineteenth century to that of Lipitor and Vioxx in this century.[12]

In 1804, there were some ninety over-the-counter proprietary medicines listed in New York. By 1857, this had swollen to more than fifteen hundred countrywide. The growth in business paralleled the growth of the press and literacy. Where there were two hundred newspapers in 1800, there were four thousand by 1860. The proprietors of these remedies took advantage of this explosive growth and were among the first to market nationally. They also marketed heavily: the proprietary medicines industry spent more than any other industry on advertising in the second half of the nineteenth century. By the end of that century up to $1 million was being spent on telling the American people about the benefits of Scott's Emulsion, just one of an estimated fifty thousand compounds in a trade that had a retail value of several hundred million dollars.[13]

The proprietary medicines industry was the first to market lifestyles rather than the compounds per se—this was marketing before the modern term had come into being. There was a simple reason for this: there was little if any value in these substances. The key ingredients were on the bottle rather than in it—the branding. It was no accident that one of the leading early lights in advertising, Claude Hopkins, would say that "the greatest advertising men of my day were schooled in the medicine field"[14]—schooled, that is, in how to persuade the public that Carter's Little Liver Pills, Lydia Pinkham's Vegetable Compound, Clark Stanley's Snake Oil Liniment, or Coca Cola or, later, 7-UP would restore health or beauty, resolve halitosis, conquer fatigue, or ward off calamity. The money thrown into the marketing campaigns came from huge markups in the selling price of these compounds, typically inflated to five times their cost of production.[15]

Marketing does exactly the same thing today when it gets us to believe that a particular running shoe or music system is not only necessary for its stated function but will deliver what we desire more generally in life—our unmet needs. These are the suggestions that underpin the marketing of bottled water and other such items that most people for most of the twentieth century never imagined could be marketed. And

as the bottled waters of the twenty-first century along with the proprietary medicines of the nineteenth century (which contained little more
than water) show so clearly, the differentiation between one product
and another is seldom based on actual differences in the products but
hinges rather on brand recognition, on how effective competing marketers are in encapsulating wish fulfillment, and in saturating potential
purchasers with their message.

While there were differences in emphasis between medical men like
Cabot and Worcester, during the period from 1850 to 1950 medicine was united in an implacable opposition to medical quackery
and proprietary remedies—and by extension to marketing. In early
nineteenth-century Europe and the United States, there was no licensing of
physicians and no training in science as part of their education. Hospitals were almshouses for the poor rather than institutions with a mission
to treat effectively. When people got sick, they increasingly turned to the
remedies being advertised nationally and sold by salesmen, who peddled
everything from cures for cancer to elixirs for love or eternal youth.

Faced with a proliferation in wild claims for cures for everything from
consumption to nervous problems, the first European and American
associations of physicians that emerged in the mid-nineteenth century
committed themselves to ensuring medical doctors knew what they were
prescribing and knew what there was to know about the conditions
they were treating.[16] In cases where no treatment seemed to work any
better than judicious waiting, the new breed of doctors were educated
in the virtue of waiting with their patients, trained to recognize as had
Philippe Pinel that there was often a greater art in knowing when not
to prescribe than in prescribing.

In Europe the greatest concern regarding these remedies was voiced
over markups of 500 percent or more for compounds that contained
little that might actually help patients.[17] In the United States, where
the proprietary industry flourished to the greatest extent, physicians
expressed greater concern over the injuries some of these potions could
cause. As Oliver Wendell Holmes put it at a meeting of the Massachusetts Medical Society in 1860, "I firmly believe that if the whole *materia
medica* [the available drugs] could be sunk to the bottom of the sea it
would be all the better for mankind—and all the worse for the fishes."[18]

Medical concerns about these proprietary medicines led to calls for
their regulation. This resulted in the establishment in the United States
in 1906 of the Chemical Bureau, the first regulator of medicines, the
forerunner of the Food and Drug Administration (FDA), established in

1938, and all such regulators since.[19] The Chemical Bureau was set up to force companies marketing medicines to specify on the label what the product contained. This minimal intrusion into the market ironically initiated a process whereby increasing regulation forced smaller companies unable to meet the demands of regulation out of the market and the consequent growth of the surviving corporations, with ever greater marketing capabilities, that have a century later brought us to the brink of Pharmageddon.

Having fought for over 150 years against quackery first and alternate or complementary medicines latterly, it has become part of the medical profession's self-image that it has nothing to do with the kind of marketing that makes extravagant claims for spurious remedies. Buyers might have to beware in other domains of life but not when it comes to medical care.

This confident self-belief can still be found in most everyone involved in healthcare, from doctors and administrators to nurses, and it is taken at face value by a wider public. The idea that most doctors have been body-snatched and replaced by someone working for a faceless marketing department seems at first inconceivable to most people, the germ perhaps of an amusing idea for a television series, but nothing more.

Doctors, and many of the rest of us, think we see the marketing in medicine—some free pens and lunches, plenty of free samples, perhaps golfing trips for some select doctors to the Caribbean—and feel able to discount this. Modern safeguards are supposed to be in place to manage anything a marketing department dreams up. Our drugs have to pass the scrutiny of regulators and they can only do this if there are controlled trials to show that they work. After that they are available by prescription only from doctors who are increasingly constrained in what they can do by guidelines drawn up by experts on the basis of these treatment trials. These guidelines are built into standards of care across all areas of medicine, and doctors straying from these standards in response to some marketing gimmick risk being sued or losing their medical license.

With these safeguards in place, the idea that medicine could be sucked into a machine that has as little interest in the health of the people who consume its products as a shoe company has in their fitness but that has a lot of interest in using disease and ill health to distinguish drugs that are often as indistinguishable in their effects as one brand of bottled water is from another will be met with incredulity or incomprehension in many quarters. It doesn't make sense that seriously ill people would pay more heed to the color of the pill or its brand name than to the question of whether the treatment they are on is likely to do more good than harm. Marketing, after all, has little impact in states of famine. Starving people don't hold out for paninis or rye bread.

But this is to miss the point. In the current setup, it is the doctor not the patient who consumes, and the doctor is rarely in extremis. What doctors dispense will have a branded glow to it. They will be giving it for a condition as likely as not that they were never taught about in medical school, a condition, in fact, now being marketed by some company. Neither the doctor nor the patients who receive a treatment, nor those who draw up the treatment guidelines, are likely to find out that this treatment may actually be less effective than older treatments recently retired medical colleagues might have prescribed. The doctor is also unlikely to be aware that the markup on drugs like Lipitor, Prozac, and Nexium may be up to 2500 percent. In 1912, medical associations inspired major changes by questioning a markup of 500 percent on proprietary medicines of the day. In 2012 there is close to silence on markups of 2500 percent. This silence is linked closely to the failure by medical practitioners to understand how industry now brands its products.

THE ONCE AND FUTURE BRANDS

Philippe Pinel working in Paris in 1809 had few effective treatments aside from some herbs and metals, along with remedies drawn from opium for pain relief or sedation, willow bark also for pain, fever bark for malaria, and foxglove for heart failure. A few years later, in the 1820s, advances in chemistry made it possible to extract opiates from opium, quinine from fever bark, and digitalis from foxglove, so that standard doses of treatments could be given. Then in 1860, just as Oliver Wendell Holmes was consigning almost all available drugs to the bottom of the sea, a new set of medicines emerged, giving doctors like Worcester and Cabot by the 1890s new therapies to employ and the hope of more to come.

In the second half of the nineteenth century, a series of mostly German chemical companies, such as Bayer, BASF, and Hoechst grew rapidly because of the newfound ability to synthesize dyes from coal tars. These dyes transformed our wardrobes from a series of drab brown and green outfits to yield the blues and pinks and yellows we now have. They also allowed human tissues and cells to be distinguished, giving rise to histology, and bacteria to be stained, creating bacteriology. The ability to distinguish among bacteria made it possible for doctors to differentiate between diphtheria, the most common cause of childhood mortality, and other throat infections, for instance. Doctors like Worcester had been called repeatedly to homes to try to save the lives of children being literally garroted by membranes from the diphtherium bacteria forming deeper and deeper down in their windpipe. They would cut open the child's throat and pass in a tube and hope no membranes formed even lower down, though all too often this failed. Distinguishing diphtheria from other bacteria led to the synthesis of diphtheria antitoxin in 1894. As the membranes from the illness faded in response to an injection of the antitoxin, so also the nightmare of diphtheria began to fade away in areas where the antitoxin was available.[20] Successes like this heralded a future of pharmaceutical magic bullets.

Discovering a new dye or drug in Germany of the late nineteenth century did not give a company sole rights to that product. If another company could demonstrate that it was able to produce the compound by a different process than that specified by the original company, the second company was entitled to manufacture its version of summer blue, say, or acetylsalicylic acid. When acetanilide, one of the drugs derived from dyes, was shown to be antipyretic (fever reducing), for example, well over ten companies found different ways to produce it. No company could easily make a blockbuster drug in these circumstances. Faced with this scenario, in 1886, another German company, Kalle, borrowing a practice from the proprietary industry, trademarked the name of their version of acetanilide—Antefebrin. Sales boomed. Other companies took note, and Bayer followed by registering Aspirin and Heroin in 1898, names with far more resonance to this day than acetylsalicylic acid or diacetylmorphine. The basis for both of these painkillers had first been created close to fifty years earlier, so Aspirin and Heroin were new social rather than pharmaceutical creations.[21]

The first brands had got a foothold within medicine, and the medical profession began to make an uneasy accommodation to this changed reality. Medical students were taught to refer to the generic names of drugs—diacetylmorphine rather than Heroin. For almost a century this denial of brands worked passably well, but to continue to pretend that doctors today typically still prescribe generic drugs rather than brands passes beyond denial into fantasy.

This denial was helped by the fact that the focus in promoting the new magic bullets from diphtheria antitoxin to Heroin was directed toward doctors rather than the public at large, and toward conquering the scourge of disease rather than capitalizing on the discontents of everyday life. Sales of these new compounds were promoted by visits from company representatives to doctors and ads in medical journals, rather than the hoopla customary to the proprietary medicines' industry. There was minimal effort to subvert medical judgment, in part perhaps because until the 1940s there was relatively little to sell.

Then, in 1937, prontosil red, a dye produced by the pharmaceutical conglomerate IG Farben, gave rise to the sulfa antibiotics, which had as great an impact on lethal conditions like bacterial endocarditis, an infection of the lining of the heart, as diphtheria antitoxin had on diphtheria forty years earlier. Other antibiotics followed in the 1940s and from the sulfa nucleus came a host of other drugs, including diuretics to remove excess body fluid in heart failure, antihypertensives to lower blood pressure, and oral hypoglycemics to lower blood sugars. In the 1950s, dyes such as methylene blue and summer blue led to the antipsychotics and antidepressants.

These new drugs all came branded by their manufacturers. These were brand names that spoke of medical diseases and or chemical contents rather than the old style panaceas whose promises were in inverse proportion to their efficacy. Thus just as Kalle had given doctors Antefebrin (antifever), Merck in the 1960s gave them Diuril (for diuresis), and Tryptizol (amitriptyline) as an antidepressant. Initially, as with brands such as Hoover and Mercedes, these new brands traded on quality. The brand stood for the fact that the drug was produced by a reputable company that was linked to previous breakthroughs and doctors could accordingly be confident about the pedigree of the product. This was an era of "magic bullets"—penicillin, the thiazide antihypertensives, and antipsychotics such as chlorpromazine—which would have marketed themselves, branded or not.

Indeed, by the 1960s it seemed to many doctors as if medicine had faced down the destructive forces of marketing as the proprietary medicines industry withered away with the advent of these new magic bullets. Few drug company invaders in the 1950s and 1960s in dead of night appeared to crawl out of the Trojan horse that brands had introduced to the medical citadel. But the fatal breach had been effected. Changes to the patent laws in the 1960s, allied to the fact that these new drugs were available by prescription only, laid the basis for the emergence of blockbuster branding in the 1980s.

PATENT MEDICINES

Patents offer an exclusive right to produce a good or service. They are granted by a state, are even older than brands, and once provoked almost as much hostility within medicine as brands. Patenting drugs, and thereby restricting access to them either physically or by virtue of the increased price that comes with a monopoly, was for centuries regarded as incompatible with a vocation to alleviate disease. In the case of modern drugs, this period of monopoly lasts for twenty years.

The first patent law was enacted in Venice 1474, and the idea then spread rapidly throughout Europe.[22] In Britain, after widespread complaints about abusive patent monopolies being granted by the Crown for long-existing technologies, the law was tightened in 1624 to limit grants of monopolies to "the sole working or making of any manner of new manufactures within this realm, to the true and first inventor and inventors of such manufactures."[23]

Being the exclusive patent holder of a good or service meant that you could produce it at a higher price than was possible in a competitive market. This, it was hoped, might lure innovative producers to Britain, and their activities would in turn stimulate commerce and improve national revenues.[24] However, in return for this benefit the producer had to show plans to create something novel that plausibly brought some benefit to the wider community.

In Britain, patents went hand in hand with the enclosure of common lands in the sixteenth century, and critics of patenting since have referred to the anticommons effect of the practice. Because science hinges on common access to all data, many scientists and free market advocates have been hostile to patenting. But the deepest hostility to patents throughout the nineteenth and twentieth centuries came from within medicine. Neither the doctors who treated patients nor the pharmacists who dispensed remedies a doctor ordered regarded the remedies they gave as industrial or commercial products or their own activities as either industrial or commercial.

In France, the Revolution led to promulgation of a new law in 1791 that permitted drugs to be patented.[25] Chemists and trade associations on the one hand argued at the time for the rights of inventors to be recognized. But French physicians and pharmacists argued against patents; their vocation, they said, was to treat the sick, not to make a profit. Furthermore, patents, they predicted, would lead to an increase in the price of medicines, which would be detrimental to public health.[26] In 1844, the French National Assembly reversed the 1791 law and removed medicines from the domain of patentable products.

German law did not permit drugs to be patented, but it did allow companies to defend their product by taking out a patent on the process used to make the compound. Another company could get around the monopoly that these patents created, if they could find another way to make a compound. In some cases, as with acetanilide, this was easy, and it was this that led Kalle and Bayer to trademark their new compounds, which gave them exclusive use of the brand name they chose for their product.

American law, in contrast, allowed patents to be taken out on drugs, even though some of the fathers of the Republic were hostile to patents. Benjamin Franklin refused to take out a patent on a stove he invented while Jefferson, referring scornfully to England's willingness to let anything be patented, refused to patent a hemp-brake he invented, stating that "nations which refused monopolies of invention are as fruitful as England in new and useful devices." In this spirit, the nation's patent office was initially stringent in its review of applications for drug patents. In 1922, for example, Lilly attempted but failed to get around the patent on the production of insulin held in the public interest by the University of Toronto.[27] When in the following year, Harry Steenbock discovered that ultraviolet light activated vitamin D and sought to patent this use, he found himself accused of attempting to patent the sun and the application was thrown out. Referring back to this case in the 1950s, Jonas Salk exemplified the attitude of many American doctors at the time when he refused to patent the polio vaccine.[28]

The issue of patents came to a head in Britain during World War II, when Ernst Chain and Howard Florey at Oxford University demonstrated penicillin's efficacy for bacterial infections and came up with a method to produce it. Chain suggested patenting the method but Florey and the rest of the group, along with the Medical Research Council that funded the research, were opposed to patenting something so important for clinical care. This was later seen by many as a lost national opportunity, and a new law was passed in 1949 that permitted patenting of medical products.

After the war, the position of an American or British company with a patented product was more secure than a German company with a process patent, but still these patents only applied to a national territory and so the monopoly they offered was limited. For example in the case of amitriptyline, the best-selling antidepressant during the 1960s, Merck held a patent on it in the United States, Roche (in fact the first to make the drug) held one in Switzerland, and Lundbeck in Denmark, as did a laboratory in Czechoslovakia.[29] Given the possibility that others might be able to make the very same product, no company could plan to market the drug profitably throughout the developed world. As a result, while some compounds that came to market during the 1950s and 1960s did extremely well, it didn't make sense for companies to invest huge effort in any one compound; except within the United States and Britain, there was no protection against another company making the same drug and cutting into profits.

The important patent changes in international drug markets came in 1960 when France, the country that had been most opposed to patenting medicines, switched to product patents, followed in 1967 by Germany, the country that had developed more pharmaceuticals than all other countries combined. Once companies knew that applying for product patents in all major countries simultaneously blocked the development of any competing products, the way was cleared for the development of blockbusters. The possibility of truly global blockbusters came in the 1980s with the creation of the World Trade Organization's Trade Related Aspects of Intellectual Property Rights (TRIPS), which extended patent protection worldwide.[30] If the patent is valid, this gives a company the possibility of a monopoly on a new product worldwide for twenty years from the date of filing. From that point onward, there could only be one Lipitor, one Nexium, one Prozac, and the way was open for a company to maximize the possibilities inherent in branding—and to go as global as Coca Cola.[31]

Compared with the vigorous debates in France that led in 1844 to a rollback in patenting medicines and the discussion of the moves that blocked the patenting of penicillin in Britain and polio vaccine in the United States, there was virtual silence in the face of these more recent changes. No one argued that patenting and commerce were incompatible with progress in science and the principles of medicine, as they had earlier.

Several historical factors probably contributed to the silence. World War II had seen heavy state investment in medical research. This investment created partnerships between scientists, universities, and pharmaceutical companies that capitalized knowledge and contributed to the development of what is now termed the knowledge economy. This led in the 1940s and 1950s to an astonishing development of truly novel and extremely effective agents, from the antibiotics and cortisone to the diuretics, antihypertensives, hypoglycemics, and psychotropic drugs, as well as the first chemotherapy for cancer. It seemed we were set on a course in which genuine developments would succeed each other for years to come. The era of snake oil was over. Academic understanding and medical research had developed as never before, laying the basis for real progress, and pharmaceutical companies had played a part in this progress. Besides, even with the change in what could be patented, the spirit of the patent laws and the expectations of the medical community at least notionally remained aimed at providing businesses with a period of monopoly but only in return for a genuine novelty that offered a distinct benefit to the public. Such an arrangement seemed to be an engine for harnessing commercial vigor to public purpose.

It hasn't turned out that way. When assessing the patent application for a drug, the examining officer is supposed to look at whether the structure of a molecule is substantially different from compounds already on the market, and whether it provides a clear clinical benefit, a solution to a problem of medical care for which we have not previously had an answer.[32] It is in the interest of a drug company, however, to argue that differences that may appear to be trivial are in fact substantial and innovative, as in some cases they are. But, if a country wishes to build up its pharmaceutical sector, as the United States was intent on doing in the postwar decades, one way to do so is to make it easy to take out patents. The notions of benefit to the community and of novelty can be shaved, so that companies might be awarded patents for trivial variations on a compound that does not clearly confer any benefit in terms of health or other public value.

Against this background let us look at the patenting of Depakote. The American patent on Depakote was taken out in 1991 but the drug in fact came from a French anticonvulsant, sodium valproate, first produced in 1962. By the mid-1960s, it was known that the sedative effects of sodium valproate could be useful in the treatment of mania. When Abbott filed for a patent on semi-sodium valproate in 1991, it was on the basis that minimally reducing the amount of sodium in the compound, which was completely irrelevant to the mode of action of the drug, made it novel. Had Abbott proposed to test this compound, which was trivially different from sodium valproate, for a hitherto incurable disorder, such a stretching of the spirit of the patent law might have been warranted on the basis of clinical need. But all Abbot planned to do was to put it into trials for use in mania, with a result that was a foregone conclusion. That Depakote was granted a patent is indicative of how lax the application of American patent law had become. The reason to go to all this trouble was that sodium valproate was now off-patent—any company could make it—and without marketing exclusivity Abbott thought that it could make little or no money.

Faced with an application for its use in mania, the FDA then licensed Depakote. Surely clinicians would not use the much more expensive on-patent semi-sodium valproate over the far less costly off-patent but essentially identical sodium valproate? Such a prediction ignores the power of the kind of branding that product patents made possible. Clinicians were faced with a brand new compound, a brand new class of drug—a mood stabilizer—and a brand new illness—bipolar disorder—and they fell hard for the package. Depakote became a billion dollar global blockbuster and manic-depressive illness was consigned to the dustbin of history, greatly increasing the costs of healthcare in the process. The success of Depakote lay entirely in Abbott's ability to distinguish between two drops of water—but it was the ability to take out a product patent with global reach that made it worth their while to do so.

In the case of Zyprexa, an antipsychotic and mood stabilizer, the story is as extraordinary. The first generation of antipsychotics ran into problems in the 1970s with million-dollar legal settlements against their manufacturers for a disfiguring neurological side effect of treatment—tardive dyskinesia. This led to a period of almost twenty years when no new antipsychotic came on the market. The only antipsychotic that did not cause this problem was clozapine, but clozapine had been withdrawn in 1975 because it was associated with a higher rate of mortality than other antipsychotics.

The way forward seemed to lie in producing a safe clozapine. There were two ways to attempt this. One was to develop a drug that bound to the key brain receptors that clozapine bound to; this method underpinned the patenting of Risperdal (risperidone) and Geodon (ziprasidone). Another way was to make minor adjustments to the clozapine molecule. Tweaking a molecule risks producing a compound with all the hazards and none of the benefits of the parent. This is what Lilly did: in 1974 the company produced a series of compounds that were all abandoned because of toxicity.

As the patent life of that series ebbed away, Lilly had to decide whether to abandon the hunt. This was a company in serious financial trouble, facing potential takeover. On April 29, 1982, they opted to move forward with a compound from the original series that by definition was not novel—olanzapine, later branded as Zyprexa. To make Zyprexa commercially viable, they needed a new patent, which meant demonstrating some benefit not found with other antipsychotics. In 1991, the only novelty presented in the company's new patent application, which was approved, was a study in dogs in which Zyprexa produced less elevation of blood cholesterol levels than another never-marketed drug.

Zyprexa has since turned out to be one of the drugs most likely in all of medicine to increase cholesterol levels in man. Lilly has settled over $2 billion worth of claims that Zyprexa has raised cholesterol and caused diabetes and other metabolic problems. There was arguably a better case to be made for patenting it to raise cholesterol than to treat psychosis.[33] Lilly's patent was declared invalid in Canada, though not in the United States or Europe. Despite this, Zyprexa has been one of the biggest selling drugs of all time, grossing $4–5 billion per annum from the late 1990s through 2010. There was no basis to think this drug was any more effective than dozens of others and a lot of reasons to think it was more problematic for patients, but the marketing power that came with its patented status enabled Lilly to hype its benefits and conceal its hazards and steer doctors to write enough Zyprexa prescriptions to save the company.

In our brave new world, companies can make blockbuster profits out of a Depakote or Zyprexa. If these two compounds were exceptions, the price might be worth paying for a set of drugs that were otherwise innovative and were leading to treatments for serious conditions that previously went untreated. Many might sigh but most would reconcile themselves to the situation—this is the way the world works. But that world does not seem to be working anymore. Where there were a handful of new tranquilizers, antipsychotics, antidepressants, and stimulants introduced annually year after year from the 1950s onward, the flow of novel psychotropic drugs dried up in the mid-1980s.

The decline of the antidepressants illustrates this all too well. The antidepressant drugs produced from 1958 to 1982 were used primarily for severe mood disorders and as such had a much smaller volume of sales than the benzodiazepine group of drugs, of which the best known, Valium and Librium, quite literally became household names—these were mother's little helpers. Valium and the other benzodiazepines were marketed as tranquilizers for anxiety from 1960 onward. In the 1980s, claims that they caused dependence led to a backlash against the benzodiazepines, leaving the market open for a new group of drugs which, however, could not be called tranquilizers as this term was now too closely linked to dependence and withdrawal. The strategy seemed clear to the major drug companies—to persuade doctors that behind every case of anxiety lay a case of depression. And to persuade them that a new group of drugs, the SSRIs (selective serotonin reuptake inhibitors), were both antidepressant and a therapeutic advance, when in fact the companies had almost consigned the SSRIs to the dustbin in the early 1980s as they were not as effective as either the tranquilizers or older antidepressants. They were also not especially novel, most of them being simple derivatives of preexisting antihistamines, many of which work as well as the SSRIs for nervous problems. Nevertheless this molecular group appeared to offer a modest but patentable amount of novelty and therapeutic benefit. The profits that came with the patent status, amounting to $15 billion per year for the group as a whole, provided the means to transform psychiatry's views of common nervous disorders—until the patent on these drugs expired soon after 2000 and clinicians had to be reeducated that the very same patients were now suffering from bipolar disorder and in reality needed a mood stabilizer.

If the SSRIs had been a bridge to a more effective group of compounds this again might have seemed acceptable, but since 2000 almost the only novelty has come from three isomers of earlier SSRIs. Many drugs come in mirror image, or left and right hand (isomer) forms. Typically only one of the hands is active. Until the 1990s it was inconvenient to attempt to separate these isomers. But then in the mid-1990s Sepracor isolated esfluoxetine and dexfluoxetine (Zalutria) from Prozac (fluoxetine). Lundbeck isolated escitalopram (Lexapro) from Celexa (citalopram), and Wyeth isolated desvenlafaxine (Pristiq) from Efexor (venlafaxine). The astonishing thing is that companies have been permitted to take patents out on these compounds, which are as alike to the parent compounds as two drops of water.[34]

The paucity of genuinely new drugs coming on the market in recent years is not some odd quirk of psychotropic drug development. The best-selling drug for minimizing acid secretion in the gut in the 1980s and 1990s was the proton pump inhibitor Prilosec (omeprazole). Before the patent on omeprazole expired in 2002, its parent company, AstraZeneca, simply introduced Nexium (es-omeprazole), an isomer of Prilosec, and clinicians shifted from a cheap drop of water to an identical but vastly more expensive drop of water. If a drug does not come in isomeric forms, companies have instead in recent years patented the metabolites of a parent compound and released these as a novel drug with the approval of the US patent office and almost no resistance from medicine.

When the breakthrough drugs of the 1950s emerged, there were great hopes that not only would they offer remedies for illnesses that we did not have treatments for, but they would also shed light on the nature of the illnesses being treated. In 1896, the advent of diphtheria antitoxin had demonstrated that not all throat infections were diphtheria, thus opening up the idea that bacteriology would be able to carve a mass of respiratory, gut, and other problems into a series of discrete illnesses each of which could be tackled individually. In the 1950s, there were great hopes that the new treatments for disorders like arthritis, depression, hypertension, or schizophrenia might similarly clarify whether these were single diseases or the end result of common pathways into which several different diseases fed.

The new drugs, to use a celebrated phrase, would help us carve nature at its joints, just as distinctions among bacteria had enabled us to carve infectious diseases at their joints. But we have now arrived at almost the precisely opposite point. Rather than drugs being used to carve nature at its joints, nature instead is being used to differentiate drugs whose differences are essentially trivial.

With the new possibilities for profit opened up by a lax to non-existent application of patent laws, the medical arena has ceased to be a domain in which scientists using new molecular tools push back boundaries. Indeed since the passage of the Bayh-Dole Act in 1980, which encouraged scientists, including medical academics, to consider patenting the products of their research, clinicians and scientists have seemed keener on making patent applications themselves and setting up start-up companies than in advancing medical knowledge or healthcare. Pharmaceutical companies meanwhile have no interest in what molecules might reveal about how humans work. Molecules are only interesting insofar as they can be used to capture market niches. Medicine may look the same as it has always done to onlookers; the marketers know it's not.

BRANDS AND PATENTS

The emergence of product patents transformed the importance of branding. By the 1980s, when H-2 blockers for ulcers, statins for cholesterol, SSRIs for depression, and other drugs were in the pipeline, branding had become so important to companies that the job was outsourced to specialist Manhattan-based companies like InterBrand and MediBrand. No longer would drugs be called Diuril or Tryptizol. We were about to get Prozac, Viagra, Zestril, and Nexium, names that bore no relation to the underlying chemical or disease but were aimed at differentiating between the new Nikes and Reeboks of the medical world and hinted at the restoration to youthful vigor that nineteenth-century brands had shamelessly promoted.

Branding now extends far beyond generating and market-testing fancy names for drugs. Brands nest within brands. The new marketers brand drug classes and diseases with far-reaching implications for medicine and society.

For instance when the makers of the new antidepressants of the 1990s needed to distinguish their drugs from older drug treatments, the term SSRI (selective serotonin reuptake inhibitor) emerged. This is not a medical or scientific term. Serotonin is a neurotransmitter in the brain, but both new and old antidepressants acted on it and the new drugs were in fact no more selective than some older drugs. The term SSRI came from the marketing department of SmithKline Beecham as part of their effort to distinguish their Paxil from Lilly's Prozac and Pfizer's Zoloft, but all three companies used the term to create the appearance of a new class of drugs and provide a common platform from which to launch marketing efforts designed to marginalize older—and demonstrably more effective—treatments.[35]

To this day, the brand names of drugs do not feature in medical textbooks, but these same books all include sections on statins, SSRIs, and ACE (angiotensin-converting enzyme) inhibitors as though these are medical terms, when in fact they are brand-like names that replace medical terminology. Statins such as Lipitor are just one subset of lipid-lowering drugs that include equally effective older drugs such as nicotinic acid. Zestril and its sister compounds hit the market in the 1980s as "ACE inhibitors," rather than simply as antihypertensives, and became bestsellers as the SSRIs did—replacing cheaper and more effective antihypertensives.

One of the most striking instances of the branding of a new drug class has been creation of the idea of a "mood stabilizer." This once rarely used term was summoned up by Abbott Laboratories in the 1990s and pressed into use in the marketing of their newly patented Depakote. Depakote as we have seen was approved by the FDA in 1995. But it was only approved for the treatment of the manic pole of what was once called manic-depressive illness. Such approval was not surprising—giving any sedative to manic patients will produce a change that can be portrayed as a benefit. More surprising was the company's application for approval. There are comparatively few manic patients, and a lot of sedatives were already in use to manage their illness. If there was to be any serious money in Abbott's move, it had to lie in the much larger market of people whose moods could be portrayed as fluctuating unhelpfully, who were in need of "mood stabilization." But Abbott's license did not include warrants to claim Depakote was prophylactic—they couldn't claim it would stop moods swinging—or indeed even that it was a treatment for manic-depressive illness.

However, from the start ads for Depakote carried a claim that it was a mood stabilizer. Had Abbott said prophylactic, indicating that this drug had been shown to prevent mood swings, they would have broken the law. The beauty of the term mood stabilizer is that it had no precise meaning. But what else would a mood stabilizer be if not prophylactic? And this verbal construction would lead prescription writers to use it for that purpose, even though no controlled trials have ever demonstrated Depakote to be prophylactic. Far from being a well-grounded scientific idea, the term mood stabilizer was an almost perfect advertising term— as successful a brand as the term tranquilizer had been in the 1950s and SSRI in the 1990s.

All of a sudden everyone seemed to know what a mood stabilizer was. There was an exponential increase in the number of articles in medical journals with this term in the title—from none in 1990 to over a hundred per year by 2000. Within a few years, all psychopharmacology books had sections on mood stabilizers. It was as if in the middle of a TV drama series like *Buffy the Vampire Slayer* the main character is given a sister she never knew she had. When it comes to entertainment we can accommodate developments like this without blinking, but it is not the kind of thing we expect to be happening in science or medicine without solid evidence.

The emergence of mood stabilizers coincided with increasing estimates of the prevalence of what, in another successful piece of rebranding, was now almost always called bipolar disorder. Up to the launch of Depakote in 1995, almost everyone had heard of manic-depressive illness but soon this term all but disappeared, replaced by bipolar disorder. By 2005 over five hundred articles per year in the medical literature referred to bipolar disorder in their titles, with almost none mentioning manic-depressive illness.

This rebranding reengineered the disorder from the ground up. Manic-depressive illness had been a rare and serious condition affecting ten people per million, who invariably had to be admitted to hospital. Bipolar disorder, in contrast, supposedly affects up to 50,000 people per million, and efforts are now underway to persuade primary care clinicians that a wide range of the minor nervous problems they see are indicative of underlying bipolar disorder rather than anxiety or depression, and that these patients should be treated with newer and more costly mood stabilizers, such as Zyprexa or Seroquel, rather than older and cheaper antidepressants or tranquilizers.[36]

Bipolar disorder became intensely fashionable with extraordinary rapidity, promoted by assiduous disease awareness campaigns through direct-to-consumer advertising on television in the United States, and patient educational material in Europe, encouraging patients to complete self-assessments and ask their doctor whether bipolar disorder might be the cause of their problems. It became fashionable to the point where clothes and accessories could be bought online celebrating the wearer's bipolarity.[37] Within a decade, one of the most serious of mental illnesses had gone from being a devastating disease to being a lifestyle option.

Everybody, it seems, stood to gain—physicians, companies, and patients. Bipolar disorder could be portrayed as a genetic disorder—not a parent's fault. While no one likes to have a biological disease, this one was portrayed in pharmaceutical company sponsored booklets[38] and ads as a disease linked to creativity that supposedly had affected major artistic figures of the nineteenth and twentieth centuries from Vincent Van Gogh and Robert Schumann to Robert Lowell and Sylvia Plath. Public authorities meanwhile could support screening programs such as Teenscreen, introduced in many American schools beginning in 2005, to detect the condition and trigger treatment as early as possible in order to avoid any number of social and individual ills such as suicide, divorce, career failure, crime, and substance misuse that might stem from a failure to detect and treat.[39]

For the specialists new journals appeared—*Bipolar Disorder, The Journal of Bipolar Disorders, Clinical Approaches in Bipolar Disorders,* and others. made possible by unrestricted educational grants from pharmaceutical companies. From 1995 onward a slew of societies and global conferences appeared as well—The International Society for Bipolar Disorders, The International Review of Bipolar Disorders, The International Society for Affective Disorders, The Organization for Bipolar

Affective Disorders, The European Bipolar Forum, The Australasian Society for Bipolar Disorders, and many others.

In just the same way impotence vanished and was replaced by erectile dysfunction, frigidity by female sexual desire disorder, boisterousness in children by ADHD. The skill lies in understanding the market and positioning a drug accordingly. In 1980, for instance, the newly created panic disorder was viewed as a severe form of anxiety; the marketing goal for Upjohn was to get Xanax on the market for panic disorder in the expectation that creating the perception that Xanax was good for severe anxiety would lead to leakage into prescriptions for other forms of anxiety also.[40] As we shall see in later chapters, marketing like this can conjure diseases like osteopenia, restless leg syndrome, and fibromyalgia out of thin air. This is now called disease mongering. But even more alarming, an "opportunity cost" of marketing like this is that medical diseases with a pedigree going back two millennia, such as catatonia, can vanish if no company stands to make money out of helping medical or nursing staff to recognize its presence and as a result patients may die, when the means to treat them may be lying inches away.[41]

Once the addition of a branded drug to a doctor's arsenal was a minor addition to medical culture, but now the insertion of a Viagra or a Vioxx into the medical marketplace will often replace existing medical culture in an area of treatment, as the examples of mood stabilizers and bipolar disorders illustrate. Disorders that were once defined by patients' needs for medical services and doctors' perceptions of their pathology are now increasingly defined by the goals of marketers. Furthermore this now happens on a global basis. Whereas once the brand names of drugs differed from country to country and huge differences existed between Japanese and American medicine, say, and between French and German medicine, from the mid-1990s drugs like Zyprexa, Lipitor, and Viagra have been launched globally with essentially the same marketing in every country. Partly as a result of these onslaughts, differences in medical cultures are flattening down to a common pharmaceutical denominator. Where almost no one had bipolar disorder, osteoporosis, or female sexual dysfunction two decades ago, these new conditions are now global epidemics.

Claims like these are cheap. If it were so simple to capture the institution of medicine just by coming up with fancy names for drugs, drug classes, and diseases, the proprietary medicines industry of the nineteenth century would never have died out. But driven by a real desire to care for the most vulnerable in society and a commitment to science, medicine eliminated these imitations of medical remedies for a century, with the exception of some holdovers from the former era such as Listerine and Clearasil. Good medicines clearly pushed out bad ones, in large part because they were based on good science. And good science continues—we now have astonishing developments in genetics and in medical imaging, so the argument presented here needs to pull back the curtains on the tricks of the pharmaceutical trade and show not only how modern marketing has closed in on the holy grail of fooling all of the people all of the time, but also why there has been so little resistance among doctors.

A great deal of the marketers' sleight-of-hand has involved a manipulation of the appearances of science. There is the early twentieth-century science that produced the sulfa drugs and other antibiotics such as penicillin that let the dying rise from their deathbeds. Science like this cuts across marketing. The results were so dramatic that the drugs in effect sold themselves. But the best-selling drugs today aren't like this. They come wrapped in numbers that appear to come from science but that have been fashioned by marketers to indicate abnormalities of lipids, blood pressure, blood sugar, mood, bone density, and respiratory flow, as well as penile stiffness and clitoral sensitivity that their company's drugs just happen to treat.

But science on its own, however artfully presented, would not have produced the comprehensive shift toward lifestyle drugs we have seen in recent decades or permitted pharmaceutical companies to penetrate the inner sanctums of medicine and transform it from a profession deeply hostile to marketing into a marketer's dream. There has been more involved. We have dealt with one structural element—the change in patent laws. We will now move on to two others—the emergence of prescription-only status for new drugs and the turn to controlled trials in the evaluation of drugs.

CLIMATE CHANGE

In retrospect the twenty-five years stretching from 1937 when the sulfa drugs were first introduced to 1962 when the US Food and Drugs Act was revised to tighten up regulations governing pharmaceuticals seems like a golden age. There were more novel agents introduced during this period than at any time before or since—the first antibiotics, antihypertensives, antipsychotics, and antidepressants, and the first oral antidiabetic drug. The period had not started well, however. Soon after sulfanilamide was introduced in 1937, a pharmacist in Oklahoma, unaware of the risk of ethylene glycol, sold sulfanilamide made up in this solvent, leading to over a hundred deaths.[42] In response, in 1938, American politicians stepped in to regulate commerce in medicines, through the Food, Drugs and Cosmetics Act. In 1962, American politicians stepped in again to regulate the industry with consequences that will follow us through to the end of the book.

Up to the late 1950s, prior to the passage of the 1962 amendments, in a history all but forgotten, the American Medical Association (AMA) had laboratories where they conducted their own testing of new drugs. They vetted any advertisements run in their journal, the *Journal of the American Medical Association (JAMA)*, for accuracy and only permitted those that earned their Seal of Approval. They regularly ran assessments of new treatments that were not beholden to the pharmaceutical industry. They were known for their support of generic formulations of drugs in preference to branded drugs. But in the 1950s these curbs on promotion stopped. The Seal of Approval scheme was watered down as the AMA sought further advertising revenue from pharmaceutical and other companies to fight Democratic plans to introduce a bill for Medicaid in Congress. With the new advertising, their revenues doubled.

In the 1950s there emerged a new set of discontents with the practices of the pharmaceutical industry and the prices these companies were charging for their drugs. The discontents were brought to public focus by the Democratic senator from Tennessee, Estes Kefauver. Kefauver's interest was stimulated when members of his staff found that several versions of the same antibiotic, marketed by different companies, had identical prices, and that the prices being charged were of the order of a 1000 percent of the price of manufacture. As they explored the issues, Kefauver's staff found compelling evidence that companies were secretly engaging in cartel practices to maintain the price of medicines and corrupting doctors with backdoor payments to prescribe on-patent and more expensive drugs. There seemed to be, as Kefauver put it, "an upside down competition where prices continue to go up even when production remains low or declines."[43] As the chair of the Senate antitrust and monopoly subcommittee he had the mandate to investigate what might be behind the apparent price-rigging.

Another concern of Kefauver's was the advertising for drugs. There was the sheer volume. As Walter Griffith of Parke Davis told Kefauver, "the ethical pharmaceutical industry of this country" had turned out "3,790,908,000 pages of paid journal advertising" and "741,213,700 direct mail impressions."[44] But of greater concern was that the ads were commonly misleading and in many cases downright fallacious. Kefauver's staff unearthed one ad for an antibiotic which displayed two chest X-rays, giving the impression of clinical improvement when the X-rays in fact came from two different patients neither of whom had had the antibiotic featured. As Dale Console, a former medical director at the Squibb pharmaceutical company later put it at Kefauver's Senate hearings, "If an automobile does not have a motor, no amount of advertising can make it appear to have one. On the other hand, with a little luck, proper timing, and a good promotion program, a bag of asafetida with a unique chemical side chain can be made to look like a wonder drug."[45]

Yet other concerns lay in drug company practices of withholding safety data on drugs, their lack of testing of new drugs on animals prior to marketing to humans and, more problematically, the fact that the regulators had no procedures in place to ensure a drug worked. The 1938 Food, Drugs and Cosmetics Act solely required companies to demonstrate safety in a number of patients without even basic toxicology testing in animals. As Kefauver's staff noted, if a drug didn't work for a condition for which it was marketed or worked less well than an already available product, then it was inherently unsafe. These discontents led in 1959 to the establishment of the Kefauver–Harris Senate hearings on pharmaceutical practices.[46]

Kefauver's main target was the patent system, which he thought was primarily responsible for the artificially high prices American patients uniquely faced. At the hearings, he elicited some revealing testimony from Frederick Meyers, a University of California professor of pharmacology who admitted that "most of the program [in drug research] has come from European and British researchers." The purpose of much of the work done by American drug firms was, according to Meyers, "partly to exploit and market" these foreign products but "mostly to modify the original drug just enough to get a patentable derivative."[47] Was this a good idea? Kefauver's staff produced figures to show that out of 77 countries surveyed, 28 allowed product patents and in these countries the prices of drugs ranged from 18 to 255 times higher than in the nonpatent countries, with both American-made and European-made drugs costing far less in Europe than in the United States.

But as Kefauver found, "These drug fellows pay for a lobby that makes the steel boys look like popcorn vendors . . . anyone who dares seek the truth will be accused of being a persecutor."[48] Up for reelection in 1960, he found himself branded a "socialist hell-bent on ruining healthcare." He was reelected comfortably, but when it came to his bill, despite having been the 1956 Democratic vice-presidential candidate, Kefauver had no support from the Kennedy administration, who were at the time trying to get Medicaid through Congress and did not want to antagonize the pharmaceutical industry. He also had no support from the American Medical Association, even for something as basic as a requirement that companies prove their drugs work before they are let on the market. The AMA was gearing up to fight Medicaid and was dependent on the increasing revenue it was receiving from pharmaceutical companies advertising in its journals.

Kefauver's bill (S.1552) was rewritten by his congressional opponents to make it more company friendly and in this form it seemed to have good prospects of passage. But then reports began to surface from Germany of the effects of a drug called thalidomide. Thalidomide was a sleeping pill sold over the counter in Germany and about to be marketed in the United States by Merrell Pharmaceuticals, when it was linked to a new and disturbing problem—babies of mothers who had taken the drug were born limbless or with useless flippers (phocomelia) where limbs should have been. The makers, Chemie-Grunenthal, fought the linkage to their drug and only removed thalidomide from the German market under pressure. Almost a year after the first reports, Merrell were mailing samples of the compound to American doctors, even though it had still not been licensed in the United States.

These events transformed the political imperative. Kefauver's bill was resurrected and rushed through both House and Senate, resulting in the 1962 amendments to the Food and Drugs Act. This mandated proper animal testing of drugs for toxicity before launch, and gave the FDA control over advertising. The new bill contained three further provisions whose far-reaching ramifications will be explored in chapters 2 and 3—it maintained prescription-only status for all new drugs, it required that companies demonstrate their drugs worked for a specified condition (where before they only had to prove safety), and it required companies to use controlled studies to demonstrate drug benefits. Kefauver's bill, however, was stripped of its provisions to change patent law, despite support from the Chief Patent Officer. And because the patent law wasn't changed, the 1962 amendments had no effect on Kefauver's primary target—control of the prices of drugs.

While it failed in its primary objective, the stripped-down bill was passed to wide acclaim. Kefauver, flanked by the junior senator from

Tennessee, Albert Gore, Sr., had been given the honor of speaking to it on the Senate floor. The disturbing changes in the climate of medicine would be stopped or even reversed, he hoped. Kennedy and Kefauver basked in the glow of success. Frances Kelsey, a staffer at the FDA, whose bureaucratic delay in reviewing and handling the license application for thalidomide undoubtedly restricted the number of American children exposed to the drug in utero, received a President's Award for Distinguished Federal Civilian Service. The reforms to the FDA were copied by other regulatory agencies worldwide. When it came to drugs, the management of pregnancy became the one area of medicine that most closely conformed to Pinel's hopes for all of medicine—that doctors in knowing when not to prescribe would demonstrate the highest medical art. Many still think this to be the case, but today's reality is quite different.

2

Medicine and the Marketers

When she became pregnant in 2004, 38-year-old Gina Fromm did a range of things that few women would have done in the early 1960s—she took cold rather than hot showers in case she might harm her baby, stopped eating yogurt and incinerated chicken because of the risk of bacterial infection, from listeria to salmonella. She balked at taking prenatal vitamins, though she had been taking Paxil following a fleeting episode of anxiety. She continued to take it through her pregnancy; she had found stopping difficult and her doctor reassured her it posed no risk to her baby. On February 2, 2005, her son was born with congenital heart defects.[1]

In the decades following the passage of Senator Kefauver's bill, women were far less likely to smoke, drink alcohol or coffee, or take painkillers while pregnant. Nevertheless, Paxil and other SSRI antidepressants, among the direct successors of thalidomide, were on their way to becoming the most commonly prescribed drugs in pregnancy—especially in the United States. In 2006, forty-four years after the 1962 amendments to the Food and Drugs Act, the first legal actions were filed for birth defects induced by SSRI antidepressants, resulting in verdicts against GlaxoSmithKline and huge settlements, but this made little dent on the prescribing of SSRIs in pregnancy, which continued to mount.

Nothing about the 1962 amendments obviously predicted the replays of drug-induced birth defects we now have. Medications continued to be available on a prescription-only basis. With the 1962 amendments to the Food and Drugs Act, companies were to be restricted to selling medications for real diseases rather than for trivial indications like halitosis or fleeting anxiety states. Furthermore, from 1962 onward, companies had to demonstrate by means of controlled trials that their remedies did in fact work.

There can be few better symbols of Pharmageddon than prescription-only drugs becoming among the most consumed drugs in pregnancy in the face of strengthening warnings that they cause birth defects. The answers to how this could happen lie in great part in how the pharmaceutical companies have managed to capitalize on the very protections put in place by Senator Kefauver in his 1962 bill and in the reforms that defeated him. Prescription-only status has made doctors the targets of a marketing exercise that is far more sophisticated than placing even billions of pages of advertisements in medical journals and bribing doctors to use drugs. As outlined in chapter 1, the patent status of drugs has given companies an incentive to chase blockbuster profits—doing so regardless of patient welfare. Controlled trials have given the companies a means to persuade doctors that snake oil works so well that withholding it in pregnancy would be unethical, and also a means to make problems consequent on treatment vanish. But all of these hinge on the fact that these drugs are available by prescription only.

WHAT THE DOCTOR ORDERED

When Alfred Worcester or Richard Cabot wrote a prescription for a remedy at the dawn of the twentieth century, they were following a centuries-old tradition of asking an apothecary to take certain ingredients and mix them according to a formula (Rx = Recipe). If there was more than one ingredient in the mix, each should have a particular purpose. If the remedy worked, patients were able to take the prescription back to the pharmacy on numerous occasions asking for refills for themselves without further endorsement from the doctor. Alternatively, having once obtained something by prescription that worked, they could revisit the pharmacist and ask for the same medicines again, for family members. A prescription from a doctor was only one means by which people could access the drugs they believed they needed.

Because in Cabot's day all medicines, including opiates, bromides, barbiturates, chloral hydrate (used for sedation), antiseptics, remedies for the gut, urinary system, and heart and respiratory system were available without recourse to a doctor, the threshold for visiting a doctor was far higher than it is today. Until the middle years of the twentieth century, there was no one being treated for latent diabetes, latent hypertension, or raised lipids. Aside from a few wealthy people engaged in psychoanalysis, no one had contact with the mental health system other than those relatively few who had psychoses and were committed to asylums.

When the US Congress passed the 1906 Food and Drugs Act, it contained no prescription requirement, only a requirement that medicine manufacturers state the contents of the product on the label. The pharmaceutical industry lobbied hard against the act, but once it was in place many enterprising manufacturers found ways of working the new situation to their advantage, for instance, by labeling their product "as approved by the Chemical Bureau."[2]

There were no implications here for traditional medical practice. But another regulatory step taken soon thereafter had profound implications. The nineteenth century saw a growing concern about opiate and cocaine abuse, as well as alcoholism. These problems had been of little concern to medicine. Drug addiction, like alcoholism, was considered a social problem, except where the affected people became patients by virtue of cirrhosis or psychosis. After a variety of social approaches to treating the problems of addiction floundered, in 1914 the US Congress passed the Harrison Narcotics Act, which introduced prescription-only status for opiates and cocaine.[3] The problem of addiction would be managed, or so it was thought, by making these drugs legally available only through a medical practitioner.

After the contaminated sulfanilamide tragedy of 1937, the 1938 Food, Drugs and Cosmetics Act encouraged a move toward making new drugs available by prescription only. The calculation was that the sulfa drugs were better categorized with insulin and the steroid and thyroid hormones, which were typically if not exclusively administered by doctors. After World War II, in 1951, the prescription-only status for new medicines in the United States was copper-fastened in place with the Humphrey-Durham amendments to the 1938 act, despite vigorous, sustained, and widespread opposition to the move. Critics complained that a system put in place for addicts was inappropriate for free citizens. But by the early 1950s, one of the side effects of having medicines that really worked was becoming clear—drugs that could really benefit, could really harm also. In 1952, Leo Meyler's *Side Effects of Drugs* appeared, a first-ever medical compendium of drug-induced injuries.[4] This new potential for harm took dramatic shape in 1961 with limbless babies born to mothers who had taken thalidomide during pregnancy as a supposedly safer hypnotic than the older barbiturates.[5]

When it came to his hearings in 1959, Senator Kefauver was exercised by the prescription-only status of the new drugs, a unique characteristic found in no other market. As he put it, "He who orders does not buy; and he who buys does not order." As a consequence, when it came to drugs available by prescription only ordinary consumers could not protect themselves against the monopoly element inherent in trademarks or patents. Patients were critically dependent on their doctors to be uninfluenced by trademarks, patents, or marketing ploys. Doctors had a choice whether to give their patients the latest on-patent and branded drug or perhaps an older, more effective and less expensive drug, but patients had little choice other than to do as prescribed by their doctor.[6]

Thalidomide had been available over the counter in many European countries but exactly the same problems arose in the United States where the premarketing samples were available by prescription only. Indeed the problems may have come to light as quickly as they did because doctors in Germany were not inhibited in recognizing the potential for harm of an over-the-counter drug, as they might have been in the case of a drug essential to their livelihoods. But in the United States in 1962, in the face of the thalidomide disaster, retaining the prescription-only status of drugs seemed to make sense: doctors retained some patina of skepticism about drug claims due to medicine's long-standing opposition to quackery, and doctors appeared to be the people who would be able to quarry information from drug companies about possible adverse side effects of their products.

Before 1962 prescription-only status was still something of a novelty—after 1962 it became the center of the distribution system for new drugs when companies were required not only to make their drugs available only through doctors but also to prove that their drugs worked for some medical condition in order to get FDA approval. This combination of controls must have looked pretty foolproof in 1962, but it has not turned out to be an effective way to constrain the pharmaceutical industry within a medical framework. Quite the reverse. When a pharmaceutical company gets a drug on the market for lowering cholesterol, for osteoporosis, or for erectile dysfunction, this now marks the point at which the company begins to sell the condition, the point at which they can gear up to reengineer the medical marketplace to suit their product, as Abbott did with bipolar disorder to make it Depakote-friendly. It seems extraordinary now that no one in 1962 seems to have realized that if pharmaceutical companies were restricted to marketing drugs for diseases, they might start to market diseases.

Had pharmaceutical companies not been required to demonstrate a drug's efficacy in treating a particular disorder, we might all have ended up with a lot fewer diseases recorded in our medical records. The first antidepressants would have been marketed as tonics or stimulants. To get St. John's wort, an herb with SSRI properties, we just have to feel stressed and buy it over the counter where it is sold as a tonic, but to get Prozac now, we have to be officially diagnosed as depressed. In a similar fashion, the statins might have been marketed on the promise of restoring inner youthfulness, or getting our arteries in shape, rather than for a supposed cholesterol disorder, or the biphosphonates might have been aimed at restoring youthful bones rather than for osteoporosis. As insurance companies reimburse in response to diagnoses, fewer diagnoses would likely have reduced our need for doctors in addition to reducing the number of diseases.

The third medical requirement of the 1962 amendments was that companies demonstrate their products worked in well-controlled clinical trials. This was smuggled into the final bill through the efforts of Louis Lasagna, a professor of pharmacology and a believer in controlled trials, who was attempting at the time to encourage some use of controlled trials, rather than trying to make them mandatory.[7] Lasagna himself had undertaken the only controlled trial of thalidomide ever done, through which it sailed—an effective hypnotic free of significant side effects.

The copper-fastening of prescription-only arrangements that came out of the Kefauver hearings would alone have put doctors in the sights of pharmaceutical company marketing departments in a way they had never been before. But constraining companies to market their drugs for diseases and to demonstrate their efficacy through what was then a new medical invention, the controlled trial, made it necessary for companies not just to have doctors in their sights but to understand doctors better than doctors understood themselves.

In the case of some hugely profitable trademarked drugs, such as Marlboro, medicine has played an honorable part in bringing lethal problems to light. But what would have happened had tobacco been available by prescription only? It is clearly helpful for ulcerative colitis. In all probability it could be shown to be just as good an antidepressant as Prozac and the SSRIs—so the market might have been substantial. How quick then would doctors have been to do the independent studies that pinpointed the problems linked to smoking or to insist on the seriousness of the risks while the tobacco industry was systematically creating doubt about those risks?

Doctors don't view themselves as consumers, subject not only to the extraordinary pressures that modern marketing can bring to bear on any consumer but also, by virtue of prescription-only arrangements, to these forces in the most concentrated form that exists anywhere on the globe. Typically, they blithely go their way without seeing the need to understand marketing. They bunker down behind a Maginot Line of what they believe are untainted controlled trials and evidence-based medicine, unaware that the tank divisions and air force of their opponents give daily thanks for that Maginot Line.

THE RISE OF THE BLOCKBUSTER

The possibilities for a new generation of branded medicines—and extraordinary sales—that opened up on the back of a regime that allowed drugs to be patented and that made these drugs available on a prescription-only basis were first revealed in the course of a battle in the 1980s between pharmaceutical giants Glaxo and SmithKline over the ulcer drugs Tagamet (cimetidine) and Zantac (ranitidine).

James Black was one of the most successful medicinal chemists ever; he was also one of the first to win a Nobel Prize while working in the pharmaceutical industry. Black had initially worked for Imperial Chemical Industries, where he had developed the concept of a beta-blocker. These drugs, which blocked the beta-adrenergic receptors on which stress hormones like epinephrine exert their effects throughout the body, turned out to be particularly useful for treating hypertension, the most rapidly growing medical market in the 1970s.

Black then moved to SmithKline, where he turned his attention to the antihistamines, helping to distinguish among two different histamine receptors, H-1 and H-2. This opened the way to develop H-2 blockers that would target histamine receptors in the gut, reducing gastric acid production, then thought to be responsible for ulcers. Tagamet was the result, a drug that embodied a genuinely novel approach to the treatment of duodenal ulcers, then one of biggest problems in internal medicine.[8] Within a few years of its introduction, surgery for ulcers had become a rarity—had Tagamet been available earlier, it would have saved my mother much misery. This epitomized the best hopes of both science and industry—new and innovative products making it into healthcare and making a big difference to patients.

In the course of developing Tagamet, Black presented details of his experiments at scientific meetings, stimulating interest among chemists at Glaxo, who also determined to develop an H-2 blocker. Glaxo's efforts led to Zantac, a drug almost identical to Tagamet. Since Tagamet had been the breakthrough compound and had come on the market in 1979, six years before Zantac, and with the prestige of Black's endorsement, few doubted that Tagament's sales would vastly outstrip those of Zantac.

Glaxo, far from undercutting the price of Tagamet, as might have been expected in a normal market, decided to make Zantac pricier. And it put huge resources into marketing, which focused on minor differences in the side-effect profiles of the two drugs. Much to the surprise of observers, Zantac's revenues soon outstripped Tagamet's, and it became the first blockbuster—a drug that makes at least a billion dollars per year.[9]

Glaxo and SmithKline merged at the turn of the millennium to become the biggest pharmaceutical company in the world. But before they did, Glaxo's response to an exciting development in the science of ulcers is indicative of important shifts that were taking place in the world of medicine and corporate interest. In Australia, Barry Marshall, then a medical resident in Perth, spotted an unusual bacterium, *helicobacter pylori*, in tissues removed from ulcers. This led him to a series of experiments where he cultured helicobacter, drank it, produced an ulcer, and later cured his own ulcer with antibiotics.[10]

Marshall made overtures to Glaxo but found they had no interest in a cure for ulcers. The beauty of H-2 blockers was that once they began taking them, many patients remained on them indefinitely. Actually eliminating ulcers, the treatment of which had just become the cash cow of the pharmaceutical industry, was not what Glaxo had in mind. The decade between the contrasting scientific experiments of James Black and Barry Marshall had propelled medicine into a new world, one in which it could not be assumed that science and business were on the same side, as they had appeared to have been over the previous three decades.

Zantac was a brand like no other. It came with attention to color coding, with free pens and trinkets for doctors, and a lot of support for doctors to attend educational meetings nationally and internationally. It set a template for aggressive drug promotion. Its very success led, in reaction, to movements like No Free Lunch, a group set up by Bob Goodman to persuade doctors to remain independent of pharmaceutical companies by refusing the free pens, lunches, and the like that companies handed out so liberally. Glaxo's aggressive marketing at the end of the 1980s also made many doctors more receptive to the idea that evidence-based medicine, which emerged in the 1990s, could be used as a way to contain the power of marketing.

But No Free Lunch and similar efforts to eliminate conflicts of interest fail to ask just what it is that would make a brand appealing to doctors. A brand is something whose value lies in the perception of the beholder—and in this case doctors repeatedly tell us that the evidence about a drug's benefits and risks trumps the color coding of the capsule or the lunches, no matter how good they might be. And insofar as creating a brand involves building a set of exclusively positive associations and eliminating any negative associations, this is not going to be done by getting the color right.

The problem is that a brand is meant to be an uncomplicated good. It is a partial truth that seduces by directing our attention away from any messier realities. It doesn't fart; it doesn't have body odor. Against a background of clinical complexity it offers a point of reassurance. But it is, by this definition, incompatible with a medicine, which is—or was—understood to be a poison whose delivery involves a judicious balancing of risks and benefits.

The combination of brands like this and prescription-only privileges leads to a tragedy in the classic sense of that word—as with Hamlet, "whose virtues else be they as pure as grace as infinite as man may undergo, shall in the general censure take corruption from the particular fault." Here's how. Brands married to product patents have created the conditions that have made blockbusters possible, and the fortunes of pharmaceutical companies increasingly now depend on the success of these blockbusters and their branding. They have to be hyped to the max and their hazards concealed. These dynamics of brand creation are, through prescription-only status, welded to an profound bias in medicine—doctors tend to attribute any benefits in a patient's state to what they have done and couple this with a tendency to overlook any harm they might have done. Doctors have to be enthusiastic about treatment—their very enthusiasm can make the difference between success and failure. Being readily able also to spot the harms they do would likely in many cases lead to clinical paralysis.

The fortunes of pharmaceutical companies hinge on this weld holding fast. The tragedy is that there is little risk of it coming undone: both companies and clinicians are biased to attribute any harms to the disease being treated—it is depression that gives rise to suicidality in patients on antidepressants, not the drugs; it is the poor state of a person's arteries that leads to coronary artery bypass surgery and is responsible for any confusion after the surgery rather than anything that happened on the operating table; it is schizophrenia that gives rise to a disfiguring neurological condition, tardive dyskinesia, rather than treatment with antipsychotics. For thirty years the outcomes for lung cancer have remained almost unchanged. Millions of people have died during this period, after having radical surgery, intense radiotherapy, or intense chemotherapy. If these treatments extended the life of some yet overall life expectancy remained the same, there must also be an equal number whose lives were shortened by treatment, but you will hunt high and low to find any whose deaths are attributed to the treatment rather than the disease.

When it comes to the harms following ingestion of over-the-counter or illegal drugs, from the end of the nineteenth century the medical profession had no difficulty seeing their problems and expressing opinions through bodies such as the AMA. But once the drugs are made available by prescription only through the clinician, there is no independent voice of any standing to urge caution. Against this clinical background, the dynamics of branding produce something close to a pure toxin for medical care.

The contrasting fates of reserpine and Prozac bring this out. In the early 1950s, reserpine, one of the first antihypertensives and first tranquilizers, was linked to suicide induction. Owing to the differing patent regimes at the time, twenty-six different companies produced reserpine and so no one manufacturer could have made it into a proprietary blockbuster. Therefore no company had an incentive to defend it to the death, and as a result while many doctors refused to concede a treatment they gave might have caused a problem, the views of others could be heard. A link between reserpine and agitation was established and reserpine fell into disfavor.

But in 1990, when similar concerns erupted that Prozac could trigger suicides, the situation was quite different. There was and could be only one Prozac, and Lilly had all their eggs in the Prozac basket. They could not readily admit their brand might have a flaw. As Leigh Thompson, Lilly's chief scientific officer put it in an internal e-mail that later came to light in a court case:

> I am concerned about reports I get re UK attitude toward Prozac safety. Leber (FDA) suggested a few minutes ago we use CSM database to compare Prozac aggression and suicidal ideation with other antidepressants in UK. Although he is a fan of Prozac and believes a lot of this is garbage, he is

clearly a political creature and will have to respond to pressures. I hope Patrick realizes that Lilly can go down the tubes if we lose Prozac and just one event in the UK can cost us that.[11]

Several years later company documents for Lilly's post-Prozac blockbuster Zyprexa made it clear that

The company is betting the farm on Zyprexa. The ability of Eli Lilly to remain independent and emerge as the fastest growing pharma company of the decade depends solely on our ability to achieve world class commercialization of Zyprexa.[12]

Prozac, Zyprexa, and other such blockbusters are products that come with a life plan that covers their use in all global markets.[13] Even before the launch of potential blockbusters, ways of promoting their use in children and the elderly, without undertaking clinical trials to demonstrate efficacy or safety, is envisaged. The necessity of acknowledging a side effect that might restrict this use is not part of the plan. When a company is faced with defending a brand that is essential to its survival, commercial logic dictates that it will take any steps necessary to preempt the emergence of a hazard, including doctoring the evidence. This commercial logic led to a relentless marketing of Zyprexa that ultimately saw it being given to children as young as twelve months of age, its clinician prescribers seemingly unable to see the massive weight gain it produces, the diabetes it triggers, the raised lipids it leads to, and the premature deaths it causes.[14]

As the story of H-2 blockers and the treatment of ulcers suggests, drug companies have little interest in innovative treatments that would eradicate a condition for which they have on-patent drugs that manage it after some fashion. When ulcers vanished, after the introduction of antibiotics, companies like Astra-Zeneca with a new generation of gastric acid antagonists, such as Prilosec, turned to GERD (gastro-esophageal reflux disease) to replace it. This disease, which now seems so widespread and crippling, was infrequently encountered when I was training, and as such it is difficult to believe it doesn't stem at least in part from our increasingly unbalanced and artificial diets and lifestyles. While there are unquestionably severe cases that need urgent medical treatment, it also seems the case that a large number of digestive discomforts that might be better handled by changing lifestyles have now been medicalized and are managed with medication.

Quite extraordinarily GERD has even spread into infancy, incorporating colic, a disorder that lasts a few months and responds to care in the real sense. The first drug treatment for GERD in infants—Prepulsid (cisapride)—killed significant numbers of children where colic had never been known to kill children before.[15] The shock of Prepulsid-induced deaths did not lead to a return to traditional medical care of colic—children instead are now getting Prilosec (omeprazole) and other successors of Zantac.

At the eighteenth annual Pharmaceutical Conference in Paris in June 1990, Christopher Adam, then the head of marketing at Glaxo told the meeting "we are moving into the mega-product age."[16] Right he was. Zantac had just become the first blockbuster. The next year all blockbusters combined only comprised 6 percent of the market, but by 1997, when SSRIs like Prozac were the darlings of the media, this had grown to 18 percent, and by 2001 to 45 percent, under the impact of Lipitor and the statins.[17] There is no blockbuster that is a life-saving drug. They are all lifestyle or risk management drugs.

In 1990, market analysts perceived two threats to Glaxo's position as the largest drug company in the world—the possible expiry of its patent on Zantac and the emergence of Prilosec, a new drug for ulcers. In fact the danger came from Barry Marshall's research. Prilosec did displace Zantac but for the GERD rather than the ulcer market, forcing Glaxo into a series of mergers in order to sustain its position among the leading companies. In 1995, it merged with Burroughs Wellcome, at which time its chief executive, Richard Sykes, made it clear he still regarded the company as a serious research company that would have nothing to do with lifestyle drugs like Prozac. Five years later it merged with SmithKline Beecham, whose fortunes rode on Paxil, the company's biggest earner since. By this time Sykes was gone. The market was changing the character of drug companies and in turn the shape of medicine.

THE FACE IN THE MIRROR

The idea that brands such as Lipitor, Paxil, and Fosamax might now have penetrated medical practice in a way that brands like Clark Stanley's Snake Oil or Beecham's Pills never did and that these modern brands might now play as big a part in medicine as Nike and Reebok do for running shoes and Lexus and BMW do for cars is not an idea that sits comfortably with the medical profession's idea of itself.

In the world of medicine most doctors come from, drugs are good, though they are unfortunately sold by slick if rather sleazy salespeople to whom doctors might try to be polite but whom they otherwise try to avoid—unless "these people" are picking up the drinks tab. But in the new world of medicine, the person doing the selling is not the sleazy-looking suit standing by the exhibit. That person is there to distract attention from the fact that one by one doctors are having marketed back to them exactly what they say are the things that count for them. The industry needs a person out there whom the doctor can identify as a source of corruption, someone they can resist, the way they might resist an obvious honeypot. In this new world, if a group like No Free Lunch didn't exist, the pharmaceutical industry would have to invent it.

In other industries, when companies manufacture a product they have to move it from factory to retail outlets where it competes with other products and they have to generate demand among consumers. The ideal arrangement is to have a dedicated showroom, such as automobile makers and Apple do, where purchases become almost inevitable as there are no competing brands in sight and, in the case of cars, nothing praising the virtues of walking, running, cycling, or any other means of transport. In the case of a branded drug, the task is to get on a hospital's or managed care company's list of approved drugs as well as into national guidelines and to have key articles placed in all the prominent journals. We shall see in chapters 4 and 5 how companies manage this and manage to eliminate competing influences, so that when the doctor gets to the point of purchase, the purchase is as inevitable as it is in a car showroom, but here let us focus on the doctor before he walks into the showroom.

He will likely think he is not particularly influenced by the ads for drugs he sees. And in this he is undoubtedly correct to a point—at least three-quarters of the ads for a drug are not aimed at him. He may even think that most ads make him less likely to prescribe rather than more likely. He will be unaware that just as marketers distinguish between women and men, or between those of us who want high-tech versus retro running shoes, so they also have learned to distinguish between "high-flyers," "skeptical experimenters," "rule bound," and "silent majority" doctors.[18] Few doctors have any idea how the marketers have pigeonholed them and as a result will not be able to pick out the ads aimed at them from the ones aimed at others that serve a secondary function of throwing any particular doctor off the scent.

High flyers are the doctors keen to try new things. They don't want to hear what is in guidelines or what colleagues are doing. They are interested in the latest reports that promote a drug for something new, or in a different cocktail with other drugs, or in a higher dose than previously recommended. These are doctors that companies term "early uptakers" and they are important to getting a new product adopted. Skeptical experimenters are similar but more likely to temper their prescribing practices on the basis of experience.

In contrast to these two types, marketers identify most doctors as either rule bound or silent-majority conservatives. For the rule bound, regulatory approval of a drug means the drug should be used for the stated purpose and for that purpose only, and in accordance with the latest guidelines. The conservative majority want everything kept simple. They pick a drug and stick to it; they're most interested in aspects such as whether the drug comes in a new formulation that might enhance compliance—a tablet that dissolves instantly in the mouth, for example, so that patients cannot but comply.

Where doctors, the media, and others see a salesperson visiting a physician with free pens and an offer of lunch, with a pitch based perhaps on the results of some recent clinical trial on a drug, the key exchange is of a different order: it is not what is handed over to the doctor but how he or she responds to various probes and what is then fed back to the company. After that, the pitch to a high flyer will be as different as the one to a rule-bound doctor just as a car salesman's pitch is different to someone keen to buy a sports car compared to someone who wants to buy a family car.[19] The ads and the patter directed at high flyers will show a doctor on a mission to tackle the scourge of disease, a mission that sometimes justifies extreme measures, where the ads to the rule bound may feature the latest authoritative guideline. The idea is to get the mood music right in the showroom, to get the brand speak in the right tone of voice.

Doctors won't have to make their own way to the showroom—they will likely be transported there even if the showroom is in a different country, being wined and dined en route. Once in the showroom, a doctor won't meet a salesman but instead, colleagues, or a local professor, or some medical eminence. The knowledge needed to construct a blockbuster brand is derived almost entirely from the physicians to whom the product is being sold. The careers of Lipitor, Nexium, Vioxx, Prozac, and Depakote make this clear. Doctors tell the company what they, the doctors, want to hear.

In the course of a drug's development, panels of medical academics—opinion leaders—are convened to see what the consumer wants. Pharmaceutical companies do nothing so crude as call these focus groups, but this is essentially what they are. The consumers being courted are jobbing doctors, and the process is aimed at guessing how these clinicians can be influenced. At the 1990 Paris pharmaceutical conference, Glaxo's marketing chief told the audience "concepts sell drugs."[20] The academic focus groups are where a company will find out just what concepts are current. After the demise of Vioxx, doctors needed something new for pain relief but rather than sell them Lyrica, a not very good analgesic, Pfizer married Lyrica to fibromyalgia and sold this combination. Fibromyalgia is a suitably vague condition characterized by nonspecific complaints of pain that had been knocking around medicine for a century.[21]

The new role of medical academics is to broker this process. Where once these academics were the repositories and creators of medical culture, they are now a resource to be plumbed by companies to establish what prescribers can be induced to want rather than what's best for the patient. The key thing is to establish what prescribers do want from a drug and ensure they appear to get what they want, whether or not there is much basis in the drug to think it might do what the prescriber wants. If pain has become an issue for doctors, the marketing of a new product will emphasize this quality even if there is nothing to recommend the new product for this purpose compared with older products. Companies trumpet the huge research and development budgets needed to bring a drug to market today. But it costs very little to make these medications. Research is undertaken on the new pill, but most of the studies are designed to secure therapeutic niches rather than to advance medical knowledge. The real "research" budget is devoted to establishing the mindset of clinicians at the time of launch. In 2003, it was estimated that thought-leader development in the United States accounted for a stunning 20 percent of marketing costs and was rising,[22] compared with 14 percent put into direct-to-consumer ads.[23]

Take the bladder stabilizer Yentreve (duloxetine). Lilly had jettisoned duloxetine as a potential antidepressant in the 1990s because it triggered urinary retention among other effects, but then brought it onto the market in Europe as a bladder stabilizer. When Prozac went off patent in 2001 and its designated successor, Zalutria, appeared to produce cardiac problems, Lilly opted to bring duloxetine back to antidepressant life as Cymbalta. Cymbalta was marketed heavily as a pain reliever in addition to helping depression. Why? Because doctors had told market surveys they often have patients in pain of one sort or another and were uncertain how to treat them.

Luckily for Lilly, just as Cymbalta was coming to market, the leading painkiller Vioxx was withdrawn from circulation because research showed it caused heart attacks. Anything that would help pain was catapulted forward in the promotions of all companies, and Cymbalta was certainly no exception.[24] As a result, a great number of patients attending pain relief clinics or visiting internists or primary care practitioners and complaining of pain were put on it, even though they showed no signs of depression. What doctors were hearing when they listened to the siren song from Cymbalta were their own needs. Duloxetine had nothing to recommend it for pain beyond what other antidepressants have, but Cymbalta relieved doctors' worries about pain.[25] Such marketing might have been developed for Zalutria and simply switched to Cymbalta in just the way that the marketing for one brand of bottled water could be applied to any another. There is nothing in the water that gives substance to any of these perceptions.

The patient given Cymbalta for pain relief is not to know that it is more likely to lead to agitation, sometimes severe enough to trigger thoughts of suicide—and that the FDA banned its use for urinary incontinence for this very reason. They are not likely to know that Cymbalta is more likely to cause urinary retention than it is to ease pain. But the patient is not the consumer, the doctor is, and his pain is eased by Cymbalta without any side effect to cloud the picture.

Once the distinguishing feature of a marketing campaign has been identified, the appearances of scientific support are manufactured. A clinical consensus for a drug such as Lyrica (Pfizer's drug ostensibly to treat fibromyalgia) or Cymbalta for pain, for instance, is built by means of scientific symposia, with articles apparently written by opinion leaders but usually ghostwritten, or by educational initiatives featuring well-known academics.

Ultimately branding of this sort feeds off blue-skies research and medical education funded by governments in the United States and Europe. Without this there would be very little understanding of the effect a medication has on lipids or bones or blood pressure and as a result very little language available with which to describe the effects of the drugs for marketing purposes. From the point of view of marketing, the advantage of the medical sciences is not that they might lead to better drugs but rather that they provide concepts and languages for marketers to use.

One of the best examples of this process has been the creation of the notion of chemical imbalance. Neurotransmitters were identified in the brain in the early 1960s. By 1965, this led some to hypothesize that the amounts of one or another of two common neurotransmitters, norepinephrine and serotonin, are lowered in depression and that antidepressants could top them up. By 1970, psychopharmacologists had abandoned these hypotheses because of clear inadequacy.[26] But twenty years later, the idea that serotonin was low in depression and restored to normal by treatment was resurrected within the marketing departments of SmithKline Beecham, Lilly, and Pfizer, as part of the sales pitch for Paxil, Prozac, and Zoloft. It was marketing copy par excellence, too tempting to spurn. In fact, mindless patter about restoring chemical balances did a great deal to make the SSRIs among the most profitable income streams for the pharmaceutical industry from 1990 onward. In similar fashion when selling drugs for osteoporosis, cholesterol reduction, asthma, and other conditions, marketers cherry-pick from the language of the appropriate science to dress up their products. As they put it themselves, they leverage the bits of the science base that suit them.

In addition to using information from the basic sciences, one of the clearest strategies companies use is to market diseases in the expectation that sales of the pills promoted for them will follow. This has happened from the 1950s onward, when Merck educated physicians to recognize raised blood pressure (hypertension) and its consequences after their new diuretic agent, Diuril, turned out to have antihypertensive properties. They convened symposia and sponsored studies on the benefits of monitoring hypertension.[27] This approach speaks directly to clinicians in clinical language. It also puts an ethical onus on them to eliminate a disease by prescribing a pill—one that comes sanctioned by the experts in the field.

Patients also have to be softened up so they are receptive to the idea of being prescribed a statin, or an antihypertensive, or a biphosphonate for their bones. In the United States direct-to-consumer advertisements school people on the importance of their "figures"—their lipid levels, blood pressure, and bone densities—or alert them to the possibility that what they regard as restless legs may be in fact be an illness,[28] or that feelings of urgency as regards micturition, low grade pain, or less than perfect sexual potency may be illnesses that can be treated. Ask your doctor if . . .

Elsewhere in the world promotional stories appearing in the health pages of newspapers and magazines fulfill the same function. PR firms place stories in the media and help sponsor books such as *Listening to Prozac,*[29] while marketers increasingly utilize Internet sites where patients can diagnose themselves and take the resulting information back to their doctors. If there is a buzz around some disorder the British, Australian, or French media are naturally going to be interested to feature it, even though direct-to-consumer ads are not permitted in these countries. They may portray the condition as one that may be as effectively treated without medication, or indeed the program may come out vigorously against regarding certain states as disorders in need of treatment, but simply raising consciousness about the condition is taken advantage of by clever drug marketers. The company touch is subtle—sponsored symposia, for instance, will regularly feature talks by academics advocating nondrug approaches to an illness. These talks fill the same role as the comic at a burlesque show—a straight man is needed at intervals between the disrobing women.[30]

Capturing understanding is the prelude to selling pills. The marketer aims to convert people from thinking that childhood has its vicissitudes and developmental stages and that most distress and abnormalities are transient to thinking in terms of diseases and chemical imbalances that cry out for treatment, from depression to ADHD, autism to juvenile bipolar disorder. The normal elevations of blood lipids and thinning of bones that go with age are transformed into diseases—moreover, diseases that have become as much commodities as are iPods and as subject to fashion, with the main determinant of the fashion cycle being the patent life of a drug.

So successful have the marketers been that it is now common practice among them to assume that few if any doctors will have any medical thoughts in their mind other than what is put there by either their own company or one of their competitors. They find even fewer physicians aware of how they are being sold pills, much less able to put up a challenge. Even if there were a challenge, just as Che Guevara has ended up as an establishment logo, so also can many forms of protest be incorporated by the marketers' machinery.[31] Just as a hostile review can sell books, companies have even learned how to increase sales in the face of FDA requirements to issue warnings about hazards such as birth defects due to Paxil, by "controversializing" the issues.

BRAND NEW MEDICINE

When asked to comment on the significance of the French Revolution, Mao Tse-tung and Chou En-lai are reputed to have said it was still too soon to judge. Two hundred years ago, in the midst of that revolution, Western medicine took on much of its modern character. In addition to the traditional and private relationship between doctor and patient, a new duty to look after the health of the wider population emerged, setting up new relationships between doctors and their patients and the state. One of the key players in shaping the new medicine was Philippe Pinel, among the most prominent of a new breed of doctors who stood in contrast to the society doctors of the eighteenth and nineteenth centuries that made a living treating wealthy patients with hypochondriacal ailments.[32]

Faced with the competing pressures on doctors, Pinel stressed that physicians needed to combine their roles as givers of care and as scientists. It was only through the application of science, he said, that doctors would be able to distinguish among the conditions they were treating and establish the natural history of each. This would give them the best chance to discover the anatomical basis of these conditions and might lead to new therapies for both individual patients and the wider community.

Pinel's approach both to science and its public dimension was vindicated in the 1880s, when laboratory science began to demonstrate links between diseases and microbes. Once it was clear infections were transmissible, medicine had to have a public dimension. In our day this dimension is global. Drug-resistant tuberculosis in Russia and AIDS in Africa pose threats to all of us.[33]

If in principle the mission of medicine has been to treat the diseased and dying wherever they are, that of the pharmaceutical industry has increasingly been to protect its patents and its profits. The clash of these values came to a dramatic head in the late 1990s with the struggles to make antiretroviral drugs available in sub-Saharan Africa for the treatment of HIV-AIDS, just as Glaxo Wellcome and SmithKline Beecham were in merger talks. The first of the antiretroviral drugs, zidovudine, also called AZT, was developed in university laboratories with public funding—the first of which, for marketing and distribution purposes, was offered to Burroughs Wellcome (prior to the merger with Glaxo) to patent, which it did and then marketed as Retrovir.[34] The fear of AIDS in the 1990s ensured that Glaxo Wellcome and other companies marketing these drugs had a rich return on these products.

In the early 1980s AIDS appeared to be confined to the United States or the Western Hemisphere, but by the 1990s it was clear that there were far higher rates of infection in Africa and a risk of the disorder spreading to Asia and elsewhere. The rates were so high that many African countries faced being crippled by the disease. Supported by all other companies, GlaxoSmithKline (GSK) refused to either permit other companies to offer the drug in generic form at much lower prices or to lower the price on AZT themselves to a level that would make it possible for the hundreds of thousands suffering in Africa to benefit from it and thereby stem the tide of an enormous tragedy. To do so, GSK argued, would breach patent law in a manner that would compromise future drug discoveries. It was as though the companies who produced diphtheria antitoxin a century earlier had refused to make it available. The outrage of almost the entire world forced GSK to back down.

Glaxo and other pharmaceutical companies have been willing to treat the West and, more recently, the wealthy parts of China, India, and Brazil, as gated communities, within which one form of healthcare will be available and outside of which no questions will be asked. Some of those inside the gates may regret this policy, but provided their children and families are not the ones dying from diphtheria or AIDS these regrets are unlikely to lead to action. But this is short-sighted in the extreme. The same patent and marketing factors that have led companies to lose interest in developing drugs for Third World diseases if these do not afford a sufficient return on investment by today's blockbuster standards, mean that the drug companies are no longer likely to play the kind of role they once did in eliminating disorders like diphtheria or bacterial endocarditis. Indeed, they didn't develop AZT or the other retrovirals for AIDS; these applications were developed elsewhere with public funds. They are not likely to develop better anticonvulsants for epilepsy or bring treatments for multiple sclerosis on the market, since even within the gated communities of the developed world the incidence of these conditions is such that it is not worth their while to make the investment. Return on investment rather than elimination of disease is, after all, what drives a pharmaceutical company.

This philosophy is as diametrically opposed to that of Philippe Pinel, Alfred Worcester, and Richard Cabot as it is possible to get. For over a century patients have assumed that the knowledge a doctor like Cabot brings to helping them stems primarily from what is known about the condition being treated or that what a doctor like Worcester brings stems from a judicious appraisal of the limits of current knowledge and treatments. But in the past two decades what is "known" has come increasingly to be dominated by the self-interested constructions of the pharmaceutical companies, through the activities they sponsor, the kind of research they promote, and the information they choose to reveal—or conceal. Under siege, doctors like Dr. N have turned to the appearances of science and spend their time filling standardized forms in medication clinics rather than talking to or looking at their patients. In this process they have become the faithful if unwitting collaborators of the pharmaceutical companies, almost as though the debates between Cabot and Worcester about the purpose of medicine had not taken place a century ago—or worse, almost as though Clark Stanley marketing snake oil or Thomas Beecham marketing his pills had not faded away in the face of developments in medical science or a growing commitment to medical care of the type Pinel and Worcester advocated but had instead taken over the health service business.

In 1909 Beecham's Pills ran into trouble when their claims to be a cure-all for lifestyle problems included suggestions that this combination of aloes, ginger, and soap, whose retail price was 500 percent of its costs of production, might be useful for "maladies of indiscretion."[35] This claim was read as offering a "morning after" service. In 2009, GSK, whose fortunes at the time of the patent disputes over AZT rested on the SSRI Paxil, a drug a former CEO had derided as a lifestyle drug but which Glaxo had inherited when taking over SmithKline Beecham, lost a legal verdict to Michelle David, who claimed Paxil had caused congenital heart defects in her son Lyam Kilker.[36] The evidence in this, and Gina Fromm's subsequent case, made it clear that in addition to doubling rates of congenital malformations it doubles the rate of miscarriages and increases voluntary terminations of pregnancy.

Yet extraordinarily in the face of this evidence not only doctors but even ethicists line up to say antidepressants are being underused in pregnancy.[37] There is a suspension of common sense here that has been brought about by company marketing of controlled trials and evidence-based medicine. Ironically a requirement for controlled trials was built into Senator Kefauver's 1962 amendments as this seemed a method to limit rather than promote treatments, but these trials have in fact become the primary marketing tool of pharmaceutical companies. The marketers have selected the trials that suit, had them polished by ghost-writers just as much as a political speech might be, before smuggling them past the peer review systems of academic journals and meetings. But none of this would have the power to influence doctors had the very meaning of clinical trials not been turned inside out.

3

Follow the Evidence

When a journalist jumps out from behind a hedge on the eleventh hole of a Caribbean golf course to ambush a professor of medicine from one distinguished university and a professor of psychiatry from another after both gave brief lectures that morning, and he asks the men whether their company-sponsored trip would influence their judgment, the response will be "Of course not!" If asked what does influence them, these academics will confidently point to the published evidence. They follow the evidence, not the money. Even if a doctor is pocketing the lecture fee rather than putting it into a research fund, the answer will still be the same:

There is a rich literature on how even minor gifts can hugely influence the recipient,[1] and an equally rich literature on how doctors, when asked, readily agree that their colleagues are swayed by favors while still denying that they themselves can be influenced.[2] That gifts can corrupt seems so obvious to everyone except doctors that in 2009 a Sunshine Act was introduced in the US Senate to mandate disclosure by pharmaceutical companies of money or other gifts given to doctors or medical academics.[3]

The response from the medical community to moves like the Senate's bill that seem to impugn medical professionalism is bewilderment. While traditionally doctors have put great store in professionalism, at least as important in their response to this issue is their belief that scientific research is immune to gifts, biases, or conflicts of interest. It's taken for granted that data don't lie, and this leaves medical personnel and their academic colleagues sanguine about gifts, from pens to all-expenses-paid conferences in the Caribbean. If anyone in the media can point to a mismatch between what doctors on the golf course prescribe in their practice and the published evidence, that would be another matter—but until Birnam Wood comes to Dunsinane there is no reason for concern.

These days, almost as though Macbeth's witches had invested in the fixedness of Birnam Wood, pharmaceutical companies also take their stand on the published evidence. From senior executives mingling with medical academics to drug reps visiting medical trainees, company personnel tout the virtues of controlled trials and exhort doctors to practice evidence-based medicine at every turn.

In its first manifestations, controlled trials and evidence-based medicine were known for demonstrating that fashionable treatments did not work. If now pharmaceutical companies invoke what they call evidence-based medicine to justify the status quo, that should at least raise some suspicion about what might be going on. In chapter 4 and 5 we will look at how companies cherry-pick the trial data that suits them, leaving inconvenient data unpublished and making a mockery of science. But in this chapter the focus is on how they have managed to turn controlled trials inside out, neutering their potential to show that some currently fashionable drugs don't work and transforming them into a means to sell worthless remedies.

THE TURN TO NUMBERS

Insofar as the Hippocratic dictum of "first do no harm" appears a good idea, we should adopt the view that we know very little. But faced with real diseases from Alzheimer's dementia to malignant cancers to rheumatoid arthritis, when both those affected and their doctors become desperate and vulnerable, remaining calm and skeptical is easier said than done. This is precisely why we need to pin down how much we do know about medical treatments, and for this purpose controlled trials can be a godsend.

There are many situations where it is not difficult to know when a drug or a medical procedure works. In the case of alcohol, for instance, we comfortably base our judgments on the fact that we can see certain effects occur reliably soon after intake of the drug, with some relationship between how much we imbibe and the effects we experience. We know about the analgesic effect of opium and the sedative effects of the barbiturates in the same way as we know about alcohol and about the benefits of having a dislocated shoulder popped back into place or a kidney stone removed, from the immediate relief.

Not all treatments have effects that are this clear-cut, though, nor are all the effects even of alcohol or sedatives self-evident. While a sedative may be usefully sedating and in this sense work, it still may not be all that useful in the long run for nervous conditions. Even bigger problems arise when the beneficial effects of a treatment are less immediate than those of alcohol or opiates, or when there are substantial differences in the effect of a treatment from one person to the next, or when the natural history of a condition is such that some people would have recovered anyway. In these cases, treatments may appear to be linked to cures and doctors or patients, who understandably want to see a treatment working, may jump to the conclusion that the treatment has worked when in fact it hasn't. This is a gap that quacks and charlatans exploit. In a world where nothing much worked, the charlatan engendered many false hopes. In today's world, where getting the wrong prescription may mean you needlessly suffer harmful side effects or miss out on a treatment that really would have helped, the consequences may be more serious.

In these more ambiguous cases—of which there are many in medicine—how do you know whether or not a treatment is likely to have any benefits and what hazards it may entail? For several centuries at least some physicians appreciated that before a proposed new remedy could be accepted, its effects would need to be observed under controlled conditions. There would need to be some way to demonstrate that any improvement in patients was due to the remedy, and not to some other factor, or even to chance. Some group of patients living under similar conditions that could be divided into comparable groups, only some of which were given the remedy, would be needed. But short of imprisonment or quarantine, this is not easily done.

In 1747, James Lind, the Scottish physician who served as ship's doctor on the South Seas–bound *Salisbury,* was given the perfect opportunity. Some of the sailors developed scurvy, a fearsome disease that caused tissue breakdown—wounds failed to heal, teeth fell out, and victims began to bleed into their skin or from their bowels. In some long-distance sea voyages up to half a ship's crew might die from it. Faced with twelve sailors whose "cases were as similar as I could have them" and who were all on the same diet, Lind was able to give two of the men cider, two vitriol, two vinegar, two sea-water, two oranges and lemons, and two a mix of nutmeg, garlic, mustard seed, and balsam of Peru. Those given the oranges and lemons improved rapidly, the others languished.[4] Even though there was limited scope for any other explanation of these recoveries, many attributed the improvement to ventilation (although that was the same for all twelve patients), while even Lind himself was slow to credit the citrus fruits for the favorable response. It took the British navy another fifty years to include lime juice in the provisions for a voyage, after which British sailors were widely termed limeys. In this case, when faced with a choice between their expectations and the evidence, observers at first clung to their expectations—a pattern we shall see again and again.

On a much grander scale, but in a less controlled fashion, in 1802 in the midst of the revolutionary ferment in France, Philippe Pinel, the general physician now commonly seen as the father of modern psychiatry, working at the Salpêtrière asylum, became the first to commit medicine to an evidence-based approach. At the time typical treatments for mental illness included bloodletting, brutality, forced immersion in cold baths, being hosed down with water jets or subjected to a variety of purgatives, emetics, diuretics, and other drugs. Although there were elegant rationales for some of these treatments, and in some cases the treatments stemmed back to antiquity and had been advocated by history's most distinguished medical names, Pinel was skeptical. Patients often seemed to get better when the doctor waited to intervene, he had observed. Learning the typical course of a disorder, he reasoned, would make it possible to predict when patients might turn a corner for the better on their own. This appreciation underpinned his dictum that the greater art in medicine lay in knowing when to refrain from treatment.[5]

Between April 1802 and December 1805, 1,002 patients were admitted to the Salpêtrière, and Pinel was able to follow these individuals during their stay to see who recovered and who didn't, whether patients in particular diagnostic groups fared better than others—and hence whether diagnoses in use at the time were worthwhile or not. This was a first example of what later came to be called a statistical approach to illness. Why do it? Pinel laid out his reasons.

In medicine it is difficult to come to any agreement if a precise meaning is not given to the word *experiment*, since everyone vaunts their own results, and only more or less cites the facts in favor of their point of view. However, to be genuine and conclusive, and serve as a solid basis for any method of treatment, an experiment must be carried out on a large number of patients following the same rules and a set order. It must also be based on a consistent series of observations recorded very carefully and repeated over a certain number of years in a regular manner. Finally it must equally report both events, which are favorable and those which are not, quoting their respective numbers, and it must attach as much importance to one set of data as to the other. In a nutshell it must be based on the theory of probabilities, which is already so effectively applied to several questions in civil life and on which from now on methods of treating illnesses must also rely if one wishes to establish these on sound grounds. This was the goal I set myself in 1802 in relation to mental alienation when the treatment of deranged patients was entrusted to my care and transferred to the Salpêtrière.[6]

There had never been anything like this in medicine before. Overall, 47 percent of the patients recovered, Pinel found, but of those who had been admitted for the first time, who had never been treated elsewhere, who had a disorder of acute onset, and who were treated only using Pinel's methods, up to 85 percent responded. When left to recover naturally, many more of the first-timers did so than did those among the patients who had been treated previously by other methods. Not only that, within a short time of admission Pinel could tell who was likely to recover and who was not based on their clinical features. In other words there seemed to be different disorders, and people suffering from some types would recover if left alone while inmates with some other types would not regardless of what treatments they were given. Finally, following the patients after discharge brought a whole new group of periodic disorders into view for the first time, laying the basis for the later discovery of manic-depressive illness and other recurrent mental disorders.

Aware of the pioneering nature of his research, Pinel presented his data, on February 9, 1807, to the mathematical and physical sciences faculty at the National Institute of France rather than to the country's Academy of Medicine. This was hard science and the first time in medicine that results were presented as ratios across a number of patients studied, rather than as accounts of individual cases.

In reporting these findings, Pinel showed that he was well aware that his personal bias could have colored the results. But, as he noted, while an individual patient in London could not properly be compared to one in Paris or Munich, the results of complete groups of patients could be, and the registers of Salpêtrière patients were publicly available. So he confidently challenged others to contest his findings based on their outcomes.

The scientists were impressed. The physicians weren't. It took thirty years before another French physician picked up the baton and further unsettled the medical establishment with numbers. In 1836, Pierre Louis outlined a new numerical method that controlled for variations by using large numbers of patients: "in any epidemic, let us suppose five hundred of the sick, taken indiscriminately, to be subjected to one kind of treatment, and five hundred others, taken in the same manner, to be treated in a different mode; if the mortality is greater among the first than among the second, must we not conclude that the treatment was less appropriate, or less efficacious in the first class than in the second?"[7]

The treatment Louis assessed was bleeding—which in fact works well in disorders such as heart failure. But when he compared bleeding to doing nothing in a sufficiently large number of patients during the course of an epidemic, he sparked a crisis in therapeutics. Doctors expected bleeding to work better than doing nothing, but "the results of my experiments on the effects of bleeding in inflammatory conditions are so little in accord with common opinion [those who were bled were more likely to die, he found] that it is only with hesitation that I have decided to publish them. The first time I analyzed the relevant facts, I believed I was mistaken, and I repeated my work but the result of this new analysis remains the same."[8]

These results led to howls of outrage from physicians who claimed that it was not possible to practice medicine by numbers, that the duty of physicians was always to the patient in front of them rather than to the population at large, and that every doctor had to be guided by what he found at the bedside.

Ironically, it was Louis and Pinel who were calling on physicians to be guided by what was actually happening to their patients, not by what the medical authorities traditionally had to say. As the marketers from GlaxoSmithKline and other companies might have told Louis and Pinel, though, for many physicians to be convinced there has to be a theory, a concept about the illness and its treatment, to guide the doctor. "The practice of medicine according to this [Louis's] view," went one dismissal, "is entirely empirical, it is shorn of all rational induction, and takes a position among the lower grades of experimental observations and fragmentary facts."[9]

Louis's struggles in Paris had their counterpart in Vienna where, in 1847, Ignaz Semmelweis noted that mortality was much higher on an obstetric ward run by physicians and medical students than one run by student midwives. Suspecting that the physicians were coming to women in labor with particles of corpses from the dissection room still on their hands, he got them to wash more thoroughly with a disinfectant and was able to show that antiseptic practice made a difference. No one paid any heed. A few years later, in 1860, Joseph Lister introduced antiseptic practice to the Glasgow Royal Infirmary, and postoperative putrefaction rates subsequently declined. The later discovery that infection with bacteria led to putrefaction provided a concept to explain these observations, but until then Lister, like Semmelweis, had trouble getting his colleagues to take his findings seriously.

One of the weaknesses in these early manifestations of evidence-based medicine, as the examples of Pinel, Louis, Semmelweis, and Lister make clear, was their inability to shed much light on what lay behind the figures—they showed associations but explained nothing about cause. There are commonly tensions between broad associations of this type, the specific evidence that comes from laboratory experiments, the evidence of our own eyes, and what currently dominant theories may dictate. To the relief of most doctors, the tensions between broad associations and more specific evidence were eased to a degree with the emergence in the second half of the nineteenth century of laboratory science, which more clearly linked cause and effect.

THE CAUSES OF DISEASES

In the 1870s, a set of laboratory sciences emerged to form the bedrock of the new scientific and diagnostic work that would transform much of medicine and underlie the practice of doctors like Richard Cabot and the rise of hospitals such as Massachusetts General, as noted in chapter 1. Advances in bacteriology were among the key scientific developments that led to new treatments as well as hope that science would lead to further breakthroughs. In France, Louis Pasteur provided the first evidence that germs, later called bacteria, were the causative factors in a series of infections such as rabies,[10] and he supplied both evidence and a rationale for vaccinations and antiseptic procedures.[11] In Germany, Robert Koch set up the first laboratory dedicated to the pursuit of the microbial causes of disease, and his most famous protégé, Paul Ehrlich, who more than anyone else developed the dyes that helped distinguish among bacteria, later developed the drugs that killed some of them. It was Ehrlich who coined the term magic bullet, for a drug that would specifically target the cause of an illness and leave the patient otherwise unaffected.[12] For generations afterward, until the 1960s, the glamour and importance of their discoveries and those of their successors, written up in books such as the *Microbe Hunters,* attracted students to medicine.[13]

In 1877, Koch transmitted the lethal disease anthrax by injecting noninfected animals with the blood of infected animals; he then isolated anthrax spores and demonstrated that these spores, if grown in the eye of an ox for several generations, could also cause the infection. Where Lister met resistance for recommending an antiseptic approach in surgery on the basis of a comparison of the numbers of infections with and without antiseptic conditions, Koch could show the existence of bacilli under a microscope and later growing on a Petri dish, and then demonstrate the efficacy of sterilization in killing the bacillus. Where it had been difficult to overcome resistance to revolutionary ideas about antiseptics using only comparative numbers, for many seeing was believing.

The impact on medicine of this new science of bacteriology and the germ theory of disease can be seen with wonderful clarity in the case of cholera. From the 1830s to the 1860s, before the role of germs in disease was recognized, a series of cholera epidemics struck Europe, killing tens of thousands. Because no one knew what caused this plague or how to protect themselves from a grisly death, there was widespread public panic. In 1856, in a now-celebrated series of investigations John Snow, a London physician, mapped the appearances of the disease around London. He made a connection between clusters of those with the disease and contamination of the water supply and famously recommended removal of the handle from the pump in Broad Street so residents would get their water from other sources.[14]

Snow's work rather than that of Pinel, Louis, or Semmelweis is often cited as the first step in a new science of epidemiology, which maps the progress of a disease (or a treatment) through a population to pin down its course and its effects. But, while Snow is celebrated now, he was ignored at the time and the handle was not removed at the time because he could not point to a cause. The association he proposed was but one of many competing theories at the time. The data alone were not persuasive.

The later detection by Koch's group of a cholera bacillus in the drinking water of people who became ill both confirmed and undercut Snow's work. It confirmed Snow's suggestion of a link to the water supply rather than the other theories prevalent at the time. But it also made an approach to a disease like cholera that required tracking what happened to thousands of people over whole areas of a city seem crude and needlessly labor-intensive. Snow died two decades before Koch's work, but Lister, who in his antiseptic investigations had done something similar to

Snow, came over to the bacterial theory of infections when it was demonstrated to him that bacteria caused putrefaction. Louis's and Snow's figures provide part of a story that needs to be matched with the evidence of our own eyes and the evidence that comes from the laboratory.

Koch's laboratory (or, experimental) approach didn't triumph without a fight, however. Many at the time refused to believe bacteria caused disease. Max von Pettenkoffer, a professor of medical hygiene in Munich, for example, argued that cholera was not caused by Koch's recently isolated bacillus but depended on an interplay of factors, many of which lay within the host. To demonstrate the point he brewed a broth of several million "cholera" bacilli and drank them, without suffering significant consequences. Faced with this challenge, Koch was forced to grapple with how we know something has caused something else. In von Pettenkoffer's case, Koch argued that stomach acid had likely killed the bacillus; still, there was room for doubt.[15]

Koch's solution to von Pettenkoffer's challenge and to the general problem of how to link cause and effect was to outline a number of rules. First, if you challenge (expose the person) with the cause, the effect should appear. Second, remove the cause and the effect should go. Third, a rechallenge should reproduce the effect. Fourth, the greater the exposure to the cause (the higher the dose), the more likely the effect should be. Fifth, an antidote to the drug (or bacterium) should reverse the effect. Sixth, there should be some temporal relationship between exposure to the drug or bacterium and the appearance of the effect. Finally, there should be some biological mechanism that ideally can be found that links the cause to the effect.

These are just the rules we now apply to deciding if a drug like alcohol or an industrial chemical has a particular effect on us and whether a controlled trial has shown a particular drug produces a benefit in a disease. Doctors attempting to make sense of what is happening to the patient in front of them will also use just the same rules. Whether direct observation by a doctor or a controlled trial run by a pharmaceutical company in hundreds of patients is the better approach depends on the question you're addressing. In the case of a patient with a suspected adverse drug reaction, when it is possible to vary the dose of treatment or stop treatment and rechallenge with a suspect drug, direct observation is just as scientific and may be much more informative than a controlled trial. In practice, however, if a hazard of treatment has not been revealed in what results of a controlled trial have been published, doctors are likely to deny it is happening, despite the evidence of their own eyes. To see how this situation has come to pass we have to turn to the study of fertilizers and the origin of randomized controlled trials.

FERTILIZERS IN MEDICINE?

In the best possible sense, doubt is the business of an epidemiologist. From John Snow onward, statistical epidemiologists worth their salt can provide several explanations that might account for the associations found in a quantitative study. Ronald Fisher (1890–1962), a Cambridge mathematician who did most of his key work in developing modern statistical methods from the 1920s to the 1940s while associated with an agricultural college, was typical of the genre. Photographs commonly show him smoking. To the end of his life in 1962, at the age of 72, he argued that lung cancer was not caused by smoking, that all we have for evidence are numbers linking people who smoke and cancer but that may simply mean that people prone to cancer were also more likely to smoke, and that correlations are not proof of causation.

Fisher's work centered on the question of whether the application of various fertilizers might improve grain yields. In grappling with how to determine this he introduced two ideas—randomization and statistical significance—that have come to dominate modern medicine. Indeed, they extend well beyond medicine and are worth looking at because they underlie so much of what is reported about science.

Misleadingly, a fertilizer may appear to increase the yield of grain if spread in an uncontrolled way: a myriad of soil, light, drainage, and climate factors might come into play, for example, and bias the results. Just as when trying to determine whether a drug works or not, the experimenter has to control for these known unknowns. Fisher anticipated Donald Rumsfeld's unknown unknowns by eighty years. But his key insight was how to control for these factors that he didn't know about—the way to do so was to allocate fertilizer randomly to the plants under study.

In early controlled drug trials, investigators allocated one male, say, to the new drug, the next one to placebo (a dummy pill), and so on, while also attempting to ensure there were an equal number of people of one age on the new treatment as on the control, or placebo, treatment. Now, in contrast, patients are divided into treatment and control groups according to a sequence of numbers that have been generated randomly before the trial starts. After the randomized controlled trial is over, investigators can check whether obvious factors like age and sex are distributed equally across treatment groups—which they invariably are. In one go, random allocation takes care of both the known and the unknown unknowns.

In addition to taking care of the unknown unknowns, randomization greatly reduces the number of subjects, whether plants or people, that need to be recruited to a study to get a clear-cut answer. At a stroke, the advent of randomization in controlled trials in the 1950s turbocharged epidemiology. It did away with the need to carefully balance controls by age, sex, social class, and ethnicity that made a nonrandomized approach slow and cumbersome because of the requirement for huge numbers of patients to produce a clear result.

Random assignment helped Fisher decide whether a fertilizer worked or not. But there is a key point to note. The question facing Fisher was whether a fertilizer would increase yield. Would there consistently be more bushels of grain, say, in the fertilized patches than in the unfertilized ones? This question is straightforward when the outcome of interest—in this instance, bushels of grain—is the only criterion. What, however, if the yield was greater but much of the grain was moldy? Would one still say the fertilizer worked?

Asked what it means to say a medical treatment works, most people would respond that it saves lives. Even if a treatment comes with side effects, staying alive ordinarily trumps these, and conversely death trumps any benefits. But many medicines, perhaps most, do not save lives. Once we look at outcomes other than death, we move into an arena where competing values come into play. We may not want the type of sleep induced by a hypnotic or the sex life produced by Viagra. The extreme, as we shall see in later chapters, is when we end up with claims by companies that a new treatment "works" because it can be shown to have effects on things the company values—even though the same clinical trials throw up more dead bodies on the new drug than on the placebo, as is the case for the cholesterol-lowering statin drugs, the Cox-2 inhibiting analgesics, blood-sugar-lowering drugs, beta-agonists for asthma, along with various antidepressants and antipsychotics. This happens when trials throw up a trivial but clear-cut and marketable benefit, with indicators of more problematic risks that companies ignore. This complex mix of benefits and risks is in fact the case for almost all of the current best-selling drugs in medicine, but all most doctors or patients get to hear about are the benefits.

In cases like these, the word "works" becomes ambiguous. When a life is saved, we know where we stand and all observers can agree on what has been done. When there is an obvious and immediate benefit, such as the effects of Viagra on a penis, or the sedative effect of a sleeping pill or anesthetic, we can all agree these effects are present and many of us feel we can make up our own minds as to whether we want such an effect. But few of the currently best-selling drugs in medicine have benefits as obvious as these.

An early indicator of this new world into which medicine began moving in the blockbuster era comes from a 1982 English study in which Sanjeebit Jachuk and colleagues looked at the perceptions of seventy-five doctors, seventy-five patients, and seventy-five relatives of the effects of propranolol, the beta-blocker for which James Black won a Nobel Prize. All the doctors surveyed reported propranolol was an effective antihypertensive: they saw the column of mercury in the blood pressure apparatus falling from visit to visit when they examined the patients, which was what they were hoping to see. The patients split down the middle in their responses to the drug they were taking: half reported benefits, half reported problems. Aside from thinking the drug was working because their doctor was happy, it's difficult to know why the patients reported benefits: raised blood pressure (hypertension) has no symptoms, so no one will have felt better on that account. But the investigators also consulted relatives, and all bar one of these reported that treatment was causing more problems than benefits—patients were now either complaining of treatment side effects or the process of diagnosis had made them hypochondriacal.[16]

So who—doctor, patient, or relative—was right? Reducing blood pressure can save lives, by reducing the likelihood of heart attacks and strokes, although statistically it may require hundreds of patients to be treated to save a life compared to people not on the drug. Companies don't collect data on outcomes like quality of life, novel side effects or relatives' impressions of benefits, however. When we are not in a position to make up our own mind about a benefit on the basis of seeing people get up off their death bed and walk or seeing the obvious effects of a hypnotic or Viagra, we become more dependent on the interpretation and judgment of our doctors, who in turn have become ever more dependent on pharmaceutical companies to interpret the effects of the drugs they produce. At the heart of those drug-company interpretations lies their use of Fisher's second innovation, the idea of statistical significance, a technique used to hypnotize doctors into focusing only on the figures that suit companies.

HYPNOTIZING DOCTORS

Fisher was an unlikely ally for a pharmaceutical company. He was a skeptic. His basic approach was to assume a new fertilizer didn't work. This is called the null hypothesis. It was only when the yield from plots fertilized with the new agent beat the plots with no fertilizer in nineteen cases out of twenty that he thought we can rule out the play of chance in the results and should concede that the new agent plays some role. When the yield from the fertilized plot is greater nineteen times out of twenty, by Fisher's determination, the result is said to be "statistically significant." All this means is that the higher yield of the fertilized fields is unlikely to be due to chance. When applied to a drug and a placebo, a meaningless difference may be significant in this sense—but calling it significant leads most people to assume that there is in fact a substantive difference.

Ironically, statistical significance was a side issue for Fisher, for whom the key issue was whether we could design good experiments or not, ones that would yield similar results time after time. As he put it, "No isolated experiment, however significant in itself, can suffice for the experimental demonstration of any phenomenon. . . . In relation to the test of significance, we may say that a phenomenon is experimentally demonstrable when we know how to conduct an experiment that will rarely fail to give us a statistically significant result."[17] Perhaps because they can design conclusive experiments, branches of science such as physics and chemistry rarely use the concept of statistical significance.

The idea of significance testing was picked up from the 1950s onward primarily in sociology, psychology, economics, and medicine, disciplines where designing conclusive experiments is much harder because of the complexities involved. It may have triumphed in these arenas because it appeared to offer scientific rigor,[18] The procedure creates the impression that the scientists have been forced to stand back and let the testing procedure objectively bring out what the data demonstrate. This can send a powerful signal in arenas that are heavily contested—but the signal is a rhetorical maneuver rather than something that in fact does guarantee objectivity. In many instances significance testing in these sciences has become a mechanical exercise that substitutes for thought. Experiments are considered good, it seems, if they throw up "significant" findings, even if the findings are trivial and cannot be reproduced.

When drug trials throw up a "significant" finding on cholesterol levels or bone densities, say, companies rush out a story that their drug "works," even though in 50 percent of the trials they've run, the drug may not beat the placebo, or there may be more dead bodies in the treatment group than in the placebo group. Companies can do this in part because regulators in the United States such as the FDA, and in Europe, have established an incredibly low bar for a drug to be allowed on the market: only two trials with statistically significant positive results are needed to let a pharmaceutical company put a drug on the market, even though there might be up to ninety-eight negative studies. Given that Fisher expected that five in a hundred studies might be positive by chance, this turns the idea of statistical significance inside out. Of the studies done with the antidepressants, for instance, 50 percent show no benefit for the drug compared with the placebo. Fisher almost certainly would have thought that those investigating such drugs simply did not know what they were doing scientifically.

Significance testing also explains how companies are able to get away with claims that treatments work even when more people die who are given the drug in a trial than those given a placebo. Trials will be set up so that findings of lowered cholesterol levels with treatment, for example, will be statistically significant while the increase in dead bodies may not be. Doctors, like many others not well versed in mathematics, clutch at the illusory certainty offered by findings that are statistically significant, even if these are trivial, on the grounds that these results *could not* have arisen by chance. Fascinated with significance, they also tend mentally to dispose of any evidence of accumulating harms brought on by the same treatments, as we shall see in chapter 7, by denying they exist—on the basis that findings that are not statistically significant *could* have arisen by chance. They are hypnotized.

There has always been a deep-rooted tension between medical care and medical business. Good medical care once firmly embraced the idea that every remedy was a potential poison that inevitably produced side effects—the trick lay in knowing how and to whom to administer this poison in order to bring about a benefit that warranted these side effects. But insofar as they are looking after their business interests, medical practitioners have always been inclined to embrace new drugs, and most doctors want more of them if they can be convinced, or can convince themselves, that they have some positive effect. This produces a bias against seeing when these very same drugs shorten lives. In the era of evidence-based medicine, the marketing barrage of the pharmaceutical companies and the promise of statistical significance have led doctors into a world in which they regard treatments more as fertilizers or vitamins that can only do good if applied widely. As a profession, medicine is thereby losing any sense of the treatment as poison, and controlled trials, which began as a method to protect patients from the biases of doctors, have become instead a method to enhance business in great part because drug companies have managed to hook doctors to the crack pipe of statistical significance.[19]

TAMING CHANCE

Because it was fatal in miniscule doses, strychnine was a favorite of poisoners. In 1852, Pierre Touery claimed that activated charcoal could act as an antidote to strychnine, but his medical colleagues were not convinced. To prove his point, Touery, in front of a large audience on the floor of the French Academy of Medicine ingested some coal tar and then drank ten times the lethal dose of strychnine—without any ill effects. Nobody is likely to think now that we need a randomized controlled trial to make a convincing case for using coal tar in a situation like this. Neither Worcester nor Cabot nor any of their colleagues in Massachusetts pressed for controlled trials for diphtheria antitoxin after its introduction in the 1890s, when the garroting membranes the illness produced could be seen to dissolve almost immediately after the treatment was administered.

When treatments are unambiguously effective, we don't need a controlled trial to tell us so. But randomized trials have become such a fetish within medicine now that it's become the source of parody. A 2003 *British Medical Journal* article, for example, suggested that we should not be using parachutes because their efficacy hadn't yet been demonstrated in a placebo-controlled trial.[20]

The perverse humor here extends into almost every encounter between doctors and patients today. If tomorrow our doctor suggested putting us on a treatment that he said had not been shown to work in a controlled trial but that he had seen work with his own eyes, most people would likely refuse. In contrast, we would likely be reassured if he suggested he was only going to treat us with drugs that had been shown by controlled trials to work. We would be even more reassured if he told us that thousands of people had been entered into these trials, when almost by definition the greater the number of people needed in a trial, the more closely the treatment resembles snake oil—which contains omega-3 fatty acids and can be shown in controlled trials to have benefits if sufficiently large numbers of people are recruited.

How has it happened that our understanding of trials has in some sense been turned inside out? The story starts with the discovery of the antibiotics. The first real magic bullet that made the rest of modern therapeutics possible came in 1935 with the discovery of the sulfa drugs.[21] Before the antibiotics were discovered a range of bacterial infections leading to conditions such as bacterial endocarditis (an infection of the lining of the heart), puerperal sepsis (an infection of mothers after childbirth), and septicemia (an infection of the blood stream) were commonly fatal. Sulfanilamide and, later, penicillin transformed this picture. Patients who were expected to die got up off their bed and walked out of the hospital. Neither doctors nor regulators required trials to show these drugs worked—the only onus on companies was to establish that their treatment was safe.

Wonderful though drugs like penicillin were, they failed when it came to the infection that terrified people at the time more than any other—tuberculosis—and it was this failure that led directly to the first randomized controlled trial in medicine. Part of the problem was that tuberculosis was a more chronic and insidious infection than bacterial endocarditis or puerperal infections, so it was harder to tell when the treatment was working. Where other infections came on dramatically and either cleared up or killed quickly, tuberculosis crept in on its victims, who might then have good spells and bad spells. Even sputum samples clear of the bacterium did not provide a foolproof answer to the state of the illness.

Every new treatment devised at the time was tested against tuberculosis—even the first antidepressants and antipsychotics—many of which worked in the test tube but not in patients. There had been endless claims for cures which had been shown repeatedly to be hollow in clinical care. So when Merck developed a novel class of antibiotic in 1945, of which streptomycin was the prototype, skepticism was called for. Austin Bradford Hill, who became the statistician at Britain's Medical Research Council (MRC) because tuberculosis had ruled him out of a career in medicine, suggested a controlled trial of the new drug using Fisher's ideas about randomization.

There were concerns about the ethics of what Hill was proposing. If the drug in fact turned out to be effective, were those who got the placebo being denied critical care? It was one thing to allow unfertilized plants in an agricultural field to languish but treatment trials had never left sick people untreated before. As it turned out, streptomycin wasn't as effective as penicillin for bacterial endocarditis, but it couldn't be said the drug didn't work for tuberculosis. The trial demonstrated that streptomycin made a difference to the patient clinically, reducing the amount of tubercle bacillus growing in sputum, and the number of tubercular holes visible on X-ray, and more patients on streptomycin survived. Running a randomized controlled trial in this case brought the effects of streptomycin into view in a way that would not have happened otherwise.

In the 1950s, even in the case of such clearly effective drugs as penicillin, the antipsychotic chlorpromazine, and the amphetamines, which, once developed, swept around the world, crossed frontiers and language barriers with little or no need for marketing, trials offered something useful. While there was no question penicillin worked on some bacteria, it was clear it did not work on all. And while chlorpromazine tranquilized, there could be real questions about which patients would most benefit from it. Similarly, the amphetamines obviously increased alertness and suppressed appetite, but did they make a difference in a medical condition? When controlled trials were conducted, it turned out that amphetamines were of benefit for narcolepsy, a condition where people abruptly fall asleep sometimes in mid-conversation, and possibly produced benefits in some neurotic states but did surprisingly little for severe depressions.

In assuming treatments don't work, controlled trials challenge therapeutic enthusiasm. Because surgery is such a clear physical stress to any body, many supposed that pre- and post-operative treatment with beta-blockers such as propranolol, which counter the effects of stress hormones on heart rate and blood pressure, could only be a good thing. This was so logical, it had become standard practice. But when the proper study was finally done, it was found that there were more deaths in the beta-blocker group.[22] Similarly, it seemed obvious that treating the anemia that develops in the wake of renal failure would be helpful and likely prolong life expectancy, but when the first randomized trial was undertaken more patients died on the high-cost treatment (Aranesp) to relieve anemia than died in the placebo group.[23]

Demonstrations that treatments don't work typically come in trials sponsored by national health organizations or other not-for-profit research institutions rather than company trials. But there are exceptions. Given strong suggestions that anti-inflammatory drugs might help Alzheimer's disease, Merck decided to pursue a jackpot by investing millions of dollars in a trial to see if Vioxx would reduce the incidence of or slow the rate of progression of dementia. In fact on Vioxx (and later

Celebrex), more patients developed Alzheimer's, the disease progressed more rapidly, and more patients died than on the placebo.[24]

If all medicines are poisons, an outcome like this is not surprising. Simply recognizing that biology is complex highlights the risk of intervening and the need to test our assumptions and practices, no matter how benign the rationale for a particular approach might sound. An insistence on testing is exactly the spirit that gave rise to randomized controlled trials. They began as a means to control therapeutic enthusiasm, whether this enthusiasm came from the good intentions of physicians or from the greed of hucksters. What is there, then, about these trials that make companies so interested? ·

MIND THE GAP

In between treatments that are so obviously life-saving that trials are not needed and proposed remedies where trials save lives by demonstrating that the treatment doesn't work, there is the huge gap in which we have treatments that ease pain or restore function or promise some other benefit, even if a modest one. In the case of treatments that do not necessarily save lives but which equally cannot be dismissed as doing nothing, we are in much less certain waters than is usually realized. Controlled trials in these instances function primarily to bring to light both positive and negative associations between treatment and changes on a blood test or rating scale. It is in these waters that pharmaceutical companies have become adept at turning the evidence to their advantage.

Imagine an orthopedic department starting a trial on plaster casts for fractures of the left leg. As their placebo treatment they opted to have a cast put on the necks of the control group but in the active treatment group they randomly put casts on the right arm or leg, or left arm or leg of the patients, all of whom had broken left legs. The active treatment group in this case would do statistically significantly better than the placebo group but to advocate treating left leg fractures by indiscriminately putting a cast on any of four limbs on the basis that a randomized controlled trial had clearly shown this had worked would be nonsensical.[25] Medicine in thrall to randomized controlled trials increasingly lets companies get away with just this, partly because an artful use of rating scales or blood tests conceals the fact that we don't know what we are doing. When we do know what is wrong the absurdity of simply practicing according to the figures becomes clear.

The plaster-cast example is not much more extreme than what in fact did happen in the case of the antidepressants.

When companies or their academics say today that a drug "works" what is commonly meant is that there is at least a minimal difference that is "statistically significant" between the effects of an active drug and a placebo on a blood test or rating scale. Evidence like this rather than evidence of lives saved or function restored, is all that the regulators need to let the drug on the market. Once approved for the market, the drug, be it for osteoporosis, cholesterol regulation, depression, or hypertension, is sold as though using it is the equivalent of being given penicillin or insulin. The problem is that increasingly, under the influence of company spin as to what the figures show, clinicians seem to prescribe drugs like the statins or antidepressants as though a failure to prescribe would leave them as open to a charge of clinical negligence as failing to prescribe insulin or penicillin would. The magic for companies lies in the fact that the numbers of patients recruited to the trials can be such that changes in rating scale scores or bone densities are statistically significant, whereas increased rates of death or other serious adverse events on treatment may not be.

When it comes to treating people who are supposedly depressed, antidepressant credentials in the form of comparable changes on depression rating scales have been generated for most of the benzodiazepines, for a number of antihistamines, for almost all the stimulants, as well as for the antipsychotics and anticonvulsants,[26] and they could be generated for nicotine or indeed for snake oil, whose omega-3 oils appear to have some psychotropic properties. A key difference between these diverse drugs and the selective serotonin reuptake inhibitors (the SSRIs) such as Paxil, Prozac, and Zoloft, was that the SSRIs were newly patented for treating depression, while drugs like nicotine or the antihistamines were unpatentable for this purpose. There was no incentive for companies to bring these latter drugs to the market but no reason to believe these drugs would be any less helpful than Prozac for depression. In the case of Prozac and Paxil, there is evidence of a weak association between treatment and a change on a rating scale but the question is what lies behind that change. The fact that so many quite different drugs can also be linked to a comparable benefit shows we know next to nothing about what is going on.

This is where the role of a mythic image of what a drug is supposed to do (a concept) can be of great importance to a marketing department. No one claims nicotine or benzodiazepines correct a lowering of serotonin in depression, whereas the SSRIs supposedly do. The idea that there is an imbalance of serotonin in depression is completely mythical. It arose in the marketing department of SmithKline Beecham, the maker of Paxil.[27] The key thing about this myth is that it provides an image that functions like the imagery of bacterial colonies in a Petri dish shrinking back from an antibiotic, or images of cholesterol levels declining following treatment with statins, or bones becoming denser with biphosphonate treatment for osteoporosis. These images help create the impression that drugs "work," when in fact the data from trials show these treatments have relatively minimal effects. These images create a spin that no data can overcome. Myths always have the last word.

How minimal are the treatment effects? In 2006 the FDA asked companies making antidepressants to submit all placebo-controlled trials to the agency. Just as some people recover from infections without treatment, based on 100,000 patients who had been entered into these antidepressant trials, the data showed that four out of ten people improve within a few weeks whether treated with a drug or not.[28] This may in part be due to the natural history of depressions in which 40 percent recover within a few months whether treated or not. Advice from a clinician on diet, lifestyle, alcohol intake, and problem solving on work and relationship issues may make a difference. Perception by patients that they are being seen and cared for by a medical expert may also make a difference, and this effect may be enhanced by being given a substance they think will restore some chemical balance to normal—even if that imbalance is mythical and the substance a placebo. On the active drugs, five out of ten apparently responded. But what comparing an active drug to a placebo shows us is that of these five, four (80 percent) of apparent responders to an antidepressant would have improved had they received the placebo. In other words, only one in every ten patients responds specifically to the antidepressant, whereas four in every ten treated with a placebo show a response.

If clinicians were really following the evidence, they should say that it's wonderful to have some evidence that antidepressants have benefits, but they would hold back on prescribing them indiscriminately and give a number of their patients a chance to recover without treatment. There is good reason to believe that many of those who recover without drug treatment are less likely to relapse in the longer run, which provides even more reason to wait judiciously in at least some cases.[29] Given that the benefits obtained in the one out of ten are bought at a cost—overall more die on treatment than on placebo, more become dependent on treatment than on placebo, more on treatment have children born with birth defects than do those on placebo, and have many other side effects—the antidepressants arguably provide the perfect set of data to support Pinel's dictum that it is important to know when not to use a treatment.

On grounds of self-interest, there are good reasons for doctors to wait in many nonacute cases. Until recently the magic was in the therapist, who might also give pills, which were an extension of his or her impact on us. Now the magic has passed into the capsule and the physician often seems little more than a conduit for medication. Therapists have forgotten how influential they might be in promoting healthier lifestyles for conditions from raised cholesterol to the inevitable but relatively inconsequential thinning of bones that happens after the menopause. With the focus that both doctor and patient now have on taking a pill, seldom do either heed the context in which a person has become distressed or unhealthy. Neither doctor nor patient appears to see how small a contribution this chemical manipulation is likely to make or to see the potential for a chemical manipulation to make things worse. In practice, doctors end up so often doing what suits drug companies– they persuade patients to go on treatments. Why? In no small part because they have become convinced that these treatments have been shown in randomized controlled trials to work.

A consideration of these nondrug aspects of medical care doesn't just apply to drugs like the antidepressants. An antibiotic like penicillin might make a life-saving difference, but it's important to note that this may not be the only route to saving a life. Once the infection begins, an antibiotic may be by far the best way to help, and we would sue a doctor who let a patient die without treatment. But in the case of puerperal infections, long before the advent of penicillin, it had become clear that women were only likely to contract these disorders if they gave birth in hospitals where the infection could be transmitted readily from one woman to the next. Strict antiseptic procedures in hospitals could help, but giving birth outside the hospital made an infection much less likely.

At the moment doctors appear to be under increasing pressure from insurance managers, hospital bureaucrats, and others to hand out drugs in response to medical problems. If patients aren't on a treatment, they aren't in treatment. No one, not even an insurance manager, would want to be linked to unnecessary deaths. In using drugs that have been shown to "work" in a statistically significant fashion, all concerned think they are avoiding this possibility. But while penicillin can clearly be shown to save lives, the same clarity can't be found with antidepressants, statins given to people with no prior cardiovascular events, asthma drugs, or treatments for osteoporosis and many other conditions. In all these cases, a shrewd selection of statistically significant changes on rating scales or blood tests as evidence that the treatment "works" has been used by pharmaceutical companies to mesmerize all the key players.

"Working" in the case of all the best sellers in medicine, it bears repeating, means the drug produces changes on some measurement of interest to a drug company, rather than indicating the drug saves a life or returns someone to employment, or is better than an older drug in the field, or even makes a person simply feel better. When in the course of these trials patients are allowed to rate whether their quality of life has been improved, in results reminiscent of Sanjeebit Jachuk's study of propranolol, antidepressants, for instance, don't show any benefit over placebo. Such quality-of-life data from antidepressant trials are little known, however, because they remain almost universally unpublished.[30] The bottom line is that while placebo-controlled trials have created appearances that the drugs work, with a few changes to the choice or rating scales or blood tests in these studies or taking into account the withdrawal effects many of these drugs have, it would be possible to show just the opposite for most of medicine's blockbusters.

There is a fundamental psychological issue here on which companies play, an issue illuminated by a series of experiments Daniel Kahnemann and Amos Tversky conducted in the 1970s on what happens when we are asked to make judgments under conditions of uncertainty.[31] Kahnemann and Tversky, who won a Nobel Prize for their work, gave descriptions of a shy, retiring, and bookish personality to their test subjects and asked them to judge whether the person was a nurse or a librarian, having told them the personality profile had been drawn from a group that contains eight nurses and two librarians. Their subjects confidently said the person described was a librarian, when, given the probabilities, they should have said nurse. In the same way, statistics like those mentioned from the antidepressant trials (in which five out of ten seemed to improve from the drug, but closer inspection revealed that improvements in four out of those five could as well be due to placebo effects) should lead us, given the overwhelming odds, to attribute a positive response in a patient to a placebo effect. But like the subjects who chose librarian, we're more likely to jump to the conclusion that the antidepressant must have been the cause.

As drug marketers know, we are all more confident with stereo-types than with rational analysis of the probabilities of a situation. When we see patients on a pill recover, probably because of powerful examples like those of penicillin and insulin, we assume the recovery has come about because of the pill. This bias may be reinforced by hearing "experts" claim that antidepressants or statins work or by seeing these claims in what are considered authoritative publications. A mythic image of increasing bone density or normalizing serotonin levels or lowering cholesterol levels helps increase our certainty.

Neither clinicians nor patients are well equipped to make judgments based on data. Our psychology biases us against seeing what the data actually show, and this bias is aggravated by the selective publication of company trials that indicate a "positive" response to the drug and, ironically, by an apparatus put in place to ensure doctors adhere to the "evidence." These factors have increasingly led to an almost automatic prescription of the latest drugs whether they are statins, hypoglycemics, biphosphonates, or psychotropic drugs.

COMPANY TRIALS

The job of medicine is to save lives, restore function, or improve on treatments already available. The aim of a drug company is to get their drugs on the market and generate profits by so doing. To see if a new treatment saves more lives or performs better than an older treatment, the obvious step is to compare the two. To get on the market, you could demonstrate superiority to an older treatment, but to satisfy the FDA or regulators in Europe or Japan you only have to beat the placebo. And if you recruit ever larger numbers of patients to trials, ever less clinically significant differences from placebo can become statistically significant. Perversely this will lead to the newer and weaker drug selling even better than the older one.

Almost all the drugs trials now conducted are done by their manu-facturers to get their compounds on the market or to establish a market niche. Once completed, these trials mark the point at which any science stops—a drug has been shown to "work," companies say, and the job of doctors is now to prescribe it—whereas entry into the market should mark the point where science begins to establish who benefits from which drug. If only a small number of people respond specifically to a statin for cholesterol levels or a biphosphonate for osteoporosis, we should be identifying who these specific responders are. Until we answer this we remain in the position of congratulating ourselves on the use of plaster casts when in three out of four cases they have been put on the wrong limb—but of course this is the question no company wants answered.

Even without fully understanding why a treatment helps, though, more can be done to improve how it is used. For instance, we have many different kinds of blood pressure medication, but almost no research to discover how they compare or who they suit. The first thiazide antihypertensives in the 1950s were succeeded by James Black's propranolol in the 1960s and 1970s, the ACE inhibitors in the 1980s, sartans in the 1990s, and a string of others, with each new drug marketed as the best. When the first proper head-to-head studies were done fifty years later, they showed that, in fact, the thiazides were the most effective and the safest.[32] For fifty years we have used a succession of ever more expensive treatments, while the best and safest and least expensive treatments fell out of favor.

Similarly, the SSRIs in clinical trials got far fewer severely depressed patients well than older antidepressants.[33] But to get on the market they did not have to be compared to an older drug; they had only to beat the placebo. As a result of marketing, the more recent drugs have almost completely replaced older antidepressants, even for the most severe depressions, for which there is not a scrap of evidence the newer drugs work.

The story is similar for the analgesics, drugs for osteoporosis, blood-sugar-lowering drugs, the antipsychotics, and almost every other best-selling drug. Best-sellers are not best sellers because they are in fact better than the drugs previously available. Yet in all these areas of treatment, doctors who are supposedly following the evidence make the latest drugs into best sellers.

There is more going on here than simply squandering money in the pursuit of the trivial (though profitable) new drug or giving patients suboptimal medicine. Company trials have radically changed how doctors treat patients. Before 1962 when the FDA stepped in and required companies to provide evidence of trials to bring their drug on the market, doctors for centuries had to learn how to use a drug when it became available. Digitalis offers a good example. This drug works by removing excess fluid from the body in cases of heart failure, but as with all drugs, digitalis came with problems. So doctors, when giving it, would typically start at a low dose, and work upward depending on how the patient responded.

But in company trials, no company is prepared to take a chance that their drug won't beat the placebo, so they err on the side of a higher or more poisonous dose. If these studies get the drug on the market, the trial results are then taken to mean that doctors should use the dose of the statin, analgesic, or antidepressant used in the trial, even though it is likely to be too high for many people. On the basis of early trials, the thiazides were given for hypertension in doses ten times higher than necessary, for example, while the lowest dose of Prozac for depression was four times higher than many people needed.[34]

Once a drug is launched, companies could run studies to find the right starting dose or determine which drug suits which kinds of patients, but marketing departments have resisted studies of lower doses of a drug—on the grounds that they want to keep things simple for doctors. Their dream is one-size-fits-all treatment, and they refuse to make lower dose formulations of a medicine available. In this way companies are, in essence, removing the craft as well as the art from medicine and encouraging overmedication.

But there are even bigger problems than this. Company trials trap both doctors and patients into treatment with the wrong medication. The antipsychotic group of drugs shows how badly wrong things can go. The first of these was chlorpromazine, a drug discovered in 1952 and widely cited as rivaling penicillin as a key breakthrough in modern medicine. It and succeeding tranquilizers had a magical effect on manic and delirious states and on some acute psychoses, sometimes restoring patients to normal functioning within days, or weeks, sometimes in hours. This was not a matter of small changes on a rating scale; there was no question but that chlorpromazine worked.[35]

Its French discoverers were sure, however, that it was not a cure for schizophrenia. In some cases it provided a useful tranquilization, but in up to a third of schizophrenic patients it made their condition worse, and in a further third the benefits were minimal. Nevertheless, most company trials to bring the successors of chlorpromazine to the US market were undertaken in schizophrenia. When responders, minimal responders, and those who got worse were combined, the results for these drugs could be shown to be, on average, marginally better than for the placebo—which was all it took to get these drugs on the market. These results, reinforced by rebranding the tranquilizers as antipsychotics, made it seem these drugs "worked" for schizophrenia. For the FDA, and most doctors, the one in three patients who got worse on treatment vanish into a statistical ether—but these patients don't vanish from the hospital and the clinic.

The antipsychotics are drugs to use judiciously. They increase rates of heart attacks, strokes, diabetes, and suicides. Studies that have examined longer term outcomes for patients on these drugs universally show a reduction in life expectancy measured in decades, not just years.[36] This is not an argument against their use, but it is definitely an argument for ensuring that they actually are producing benefits that warrant the risks undertaken. Unfortunately, even when faced with a patient who is not responding or responding negatively and for whom therefore the treatment should be stopped, the drug often keeps being given. Nursing staff, hospital administrators, relatives, and other doctors find it inconceivable that a doctor might not give a drug that "works" to a patient who is so clearly ill with the condition that the drug supposedly benefits—to the point that a refusal to prescribe is in many settings getting ever closer to being grounds for dismissal.

In similar fashion, the company trials of statins for lowering cholesterol, biphosphonates for osteoporosis, and for other medicines that suggest these drugs "work" exert pressure on clinicians to prescribe and patients to acquiesce in treatment. This pressure cannot simply be put down to corruption by the pharmaceutical industry. No one, it seems, wants a doctor to wait judiciously to see if a treatment is really warranted. We might like the idea of an Alfred Worcester in books or movies but not in real life.

In addition to these serious consequences for medical care, there is a huge ethical problem with company trials. Randomized controlled trials began in conditions of scarcity after World War II, when those who volunteered to be left untreated or to get a potentially dangerous new treatment did so for the sake of their families, their relatives, or the communities from which they came. They consented, in other words, because they thought they were helping to improve medical care, and in so doing they did in fact lay the basis for our current freedom from infectious diseases, malignant hypertension and other disorders, and our better life expectancies in the face of tumors. The same spirit is now invoked when patients are asked to consent to company-run trials. But they are not told that these studies are designed to secure a business advantage, that they will lead to marketing that often substitutes giving drugs for caring, that far from benefitting their communities the studies may result in treatments that shorten lives, or that data from these studies may be sequestered so that nobody ever finds out about the side effects of treatment. They never get a chance to decide freely whether to consent to this or not.

If the primary ethical as well as scientific purpose of controlled trials was initially to debunk unwarranted therapeutic claims, companies have transformed them into technologies that mandate action. The method originally designed to stop misguided therapeutic bandwagons has in company hands become the main fuel of the latest bandwagons. A method that is of greatest use when it demonstrates drugs either do not work or have minimal effects has become a method to transform snake oil into a must-use life-saving remedy. In the process, evidence-based medicine has become evidence-biased medicine.

EVIDENCE-BIASED MEDICINE

In 1972, two decades after randomized controlled trials came into use, Archie Cochrane, a physician based in Cardiff, Britain, who had worked with Austin Bradford Hill when the first clinical trials were being set up, published an influential book on the role of evidence in medicine. The vast majority of medical services and procedures still had not been tested for their effectiveness, he noted, while many other services and procedures that had been tested and shown to be unsatisfactory, still persisted.[37] Cochrane was a randomization extremist; in his view, not only doctors but also judges and teachers should be randomizing what actions they took to see what worked, but all three unfortunately had God complexes—they "knew" what the right thing to do was. As late as the 1980s, Cochrane claimed fewer than 10 percent of the treatments in medicine were evidence based.[38]

Cochrane made it clear that using controlled trials to evaluate treatments was not a matter of dragging rural hospitals up to the standards of Harvard or Oxford. Rather, mortality often seemed to him greater where there were more medical interventions rather than fewer. After coronary care units (CCUs) came into fashion in the 1960s, for instance, he suggested randomizing patients who were having heart attacks to treatment in a CCU versus home treatment. Cardiff physicians refused to participate on the grounds that CCUs were so obviously right. Cochrane ran the trial in neighboring Bristol instead. When he first presented the results, he transposed them so that the home treatment results, which were actually the better ones, appeared under the CCU column and vice versa. His audience demanded an instant halt to home treatment. But the response was quite different when the "error" was corrected and it was made clear that the data favored home treatment. To this day there is a reluctance to believe that home care might be better than care in a CCU.

Iain Chalmers, a perinatologist and health services researcher from Oxford picked up the baton from Cochrane. He was similarly struck that physicians often seemed slow to implement procedures that had been shown to work and instead stuck with approaches that had not been shown to work or had been shown not to work. His concern lay not just in encouraging trials but in accessing the information from trials that had already been done.[39] Everyone knew there had been an explosion in the medical literature since World War II, but efforts to collect reports of clinical trials began to reveal that there were far fewer published trials than many had thought. Some of the trials done had been published multiple times, while others had not been published at all.

Many of the articles that dictated clinical practice, furthermore, were framed as review essays, published under the names of some of the most eminent academics in the field, but on closer inspection, these often lengthy articles with their impressively long reference lists espoused only one point of view of a topic. These academics were not systematically considering all the available research, in other words. These were not scientific reviews—they were rhetorical exercises. Recognition that a scientific review should be systematic led Chalmers to set up the Cochrane Center in 1992 dedicated to amassing all available clinical trial evidence in every branch of medicine, even when the evidence had not been published.

It was David Sackett at Canada's McMaster University, outlining a program for educating medical students to practice according to the evidence, who branded the new dispensation evidence-based medicine.[40] When it came to considering the evidence, Sackett drew up a hierarchy in which systematic reviews and randomized controlled trials offered gold standard evidence, while at the bottom of the hierarchy came individual clinical or anecdotal experience. This was a world turned upside down. Just a few years earlier, clinical judgment had been seen as the height of medical wisdom.

The implication was that we should submit every procedure to controlled trial testing. Even if newer treatments were more expensive as a result, in due course the health services would gain because money would be saved as ineffective treatments were abandoned and better treatments reduced the burden of chronic illnesses. This seemed to be a win-win claim for those paying for health services, for physicians and their patients, as well as for scientific journals. It quickly became almost impossible to get anything other than clinical trials published in leading journals.

When Cochrane advocated for randomized controlled trials, Chalmers campaigned for comprehensive collection of their results, and Sackett drew up his hierarchy of evidence placing trial results at the top, no distinction was drawn between independent and company trials. Controlled trials were controlled trials. It seemed so difficult to get doctors to accept the evidence that their pet treatments didn't work, that any indication that doctors were practicing in accordance with clinical trial evidence seemed a step in the right direction.

There are two problems with this approach. The first applies to both independent and company trials—namely, that we appear to have lost a sense that, other than when they demonstrate treatments don't work, what controlled trials do primarily is to throw up associations that still need to be explained. Until we establish what underpins the association, simply practicing on the basis of numbers involves sleepwalking rather than science—equivalent to using plaster casts indiscriminately rather than specifically on the fractured limb.

The second is that in the case of company trials, the association that is marketed will have been picked out in a boardroom rather than at the bedside. One of the most dramatic examples of what this can mean comes from the SSRIs, where the effects of these drugs on sexual functioning are so clear that controlled trials would be merely a formality. In contrast, hundreds of patients are needed to show that a new drug has a marginal antidepressant effect. Yet the marketers know that with a relentless focus on one set of figures and repetitions of the mantra of statistical significance they can hypnotize clinicians into thinking these drugs act primarily on mood with side effects on sexual functioning when in fact just the opposite would be the more accurate characterization. Because it has become so hard to argue against clinical trials of this nature, there is now almost no one at the séance likely to sing out and break the hypnotic spell.

A cautionary tale involving reserpine may bring home how far we have traveled in the last half century. In the early 1950s, medical journals were full of reports from senior medical figures claiming the drug worked wonderfully to lower blood pressure; what was more, patients on it reported feeling better than well.[41]

Reserpine was also a tranquilizer and this led Michael Shepherd, another of Bradford Hill's protégés, in 1954 to undertake the first randomized controlled trial in psychiatry, in this case comparing reserpine to placebo in a group of anxious depressives.[42] While reserpine was no penicillin, some patients were clearly more relaxed and less anxious while on it, so it was something more than snake oil. Shepherd's trial results were published in the *Lancet,* a leading journal; nevertheless, his article had almost no impact. The message sank without trace, he thought, because medicine at the time was dominated not by clinical trials but by physicians who believed the evidence of their own eyes or got their information from clinical articles describing cases in detail— "anecdotes"—as they would now be called.[43]

Ironically the two articles preceding Shepherd's in the same issue of the *Lancet* reported hypertensive patients becoming suicidal on reserpine.[44] Reserpine can induce akathisia, a state of intense inner restlessness and mental turmoil that can lead to suicide. The case reports of this new hazard were so compelling, the occurrence of the problem so rare without exposure to a drug, and the onset of the problem subsequent to starting the drug plus its resolution once the treatment was stopped so clear that clinical trials were not needed to make it obvious what was happening. On the basis of just such detailed descriptions, instead of becoming an antidepressant, reserpine became a drug that was said to cause depression and trigger suicides. But the key point is this—even though superficially contradictory, there is no reason to think that either the case reports or the controlled trial findings were wrong. It is not so extraordinary for a drug to suit many people but not necessarily suit all.

Fast forward thirty-five years to 1990. A series of trials had shown Prozac, although less effective than older antidepressants, had modest effects in anxious depressives, much as reserpine had. On the basis of this evidence that it "worked," the drug began its rise to blockbuster status. A series of compelling reports of patients becoming suicidal on treatment began to emerge, however.[45] These were widely dismissed as case reports—anecdotes. The company purported to reanalyze its clinical trials and claimed that there was no signal for increased suicide risk on Prozac in data from over three thousand patients, when in fact there was a doubling of the risk of suicidal acts on Prozac but this increase was not statistically significant and thus was ignored. Even if Prozac had reduced suicide and suicidal-act rates, it would still be possible for it to benefit many but pose problems to some. But the climate had so shifted that instead the fuss generated by the Prozac case reports added impetus to the swing of the pendulum away from clinical reports in favor of controlled trials.

But as we saw in the analysis of antidepressants, in addition to the 40 percent who responded to placebo, a further 50 percent of patients (five out of ten) did not respond to treatment, so that in only publishing controlled trials and not the convincing reports of hazards for treatments like the antidepressants, journals are privileging the experiences of the one specific drug responder over the nine-fold larger pool of those who in one way or another are not benefitting specifically from the drug. Partly because of selective publication practices, partly because of clever trial design, only about one out of every hundred drug trials published in major journals today is likely to do what trials do best—namely, debunk therapeutic claims. The other ninety-nine are pitched as rosily positive endorsements of the benefits of statins or mood stabilizers, treatments for asthma or blood pressure or whatever illness is being marketed as part of the campaign to sell a blockbuster.

The publishing of company trials in preference to carefully described clinical cases, allied to the selective publication of only some trials of a drug, and interpretations of the data that are just plain wrong amounts to a new anecdotalism. The effect on clinical practice has been dramatic. Where once clinicians were slow to use new drugs if they already had effective treatments, and when they did use the new drug, if their patients had a problem, they stopped the treatment and described what had happened, we now have clinicians trained to pay heed only to controlled trials—clinicians who, on the basis of evidence that is much less generalizable than they think, have rapidly taken up a series of newer but less effective treatments.

The development of randomized controlled trials in the 1950s is now widely acclaimed as at least as significant for the development of medicine as any of the breakthrough drugs of the period. If controlled trials functioned to save patients from unnecessary interventions, it would be fair to say they had contributed to better medical care. They sometimes fill this role, but modern clinicians, in thrall to the selective trials proffered up by the pharmaceutical companies, and their embodiment in guidelines, are increasingly oblivious to what is happening to the patients in front of them, increasingly unable to trust the evidence of their own eyes.

We have come to the outcome that Alfred Worcester feared but not through the emphasis on diagnosis and tests that so concerned him. It has been controlled trials, an invention that was designed to restrict the use of unnecessary treatments and tests, which he would likely have fully approved of, that has been medicine's undoing.

This company subversion of the meaning of controlled trials does not happen because of company malfeasance. It happens because both we and our doctors as well as the government or hospital service that employs our physicians, in addition to companies, all want treatments to work. It is this conspiracy of goodwill that leads to the problems outlined here.[46] But in addition to this, uniquely in science pharmaceutical companies are able to leave studies unpublished or cherry-pick the bits of the data that suit them, maneuvers that compound the biases just outlined.

Two decades after introducing the randomized controlled trial, having spent years waiting for the pendulum to swing from the personal experience of physicians to some consideration of evidence on a large scale, Austin Bradford Hill suggested that if such trials ever became the only method of assessing treatments, not only would the pendulum have swung too far, it would have come off its hook.[47] We are fast approaching that point.

4

Doctoring the Data

By 1965, the flood tide of innovative compounds ranging from the early antibiotics to the first antipsychotics that had transformed medicine in the 1950s appeared to be ebbing. Desperate to continue with business as usual, the pharmaceutical industry had to decide if it made business sense to allow its researchers to pursue scientific innovations in quite the ad hoc way that had worked so well for the previous two decades. This was the question the major drug companies put to a new breed of specialists, management consultants, who were called in to help them reorganize their operations with a view to maintaining the success of previous decades. The answers these consultants provided have shaped not only industry but also the practice of medicine ever since.

In the preceding decades, scientists working within pharmaceutical companies took the same approach to research that scientists based in universities did: they conducted wide-ranging, blue-skies research out of which new compounds might serendipitously fall and for which there might initially be no obvious niche—as had once been the case for a host of drug innovations that later became huge money makers, including oral contraceptives, the thiazide antihypertensives, the blood-sugar-lowering tolbutamide, chlorpromazine and subsequent antipsychotics, and imipramine and later antidepressants. But under changed conditions and the coming of the consultants, the mission changed to one in which clinical targets were to be specified by marketing departments and pursued in five-year programs. If that meant discarding intriguing but unplanned leads, so be it.

Where once pharmaceutical companies had been prospectors for drugs, more like oil exploration companies, they now changed character. Their share prices had soared but these were now dependent on the recommendations of analysts who scrutinized the company's drug pipeline and business plans. Accordingly companies had to do business in a different way. Even though the best way to find new drugs is to watch closely for drug side effects in people who are taking them, just as simply drilling oil wells is still the best way to find oil, this avenue of drug development was cut off.

Fatefully, in tandem with these corporate changes a second wave of drug development had come to fruition. The original, serendipitous discoveries of the 1940s had not only offered stunning new treatments but also greatly advanced our understanding of biology. Out of this new understanding came a further group of compounds, like James Black's beta-blockers for hypertension and H-2 antagonists for ulcers, as well as Arvid Carlsson's selective serotonin reuptake inhibiting antidepressants (SSRIs). This second wave initially gave hope to those who like business plans—it appeared that drug development could be made rational and predictable in a manner that might fit into a business model. But since the 1970s, this new tide has also gone out. The number of new drugs registered yearly and the number of breakthrough compounds has dropped dramatically, leading companies to hunt for new solutions, one of which has been to outsource drug development to start-up companies.

While the changes in drug development programs that began in the 1960s have been enormous, the key reorganization came at the marketing and clinical-trial end of company operations, and these have transformed pharmaceutical outfits into companies who market drugs rather than companies who manufacture drugs for the market.[1] As it happened, these corporate changes coincided with three other developments that were to have far more profound effects on the drug industry than any management consultant in the 1960s would likely have supposed. It was one thing to reorganize pharmaceutical companies, it was quite another to end up with almost complete control of therapeutics.

The first of these developments was a decline in US government funding for clinical research beginning in the 1960s. If industry was already funding many studies in order to get approval for drugs, why not let them carry an even larger share of the burden? So the thinking went. For well-done randomized controlled trials, it shouldn't make much difference where the funding came from.

The second development in both the United States and Europe was a huge expansion in university training and in the health services industry. This led to a rapidly growing number of medical academics. Where before the pharmaceutical industry had been beholden to a handful of magisterial figures, any of whom could make or break a new drug, now companies could shop around among eager young academics willing to manage a trial in return for the kudos of being a principal investigator and the fees that came with the exercise. These new academics, more vulnerable in their careers and more open to the seduction of being made into opinion leaders, could be expected to accommodate them-selves to company interests in a way that their older counterparts might not. Besides, there was little these academics had to do other than be notional investigators—companies could now supply them readymade versions of clinical trial protocols that the previous generation of aca-demics had developed during the 1950s.

The third development was the increasing dispersion of the locus of clinical trials. Where in the 1950s and early 1960s trials had often been conducted in a single university or hospital, by the late 1960s they were typically multicentered, and by the 1970s they had become multinational. This did not happen because the drugs and the testing were better. Quite the contrary, the more obviously effective the drug the smaller the trial needed to demonstrate that it works, although large trials might still be needed to reveal possible hazards of treatment. The newer drugs were in fact less effective and required larger trials to show benefits that could be considered statistically significant. Increase in the number of participants in typical trials and the geographic proliferation of sites had far-reaching implications; principal investigators could no longer know all the patients, could no longer supervise all the raters, and might no longer be able to speak authoritatively to side effects that may only have been witnessed on sites other than their own. Where before investigators had the data for the whole study, now they typically had a record only of the data from their own site and just a summary of the rest. Companies or their proxies increasingly did the shuttling between sites, and it made sense to lodge the data somewhere central—such as company headquarters. When investigators requested full access to the data—the answer was no, the information was proprietary. Without accessible data, these trials had the appearance of science but were no longer science.

These three developments changed the interface between medicine and industry. Where clinical trials were once a scientific exercise aimed at weeding out ineffective treatments, they became in industry's hands a means to sell treatments of little benefit. The key to this has been— and still is—industry control of the data from "their" trials, which is then selectively described in articles designed to establish market niches by selling diseases the new drug happens to address or to counteract adverse publicity about treatment hazards.

THE APPEARANCES OF SCIENCE

As part of an effort to reengineer their drug development and marketing strategies in the 1970s, the major pharmaceutical companies began to outsource not only their clinical trial division but their medical writing division as well. The job of running clinical trials went to a new set of companies—clinical research organizations (CROs). The early CROs included Quintiles (set up in 1982), Parexel (in business since 1984), and Covance (started in 1987), with a growing number of companies such as Scirex and Target Research coming onstream in the 1990s. By 2010, the clinical trial business was worth $30 billion and CROs were running more than two-thirds of the clinical trials undertaken by industry.[2]

In the 1950s and 1960s, controlled trials involving drugs were either funded by independent agencies such as the National Institutes of Health or involved drug companies handing over supplies of new compounds to medical academics who devised the clinical trials to test out the new remedy. These professors and their colleagues personally witnessed the giving of placebos that were outwardly indistinguishable from the trial drugs, along with both older and new drugs to patients. They interviewed the patients and completed the rating scales themselves or personally taught members of their team how to do so. When the data were finally assembled, professors would analyze them and later store the data in their filing cabinet for consultation should questions arise. While some academics availed themselves of the new opportunities to supplement their income, in many instances, the investigators did the work without charge—the new drugs were unquestionably moving medical science forward, which for some was payment enough.

When a lead investigator wrote a paper for a scientific journal representing what the trial had shown, the resulting article reflected a judgment on the new compound based on familiarity with other compounds in the field. When it came to presenting the findings at an academic meeting, the professor was there to answer audience questions about potential hazards of the new compound or other issues not covered in the article or presentation. At meetings in the 1950s and 1960s, entire symposia were dedicated to the hazards of new treatments, where now it is as difficult to find mention of a treatment's hazards at major academic meetings as it would be to find snow in the Sahara.

Few clinicians or others outside industry noticed any change during the transition from the 1960s's way of doing things to the 1980s's way. The trials under CRO auspices had all the appearances of previous clinical research. But from the 1980s onward, these trials increasingly diverged from previous clinical research practices.

The CROs competed among themselves for clinical trial business on the basis not only of price but also of ensuring rapid access to patients and timely completion of competent study reports. Clinicians who enrolled suitable research subjects were paid per patient, and paid more for patients who completed a course of treatment. There was no one to keep an eye on whether those recruited and deemed to have a particular disorder actually had the disorder, however. In addition, patients were increasingly recruited by advertisement rather than from clinical care. And an increasing number of patients reported in these trials didn't exist. In 1996, as one indicator of this trend, Richard Borison and Bruce Diamond from the Medical College of Georgia were jailed for the conduct of their clinical trial business, which recruited nonexistent patients to trials of many of the antidepressants and antipsychotics now on the market.[3]

Where once clinical trial protocols had to be approved by a hospital or university ethics committee—an institutional review board—now they may be subject only to the CRO's privatized review system for company studies. And where university or hospital review boards typically commented on the science in addition to the ethics of a study, often forcing researchers to improve their designs, privatized committees may simply nod company protocols through. As the clinical trial business grew and competition for patients increased, CROs initially moved trials out of university and hospital settings and contacted physicians in general practice to get study subjects. As getting patients in the United States and Europe became more difficult, even from primary care physicians, CROs began moving trials first to the former Eastern European bloc during the late 1990s and subsequently to Asia and

Africa. Regardless of location, though, it's still likely to be a Western academic's name that appears as the notional principal investigator on the trial protocol or subsequent articles.

But the key difference in the shift toward privatization of trial research lies in what happens with the data. Where once a professor might have analyzed the data from a trial, now personnel from the CRO collect the records from each center and assemble them back at base. The events in a patient's medical records or the results of investigations are then coded under agreed-upon headings from dictionaries listing side effects. These items are then cumulated in tabular form. Such tables are the closest that any of the academic investigators are likely to get to the raw data, except what they themselves collected. If later asked at an academic meeting what happened to patients on the drug, this is what they will cite. In this way the blind lead the blind—giving a whole new meaning to the idea of a double-blind study.

For instance, academics presenting the results of clinical trials of Paxil for depression or anxiety in children wrote about or showed slides containing rates of emotional lability on Paxil and placebo. The presentations were relatively glib, and there is no record of any member of any audience being concerned by higher rates of emotional lability on Paxil, probably because none of those involved realized that emotional lability is a coding term that covers suicidality; in fact, had they had the raw records in front of them clinicians would have realized there was a statistically significant increase in rates of suicidal acts following commencement of treatment with Paxil.

Other decisions about how the data is presented can also drastically affect how a drug's effects are perceived. For instance, if a patient experiences a sequence of side effects starting with nausea, then several other side effects, and those are followed by suicidality, and the person then drops out of treatment, if nausea is listed first rather than the suicidal act that actually triggered the drop out, this patient will likely count as a drop out for nausea rather than suicide. Unless there is someone at the heart of the system who understands the issues, the default in these new trial procedures conceals rather than reveals problems.

But there is no independent academic at the helm any more. The first semijudicial setting in which these issues were tested involved Richard Eastell and Aubrey Blumsohn from Sheffield University in England in a hearing in 2009. Eastell and Blumsohn had been senior investigators on a study of the effects of Proctor and Gamble's Actonel for osteoporosis. Behind the veneer of professional ethics lies another world, as Aubrey Blumsohn found out when Proctor and Gamble set about ghostwriting articles for him. A senior company figure wrote to him "to introduce you to one of The Alliance's external medical writers, Mary Royer. I've had the great privilege of working closely with Mary on a number of manuscripts, which The Alliance has recently published. Mary is based in New York and is very familiar with both the risedronate (Actonel) data and our key messages, in addition to being well clued up on competitor and general osteoporosis publications."[4] Blumsohn found himself faced with articles written up under his name containing tables of·"data." He asked to see the raw data, but access was refused. Using subterfuge, he eventually managed to get hold of the data and found that the tables had been cropped to leave out a great deal of data; when this information was included the claims being made for the drug did not hold up.[5] He withdrew from authorship, a move that ultimately cost him his job at Sheffield.

Eastell, who was the dean of medical research at Sheffield, meanwhile had authored several papers on the same research, one of which required him to declare he had access to the data. He said he had had access. In September 2009, Britain's General Medical Council (GMC), were asked to rule on whether Eastell's behavior was appropriate or whether he should be debarred from medical practice. At the heart of the issue was the question of what are data. After two days of legal argument, the GMC came up with a formulation that most readers of this book have likely already come to—that access to the data means access to the raw medical records. Summary tables of events or results are not data. (Eastell, as one might expect, pleaded that this had not been his understanding of what the term "data" meant at the time of his declaration.[6])

If the key data are the raw medical records, who owns these data? In point of fact, no one knows. When it comes to legal cases, companies regularly keep any paperwork they have stemming from "their" trials and other data off the US mainland just in case a court should request access. If in responding to an article presenting a company's drug trial results, I were to request access to the raw data I would be told to get lost. But this is an exercise of *force majeure* rather than a position that has scientific, legal, ethical, or moral support. Companies may be practicing their version of evidence-based medicine, but they are not practicing data-based medicine, which is the soul of scientific medicine, and they are actively stopping anyone else from practicing data-based medicine.

Compared to the days in which purveyors of proprietary medicine flourished, one of the protections we now have is that someone like me cannot simply stand up at a major medical meeting and claim I have a new treatment for some condition without making the data available. I would be jeered off the podium. Practitioners of alternative or complementary therapies never get asked to medical meetings precisely because their claims are not based on data that can be examined.

Yet standing up and making claims while refusing to make the raw data available is exactly what pharmaceutical companies, and academics speaking on their behalf, do time after time. At first this wasn't much of an issue as there were only occasional reports of company-sponsored drug trials scattered among other articles in peripheral journals and occasional presentations on the program of academic meetings. Initially many people assumed that the trial data was available just as it was in other studies: the academic presenters of the material must have had access to it. When it became clear that the presenters hadn't seen it, academics took refuge in the thought that at least the regulator would have seen all the data. But now, the majority of treatment trials reported in leading journals, as well as large chunks of academic conference programs, feature company material without data access and even if regulators request all the data, they do not get all the studies and certainly do not get the data in accessible form—although few doctors know this.[7] At academic meetings and in scientific journals everyone welcomes the velvet glove of scientific appearances while ignoring the iron fist of refusal to part with data.

Access to the data of experiments is at the heart of what makes science. Right from the very first scientific meetings in seventeenth-century England in Oxford and London, there was a consensus that what made these meetings scientific and different from all previous meetings was a focus on observable evidence. Whether the subject was physics, chemistry, or biology, participants ran experiments in front of their peers. Whether by virtue of a novel technique or a new method, the experimental art aimed at generating data that revealed a formerly hidden aspect of the world. Where others talked, scientists generated data and made both the data and the method to generate it publicly available. It is inconceivable that Louis Pasteur, Robert Koch, Richard Cabot, or other medical people who came after them would have refused access to the data underpinning any scientific claims they made. Refusal to share key information, however, was precisely what characterized the purveyors of proprietary medicines.

GHOSTS IN THE MACHINE

Just as many drug companies began outsourcing clinical trials in the 1970s, they began to do the same with medical writing, giving rise to a huge increase in ghostwriting and, in a further twist, ghost-presenting. This went on quietly for more than twenty years before the issue began to surface in the academic media and later more generally.

The first companies in the medical ghostwriting business emerged in the 1970s but many more entered the market in the 1980s and 1990s; there are now fifty or so medical writing companies in the United States and Britain.[8] These specialized companies compete for drug company contracts for a series of articles on the basis not only of price per article and article quality, but also on the stature of the academic "authors" the outfit is able to recruit and the ability of the ghosts to get an article speedily placed in a prestigious medical journal. Many of these writing agencies have since become subsidiaries of public relations companies, who are in turn branches of global advertising companies such as WPP,[9] Omnicon, and Interpublic, some of whom have now taken up the clinical trial business themselves.

Axis Healthcare Communications, one such company, offers to help pharmaceutical companies "brand the science." Envision Pharma announces that "data generated from clinical trials are the most powerful marketing tools available to a pharmaceutical company." GYMR boasts that they "know how to take the language of science and medicine and transform it into the more understandable language of health. We advise clients of the best dissemination strategy for their news and make sure that the message they deliver is compelling, documented and contributes to other national dialogues in a real and meaningful way."[10] Meanwhile, Current Medical Directions offers to deliver scientifically accurate information that has been strategically developed for specific target audiences. To do this, they "write up studies, review articles, abstracts, journal supplements, product monographs, expert commentaries and textbook chapters, conduct meta-analyses, organize journal supplements, satellite symposia, and consensus conferences as well as advisory boards for clients."[11]

Who are the ghostwriters in these endeavors? They are predominantly women, with PhDs or other science qualifications. The work may offer them an opportunity to work from home, possibly on a different continent than that of either the notional lead investigator or the study site. The job requires no familiarity with what actually happened; indeed it can probably best proceed without firsthand knowledge of the trial—that's not the writer's department, as Tom Lehrer might have sung.

Most of the medical writing companies and independent writers working on contract have put in place protocols or business plans specifying what they do and do not do, and they see themselves as adhering to these specifications and standards. The protocols may, for instance, mention that they will ensure that any submission to a particular journal takes account of that journal's requirement for conflict-of-interest statements and authorship declarations. And in fact, these requirements are much more likely to be met in articles written by medical writers than in articles written by academics.[12]

The ghosts see themselves as occupying a position midway between marketing and the practice of science. They are sure that the marketers, left to their own devices, would not be able to resist overt promotion and the resulting product would be rejected at peer review for not meeting the standards of scientific presentation. Left to the academics, the articles would not be ready in even draft form in time for a drug's launch and inadvertently might put the trial's results in less than the best light. The writers see themselves as producing an acceptable compromise.

The editorial staffs of leading journals such as the *British Medical Journal (BMJ)*, *New English Journal of Medicine (NEJM)*, and others regularly attend the meetings of medical writers. They encourage writers to contact them early in a manuscript's development so that the extent of mutual interest can be gauged. If I am a ghost, I can contact the editorial desk and find out if the topic on which I'm writing would be of interest—if the journal has several articles on this already in press, for instance, they may not want more. But if they indicate interest, I am half way to having the article accepted as it is more likely to be sent out to sympathetic reviewers if this is an article the editor wants.

It is not so surprising that journals have drifted into a position of collaboration with industry. They have vested interests in getting an option on publication of the latest studies. Today, reports of randomized controlled trials stand at the top of the evidence hierarchy and the leading journals realize that their own influence and the perception of how seriously their journals are taken depend on getting access to these trials. Given that industry runs the great bulk of such trials and medical writers produce articles that tick all the quality boxes, avoid the excesses of the marketers, and turn around a product in a timely fashion, with a paper trail that makes for accountability, what's not in it for journal editors to cooperate?

When the matter of ghostwriting comes up, the medical journals seem mostly concerned with whether or not the role of the ghost should be acknowledged. Article writers, journal editors, and pharmaceutical companies all believe that prescribing doctors would find the articles less persuasive if they knew they were ghostwritten—that this would convey the message that these were commercial product placements rather than scientific articles. The implication is that if the authorship issues were managed in a better way, the system could be salvaged, ignoring the larger issues of scientific and medical integrity.

Faced, for instance, with evidence that Merck had employed Scientific Therapeutics Information (STI) to write up a series of studies on the drug Vioxx and that critical data on the hazards of Vioxx had been concealed,[13] Catherine DeAngelis, the editor of *Journal of the American Medical Association (JAMA),* in a 2008 editorial deplored the deception.[14] But she did not deplore the ghostwriting per se. She was in fact concerned for the medical writers who had actually authored the piece but had not been included on the authorship line and so had not received due acknowledgement.

The next slip down the slope from the presentation of science by scientists to our current world of scientific appearances has been from ghostwriting into ghost-presenting. There is an increasing chance that the named authors on articles in journals such as *JAMA, New English Journal of Medicine,* or the *Lancet* will know relatively little about the study they have apparently authored. Having written the article, the medical writer will often be the person best placed to answer questions arising from any publication. As a result it is not uncommon in major meetings to find poster presentations of a study's results tended by attractive, confident women whom the passing doctors will assume are postdoctoral researchers linked to the study. Far better have this kind of arrangement than some academic stumbling unconvincingly through the study design and results, drifting perhaps off message.

It is difficult to think of any other domain of professional life where this would be possible—except in the entertainment industry. A lawyer would not be able to bring in someone who "looked good" to sway a jury. If asked thirty years ago which professions could be body-snatched in this way, academic medicine would have seemed an unlikely candidate.

Until relatively recently in the biomedical sciences the most distinguished scientists in the field, Nobelists or aspiring Nobelists, might have four to five hundred articles on their curriculum vitae when they reached their sixties. The great men would often joke that if they hadn't gotten a Nobel Prize for science, they would have been in line for one for fiction. Many of today's ghostwriters in their thirties or forties will have more articles published in major journals than any of these Nobelists. But the most interesting figures are the academics still in their forties that the pharmaceutical industry has made into opinion leaders and who may as a result appear as an author on eight hundred to a thousand articles. Sometimes the marketing copy slips and such an academic figure may be described as someone whose views you can trust because they have over eight hundred articles to their name.

When it comes to choosing names to go on a paper's authorship line, the marketing department of the parent company has the key input. Companies will pay some heed to the contribution an individual may have made to study design, execution, or review of the manuscript, but they put greatest store on the profile of the academics and their ability to serve as spokespersons for the study among their peers.

When choosing a journal, companies review their portfolio of articles and decide on the mix they need for marketing purposes—some for the *New England Journal of Medicine,* some for the *Lancet,* and some for more specialized outlets. Factors such as the journal editor and the likely speed of acceptance and publication of the article make a difference too. In the case of Vioxx, Merck was interested in *JAMA,* for example, because it offers a fast-track option for "important" papers.

How many articles are now ghostwritten? In the late 1990s a document developed by Current Medical Directions, a medical writing company that was at the time coordinating a portfolio of relentlessly positive articles on Zoloft for Pfizer, surfaced that helped answer this question. Along with colleagues, I had a chance to analyze the papers being written and this made it clear that even by the late 1990s well over 50 percent of all articles on a drug such as Zoloft were likely to have been written by medical writers and over 90 percent of those appeared in major journals.

Of the eighty-five articles in the portfolio we tracked fifty-five to publication. All were devoted, it seemed, to securing marketing niches. There were articles, for example, on the virtues of Zoloft for anxiety, for panic disorder, for depression, for dysthymia, for obsessive-compulsive disorder, for children, for the elderly, and for women, along with articles on how Zoloft's metabolic profile was better than those of competitor SSRIs.[15] None of the published articles shed light on what SSRIs such as Zoloft actually do or what their hazards might be.

Two articles in particular bring out what is involved. These reported clinical trial results of Zoloft in the treatment of post-traumatic stress disorder (PTSD). At the time the portfolio was assembled these two articles were listed as written but their authors were "TBD" (to be determined). Despite this they were scheduled to appear in *JAMA* and the *New England Journal of Medicine*. (They ultimately appeared in *JAMA* and *Archives of General Psychiatry*.)

"PTSD" as a defining label only came into being in 1980, and many experts were and are still skeptical that there is any such thing, arguing instead that the patients concerned are either anxious or depressed. In any case, in the late 1990s no company had a treatment that they were entitled to claim could benefit PTSD and so all companies were scrambling to be the first with a license. The two trials on which the two articles were based were part of Pfizer's effort. If Zoloft got on the market for PTSD, then publishing studies on PTSD would become a means to sell Zoloft. At the same time, selling Zoloft would establish some legitimacy for PTSD—as doctors and patients are likely to think a condition has to be real if a drug makes a difference to it, whether PTSD, female sexual dysfunction (FSD), compulsive shopping disorder, or adult ADHD. And of course, there is something real there—people.

In fact Pfizer had conducted four controlled trials for treatment of PTSD with Zoloft. In all four the drug had proved ineffective for men, a large proportion of whom had a clear history of having experienced a traumatic event through wartime exposure. In the two studies listed in the portfolio, some women, a much smaller proportion of whom had clear-cut evidence of having experienced a traumatic event, showed sufficient response for the company to steer the drug past the FDA and get it licensed.

Some years later, in 2007, there was widespread publicity about soaring suicide rates among traumatized US soldiers returning from the Second Gulf War or on active service in Iraq.[16] Many of these will have been treated according to the best guidelines—with Zoloft or other SSRIs, even though the evidence these drugs work for men is almost nonexistent and there had been compelling evidence for some years that Zoloft and other SSRIs might trigger suicide.

A CUCKOO'S EGG IN THE NEST OF SCIENCE

In response to revelations about ghostwriting, medical journals began to put safeguards in place. The safeguards for the most part were a matter of ticking boxes by authors to say they had been involved in the study in some capacity. Safeguards of this kind tend to play into the hands of ghosts, who are more likely to adhere to the wording of the latest best publishing-practice guidelines than any academic.

The medical writers manage to see and portray themselves in general as adhering to high ethical standards, but both they and journal editors miss both how they are being used by pharmaceutical companies and the effects of such medical writing on medicine. What is at stake was brought out best in the case of Study 329 and Study 377, two clinical trials of the effects of GlaxoSmithKline's antidepressant Paxil in children that were conducted in the early 1990s and were designed to get a license for the drug to treat depressed children.

In these two studies Paxil failed to produce a clear benefit in depressed children compared to placebo, and the children on the drug, it was later revealed, became suicidal at over triple the rate of those on a comparison antidepressant (imipramine) or on placebo. Faced with these findings, an internal SmithKline memorandum from 1998 shows that company personnel decided that they could not show the data to the regulator and that their best strategy was to publish what they saw as the good bits of Study 329. Sally Laden of STI was given the task.[17]

The resulting manuscript portrayed Paxil in a very favorable light. As James McCafferty, Laden's SmithKline contact, put it in a July 19, 1999 email, "It seems incongruous that we state that paroxetine [Paxil] is safe yet report so many SAEs [serious adverse events]. I know the investigators have not raised an issue, but I fear that the editors will. I am still not sure how to describe these events. I will again review all the SAEs to make myself feel comfortable about what we report in print."[18]

The study had been multicentered, and only SmithKline had access to all the data. Thus, if a center's investigators had seen a problem or two at their location, they were not to know that the pattern was repeating at each of the other centers. Like Sheffield's Richard Eastell in the Actonel case, what these investigators saw when they thought they were seeing the data were summary tables on side effects. These tables did show an increase in emotional lability on Paxil, but few if any investigators would have known that this meant suicidality. I, for instance, was an investigator on Paxil clinical trials at this time and did not know what problems lay beneath the rock of emotional lability.

If the authors who put their names on the resulting paper saw no problem with the paper, when it went out to review a peer reviewer would be even less likely to spot problems, as the reviewers were one step further removed from the data. Similarly, when presented to audiences of several hundred at academic meetings, who if anyone was likely to be in a position to spot the problem? For anyone in these audiences who might have been suspicious, speaking up would have meant voicing doubts about a study whose authors were particularly eminent and whose article had been peer-reviewed by one of the most prominent journals in the field—not an easy thing to do.

At one center in this study, linked to Brown University in Rhode Island, we now know that some of the children who deteriorated on treatment and dropped out of the study were coded as noncompliant rather than as emotionally labile or suicidal.[19] It only takes a few misjudgments in coding like this, possibly only one per center, for the meaning of a trial to change quite dramatically. Laden did not have the records of the children coded as noncompliant—the real data. But even if she had, who was she to gainsay the judgment of a senior clinical investigator?

The article Laden wrote appeared in 2001 in the *Journal of the American Academy of Child and Adolescent Psychiatry (JAACAP)*, the most influential journal in child psychiatry. It claimed Paxil was safe and effective for children.[20] Martin Keller of Brown University was listed first in the list of twenty-two authors, among whom were some of the most distinguished names in American pediatric psychopharmacology. Laden's name did not feature on the paper.

In addition to illustrating the industrialization of clinical trials that happened when CROs took over their management and the data control and authorship tactics drug companies employ for studies like 329, this example shows how the publication of clinical trials today entails an entirely different kind of scientific article than the articles that came out of studies run by academics in the 1950s, 1960s, and 1970s. It would once have been inconceivable, and is still almost inconceivable, that academics in possession of a full set of data would choose only to publish the good bits of the data on a clinical issue this serious—if only because they knew that others could request to see all the data rather than because academics were once more ethical than they are now.

It would once have been inconceivable for academics to hire public relations companies to promote their research. But public relations companies are now hired by pharmaceutical companies to ensure both physicians and the wider public hear about company publications that support their drugs. In the case of Study 329, though GlaxoSmithKline could not legally have sales representatives talk to doctors about using

Paxil for childhood depression, they could expect that a prominently placed article suggesting such use that was backed by well-known academics would lead many doctors on their own to prescribe the drug "off-label."

Off-label use like this, which is typically based on some academic article, may account for up to half of all medical prescriptions—and more for children. Successful media coverage of a study may generate so much off-label sales that applying to the FDA for a license for some new indication of an already approved drug may not be needed. Even though company representatives cannot sell the drug directly for childhood depression, they can hand out academic articles, along with marketing copy for those articles. In the case of Study 329, the marketing copy the PR firm Cohn and Wolf developed claimed that "[in this] 'cutting-edge' landmark study . . . Paxil demonstrates REMARKABLE Efficacy and Safety in the treatment of adolescent depression."[21] The "remarkable" thing about Study 329 is how far we appear to have travelled from a negative set of data to a sparkling publication diamond whose flaws few doctors would be able to spot.

Much of the Paxil story we might not know but for a modern reworking of the Emperor's new clothes in the form of a documentary television series. Starting in 2002 the BBC ran a series of Panorama programs on Paxil that eventually brought the full details of Study 329 and other trials of antidepressants done on children to light, showing essentially that these drugs produced no benefits to warrant the risks being taken. A journalist with no medical training, Shelley Jofre, it turned out, could spot all the problems that the academic authors or readers of the article had failed to detect.

How did Jofre do it? Essentially the same way as many readers of this book might have done it. Because she was not in the field, the reputation of the journal meant nothing to her, and the distinction of the names on the authorship line escaped her. Because statistical significance was not part of her everyday world, she wasn't hypnotized into thinking that events that were not significant weren't happening. She didn't assume that emotional lability was some inconsequential change on treatment; she noticed that it was happening a lot more on Paxil and began to ask questions. The lack of sensible answers ultimately led to the discovery of company documents conceding that the data showed Paxil didn't in fact work.

Do ghostwriters lie? When asked this question straight up, they typically answer no. But they concede they have considerable skills in polishing a manuscript or inching it in the right direction. Data on a drug showing it barely beats placebo becomes evidence that the drug is effective. The writer can choose to let the world know about the side effects occurring in 1 percent, 5 percent or 10 percent of subjects. Thus a paper might avoid mention of a serious side effect that occurred at a 9 percent rate without technically lying by simply announcing that only events occurring at a 10 percent rate or more would be reported.

For the most part ghosts are likely to miss their own bias, but the process by which trials are presented is bringing us closer and closer to what we expect from politicians rather than scientists. Sally Laden caught it best when faced with a SmithKline decision to abandon a manuscript on the withdrawal effects linked to Paxil—"there are some data that no amount of spin will fix."[22] For a writer who could transform Study 329 from a failed study showing Paxil should not be used in children into an advertisement advocating its use, this is a telling admission.

What about the academics who are at least the nominal investigators of these studies? The standard response from medical writers and pharmaceutical companies is that the academics have a chance to review everything that is done in their name. In fact, however, as the Current Medical Directions material outlined above revealed, articles are often, perhaps typically, close to completion before an academic gets to see any draft, and after that it is common for the paper to be submitted without the academics making any changes whatsoever.

In a sense, however, this focus on darker arts of scientific spin misses the bigger point about lack of access to data. In the absence of the data, neither the medical writers involved nor the academics have either the ability or the incentive to make sure the paper is a reasonable representation of what took place. If no one can access the underlying data, no one is likely to be able to take issue with the paper as a fair representation of what happened in the trial.

The conjunction of medical practice and medical business is such an emotional and important arena that it is inevitably prone to bias. There is, for example, as noted before, a conspiracy of goodwill that ties drug companies to governments and both to doctors, hospitals, and patients—everyone wants to see the treatment working. And no one wants to see the harms. This bias provides a spin that in some instances no data can overcome. The point behind having full access to data is the hope that it can challenge some of our biases; that's what makes for good science and for good medicine that's based on science. But to add to this bias a systematic process aimed at eliminating or overcoming apparently inconvenient data through coding bias, selective reporting of data, lack of independent access to the data, and ghostwriting spin is the exact antithesis of science and reduces these publications to the status of marketing copy.

BEYOND CONFLICT OF INTEREST

There is today tremendous disquiet about the interface of medicine and industry, with doctors widely perceived as being too close to industry. At the same time, governments and universities advocate partnering with industry, in what both sides portray as a win-win deal.

We can bring some of our current difficulties and disquiet into focus by revisiting the relation of medicine and industry in the 1930s and 1940s. In the 1930s, SmithKline and French (SK&F) bought d,l amphetamine (Benzedrine) from its maker Gordon Alles as a treatment for asthma and other respiratory problems. In an early example of what would now be called disease mongering, SK&F in the 1940s promoted the views of an "opinion leader," Tufts psychiatrist Abraham Myerson, that anhedonia (a forerunner of today's depression) would respond to amphetamines. The company also marketed an amphetamine variant, d amphetamine (dexamphetamine, or Dexedrine), as a treatment for what they characterized and marketed as pre-obesity.

In addition to disease-mongering, the company was involved in ghostwriting and other manipulations of the literature. There is good evidence, for example, that SK&F helped draft the outlines of an article for Louis Sulman, a University of Pennsylvania otolaryngologist, who suggested that Benzedrine might prevent colds.[23] They prepared illustrations and almost certainly wrote entire manuscripts for Joseph Scarano, a Philadelphia doctor who praised Dexedrine.[24] They also appear to have been able to discourage University of Minnesota's Howard Diehl from publishing evidence demonstrating that Benzedrine was of no use for colds.[25] And they had a research contract with Dr. Ella Roberts in which the company granted itself the right to block publication of the findings of any research if it so chose.[26]

Today it is de rigueur for academics to declare possible conflicts of interest, such as their links to industry. It is no longer acceptable to do as Soma Weiss, a professor of medicine at Harvard and chair of the American Medical Association's Council on Pharmacy Approval system, did in a 1939 pharmacology review endorsing Benzedrine as one of the most promising drugs ever developed without acknowledging SK&F's five-year grant to his Boston clinic.[27] Though it is rare to find any declarations of conflicting interests in academic articles before 1990, this is not because they didn't exist.

When it comes to drug hazards, such as the possible addictiveness of Benzedrine, SK&F retained libel lawyers and threatened to sue the next periodical that suggested that Benzedrine was addictive. The company also actively supported publications from experts in the field that might suggest that concerns about Benzedrine's addictive potential were overblown.[28]

Ghostwriting, concealed conflicts of interests, obstruction of legitimate concerns about a drug's dangers, and the marketing of diseases to market a medicine are all features of the medico-pharmaceutical complex that today draw the fire of critics concerned about the corruption of medicine. The Benzedrine example indicates that such practices can be found in decades past as well. But there's a difference. Examples like these for SK&F confirmed for academics that the sales and marketing divisions of companies were populated by "scurvy knaves."[29] Up to about 1980 there had been something of a firewall between academia and industry. It was the kiss of death for any physician or scientist aspiring to an academic career to join industry. Academics were under no illusions that pharmaceutical companies were anything but a business, with a dedication to the bottom line.

But starting in the 1980s, the situation changed, giving rise at the same time to both our current concerns (and new manifestations of old ones) and the exhortations to partner with industry. The change was not that industry became more rapacious or that academics stooped to new levels of venality. The change has lain in the industrialization of a set of processes in the research, development, delivery, defense, and marketing of pharmaceuticals. Companies have not become more commercial, any more than Henry Ford was more commercial than other car manufacturers of his day when he turned to assembly line manufacture. Pharmaceutical companies may have even become more ethical and more adherent to the law's letter, but following the advice of the management consultants they hired in the late 1960s they have, like Henry Ford, turned to assembly lines.

As clinical trials became of central importance after 1962, pharmaceutical companies have dissected and reengineered their business to produce and deliver quality clinical-trial products in a timely fashion and to develop much of their marketing around them. And as clinical trials became ever more important, companies appeared to be ever more involved in doing science rather than business. Against this background efforts to encourage academics to partner with industry seemed to many less problematic.

To the major pharmaceutical companies, however, it has become increasingly clear that a prime purpose of clinical trials, beyond that of gaining regulatory approval, is to secure or maintain a marketing niche for their product and sometimes the disorder it's meant to treat along with it. Companies have no interest in doing studies to answer scientific or therapeutic questions. The only trials that count are the ones that turn up a positive result that can be published in a reputable journal with the names of leading academics as the authors. This is the process that companies have industrialized, out of which they expect quality and timely publications that optimize their ability to sell the company's product, or help them counter any claims regarding problems the drug may cause. And central to their ability to achieve these ends is the fact that they are able to sequester study data.

The many people grappling with what is going wrong on the interface between medicine and the pharmaceutical industry look at the academics who end up on authorship lines of studies like these Zoloft PTSD studies or Study 329 and to the reviewers who fail to spot problems, and instead critique the conflict of interests—the payments academics get for lectures, for participation in research, for consulting arrangements, or for the shares they may hold in pharmaceutical companies. They call for conflict-of-interest declarations or sets of rules about authorship.

The academics caught in the crossfire are often bewildered. They don't have the experience of having been paid and then changing their views—in part for the simple reason that this isn't what happens. Companies can select from among available academics those who have views that suit the task at hand. To be selected in this fashion is not a crime—some of our most celebrated scientific breakthroughs have come to light in this way. John Snow's suggestion in the midst of the 1850s cholera epidemic in London of removing the handle from the Broad Street pump was only heard because it suited the commercial interests of abattoir owners and others who were being blamed for the epidemic to sponsor a public meeting at which the finger of blame might be pointed in another direction.[30]

If there is a problem it lies in current patent arrangements that fail to pit competing drugs or companies against each other. As a result all experts for all companies sing from the same song sheet now in a way that didn't happen with John Snow. We do not have conditions in which facts are likely to be contested, but to blame this on the experts who are hired by companies seems to miss the mark.

Indeed it is almost certainly a mistake to think that scientists in general are disinterested or do things for lofty motives. The history of science makes it clear that individual scientists have often been deluded or obsessive or have pursued their hunches for a variety of motives, be it a desire for fame or money or because of a grudge against someone holding competing views. Science can harness all these motivations provided others can scrutinize the data and decide whether the claims being made actually do follow these data. The objectivity of science lies in the group rather than the individual, and in this sense paying a professor for a talk should make little difference in the larger scheme of things. The problem does not lie in the involvement of private companies in science but rather in our collective failure in ensuring that all parties, including the government, play by the rules of science.

Science is not value free. It values data. Science is not about publishing the appearances of a scientific experiment, it is about replicable data. But for some reason the normal rules of science appear to be suspended in proximity to a pharmaceutical company.

In these circumstances of inaccessible evidence and failure to sponsor open, independent tests, company trials have become the petard on which medicine is being hoisted. Where briefly in the 1950s drug companies might have seen themselves as adding to medical culture by undertaking clinical trials, this is no longer how they view things. In fact, what they do now replaces any culture there once was in medicine. Diseases of many sorts now come and go at the whim of marketing departments.

Any process that generates new insights and reveals new phenomena will inevitably throw up opportunities for commercial exploitation, and science is no exception. From the developments in chemistry in the nineteenth century that laid the basis for the creation of rubber and plastic products or in physics that underpin the computer industries or space exploration today, an ever-increasing proportion of our industries are science based. Science is also the ultimate free market, where an invisible hand does lead to progress in knowledge, whether by playing on our desire to solve puzzles or on our self-interest. As such, science might appear ideologically to be on the same side as capitalism. But insofar as commerce depends on secrecy and acquisitive self-interest rather than free communication of data and other findings, business will inevitably be as inimical to science as the Catholic Church once was to Galileo or Soviet Communism later was to evolutionary biology.

Rather than focus on this secrecy, many concerned at the growing mismatch between therapeutic success and publication rhetoric see the problem as stemming from someone somewhere being corrupted. At present the focus is restricted to the relatively small amounts of money given to some doctors to deliver lectures or participate in clinical trials. If conflict of interest is as important as claimed, then there are other areas to consider also, one of which is the availability of drugs by prescription only; prescribing drugs is a large part of their job for many doctors and prescription-only privileges keep many of them in a job worth hundreds of thousands of dollars. Another area of conflict stems from current patent law, which drives blockbuster development as well as prices of company shares. In the years covering the success of their antidepressant Prozac and the emergence of Zyprexa, 1987 to 2000, Lilly employees netted $3.1 billion from stock options they exercised, quite aside from any salaries or bonuses.[31] These payments also dwarf any consulting fees that the average academic is likely to receive.

The paradox that few grapple with is that in one sense we want conflicts of interest—a complete absence of conflicts would mean that no one has anything that works or anything about which they are passionate. The weaker the treatment, the more likely companies are to employ banks of speakers to compensate—but this only works in conditions where the data underpinning claims are inaccessible or the experts are bamboozled by the statistical decorations on the data into thinking that the latest fashion is something that is likely to protect us against the gales of a serious disease.

THROUGH THE LOOKING GLASS

Where the creation of bacteriology was one of the glories of nineteenth-century medical science, the role of epidemiology in identifying the toxic effects of lead in paint or fuel, as well as the effects of tobacco, asbestos, vinyl chloride, benzene, or other organic chemicals on respiratory function or tumor growth were among the glories of mid-twentieth-century medicine. This put medicine on a collision course with business.

In the nineteenth century Robert Koch's and Louis Pasteur's ideas about germs faced the typical resistance to new scientific ideas. In the twentieth century, corporations producing chemical pollutants, from vinyl chloride and benzene to tobacco, brought financial might to resisting the new scientific ideas that linked their products to cancers or other medical disorders. This financial might enabled companies to invade and attempt to colonize science with apparently independent but in fact corporate-sponsored research, through appeals to studies that have the appearance of research but which are in fact opinion pieces aimed at discrediting linkages between company products and ill health. The most famous of these defenses has been that of the tobacco industry which, under the banner "doubt is our product," turned scientific doubt inside out, transforming it from a means to detect truth into a means to conceal the truth.[32] And it was tobacco-company lobbying that led in 1999 to the US Data Access Act that ensures access to scientific data—company access, that is, to the data of independent or federally funded studies that have demonstrated harm from chemicals, yet with no reciprocal rights granted to the public or independent scientists for access to data from company studies.[33]

Still, medical professionals, scientists, and others who have tackled the links between polluting companies and disease have had some advantages. The people injured by chemicals have, for the most part, been healthy before exposure. This puts an elephant in the room that can't easily be ignored. In addition, while manufacture of the items of which these chemicals are typically byproducts might be good for the economy, no one thinks these chemicals are likely to be good for individuals. While not always the case, many of the classic industrial injuries induced by chemicals clustered in the neighborhood of a plant. And most importantly doctors don't make a living from prescribing vinyl chloride, benzene, tobacco, or lead.

In contrast, efforts to tackle medically induced problems have some additional hurdles to overcome. People who may be injured by *medical* chemicals typically have something wrong with them to begin with, so that any defense of the product can appeal to a patient's original sin as the real problem. And the injuries that a medicine causes are likely to be distributed right across the United States and Europe, making them harder to spot than the clusters of a new illness that pop up around a power plant or other new industrial facility. Also of great importance, doctors, who might otherwise spot the problem, not only make a living out of these same medical chemicals but prescribe them believing they are doing good for people.

A prime indicator of good medical care is an ability to detect treatment-induced injury. When an injury can be traced to a drug side effect, a clash with the pharmaceutical industry is set up. Just as in the struggles between medicine and the tobacco or chemical industries, the interaction between medicine and the pharmaceutical industry has had an extraordinarily nasty side when self-interest is seen to be at stake, with companies using gag orders, appealing to trade secrets, concealing their views as to the risks their drugs pose behind a veil of attorney-client privilege, settling legal actions out of court to hide data and documents, sometimes stalking and harassing academic critics, and co-opting universities with funding.[34]

But in this domain there is another factor not found with tobacco or industrial chemicals that isolates doctors who attempt to bring the hazards of a drug to light. The problem is that the medical body has now been infected with what could be called a clinical immunodeficiency virus (CIV). The infection enters in the drip feed of science. With industrial chemicals, the best studies systematically point to hazards where they exist, with a number of inferior, often company-sponsored "pseudo-studies" vigorously promoted to create doubt. But with pharmaceuticals, often the only studies are those of the drug companies themselves, and these studies, as one might expect, all seem to point to the benefits of an ongoing use of the very chemicals that may in fact be causing the problem.

There is another side to this infection. If the free market worked properly, given the amount of chemicals being pumped into patients in medicine, doctors eager for their fifteen minutes of fame should be hovering above their patients ready to write articles on any signs of problems stemming from treatment. But instead the literature on treatment-induced hazards is drying up, even though there are estimates that medical treatment is now one of the leading causes of death in hospitals.[35] Instead there is a growing silence, and the censorship that brings about this silence is all but invisible.

For most academics it likely seems inconceivable that scientific journals and meetings might be censored, although some might concede that political maturity requires some accommodation with commercial sensitivities. A kind of de facto censorship, for example, occurs because of the premium put on controlled trials—the hazards of treatments are virtually never discovered in controlled trials, and faced with a choice between a ghostwritten account of a controlled trial demonstrating a trivial benefit or a detailed account of a new and potentially serious hazard in a small number of patients, journals will opt for the controlled-trial account each time.

But there is more to the censorship process than this. The best way to bring home what is at stake is to turn to a series of personal examples, from one domain—the risks of SSRI-induced suicides—to illustrate a larger issue.

In 1999, having agreed to testify in a case involving homicide and suicide on Prozac, I learned of company documents showing that Lilly had been aware for years that Prozac might make some people suicidal and indicating the lengths to which the company went to avoid warning of the risk. Although the documents were in the public domain, few people were aware of them. My immediate thought was to write an article outlining the material for the *British Medical Journal*.

After the question of Prozac-induced suicide was first raised in 1990 and the first legal actions filed against Lilly, in 1991 the *British Medical Journal* carried an article by Charles Beasley and a series of Lilly-only authors. Despite the fact that the data in the article show a 1.9-fold increased risk of a suicidal act on Prozac compared to placebo, this article was widely spun as evidence that there was no risk from the treatment.[36] It drew a response from one academic who had a history of difficulties with the pharmaceutical industry: "The BMJ is a journal of distinction and, dare I say it, perhaps also of some innocence. At a time when in the United States the manufacturer of fluoxetine [Prozac] is facing litigation, the corporate defense attorneys will be pleased by the journal having published a piece authored wholly by the manufacturer's employees."[37] But even he seemed unaware the article had appeared in the very week Lilly was facing hearings at the FDA about the risk of suicide on Prozac.

The initial response from the then-editor of the *British Medical Journal*, Richard Smith, to my draft article appeared to recognize that the journal had had a role in the "mistake" in 1991. He seemed to welcome my submission and suggested reframing it as a discursive debate article rather than a data-driven research article. The reframed article was sent to a reviewer, who was apparently not told that it was an article about company behavior and not an evidence-based assessment of the case for Prozac-induced suicidality. The reviewer suggested the article had not established the case for treatment-induced problems—which it had never attempted to do. The editor rejected the piece on this basis. Mystified at the mismatching messages, I appealed, but in vain: in a phone call Smith stated that no matter what revisions I made nothing would be published.[38]

This article was published unaltered in the *International Journal of Risk and Safety in Medicine,* whose editor, Graham Dukes, also editor of the most authoritative book on drug-induced side effects in the field,[39] commented: "It seems to me your approach is original and fair. . . . I also agree with your remarks about the failure of the present overall research approach to elicit a reliable picture of adverse effects and the sometimes unrealistic defenses put up by industry when their products are the subject of injury litigation."[40]

A year later, in 2000, having conducted a blind and randomized trial in healthy volunteers, in which two volunteers had become suicidal on Zoloft, I again contacted the *British Medical Journal* about a submission. Nobody had ever accused Richard Smith of being in the pocket of the pharmaceutical industry; there are in contrast many journals whose editors have previously been employees of the pharmaceutical industry. For those who think conflict of interest is at the heart of all therapy-related problems, the prediction is clear—the *British Medical Journal* should be much more likely to take this article than a journal whose editors have been so closely linked to industry. In fact, even without review, the *British Medical Journal* declined to take the article. So I then sought publication instead in a journal whose editors had a pharmaceutical company background, which seemed to make them less rather than more nervous about offending industry. The paper was peer reviewed and rapidly published.[41]

What is going on? The following examples help clarify the possibilities. In Spring 2000, the *Hastings Center Report,* a leading bioethical journal, published a special issue, "Prozac, Alienation and the Self," featuring five articles on the drug.[42] Two of these articles suggested that Prozac was so wonderfully effective that it would be a mistake to restrict its use simply to people who are depressed; it should be available to anyone who responded to it. Two further articles argued that even though Prozac was very effective, its use should be restricted to people who are depressed. The fifth article, by me, argued that impressions of Prozac's efficacy stemmed in great part from the fact that negative trials were left unreported, that data on the hazards of the drug were concealed, and that this state of affairs was linked in part to the fact that articles on Prozac and on other psychotropic drugs were increasingly ghostwritten.

Following the publication of this issue of the journal, Lilly, at the time the biggest single outside funder of the Hastings Center, withdrew support, charging that the Center had "published articles that Lilly felt contained information that was biased and scientifically unfounded and that may have led to significant misinformation to readers, patients and the community."[43]

Subsequently, in 2003, using the Current Medical Directions portfolio of Zoloft articles noted earlier, I submitted an article to the *British Journal of Psychiatry* on ghostwriting, whose key finding was that a majority of articles that deal with pharmaceutical products in leading journals are likely to be ghostwritten and that these articles do not faithfully report the data on hazards. A clearly nervous journal staff used at least five reviewers (instead of the usual two) and had the revised article re-reviewed—making up to ten reviews. The article was subsequently referred to the journal's legal department and after that the journal's copyeditors pored over the final version for longer than any other article I've ever written. It was finally published after a change in editors.[44]

A bit earlier, in 2001, *Contemporary Psychology* requested a review of Joseph Glenmullen's *Prozac Backlash,* a book that outlined some of the hazards of treatment with SSRIs. My review outlined the book's key points, without endorsing or countering the position of the author. I also noted that I was in possession of five highly critical reviews of the book written by distinguished American psychiatrists, disseminated by public relations agencies working for Lilly who urged media outlets not to feature the book. I sent the review and the accompanying documents to the editors. Having initially been accepted, the review failed to appear. On enquiring I was told that the journal could not find a balancing reviewer and that they thus could not carry my review. The response made little sense.

In 2004 two journals, *Open Minds* and *Young Mind,* requested articles on the subject of antidepressant-induced suicidality in pediatric populations. Both journals then declined to publish what I submitted on the basis, I was told, of legal advice. They said they did not have the resources to handle any difficulties that might arise with pharmaceutical companies as a result of the articles, and this could put them out of business.

The issues here do not just affect academic journals. In 2005 the *Times Higher Education Supplement* (*THES*) featured a series of articles on the case of Aubrey Blumsohn, the man described above who had "blown the whistle" on Proctor and Gamble over the ghostwriting of articles and concealment of data on patient responses to Actonel, their blockbuster treatment for osteoporosis.[45] I wrote to *THES* to make it clear that Blumsohn's case was not unique. In the new world of medicine, data were routinely withheld and companies threatened to sue periodicals that reported on treatment risks. *THES* offered to publish an amended version of the letter, but the changes they wanted stripped the letter of its meaning. When I suggested their revisions made the letter pointless, *THES* responded, "We have also had to run these letters past our lawyers as this is, as you are aware, a very sensitive issue, and there are certain legal amendments we had to make." The key amendment seemed to be that the letter could not state that anything the journal published on this issue was constrained by threats of legal action. They did not publish my letter.[46]

A more striking instance took place in 2007, when I was approached by *Index on Censorship* for a piece outlining evidence "that pharmaceutical companies are not transparent and that medical journals allow this to happen. . . . I think to an outsider who has certain expectations of science (that data is widely available and that access to data is fundamental in terms of any credibility) it's a baffling and shocking state of affairs."

The resulting article covered the evolution of ghostwriting and the lack of access to clinical trial data, focusing on Study 329, the biggest study undertaken of the use of Paxil in children who were supposedly depressed. After much back and forth, the editor commented, "Our lawyer's just taken a look at your piece—and I do need to ask you for more chapter and verse on some points." I complied, and eventually heard this: "I realize this is taking up more of your time than you bargained for and do apologize—lawyers must make you weary by now—but am sure you'll understand that it's necessary." The process ended with this assertion: "The documents made interesting reading—and certainly answered the concerns—along with the cuts. But I've still got worries about running the piece. . . . I regret how things have turned out very much. I've appreciated all your help in finding documents and in cooperating with all my requests. As I've said before—it's a hugely important subject and we should be covering it." *Index on Censorship* self-censored.

Leemon McHenry from Los Angeles and Jon Jureidini from Adelaide in Australia also tried to publish a paper on Study 329, "Clinical Trials and Drug Promotion: Selective Reporting in Study 329," initially in the *Lancet* and later in the *British Medical Journal*. The *Lancet* sent the paper to GlaxoSmithKline, who objected, and the journal backed down. The *British Medical Journal* then contacted them saying they had heard of their paper and wanted to fast-track its publication. Six months later, the *British Medical Journal* indicated their lawyers still had concerns and they would not publish. They finally published a heavily modified version several years later.[47]

In 2005, the *British Medical Journal* had a new editor and I submitted an article on how the data on suicide and antidepressants had been manipulated. The peer reviews I received back were longer than the original paper. After answering all queries from two rounds of peer review, the paper was accepted, and proofs of the paper due to appear in the journal two weeks later were sent to me. In the middle of correcting the proofs, I received an email from the editor: "Thank you very much for all your hard work on this article. I'm afraid we've run into a legal wall with our libel lawyer reluctant for us to publish your piece. . . . I remain supportive of publication but obviously can't do this against legal advice."

I spent over a year answering legal queries and providing supporting documentation; finally, a year and a half later, the article was published.[48] Where the original had implicated both companies and regulators in concealing the problem, the wording had been altered so that the new version emphasized the failings of the FDA for the corrupted data in the public domain and deemphasized any company failings.

Where SmithKline & French once had to threaten to sue, journals now self-censor. Views not favorable to company interests seldom if ever appear in medical journals or social science journals or in any journals or other outlets. Across the board the hazards of blockbusters are notably underreported and in particular, reports of these hazards do not appear in the most influential journals. Even reviews of company documents conceding the hazards of drugs that have become available in the public domain seldom appear.

Self-censorship and ghostwriting go curiously well together—ghosts traditionally can be detected by their lack of a mirror image. Where there should be articles on the benefits of treatment mirrored by articles on the hazards, there are a rapidly diminishing number of articles on either the benefits or hazards actually authored by medical academics. When medical writers contact the offices of our most prestigious journals on behalf of corporate-sponsored projects, neither the writers nor the journals are inhibited by any considerations about incurring a legal action.

Quite the contrary. In 2006 the editor of *JAMA,* Catherine DeAngelis, tackled the issue of why leading journals could not simply ban further articles from academics who had been publicly linked to ghost-written or other tainted articles:

> Leveling sanctions against an author who fails to disclose financial interests by banning publication of his or her articles for some time period would only encourage that author to send his or her articles to another journal; it cleans our house by messing others. So what about all editors, or at least a group . . . agreeing to share the information and jointly to ban the offending authors? Those who suggest this approach have not considered the risk of an antitrust suit.[49]

This statement all but concedes that our leading medical journals will, in effect, ignore transgressions of their own rules when it comes to publishing drug company–related articles. Even though it is an essential legal and ethical duty for physicians to report on treatment hazards, journals will rarely take such reports if the material is inimical to the interests of a pharmaceutical company. In contrast, the material that increasingly fills our journals does not conform to the basic norms of science, namely to make available the full complement of data on which claims are based.

These failures to publish are not isolated anomalies. The articles cited above were all articles central to regulatory hearings or legal actions against drug companies. When Study 329 came to light, New York State took a fraud action against GlaxoSmithKline on the basis that the apparent science they had promoted led doctors to prescribe this drug and children to receive it, and the State to pay for these prescriptions, although it was likely to be ineffective. It was this money they were now claiming back. GlaxoSmithKline settled, further illustrating the failure of nerve of medical editors.

SCIENCE EX MACHINA

In striking contrast to these publication difficulties, when marketing sertraline (Zoloft), Pfizer's efforts were geared to producing an average of two to three articles per month in significant journals,[50] many of which appear to have been ghostwritten.[51] In the case of the three leading SSRIs combined, this would mean six to nine articles per month—two per week. In the case of Lilly's Zyprexa, the four clinical trials that brought this drug on the market gave rise to 234 publications, all advocating the efficacy of the compound with none containing data on the increases in glucose or cholesterol levels or rates of suicide found in these trials that have since become the subject of legal actions.[52]

As a simple matter of probabilities, therefore, when it comes to any public-domain difficulties companies may have to manage, whether arising from legal cases of treatment-induced injury or from regulatory hearings, they can almost always parade apparently new studies that portray their product in a good light. In addition to simple probabilities, companies are much more aware of the dates of trials and regulatory hearings concerning products than academics, more aware of the publication timelines of journals than academics, and unlikely to be held up by a journal feeling they need to undertake a legal review.[53] When it comes to real-time debate in the public domain, therefore, it is almost inconceivable that patients or academics will have the data or resources necessary to engage with a company.

Statements from professional bodies can be targeted with even greater precision to coincide with regulatory hearings or legal trials than standard journal articles. This is because such statements rarely go through editorial or peer review processes. In the week before the first regulatory hearing on suicidal behavior among children taking antidepressants in 2004, the American College of Neuropsychopharmacology (ACNP) sent out a press release of a then as-yet-unpublished position statement apparently from a distinguished set of academics that concluded that antidepressants did not cause suicidality in children.[54] This position statement was widely covered in the media at the time. The paper was written by a public relations agency based in Washington, DC.

Having personally written a position paper for another professional association and attended many consensus statement meetings, as outlined in the next chapter, I can vouch for the ease with which the timing of the appearance of statements from bodies like these can be controlled. Typically such statements arise from small working groups within an organization. They may be proposed by an individual, who then selects the working group. Once a position statement is formulated it is easy for a small group of individuals to target publication to an opportune date. Alternatively if a final statement is agreed upon but publication delayed, a draft can be issued directly to the media, as with the ACNP position paper.

From the time of their launch in 1987 through the end of 2009 there were four legal cases involving SSRIs, three of them centered on suicide and one, the Kilker case, on birth defects. In the weeks prior to each of the suicide cases at least one article had appeared outlining the benefits of drug treatment and claiming that antidepressants reduced rather than increased the risk of suicide[55] or proclaimed the benefits of antidepressants in pregnancy.[56]

Since 1991, there have been four regulatory hearings on SSRIs and suicidality. Two in 2004 involved children, while one in 1991 and one in 2006 involved adults. In addition to the ACNP statement that came out prior to the February 2004 FDA hearings, a paper appeared in July, prior to the September 2004 hearings, suggesting that there was no risk linked to SSRIs.[57] The Beasley paper appeared in the week of FDA hearings on Prozac and suicide in 1991,[58] while prior to the 2006 FDA hearings regarding adult suicidality on antidepressants, a series of articles was published in the *American Journal of Psychiatry* suggesting that warnings added to SSRI labels had themselves led to an increase in the rate of suicide, inferring that it would be a mistake to further extend the warning from children to adults.[59]

In close proximity to every single SSRI jury trial or regulatory hearing, therefore, one or more articles favorable to the drug company view has been published in a major journal. Pharmaceutical companies, it would seem, have refined the process of managing "science" to the point of being able to turn up papers on demand in an attempt to save the day if their product is in difficulty or under scrutiny.

DISAPPEARING SCIENCE

Revelations about ghostwriting, conflicts of interest, and hidden studies have prompted calls for reform. In the United States, Republican senator Charles Grassley has taken a lead in calling universities and professional associations to account for the undeclared conflicts of interest some of their academics have with the pharmaceutical industry[60] and for allowing members of their staff to claim authorship for articles that have in fact been ghostwritten.[61] He has sponsored a Sunshine Act in the Senate to shed light on these practices[62]—but there is no mention of shedding light on the clinical trial data without which we can never know if payment has corrupted an academic or not. The Sunshine Act focuses on rotten apples in the barrel rather than on the barrel and risks therefore suiting pharmaceutical companies rather than troubling them.

Several years before this, in 2004, documents demonstrating that GlaxoSmithKline intended to hide the parts of Study 329 that didn't suit them led New York State to take a legal action that resulted in an agreement by the company to post the results of all its clinical trials on the web. Other companies agreed to do something similar and many journals and academics expressed the view that we had turned a corner, unaware that companies intended to post study reports rather than data.

In fact, neither all of the paroxetine trials nor the underlying data from these trials has been posted as of February 2011.[63] What is posted is a set of summaries of studies, authored by company personnel. Despite repeated statements by companies that they now post their studies on the web, this has not been the case. In creating a situation where companies can convey the impression they have come clean with their data, the action by New York State paradoxically may have made things worse by enabling companies to claim they are being transparent.

There are great risks that those attempting to develop policies in these domains, if they don't fully address the deeper sources of the problems involved, will come up with answers that, like Kefauver's 1962 amendments to the Food and Drugs Act, compound rather than remedy our problems. The failure to require access to trial data in particular plays straight into the hands of pharmaceutical companies.

Within medicine, trust in "scientific" data to set us free remains strong. But by failing to challenge companies about their data, we have handed over the instrument of our freedom to company marketers and risk ending up increasingly trussed in company-generated evidence. These are the "data" that tell insurance companies that the latest block-busters work better than anything that came before and that they come with few if any serious hazards, so that their use will lead to ever shorter hospital stays. Embodied in guidelines, these "data" increasingly limit the abilities of doctors to exercise any discretion in caring for the person in front of them. These "data" should improve the quality of medical care but instead are leading to Pharmageddon.

5

Trussed in Guidelines

Bill was in his seventies, tall and relatively fit for his age if slightly overweight. His wife was petite. She gave every impression of having been dependent on a physically and behaviorally imposing husband, although their roles were now reversed. Bill had had a stroke a month earlier and Sally was distraught. She was sure that he could recover and concerned that the medical team had not referred him for active rehabilitation. He had shown no signs of recovery of function after his stroke, though. In their opinion there was nothing to build on, but they had asked me to assess if there might be psychological factors or a depression holding him back.

When I saw Bill he had no language. He appeared to be trying desperately to communicate, however, almost like Jean-Dominique Bauby in his diving bell. He had something between a cough and an effort to clear his throat that apparently had persisted for weeks. He hacked every few minutes, then fixed me with what appeared to be a pleading look in his eyes. Some patients after a stroke cannot clear saliva pooled in their esophagus, but Bill's hacking was different in its quality and persistence. "Why can't they do something about it," Sally said, "surely they can make him more comfortable."

Bill was on a cholesterol-lowering statin and an ACE inhibitor to lower his blood pressure, I discovered. The attending doctor had said it was in line with current international guidelines to put everyone who had a stroke on a statin and an ACE inhibitor.

I recommended stopping both treatments: either of these two drugs could have been holding Bill back from making some progress. The statins can cause muscle pain and weakness, which he could not now complain about. If the medical team was planning no more active intervention on his behalf, why not stop the treatment and see? All that guideline-based treatment could do, at best, would be to prolong an agonizing life. As for the ACE inhibitor, it was almost certainly causing his hacking cough—this was an unusual but known side effect of this group of drugs.

But guidelines were guidelines, and the medical team was unlikely to go against them. There was no point telling Sally that the hacking could be sorted out. Why set her against the doctors even more than she already was if they were so set in their ways? Generating hostility on their part at betrayal by a medical colleague's interference wouldn't do Bill any good, but it might compromise my ability to make a difference for someone else.

Aside from the horror of this case, few physicians would see anything remarkable in it. An unfortunate medical error in the treatment of this particular patient perhaps, but it's impossible to practice medicine without errors. Better a few have grim outcomes like this than have more lives lost because of a failure to manage patients properly after a stroke.

The problem is, the distress Bill had to put up with so that his doctors could feel comfortable and comply with ostensibly the best available evidence as embodied in the latest authoritative guideline is fast becoming the clinical norm rather than an exception. There was once only a small number of exceptions, as for instance in the case of vaccination, where medicine was prepared to inflict vaccine-induced injuries on some in the hope that a much greater number would benefit, but this ethos is changing rapidly.

Take Sheila, who had had anxiety and agoraphobia during the 1960s—she would likely have been diagnosed with panic attacks today. She had been caught up for years in what was an almost automatic prescription of benzodiazepines for anxiety and became physically dependent on them. The combination of anxiety and benzodiazepine dependence made her agoraphobic. She was scared to venture out of the house.

When her husband died two decades later, everyone feared she would become dependent on her children. Remarkably, she instead struck out on her own. She bought an apartment, some distance from any of her children, and began socializing in a way she had not done for over two decades.

When the alarm was raised in the 1980s about benzodiazepine dependence, many primary care physicians changed their patients to low doses of antipsychotics or antidepressants instead, and Sheila's new doctor was no exception.

I first met Sheila around the time that the selective serotonin reuptake inhibiting (SSRI) antidepressants came on stream. Her doctor referred her to me for review of her medications. Rather than the combination of an antipsychotic and antidepressant she was on, I started her on an SSRI. At first, she did much better. But shortly afterward she began grinding her teeth. We changed her to another SSRI. Again she initially did well, but then the grinding and restlessness commenced again. The same happened with each of the four SSRIs then available.

Sheila's teeth grinding was so intensely painful that she had to remove her dentures. With her teeth out she became more self-conscious and grew more reclusive. She was slipping back into the shell in which she had lived for over twenty years. I opted to go back to one of the older antidepressants which, in a low dose, made her less anxious without causing teeth grinding and restlessness. We met regularly thereafter for close to ten years during which time she maintained a delicate equilibrium.

Then, at the age of eighty, she had a "turn" and was brought to hospital. There were some inconclusive changes on her cardiogram, possibly indicative of a minor heart attack, and Sheila came out of hospital on both an SSRI and a statin. The SSRI had been prescribed by the hospital medical team because it was supposedly safer for the cardiovascular system than her older antidepressant, the statin because international guidelines now recommend statins for everyone who has had a cardiac event—regardless of whether the person's cholesterol levels are high.

Sheila now developed two sets of problems. Her teeth began to grind again and her legs became so weak and painful that she fell when she least expected it, so she couldn't go out to the shops or to see friends. I was asked to see her. I suggested stopping the statin as it was probably causing the weakness and pain in her legs, and switching her back to her previous antidepressant. Her primary care doctor was faced with a choice between my advice and the input from the medical team. He opted to continue the statin and SSRI prescriptions. The calculation he apparently felt called on to make was whether it was better to keep her alive, although disabled by treatment, or give her a better quality of life but risk her dying earlier than she would otherwise have done.

For over twenty years I have copied my patients on all correspondence that concerns them. Sheila had the letters to her doctor recommending that he stop her SSRI and statin. Although she told me that she was sure I was right about the drugs, she didn't demand her doctor do what I recommended. She was nervous that in her current frail state she might suddenly have a medical emergency and would be critically dependent on him. She had a niggling doubt that he might not be as quick to help her if she were a difficult patient. She was a hostage—as many patients are.

Her doctor was finally persuaded that SSRIs were no better for the cardiovascular system than her older antidepressant and might actually increase her risk of a stroke especially when combined with the aspirin she was on. Switching antidepressants improved her tooth grinding and her restlessness. But Sheila never recovered. The statin was still prescribed and her leg pains and weakness remained. Unhappy and lonely, she ended up in a residential home.

Sheila's doctor never let pharmaceutical company sales reps into his practice. He had no dealings with industry. Yet here he had been doing exactly what industry would have wanted—and seemingly oblivious to the obvious difficulties his patient was having in front of his eyes. The problem he had and the biggest problems Sheila and Bill faced had a common source: sets of guidelines produced by medical organizations, in both the United States and Europe, in the hope that these guidelines might improve medical care and provide a bulwark against company marketing. But these same guidelines have instead too often become a means to harness the medical impulse to give the best possible care to the delivery of the latest drugs, even when these offer less benefit and more harm than older treatments.

THE END OF DISCRETION

As 2009 closed a controversy erupted across the pages of medical journals concerning Tamiflu (oseltamivir), an antiviral drug produced by Roche, which had had several years of good fortune as Western governments stockpiled the drug, fearing a pandemic first of avian flu and then of swine flu. The published evidence appeared to indicate that Tamiflu reduced the likelihood of a full-blown influenza, reduced the length of a flu episode that developed, and reduced the secondary complications of influenza such as pneumonia or other respiratory disorders that might lead to hospitalization and even death in vulnerable groups. This led national governments throughout the Western world, and agencies like the Center for Disease Control in the United States, to a set of recommendations to doctors on the management of flu that hinged on a widespread use of Tamiflu. The trouble was, no one could access the data on which these recommendations were made. Furthermore, it became increasingly clear that only a fraction of the trials that had been undertaken were published, and of those published, ghostwriters had played a significant role in what was reported.[1] The more material leaked into the public domain, the less effective Tamiflu looked and the more dangerous using it began to seem—it appeared to induce neurological problems in a subgroup of patients and to make others suicidal. But a further dilemma came into view—governments had spent billions on this drug. Would they admit they had spent billions on a drug for which they had seen only a portion of the evidence and that might not work as designed? Would they pressure Roche to release all the data on the drug?[2]

Sequestering data violates a basic norm of science even if it is overlooked by law. Today when public policy at many levels is or aspires to be based on scientific data, such violations have ever greater ramifications, from the individual treatment our doctor gives us to decisions about national and international health care. To see how hiding medical data directly affects the doctors we consult and the quality of medical care we receive, we need to explore two aspects of everyday medical practice: the increasing use of guidelines and what they are based on (the subject of this chapter) and the interests behind the measurement technologies to which practitioners like Dr. N, discussed in the introduction, turn (the subject of the next chapter).

The evolution of guidelines is best told firsthand. For that reason we will focus on guidelines for the treatment of mental health disorders, but the story that unfolds here parallels developments in other areas of medicine—and it is these developments that ensnared Bill and Sheila. In every area of medicine, doctors increasingly find they have to take into account guidelines or standards that have been established, not infrequently to the detriment of the patient in front of them. It is against such guidelines that medical personnel are ever more likely to be judged by the managers of the service they work in or by the legal system should one of their patients take an action against them.

Our point of entry into the story lies in 1993 when the Janssen pharmaceutical company was hoping to bring their new antipsychotic

Risperdal (risperidone) to the market. An FDA review of this drug prior to its launch stated that "We would consider any advertisement, promotion or labeling for Risperdal false, misleading or lacking fair balance under Section 502 of the Act if there is a presentation of data that conveys the impression that risperidone is superior to haloperidol or any other marketed antipsychotic drug product with regard to safety or effectiveness."[3]

All of the antipsychotics developed during the 1990s, from Risperdal to Lilly's Zyprexa, Astra-Zeneca's Seroquel, Pfizer's Geodon, and Bristol-Myers Squibb's Abilify (among others), had been tested in premarketing trials against haloperidol, one of an earlier generation of now off-patent antipsychotics. In their trials all of the companies used a higher dose of haloperidol than clinically needed.[4] The stated rationale for using haloperidol as the comparison drug was that it was supposedly the market leader. The unstated rationale was that given the side-effect profile of the newer drugs they stood their best chance of looking good from a marketing point of view if compared to high-dose haloperidol. This kind of comparison is standard company practice for bringing any new drug to market, whether statins, antihypertensives, painkillers, treatments for osteoporosis, or for gut problems—compare your drug to some formulation of an older compound against which the new drug is already known to look good on some parameter.

On the face of it, the FDA's cautionary note, repeated for subsequent antipsychotics and in slightly different form for cholesterol lowering statins, proton pump inhibitors for gut disorders, the latest antihypertensives, the Cox-2 inhibiting painkillers, or biphosphonates for osteoporosis, looks like it should produce problems for any company wishing to market new drugs that, like Risperdal, can cost up to fifty times as much as older drugs.

There are lots of ways to get people to take a new drug that may be no more effective than an older one, however. For one thing new drugs come with a hope of superior efficacy built in that older drugs have lost, so we want them. But how to price up this hope—is the right answer twenty-five or fifty times the price of older drugs when the new drug is no better than the old drug for the same malady? Patients trade on such hopes, and one approach companies now take is to set up patient groups to lobby for the new drug. Such groups are all too willing to believe they are being denied access to the latest and best treatment on cost-cutting grounds. And it is difficult for doctors or, more importantly these days, politicians or insurance companies to resist articulate patients who question whether they are being denied the newest and best treatments on the basis of economic rationing. Doctor, what would you give to a member of your own family?

Patient hopes and expectations work in favor of a pharmaceutical company bringing a new drug to the market, but in addition since the 1990s, doctors in many countries, whether they work for a health maintenance organization or in a universal healthcare system, have also had to adhere to drug formularies (lists of approved drugs) which dictate what they can and cannot prescribe. These formularies arose in response to perceptions that healthcare costs were escalating uncontrollably and that a key element in this escalation was the price of drugs. The formularies often start with a principle that, where possible, doctors should prescribe cheaper generic rather than higher cost, branded compounds. The guidelines are intended to be both evidence-based and cost-sensitive—with some trade offs, so that if a new drug costs more but could show a real benefit over older agents, for example, it would be included on the approved list. The types of assessments pharmacists and doctors with no links to industry would make in constructing formularies, it was thought, would in general slow the entry of unnecessary new drugs to the market.

When it came to managing costs, from the 1990s onward service managers and others could, at least in theory, also turn to health economics to assess company claims that their new drugs offered good value for the money. And of course if the market really was a free market and several different companies each brought to market new antihypertensives or treatments for osteoporosis, competition should drive the price of the new drugs down—as many from Senator Kevaufer in 1962 onward have argued.[5] But this has never happened.

In the fifteen years following the FDA ruling on Risperdal and other new antipsychotics, no independent evidence appeared that any of the newer antipsychotics was superior to the older ones in terms of either safety or efficacy—even though the new treatments cost between fifty and eighty times as much.[6] But in the interim the companies managed to convert virtually everyone in the medical community from older to newer antipsychotics, and all of the new drugs made it on to hospital formularies—how? More generally, how do the pharmaceutical companies manage to market newer drugs so successfully when the cost of healthcare is forcing everyone to be aware of costs and in the face of guidelines, which ostensibly based on the evidence might be expected to come to the same conclusion as the FDA?

Part of the answer to this conundrum lies in the medical academics who, as we have seen, are among the key people who influence a doctor's view of particular drugs. Regulators have no control over what these academics say—academics, often, whom pharmaceutical companies have made into opinion leaders. In the case of antipsychotics like Risperdal, statins like Lipitor, or proton pump inhibitors like Nexium, professors of medicine, psychiatry, pharmacology, or general practice can say what they like in lectures or report what they like in medical journals. Companies can even include statements in their ads claiming that, say, Risperdal is superior to haloperidol, provided it is clear the statement has been made by an academic rather than the company. There will be a footnote in the ad to a medical article in which superiority is claimed—almost certainly a ghostwritten article.

An even more effective marketing technique is to coax support from medical academics who are not hired guns, who may even see themselves as hostile to company marketing and keen to constrain this marketing within a framework of independent treatment guidelines. It is in fact by manipulating the most independent of medical academics through guidelines that companies have been able to make new drugs from Risperdal to Lipitor, Vioxx, Nexium, and Fosamax into the most profitable drugs in the world.

CONSENSUS CONFERENCES

In the 1980s it seemed obvious to many medical academics with no links to the pharmaceutical industry that where there was a dispute about a drug or other medical treatment it made sense to bring representatives of the differing points of view together in an attempt to achieve consensus. This led to the creation of consensus conferences aimed at producing guidelines for clinical practice.[7] Initially, these consensus conferences seemed like a way to rein in the excesses of pharmaceutical company marketing departments—if we review all the evidence it will surely be clear that the benefits of a new drug are far less than the marketing hype might suggest. With this in mind, groups across medicine began to convene conferences to produce treatment guidelines on new drugs for conditions ranging from arthritis to schizophrenia.

Initially, the organizers of these consensus conferences were in the business of developing guidance for doctors rather than guidelines to be rigidly adhered to. Twenty years later the guidelines we now have still notionally offer guidance to doctors, but this is the kind of help that once led Ronald Reagan to suggest that the scariest words in the English language were "I'm from the Government and I'm here to help you."

By the time I was invited to a consensus conference in London convened by Catalyst Healthcare Communications on behalf of Janssen in 1995, drug companies far from feeling constrained by guidelines had begun to embrace them. Other invitees to this London meeting included senior psychiatrists, pharmacists, and economists. No one among the invitees would have been thought of as a friend of the pharmaceutical industry. We were presented with the published results of Janssen's trials of Risperdal. There was no attempt to stifle debate or to block us from bringing in any relevant material we might have been aware of.

The exercise involved taking the published research on Risperdal and discussing what would happen in real life if the results found in the clinical trials, which had all been reported in the better journals, applied. What effect would it likely have on the rate patients got discharged from acute hospital settings or from longer-term care facilities and on their rates of readmission to a hospital bed? When costing the outcomes, a significantly higher cost was used for Risperdal compared to the older drugs. Nevertheless, use of Risperdal came out as less expensive compared with older drugs in the long run. This result didn't make sense to me and was at odds with everything I saw about the use of Risperdal in clinical settings, where those taking Risperdal should have clearly been doing better if this "finding" was a real one.

Looking at how Catalyst pulled off this trick, it became clear that companies can almost guarantee an outcome like this. The reason: the bedrock on which guidelines depend is the published evidence from company clinical trials. If a guideline is going to be credible, its proposers should have access to all relevant trial data—exactly what the companies appeared to offer (but didn't). With this assumption, advocates of evidence-based medicine would think that, based on the data, the individual bias of participants or collective bias of the group or any bias stemming from the fact that these were company trials should have little effect on the final conclusions. A group of radiologists, doctors free of drug company influence, or even hostile to industry but prepared to go by the evidence, should come to much the same conclusion on Risperdal as our consensus group—that switching patients from older drugs to Risperdal would save money. This consensus-group meeting resulted in a publication claiming that treatment with Risperdal offered value for money.[8] It was followed over the next few years by publications on results from similar exercises undertaken with Zyprexa and other antipsychotics.[9]

Slightly over a year later I was invited to another consensus conference, again linked to Janssen and Risperdal. The procedure was the same. We had all been sent a dossier with all the published Risperdal trials as well as trials of other new antipsychotics. Any other information we asked for was forthcoming. Based on this material, we were asked what would be the optimal and cost-effective first line of treatment for patients with schizophrenia in chronic care and other treatment settings. Again based on the clinical trial data, Risperdal looked good and "our findings" were presented under our names at major international psychopharmacology settings.[10]

Pharmaco-economic evaluations like that of our consensus group were, at least on the surface, aimed at costing medical procedures to determine which offered value for money. A few voices at the time were saying that we in medicine couldn't do what the economists were purporting to do—that too little was understood about what really goes on in medical care. But it seemed clear the pharmaceutical industry was going to pull this new discipline into existence. Drugs function within healthcare the way automobiles do in the wider economy—they can be costed while the degradation of the environment or of medical care remains unmeasurable and uncostable.

Before getting involved in any of these consensus conferences, I had committed myself to the position that pharmaco-economics was bogus science in a debate over claims that the first of the new antipsychotics, Clozaril, which had been launched in 1989 with a price tag of roughly $10,000 per year compared with $100 for the older drugs, was nevertheless cost-effective.[11] It was clear at the time that Clozaril had set a price benchmark that, if it did not meet significant resistance, would become the price norm for any subsequent new antipsychotics coming on the market, with major economic consequences for individual patients and health systems in general.

As part of company marketing strategies, economic evaluations of antidepressants also began to come onstream in the 1990s. These purported to show that despite a price of $1,000 per year for a drug like Prozac, compared with the $100 (or less) price tag for older drugs, the new drugs represented value for the money.[12] Along with colleagues, I had argued that such prices were even more likely to lead to serious adverse financial consequences for the health services than the even bigger markup on antipsychotics because so many more people were prescribed antidepressants.[13] This seemed obvious, but no one else was saying it. In the face of publications in leading journals claiming the SSRIs or other new treatments would produce savings, there was no dissent.

Given my published positions, it is interesting that company personnel felt confident asking me along to a meeting on economic evaluations and consensus guidelines. Ironically, a few years later, when an independent expert for Britain's National Institute for Health and Clinical Excellence (NICE) suggested consulting me on the antidepressant guidelines NICE were constructing, the idea was shot down on the basis that Healy was too anticorporate when it came to drugs. Too anti-drug-company for NICE, but just perfect, it seems, for pharmaceutical companies.

Why go to meetings like this? It paid. For many outside observers, the repeated endorsement of on-patent products over older drugs at guideline meetings is close to inexplicable. Finding that the participants at these meetings have at some time been paid by a pharmaceutical company seems the only way to account for this. How else can you explain, for instance, the fact that in these guidelines Healy seems to be endorsing things when he has in other places appeared to say the opposite?

Another factor is lots of us want to be where the action is and industry is very good at creating action or at least the appearance of action. A further factor is friendship. Put in rooms for meetings like these, even people who have been on the opposite sides of arguments in print tend to get on. If others seem friendly in the flesh, it's somehow easier to see where they're coming from or to find a way to reconcile views. Companies excel at cultivating friendships—remembering details about you and making you feel that you count. Besides, as the taint of working with industry has receded and as more and more people are linked in, there increasingly seem to be fewer and fewer differences between "them" and "us." This is a world in which conflict of interest becomes a badge of honor, the more links to the greater number of companies the better.

These are all important issues but the conflicting interests of payment, friendship, or boredom do not explain what happens. Here's a further puzzle—the guidelines emanating from company-sponsored meetings are all but indistinguishable from those produced by committees with no links to the pharmaceutical industry. Whether the game is played by free market rules or within a socialized system, industry wins.

ONE GUIDELINE, ONE VOICE

To bring out how companies manage to win regardless of which way the game is played, let us contrast practices in the United States and Britain, in particular the operations of the British guideline system run by the National Institute for Health and Clinical Excellence (NICE), widely regarded as the most independent guideline system in the world, and the American Texas Medication Algorithm Project (TMAP).[14] TMAP was created by industry. NICE was set up in part to contain industry and has the distinction of having been sued by companies for advising against current drug treatments for Alzheimer's disease. NICE is exactly the kind of system that the Obama administration looked to put in place as part of its healthcare reform package.[15]

TMAP was set up in 1994, the year after Risperdal was launched in the United States. The project was initially funded by Janssen but soon thereafter all of the other major pharmaceutical companies had signed on as well. TMAP started with a panel of experts convened to produce a consensus on the use of antipsychotics. Later panels were pulled together to consider the use of antidepressants and mood stabilizers. Many of these consultants had prior links to Janssen and other companies operating in the mental health field, but these experts were distinguished psychiatrists and psychopharmacologists, and none have complained about having data withheld from them.

The first set of TMAP guidelines concluded that the recently launched antipsychotics—Risperdal, Zyprexa, and Seroquel—were the drugs of choice for schizophrenia. A second set of guidelines concluded that rather than older, cheaper antidepressants, the more recently launched on-patent Prozac, Paxil, and Zoloft were now the drugs of choice for depression. Further guidelines moved on to endorse mood stabilizers such as Depakote over other treatments for bipolar disorder. In each case the guidelines recommended newer drugs as safer, more effective, and better tolerated than older agents. In 1999 TMAP commissioned a set of guidelines for the management of childhood mental disorders, even though at the time no psychotropic drugs had been licensed for use in children or teenagers.[16]

In a number of states, Texas among them, legislators have the power to rule that guidelines such as TMAP's must be applied in the care of any patients receiving treatment in public facilities. The logic is that evidence-based guidelines, if they really do reflect reality, can be expected to be cost-effective over time. The legislators in Texas meet infrequently, are poorly paid, and are intensively lobbied. Perhaps because of such lobbying, or because pharmaceutical lobbyists were able to show the legislators position papers endorsed by experts, in 1999 the state of Texas endorsed, with no dissenting views, the TMAP guidelines for schizophrenia, mood disorders and for children, thus requiring state hospital doctors to prescribe the newer drugs first.

The TMAP guidelines were subsequently adopted by executive decision in a large number of other states.[17] In this way companies have effectively produced a situation in which a growing number of patients on Medicaid and other programs end up being put on and maintained on the newest and most costly of drugs.

The consequences are worth looking at. In 2004, eighth-graders in Pflugerville, Texas were screened by psychologists. Aliah Gleason, a thirteen-year-old, ticked the box for suicidality on one of the tests—probably a probe such as, Have you ever wished you were dead. Even though she was regarded as a live wire in class, this tick led to a referral to a psychiatrist and removal from her family by the child protection services. She was admitted to Austin State Hospital and within hours she was receiving the very best treatment—and did so for the next nine months. This involved all the latest antipsychotics, antidepressants, and mood stabilizers, as mandated by TMAP, costing a small fortune. These were administered not individually but in cocktails of up to five different medications daily. She gained huge amounts of weight, developed a range of side effects, and showed no evidence of progress. It took nine months for her family to get her back and begin to get her off treatment.[18]

Between 1997 and 2004, Texas Medicaid spending on antipsychotics rose from $28 million to $175 million. In the months of July and August 2004, over 19,000 adolescents in Texas were given antipsychotics, even though pharmaceutical companies had not applied for licenses to market these drugs for use in minors.

In 2003, Zyprexa pulled in $4.3 billion in sales in the United States, 70 percent of which came from state health insurance and other public health programs. It will probably come as no surprise that within all the major companies there are divisions aimed at maximizing the effectiveness of company marketing in the public sector. And it may be no accident that, in 2009, research revealed that children being treated under Medicaid were four times more likely to get antipsychotics than children not covered by Medicaid.[19]

Surely nothing similar could happen within Britain's socialized system of medicine, where the key guidelines are produced by NICE, which had been set up with a brief to make recommendations as to the most cost-effective treatments for both physical and mental illnesses? The panelists framing NICE guidelines, whether for cardiac treatments, arthritis management, or psychiatric conditions, have access to the resources of the Cochrane collaboration, the independent organization set up by Iain Chalmers initially in Britain but now with centers in all Western countries that systematically reviews the published evidence—taking pains to obtain all the published evidence and eliminate all evidence that has been duplicated to inflate artificially the apparent benefits of one drug over another. When assembling guidelines, NICE also ensures that it has a range of nonmedical participants to balance out any bias the doctors involved may have in favor of the latest treatment.

Despite this, the 2002 NICE guidelines for the use of antipsychotics came to the same conclusions as TMAP: newer agents like Risperdal and Zyprexa should be used before older ones.[20] Lilly responded to this news by incorporating symbols of NICE and NICE statements into its ads for Zyprexa, which was now supposedly a medication NICE endorsed. NICE had done for Lilly what we've seen the FDA had indicated would be illegal in the United States for the company to do for itself.

How come? The first point is that while NICE had access to all the published evidence through the resources of the Cochrane collaboration, this really didn't amount to any more than they would have been provided by the pharmaceutical companies had they asked. The Cochrane Center had made it clear that there was a great deal of duplicate publication. The four initial trials of Zyprexa in schizophrenia for instance had given rise to 234 publications of one sort or another—almost entirely company written.[21] While whittling the publications down to establish just how many trials there had been did help to qualify the apparent benefits of Zyprexa, it made no difference in NICE's overall evaluation.

What might have made a difference lay elsewhere in the vast amount of data from the four Zyprexa trials that simply could not be found in any of the 234 publications—there was nothing on suicides, diabetes, or cholesterol and little on weight gain. Not one publication hinted that patients given Zyprexa in these trials for schizophrenia had the highest suicide rate in clinical trials history; suicide was in fact rare in schizophrenia before the advent of the antipsychotics.[22] Not one publication mentioned that patients in these trials went on to develop diabetes at a rate triple the background rate in the general population, when diabetes was almost unheard of in schizophrenia before the antipsychotics.[23] The publications concealed the extent of weight gain in the patients given Zyprexa, whose weight often ballooned by anything from 20 to 140 lbs. These and subsequent publications also failed to reveal that, regardless of diagnosis, Zyprexa raised cholesterol levels more than almost any other drug in medicine—though Zyprexa had received a patent in part based on company claims that it would be less likely than other antipsychotics to raise cholesterol levels.

The figures for suicides, cholesterol, and diabetes were all buried in reports submitted by the company to the FDA. Even furnished with these reports to the regulator, it is difficult to establish what the true figures are and a good deal of data seems to be missing.[24] But NICE and TMAP didn't have the data and didn't even have these reports that were submitted to the regulator—they were working only from the published evidence. Based on a thorough assessment of the publications alone, NICE came to the conclusion the newer antipsychotics were no better than older agents. But the published evidence still suggested the new drugs provided a better quality of life and a lower burden of side effects than the older drugs, whereas the raw data point to just the opposite conclusions.

Against this background, NICE also had to manage a dynamic situation. First, how would clinicians and patient lobby groups, who had been bombarded for years with hundreds of publications extolling the virtues of Zyprexa and Risperdal and claiming these drugs liberated patients from some of the terrifying problems caused by the older agents, respond to a recommendation from NICE to use older drugs—had they chosen to give it? The 234 Zyprexa publications and further hundreds from the other new antipsychotics (Risperdal, Seroquel, Abilify, Geodon) played a great part in generating this pressure. Some of the panelists may privately have thought the older drugs were as good as the new ones, but it was difficult to offer evidence for this point of view, especially since they had no access to some of the most telling data. If NICE had come down favoring the older drugs, company-sponsored patient groups, told they should have the older drugs, would likely holler rationing, and even use this supposed rationing as an argument for desocializing healthcare. Second, just as journals do not publish articles critical of the pharmaceutical industry for fear of a legal action, so also NICE knew it stood to be dragged into a legal action if it came to a decision that was not based on published evidence. And since then, in the case of guidelines for Alzheimer's disease, it has found itself sued even though its decision is based on the published evidence.

Rumor has it that NICE was also faced with a British government that was in receipt of communications from several pharmaceutical companies threatening to pull out of the UK if the guidelines were not favorable to its products.[25]

The NICE guidelines came out in 2002. Three years later two large independent studies, one American and one European, were published showing that older antipsychotics were as effective and tolerable as any of the newer agents, and superior to some of them.[26] But if doctors wanted to follow the evidence and prescribe one of the older agents, they would have found a series of guidelines standing in their way, as these are only updated periodically.

THE GREATEST DIVIDE IN ALL OF MEDICINE

Having been invited to a number of guideline meetings, I had a chance in 1997 to convene one. As the secretary of the British Association for Psychopharmacology, I organized the first consensus conference to look at issues surrounding the prescription of psychotropic drugs to children. The growing number of prescriptions being written for ADHD (attention deficit hyperactivity disorder) had triggered the meeting, but on the day, the treatment of depression in children was the primary focus of attention.[27]

There was an important difference between this and the pediatric guideline meetings that came later. In 1997, except for ADHD, there were few published clinical trials. Furthermore when it came to depression, the clinical wisdom as of 1996 was that unhappiness in childhood was not the same as depression in adults—it was not something for which pills were the accepted answer. As a result when authoring the final document, the premium was on treating the child rather than the condition. Clinicians were recommended to lay out all the treatment options—drug and nondrug—for patients and their parents and if the first treatment didn't seem to be working they were advised to switch to alternate treatments even if not among those the doctor preferred. This was guidance rather than a guideline.

One feature of the meeting became intriguing later on. I had invited all panelists and a number of pharmaceutical companies. SmithKline Beecham were present as were a number of the clinical investigators for Study 329, SmithKline's trial of Paxil in depressed children outlined in the previous chapter. This study had been completed at the time the guidelines were written but I didn't know about it and possibly very few others did and there was not a single mention of any Paxil study on the day of the meeting.

Two years later, in 1999, TMAP issued guidelines endorsing the use of SSRIs in children who were depressed.[28] By this time a trial of Prozac in children had been reported and it was known that several other trials were underway. In 2002, the FDA endorsed Prozac for treating depression in children. The FDA had also issued a tentative approval to GlaxoSmithKline for the use of Paxil in children and was likely to do so for Zoloft. An article that had appeared in *Newsweek* to coincide with World Mental Health day in 2002 claimed there were three million depressed adolescents in the United States, who were supposedly at substantially increased risk of career failure, divorce, alcoholism or other substance misuse, and suicide, all of which could, according to the *Newsweek* article, be averted by the new SSRIs just about to be approved.[29] There was no hint here that unhappiness in childhood might be different than adult depression. The thrust of the article was that a failure to treat with medication would be equivalent to failing to give an antibiotic to a child with a life-threatening infection.

When the FDA approved Prozac, Paxil, and Zoloft for use in adults in the early 1990s, they noted that the drugs were likely to be used to treat children and encouraged companies to run studies to establish the safety of the drugs in children. Sales of SSRIs for children had been creeping up steadily through the 1990s on the back of over seventy published "open studies" of these medicines—all claiming the drugs were marvelous. Open studies are ones in which a doctor knows what the drug is and the patient may be told as well. They invariably report positive results for a drug, but companies cannot use this kind of study to get marketing approval from FDA; they can only use randomized studies.

Because there were so few good studies for any drugs in children, in 1998 the FDA Modernization Act (FDAMA) offered pharmaceutical companies a six-month patent extension for a drug if they submitted studies that examined safety issues in children. They didn't have to prove safety. They just had to test for it. If the drugs showed hazards, the company still received the patent extension but would have to incorporate the hazard information in the label.[30] This offer of patent extension gave the companies a hefty incentive to submit studies to the FDA on the effect of their drugs on children. A six-month patent extension for a Paxil or Zoloft meant easily over $1 billion in additional revenues. And there was every chance that the FDA would miss the problems.

As a result, in 2003 when NICE set about drawing up a guideline on the treatment of childhood depression, six randomized trials of SSRIs in children had been published.[31] The new guidelines were set to endorse the use of Prozac and other SSRIs for children.[32] The use of these drugs was increasing rapidly in Europe and this endorsement would likely have opened a floodgate.

In the case of Prozac there were two Lilly trials. Graham Emslie from Texas, who had participated in drawing up the TMAP guidelines for children, was involved in both. In clinical trials, it is customary to specify a primary measure of the success of treatment—such as the score on a particular rating scale or blood test—and if the drug fails to beat placebo on this measure, the trial is considered negative. On this basis, the first Emslie study, which started in 1990 but was only published in 1998, was a negative study even though the published article claimed it was a positive study.[33]

A second study published in 2002 was also negative. After the first week of the study, all children who had a bad reaction to Prozac or a good response to placebo were excluded.[34] It is common for a company to load the dice in its favor by excluding anyone who responds to placebo in the initial phase of the trial, but it was almost unheard of at the time to take the extra step and exclude patients who reacted poorly to the experimental drug during the first week of their exposure to it. If they dropped out of the study, they should be counted as dropouts for adverse events, not eliminated from the study calculations entirely. This novel tactic has since been increasingly copied in company trials of drugs for asthma, hypertension, and other conditions.

In the case of Paxil, the key study and the largest of the SSRI trials was Study 329, which as outlined in chapter 4 was a negative study that Sally Laden of Scientific Therapeutics Information transformed into an article demonstrating the remarkable efficacy and safety of Paxil. In addition to Study 329, Study 377 had also been undertaken in the 1990s but remained unpublished. Two further studies were presented at academic meetings in 2002; both claimed that Paxil was safe and effective.[35]

The third of the major SSRIs was Zoloft. The FDA requires two controlled studies to let a drug on the market. Pfizer ran two studies. In each Zoloft failed to beat placebo.[36] Just as with Study 329, these studies were ghostwritten. In this case they were published in the *Journal of the American Medical Association* and in the process transformed into one positive study—Zoloft was deemed effective and well tolerated. The design of these trials did not encourage the detection of any problems resulting from Zoloft, but even so, compared to children on placebo, there was a doubling of the rate of behavioral problems, including suicidality and aggression, in children on Zoloft and a tripling of the dropout rate for side effects.[37]

By 2003, then, a series of articles all claimed the SSRIs worked, and so an impending endorsement by NICE did not seem surprising. GlaxoSmithKline had applied to the British regulator (the Medicine and Healthcare Products Regulatory Agency, MHRA) for a license to market Paxil for childhood depression. But in October 2002 and Spring 2003 two BBC investigative journalism programs had questioned the benefits of Paxil.[38] Astonishingly, MHRA turned down GlaxoSmith-Kline's application to license Paxil, and in support of their move took the unprecedented step of posting on its website the details of fifteen controlled trials on antidepressants undertaken by a number of companies in pursuit of a license for treating pediatric depression. Depending on the way one reads the studies, between twelve and fourteen of these fifteen studies suggested the drug being tested didn't work and overall the studies showed a doubling of suicidal acts on the drugs compared to placebo. It was clear from these posted studies that there were yet further data that GlaxoSmithKline had not sent to the regulator.[39]

NICE was faced with two problems. First, they worked from the published data but the MHRA posting made it clear there were many more studies. Of the at least fifteen studies conducted, only six had been published. The unpublished studies were all negative. The second problem was that even the published Paxil, Prozac, and Zoloft studies, it was now clear, had been manipulated so that essentially negative studies were transformed into positive studies, hiding the fact the drugs didn't work and masking the problems of treatment. These revelations led researchers from NICE to pen an award-winning editorial in the *Lancet*, lamenting "depressing research."[40] This pointed to the impossible position any guidelines agency was in if companies withheld trials and distorted the data to the extent that had happened in the case of the pediatric antidepressant trials. It was left unsaid, but the position for doctors whose legitimate concerns about giving drugs like Paxil to children might conflict with the guidelines, had they been instituted, would have been even worse. The position for the children would of course have been worst of all.

For a brief moment, some of those in NICE who had gone through this crisis toyed with the idea of insisting that the status of any evidence that came from company trials be downgraded. Up to this point, the rules of evidence-based medicine had been that the results of clinical trials trumped everything else. Now it had become clear that companies were selective in what trial data they released, and thus company data appeared to be worth a lot less than had previously been assumed.[41]

But NICE dropped the idea of downgrading company trials. Could they be sure that a rule made on the back of the issue of antidepressants for children would hold water when it came to, say, trials of antihypertensives or analgesics or drugs for osteoporosis? If company evidence were to be downgraded, to what rung in the ladder should it be relegated—above or below the opinions of experts? Just how worthless was company evidence? And having dragged pharmaceutical companies into trials by insisting upon their necessity in order to gain a license, was this really the time to give them a slap in the face? Far better, surely, to work to improve company trials.

There had, moreover, apparently been one positive outcome of the debacle. The Paxil data that MHRA made public confirmed the message of an internal GlaxoSmithKline memo that had come to light in the BBC investigations: that Study 329 had shown Paxil was not effective, so only the good bits of the data would be published. At hearings the FDA held in February 2004 on prescribing antidepressants for children I made it public. It found its way from there to the offices of New York's Attorney General, who sued GlaxoSmithKline for fraud, and as part of the settlement, the company agreed to register all its trials on the web.

The idea of a clinical trial register took off. Journals indicated that they would in future only publish accounts of trials that had been registered with a central trial register beforehand and been given a unique identifier. Such an identifier would have made it easier to establish that only four trials underpinned the 234 publications on Zyprexa. But clinical trial registers and Glaxo's posting to its website do nothing to change the basic problem, which is that companies still do not made the raw data from these trials available.

NICE finally did issue a guideline on pediatric depression in 2004: they recommended against using SSRIs as a treatment. In 2004, the FDA held a further regulatory hearing in September to follow up the February hearing. These hearings on antidepressants and suicidality in children led to the highest level of warning, a black box warning, being put on the drugs indicating that they might trigger suicidality. The FDA meanwhile did not license Paxil or Zoloft or other antidepressants for use in children.

Far from this being a case of all's well that ends well, however, the use of antidepressants in children shows how far our scientific standards have slipped and how this impinges on our ability to care for some of the most vulnerable people there are. These studies of antidepressants in children offer the greatest known divide in medicine between what published reports in the scientific literature say on the one side and what the raw data in fact show, but there is no reason to think this problem doesn't extend to other treatments in other areas, from drugs for osteoporosis to treatments for asthma, female sexual dysfunction, PTSD, or other disorders. There was another landmark also—this was the only known case where all of the published studies were ghostwritten or company written.

The fifteen controlled studies of these new antidepressants should stand as a celebrated example of what controlled trials are there for—to stop bandwagons in their tracks. But instead, between ghostwriting and selective publication of the data, companies have turned controlled trials into their primary means to turbocharge sales. The published papers endorsing the use of Paxil, Prozac, and Zoloft remain in print in the best journals and continue to fuel a boom in off-label sales of these drugs to children.[42] There have been efforts to get Study 329 retracted but these have failed.[43] It continues to be built into guidelines supporting the use of antidepressants for children.

Erick Turner, formerly a reviewer with the FDA, has demonstrated that a third of the studies undertaken to get current antidepressants on the market for adults remain unpublished but even more worryingly a third of those published were studies the FDA regarded as negative but, like Study 329, companies published as positive.[44]

In other areas of medicine, where the problem has not been forced out into the open, companies can use their published studies to capture guidelines as they had almost done in the case of antidepressants given to children and, as we shall see in the next section, they continue to do in other domains. But even when the guideline is not captured, such studies and their publications transform the way we view things. In the case of antidepressants and children, for example, there is no longer any appreciation that childhood unhappiness might be anything different from adult depression. Someone attempting to express such a view today would find it difficult to get acceptance in anything other than a marginal journal.

THE CAPTURE OF THE BIPOLAR GUIDELINES

Classic manic-depressive illness, which typically leads to periods of hospitalization, was and still is rare. The recent invention of bipolar disorder obscures this but reveals much about how companies capture guidelines. When patients with the classic illness were admitted to hospital, either manic or depressed, they were typically too ill to be recruited for a controlled trial. This is not as problematic for good clinical care, including care that involves pharmaceuticals, as it may sound, however. Clinical trials rarely lead to discovery of any new drugs. Chlorpromazine, for instance, the first of the antipsychotics, was discovered in the early 1950s in Paris as a treatment for mania—but it was discovered because it made such an obvious difference to the patient in front of the doctor's eyes, not because a clinical trial showed it had an effect.[45] For the ensuing forty years, no one in medicine saw a need to conduct a trial for something as obviously beneficial as giving these antipsychotics to manic patients.

That there had been no randomized trial data for these older drugs for mania opened up a golden opportunity for pharmaceutical companies to push these older drugs out of the market, when in the 1990s the companies came out with a series of new, albeit, as it turned out, no more effective and actually more hazardous antipsychotics. The way forward led through treatment guidelines.

Here's how it happened in the case of bipolar disorder. The first step was to run short-term trials involving patients with much less severe conditions, and less certain diagnoses, using rating scales that may have reflected little more than how highly sedating were the drugs being tested. A strong sedative will always produce a "signal" on a rating scale for mania—the patient will be less active, less talkative, less disinhibited while under the influence of the drug. This is all it takes to get FDA approval for company claims their drug is antimanic. As a result of these trials all guidelines from the first formulated by TMAP in 1998 to a set of NICE guidelines in 2006 recommend the use of on-patent antipsychotics—but not any of the older antipsychotics.[46]

The second step was to run debatably ethical trials elsewhere, such as one Janssen ran in 2003 and 2004 on Risperdal for mania in India.[47] This trial became the subject of a BBC investigation into the ethics of studies for Western treatments outsourced to India. Did patients know they were involved in research? Did they consent to it? Did they know that once their participation was over they would be removed from drugs that might have been helping them? And it wasn't just ethics that was at issue. The correspondence in the columns of the *British Journal of Psychiatry* on the validity of this study was more extensive than for any other study the journal has published.[48]

In this newly globalizing clinical trial world, everyone faces a future in which the bulk of the evidence that dictates clinical practice when it comes to the use of statins, antihypertensives, painkillers, antibiotics, and practically everything else from mental health to respirology will come from settings that are very different from those in which the treatment will be given. There are likely to be many consequences for clinical practice, not least because both efficacy and side effects of different medicines may vary markedly in different ethnic groups.

As a result of the trials undertaken in India and elsewhere, only the new antipsychotics had randomized controlled trial support. The older agents hadn't. The straitjacket of current notions of evidence-based medicine, as applied by guideline bodies like TMAP or NICE, places published evidence from controlled trials above everything else—almost to the absurd point of not using a parachute until a study is undertaken to indicate formally its usefulness. What's more, the marketing departments of companies depend on our fascination with the supposed ironclad science of controlled trials and use it to capture the process of developing guidelines.

The third step involves something close to checkmate. In the case of manic-depressive illness the only agent with an established prophylactic effect is lithium. But modern guidelines also variably recommend Zyprexa, Depakote, and other new antipsychotics or anticonvulsants even though these are not licensed for this purpose. This has essentially happened because Abbott heavily advertized Depakote as a mood stabilizer in the first instance and the companies with follow-up anticonvulsants and antipsychotics followed suit. The term "mood stabilizer" generates expectations of a prophylactic effect even though none has been shown. Claiming Depakote was prophylactic would have been illegal—but there was no need for Abbott or other companies to tempt the law when a prestigious guideline recommends Depakote for a use the regulator would not let the company claim. In this case, bound by the law, the FDA is a lot more stringent than the guideline makers. This is advertising that's hard to beat.

The final step involves the use of guidelines to create new disorders. Over a century of clinical opinion has unanimously held that bipolar disorder can occasionally start in adolescence but usually has a later onset. The guidelines makers are trapped into mentioning pediatric bipolar disorder by the simple fact that companies have published a number of trials giving sedative drugs to unruly children, labeled as suffering from bipolar disorder. Being value neutral, because such trials had been run, in their 2006 guideline NICE had to mention pediatric bipolar disorder. In so doing they breached a century of worldwide clinical consensus, and all but endorsed the disorder, pushing Europe down a route the United States had already traveled.[49]

When it comes to bipolar disorder, American medicine is in the grip of an enthusiasm reminiscent of the seventeenth century Dutch tulip mania. Children as young as one year of age are being put on antipsychotics, and some clinicians even contemplate the possibility of making in-utero diagnoses. Guidelines have been a significant factor in this infection. In recent years a series of pediatric bipolar consensus conferences were organized in the United States, such as one organized by Best Practices, a marketing firm specializing in central nervous system drugs.[50] This conference was supported by all the major pharmaceutical companies, and its final recommendations were ghostwritten, but even if such meetings weren't financially supported in this way with carefully sculpted ghostwritten recommendations, the result would likely have been the same. Running trials of sedative drugs in overactive or disruptive children, who are labeled bipolar, will produce an apparent benefit. That clinical trial result in effect pulls a guideline into existence, and if there's a guideline, the condition is assumed to be real. All the marketing company need do is ensure the guideline making process happens in a timely fashion, with a consensus statement for publication and dissemination.

Once the participants agree that the guideline has to be based on clinical trial evidence, the guideline all but writes itself before the participants sit around the table. The guidelines produced by TMAP in 1998 for the treatment of bipolar disorder are essentially indistinguishable from those produced by NICE in 2006. Where in 2004 NICE were saved by a television program from contributing to making children depressed, nothing saved them in 2006. The reasons for NICE's failure to distinguish itself from TMAP in 2006 do a great deal to help explain our current healthcare problems. ·

FACTS ON THE GROUND

Across medicine, however misleadingly certain academic papers may be written, with a few exceptions, no studies allow claims that one drug is superior to another. Even so, a series of guidelines in different areas of medicine advocate newer, more expensive drugs over older ones. However well-meaning these may be, in these cases there should be suspicions that the guideline has been captured by pharmaceutical companies.

Capture is engineered by a combination of smart publication strategies and targeting trials at illnesses where there have been no trials before, whether restless legs syndrome, female sexual dysfunction (FSD), or osteoporosis. In these ways, companies can make diseases fashionable, can engineer the appearances of comparative efficacy, and can enlist academic advocates for particular treatment options. By these means, too, they have been able to control the content of guidelines and transform even independent guidelines into something close to an extension of company marketing departments.

This dynamic plays a key role in the selling of diseases from FSD to PTSD, overactive bladder, osteoporosis, and osteopenia.[51] Getting a drug licensed for FSD or osteoporosis does not mean that physicians are thereafter enabled to treat women in a more effective way than they had been able to do before. Rather, it means that Pfizer, Lilly, and GlaxoSmithKline are enabled to start marketing these disorders and in the process to convert the vicissitudes of intimate life on the one hand or the changes of middle years on the other hand into illnesses. Guidelines achieve even more for a company—they make it appropriate, indeed almost necessary, to detect and treat these illnesses. Company-sponsored and ghostwritten "scientific" papers, along with selectively presented trial results, offer the raw material out of which clinical consensus will later be manufactured. When it comes to annexing territory, this clinical consensus in the form of guidelines establishes facts on the ground.

Consider what happens when a guideline is published. For managers running healthcare institutions, there need to be standards against which the organization can be held accountable. Whether or not the current guidelines are wrong is immaterial. If attempting to implement them produces no health gain, this still makes no difference to managers, at least in their strictly institutional role. The key point is adherence.

A celebrated episode from the fourth series of the American TV medical drama *House* shows Dr. Foreman grappling with a patient's life-threatening problem. He ultimately finds an unorthodox answer to it that saves his patient's life but gets him the sack. As his boss tells him, it may have been good medicine but it was bad practice. Dr. Foreman is not alone; clinicians worldwide are increasingly faced with managers enquiring about their compliance with guidelines and more and more are getting the sack. What's a manager going to do if a doctor retorts that these ostensibly evidence-based guidelines amount to pharmaceutical marketing by proxy?

The accountants in the finance department of a healthcare organization who see the figures on newer and more costly drugs also find themselves faced with guidelines supporting the use of these drugs, issued by independent academic bodies whose stated brief is, in part, to secure cost effectiveness. The promise is that the organization will save money in the longer run by being "evidence based," as this will lead to better outcomes for diseases treated this way and to savings on not doing what works less well. The beans line up for both the accountants and the executives. Truth does not.

Articles by guideline proponents, and even the guidelines themselves, state that clinicians do not always need to adhere to the guidelines—this is guidance rather than a diktat.[52] But medico-legal articles suggest that any deviation from guidelines needs to be justified. Where a clinician wouldn't have to justify guideline-sanctioned treatment in the medical record, they are advised to justify everything that is "unorthodox." Doing anything different, then, adds to the bureaucracy, and increases the sense of risk.

An element of coercion has also emerged in many medical settings where reimbursement has been tied to guideline adherence. The element of coercion increases further if one considers that current evidence is framed within settings in which pharmaceutical companies advertise (in the United States) and set up patient groups who lobby for new treatments even though there is no evidence to believe these are any better than older treatments.

The proponents of guidelines put them forward as guidance and believed that they could only lead to improvements in the outcomes of treatment for all conditions. But a series of studies have shown that the outcomes, on average, are in general no different whether or not clinicians adhere to guidelines.[53] Soon after guidelines began to appear in the 1980s, opposition to them emerged and grew steadily.

Clinical concerns that guidelines risk becoming coercive are often met with a cynical response—of course clinicians will be worried if their autonomy is being curtailed. While not untrue, this misses an essential point. If a treatment really works, both because they want to help their patients but also for reasons of compelling self-interest, few clinicians are likely to fail to prescribe it whatever the guidelines may say. Who would not give penicillin to a patient with pneumonia or an antipsychotic to a floridly manic patient?

The problem guidelines might pose was outlined first in 1956 long before anyone had heard of them. Following the discovery of the first antipsychotic, chlorpromazine, the National Academy of Sciences (NAS) and National Institute of Mental Health (NIMH) convened a meeting to work out how to build on this discovery. Ed Evarts from the NIMH, one of the leading lights of the day, put it to his colleagues that but for an accident of history they could now be discussing the use of the new antipsychotics for the treatment of *dementia paralytica* (tertiary syphilis) rather than *dementia praecox* (schizophrenia). Tertiary syphilis had looked identical to schizophrenia and chlorpromazine would have produced a distinct benefit on this state because it controlled the hallucinations and delusions that went with the disorder, although likely at a cost of increasing mortality—but this increase in mortality would not have shown up in the short-term clinical trials that demonstrated a benefit.

Evarts pointed out to his audience that none of the rating scales, clinical trial methods, or animal models that were then being put in place as the engines of progress that would move the new psychopharmacology field forward would have helped doctors to work out that penicillin rather than chlorpromazine or psychotherapy was the right answer to *dementia paralytica*. What made the difference was understanding that tertiary syphilis was a microbial infection. He predicted that the proposed scaffolding of clinical trials, although eminently sensible, would create an academic and industrial complex that would slowly stifle progress in therapeutics.[54]

No one paid heed to Evarts. He came to the conference as a leading figure within the psychiatry of his day but vanished from the radar afterward—leaving a set of predictions that have been right on the money. Fifty years later, compulsory detentions for mental illness have risen three-fold, admissions for serious mental illness have risen seven-fold, admissions overall have risen fifteen-fold,[55] suicide rates in schizophrenia have gone up twenty-fold,[56] and diseases such as diabetes have increased exponentially among the mentally ill.[57] There has been a dramatic drop in life expectancy for serious mental illness in the United States—with a fall of up to two decades compared with the rest of the population.[58] The same has been found wherever else these things have been measured,[59] with increases in mortality correlated with the numbers of psychotropic drugs given.[60]

We have focused on mental health in this chapter, but the same is happening in other areas of medicine where there are blockbuster drugs. The interaction between the first of the blockbusters, Zantac, and the treatment of ulcers, outlined in chapter 2, bears out Evarts's prediction better than anything else. Many doctors had been using antibiotics for ulcers before Barry Marshall demonstrated that ulcers were often caused by the *helicobacter pylori* bacillus. Had there been guidelines for the treatment of ulcers then, any doctors prescribing antibiotics would have been at greater risk of a lawsuit than they might have been before the guidelines were formulated.

Current cardiovascular guidelines all mandate lowering low-density lipoprotein (LDL). Company marketing took advantage of this with Merck and Schering Plough suggesting that Vytorin (a combination of ezetimibe and simvastatin) would lower LDL cholesterol further than would treatment with a statin alone. The thrust of the guideline played into the marketing of Vytorin—until the clinical trial evidence finally demonstrated that prescribing Vytorin produced no benefit in terms of mortality.[61] Hormone replacement therapy entered guidelines as a means of lowering cholesterol, but it is now clear this increases death rates.[62] Cardiovascular guidelines also call for optimal control of blood pressure, and company marketing has suggested adding angiotensin receptor antagonists (ARBs) to ACE inhibitors as one way to do this, but the clinical trial evidence now suggests that this also increases mortality.[63]

For the treatment of diabetes, guidelines recommend tight glucose control. GlaxoSmithKline's Avandia (rosiglitazone) was promoted as doing just this, making the company billions of dollars annually in the process, until it was withdrawn following evidence that Avandia increases rates of heart attacks and death by up to five hundred cases per month above what might have been expected had other agents been used.[64] The question of whether GlaxoSmithKline knew about these risks and hid clinical trial data—just as they did with Paxil in both children and adults—became the subject of a US Senate investigation, discussed in chapter 7.[65] More generally, large-scale studies have shown that adhering to these diabetes guidelines have led to higher death rates and more hypoglyemic episodes than found in patients treated with less emphasis on tight glucose control.[66]

The country that consumes the greatest amount of on-patent medications and the greatest amount of medications attested to by the most authoritative guidelines is the United States, but over the past decade,

American life expectancies have progressively fallen behind other developed countries.[67] Over the same period of time spending on health has escalated in the United States beyond elsewhere, rising from less than 1 percent before World War II per annum to over 17 percent of GDP now. This is not what happens when treatments work. It is not what happened to the clinics and beds used to treat patients with tertiary syphilis after the discovery of penicillin, or tuberculosis after the development of streptomycin—when the patients vanished, the beds were closed down, the staff redeployed, and money was saved. The promise of the guideline makers—that if only policymakers follow the evidence (such as it is), health will improve while costs come down—has not held up.

When faced with evidence that guideline-mandated treatment with statins, antidepressants, or drugs for osteoporosis fails to make a difference, guideline makers sometimes attribute this failure to a delay in instituting treatment. In July 2008 the American Association of Pediatricians issued a new guideline on the health of children. It recommended screening children as young as eight years old for raised cholesterol levels, and then possibly instituting treatment with a statin.[68] The promise is held out that catching people ever earlier will make a difference. Similarly, advocates of mood stabilizers commonly attribute the failure of their drugs to make a difference to the delay in starting the drugs, and they suggest catching and treating ever and ever younger children. Once the disease takes hold it is supposedly more resistant to treatment.

It seems strikingly difficult for clinicians and others to ask whether robust independent assessment of drugs can be undertaken in a world where data is privately held. The reviewers for the NICE guidelines on pediatric depression teetered on the brink of making this point but backed down. The point was finally made in January 2011 by the Cochrane Center reviewers of Tamiflu, who made it clear that in the current circumstances we have little option but to recognize that independent assessment of drugs is not possible.[69] There has so far been a deafening silence from Western governments, all of whom have handed over billions of dollars to stockpile a remedy little better than one of the proprietary nostrums from the nineteenth century.

Some years ago, there was consternation in the Lake District of Britain, an area known for its narrow country roads and stone walls, as a growing number of juggernaut haulage trucks came roaring off the motorways and down the narrow roads, knocking over walls, getting stuck in the middle of towns and sometimes damaging property. The drivers were on autopilot. Alerted by their satellite navigation systems to delays ahead and advised of alternate routes, they followed the guidance. Putting patients on every drug indicated by a guideline—guidelines drawn up for diseases rather than for people—demonstrates a comparable blindness. The consequent polypharmacy constitutes a disorder in its own right if not an illness. Getting people off their medications has been demonstrated to reduce hospitalizations, reduce costs, and save lives.[70] But doctors adopting this approach are getting and will get the sack, unless they can appeal to a guideline for treating people rather than diseases.

Some of us put on a guideline-mandated treatment will know when the new treatment is causing us problems; at that point surprisingly few of us have the fortitude to insist that the treatment be changed or stopped. Children have an even more difficult problem. Their complaints have to be filtered through a parent, who may be no more likely to think a doctor would do anything that might harm their child than once they might have thought a cleric capable of abuse. Children are even more likely to be hostages than was Bill when he was put on an ACE inhibitor after his stroke or Sheila when put on a statin after her cardiac event, or as the case of Aliah Gleason, forcibly removed from her family and treated according to the latest guidelines, demonstrate.

Sheila, Bill, Aliah, and the rest of us are increasingly faced with doctors who are treating diseases rather than treating us. There are no guidelines for treating us. There are only guidelines for the treatment of cholesterol levels or diabetes or depression. These doctors are caught in the pincers of an apparatus which is now being used to give us diseases and indeed often several different diseases at the same time. This apparatus has twin pincers—one pincer lies in the guidelines, the other is formed by a series of measurement technologies that now are being used to make us ill in ways we weren't before. It is to these measurement technologies and how they are used that we now turn.

6

The Mismeasurement
of Medicine

When Jane, a woman forty-five years old, became increasingly wheezy she went to see her primary care doctor. He got her to blow into a peak flow meter, which measures the amount of air one can breathe out. She had asthma, he said, and prescribed a beta-agonist inhaler, called a reliever, that commonly has a dramatic effect on wheeziness. Even people who do not have asthma can feel they are breathing more freely after a puff of one of these inhalers. Treatments for asthma are among the current medical blockbusters, with a market value over $10 billion. Jane was also given a steroid, called a preventer, aimed at damping down the inflammatory responses that lead to asthma.

The reliever provided instant aid when she wheezed, but over the course of some months her problems get worse. Her peak flow dropped from the normal 500 liters per minute to close to 200, and sometimes she turned blue. On referral to a respiratory clinic, the specialist and nursing staff told her that it was impossible that the reliever could be making her problem worse. She was prescribed one of the latest asthma blockbusters, Advair, an inhaler that combines both a reliever and a steroid.

At subsequent clinic visits a further blockbuster, Singulair, a leukotriene antagonist, was added. In Jane's case, this produced only side effects.[1] Older agents were added to the mix, but these only made her sick. Her physician started talking about experimental techniques not in common use.

Jane had had no problems before moving to the area, and her profile of blood tests suggested an allergic component to her problem. Accordingly she eliminated certain foods from her diet and took a variety of supplements which appeared to help marginally. But the clinic seemed uninterested, she felt.

She tried a new doctor, who took her off the combined inhalers and Singulair. The mainstay of her treatment became a different steroid given alone. She improved dramatically, but her new doctor didn't seem interested either in tracking down the circumstances that made her problem worse.

Dick's case was a bit different. He was eighty-one when referred by his generalist to a respiratory clinic with an atypical wheeze. A reliever inhaler made little difference to his peak flow rate, which was in fact better than that of most twenty year olds. Nevertheless, he ended up with not just a reliever inhaler but a series of other asthma medications. Dick did not have asthma, though. His breathlessness was caused by a disturbance in the movement of his diaphragm (a respiratory dyskinesia), probably caused by a previous treatment for nausea. The only treatment for a respiratory dyskinesia is time and avoiding any unnecessary treatments, such as treatments for asthma, which worsen the problem.

Until recently, asthma was relatively uncommon. It was found most often in children, who usually grew out of it. Later-onset asthma was a serious but rare condition. The first concerns that treatment might aggravate the condition and even lead to death were raised in the late 1970s, coming to a head in New Zealand in the early 1980s.[2] These concerns might have been expected to slow the rate of diagnosis, but clinics now register cases as asthma, even ones as grossly atypical as Dick's, at a much greater rate than previously.

Many of us may suspect that synthetic chemicals, perhaps ones we're not being told about, could be causing conditions such as asthma.[3] Although toxins may play some part in the current epidemic, there is another, altogether more visible culprit at work as well. Coincident with the rise of asthma over the last thirty years has been the emergence of peak flow meters, which have given rise to norms according to which many of us are diagnosed as asthmatic though a doctor forty years ago would never have diagnosed that disease in most cases. In the 1980s, the companies marketing treatments for asthma provided peak flow meters to doctors. As a result many of us are now only one bout of wheezing or coughing away from our GP discovering we have reduced peak flow rates and then putting us on inhalers, which might initially make us feel better, whether or not we have asthma. This response cements the diagnosis in place. We will also be sent home with promotional literature sponsored by some company advising us to keep a daily chart of our peak flow rates and to increase the amount of medication we take should the readings fall. Every time we take an inhaler, we will be able to see our own peak flow rates "improve," trapping us into a medication cycle as Jane was.

It's hard to fathom the apparent lack of medical concern demonstrated in the continuing prescription of beta-agonist inhalers in the face of study data showing an excess of deaths on these inhalers compared to placebo.[4] Such lack of concern likely stems in part from the very visible short-term benefits doctors find in their patients' peak flow figures. This seems to trump all else—even death. This chapter is about the lure of such measurements on the ability of doctors to care for us.

CARING AND MEASURING

Medical matters and health in general are now among the leading media items, whether in newspapers and magazines or on television or the Internet. These are surprisingly recent developments. Only a few decades ago, healthcare was at the margin of our social awareness. There were no health pages in newspapers, no magazines devoted to health, no television or radio programs about health issues, and relatively few books about health in bookshops. But now medical breakthroughs or concerns about diseases regularly dominate the headlines. The issues may be far removed from blockbuster drugs, focusing instead on healthcare reform, insurance coverage, rising costs, or the latest pandemic of swine flu or other disorder, but the marketing of pharmaceuticals has done more than anything else to make health in general the front page news it now is.

The influence of company marketing on this shift has been profound, although not necessarily because the treatments we hear about work. In fact the less effective the treatment, the greater the need for marketing support, including a marketing of the conditions that a drug might treat. For over three decades pharmaceutical companies have been more likely than any other players within the medical arena to retain public relations companies to ensure that we all get to hear the message of salvation through the use of one or another pharmaceutical or to hear experts counteract some story that a company thinks likely to undermine sales of their drug.

As health hits the front page of our lives and healthcare becomes an ever bigger business and an arena of increasing competition, healthcare managers, clinicians, and drug marketers are faced with problems of increasing complexity. This is an arena where differing values linked to ethnic, social, or religious backgrounds, or based on class and gender, clash. Trumpeted as providing gold standard evidence, randomized controlled trials, along with the apparently objective evidence that comes from measurement, seem to offer an alluring solution to some of these complexities. These measurements have brought a standardization to medicine that has transformed the meetings between doctors and patients as well as the nature of modern medical care.

Up to the·1960s in United States and even more recently in Europe, a patient walking in to see a doctor encountered a man in a white coat, perhaps even a suit, possibly with a stethoscope dangling around his neck. Patients might have been aware of themselves as the object of attention of what social scientists in the 1960s began to refer to as the clinical gaze. Social scientists and even many physicians had a number of problems with this clinical gaze. At its worst it saw a specimen rather than a person. It noticed pallor, odd breathing patterns or fetid breath, abnormalities of gait, a lump in the throat, a mole on the skin, the shake in a hand, but might be blind to the person's social circumstances, history of difficulties, and experience of disease. But at its best, the clinical gaze encompassed all of these things, in part because of a relationship between doctor and patient that meant the doctor was noticing differences from one visit to the next, had learned more about the person and the person's family over time, and knew a lot about the circumstances in which they were living.[5] There was a clear link between this kind of doctor and doctors like Richard Cabot and Alfred Worcester from Massachusetts, over half a century earlier.

The doctor's interest in a patient's physical state might lead to the use of instruments to directly observe things—a stethoscope to listen to breath and heart sounds, perhaps an otoscope to look in ears or ophthalmoscope to look in eyes as symptoms required. Otherwise it was hands on—a feel of the abdomen to rule out acute organ pathology, a check of the glands, a tapping of the chest. A hand on the forehead to check temperature was often used rather than a thermometer. Even in teaching hospitals, like Massachusetts General, that had made their reputations on the back of diagnostic tests introduced by Richard Cabot and his successors, measurements in general were still only taken when evidence for a specific disease was being sought. The first changes to this practice came with the use of blood pressure cuffs in the 1960s in yearly insurance check-ups—but these were marginal to normal medical care. Through to the 1960s the patient might leave a doctor's office without anything being measured.

Now, medical consultations will include assessments of blood pressure and weight, and blood tests for sugars and cholesterol. In the case of women it might involve a referral for a bone scan or mammogram, or in men a screen for prostate-specific antigens. There may be some listening to breath sounds, but the person will also be invited to blow into a meter to establish their peak flow rate. While waiting to see the doctor they may have been invited to complete a series of general health questionnaires or answer questions related to mood or other aspects of their mental health.

Although doctors of an earlier time could rightly be accused of missing critical aspects of their patients' lives, today they are much less likely to notice a difference in gait or pallor that the doctors of yesteryear would have spotted, if only because the patient is less likely to see the same doctor from one visit to the next. The clinical gaze is now more akin to being on autopilot. It doesn't really matter which doctor is present. Any medical person could consult the numbers from the previous visit, even a holiday stand-in just jetted in from New Zealand. The doctor's horizon is often now numerical rather than personal.

The key group we will follow in this chapter are people who walk into a doctor's office thinking they are normal but whose "numbers" are not quite right on that day. These numbers put us at much greater risk of becoming patients than ever before. Just how this can depersonalize us becomes clearer in the case of anyone who has a chronic disease such as diabetes, hypertension, or asthma. In these cases, the disease cannot be cured but some set of numbers can be put right or at least adjusted, and doctors increasingly focus on this rather than on the messier business of what it might mean for their patients to have to live with this condition. The patient may be worried about a lot of things stemming from his illness; but the doctor looks at the computer terminal for last week's blood results, perhaps consoling herself by thinking that while she may not be addressing what is really bothering the patient, she at least is reducing the risk of problems that might bother him in the future. The fact that some numbers are going in the right direction will do something to ease her concerns about possible side effects the patient may be suffering.

She can also take comfort in the likelihood that an increasing number of her colleagues would endorse her approach. She is meeting acceptable standards of care—standards that are intimately tied to the emergence of guidelines in the 1990s but in daily practice also driven by the measurements doctors now take in clinics—often in lieu of talking to us.

STANDARDIZED MEDICINE

The roots of standardization can be traced back to the establishment of alphabets, or to the units of measurement that enabled a trade in agricultural goods, or the units of time that replaced earlier ways to map the day. In all these cases a standard approach offers a structure that facilitates interactions between communities and allows agreed-upon comparisons between things that were formerly distinct, although it may override what seem like more natural and seasonal rhythms. Some aspect of a primal Eden may be lost, but a lot is gained.

From ancient China to the modern day, those in favor of establishing more standards or spreading the reach of existing ones have proclaimed that they are needed to stop rogues. Those against increasingly elaborated standards argue that they can just as easily facilitate greater roguery and that they have a deadening effect on human interactions. Those in favor of a greater stipulation of standard procedures in medicine argue that they lift it out of parochialism, while those against argue that standards will ultimately reduce medicine to a cookbook exercise, often at the patient's expense.[6]

Prior to the development of clinical trials, medicine was one of the preeminent professions. While still prestigious, based on the technical accomplishments of heart surgeons during the 1970s, for instance, and probably better paid now than before, there has been a profound change in the degree to which a doctor can exercise discretion—once the hallmark of a professional. When you met a doctor in the 1960s you did not question his judgment or if you did, the likely response was that he would be happy to have this discussion with you when you had been through ten years of medical training.

For a state wanting to ensure good medical care for all its citizens, or for a health delivery organization keeping an eye on the legal and financial sides of its business, or for many of today's informed consumers of healthcare, the idea that you might get a completely different treatment if you go to doctor A rather than doctor B is close to insupportable. Advocates of good medical care of this kind viewed traditional medicine with its great variability based on professional discretion as something closer to a cottage industry in which patients all too often had to endure both their illness and their doctor. They see a resistance to standardization as something less than noble—an attempt to hold on to private practice—and wonder if the art of medicine in question isn't a cover for laziness and old boy networks.

There is a tricky balance here. In chapter 3, I praised the efforts of Philippe Pinel and Pierre Louis to monitor the outcomes of treatment in nineteenth century France. The response from French physicians at the time was to rail against attempts to standardize medical practice. At the start of the twentieth century in Massachusetts, the new diagnostic tests introduced by Richard Cabot and others led Alfred Worcester to complain that too great a focus on testing would lead to a neglect of the sacred doctor-patient relationship. Measurement and testing are not problems in their own right; in proper proportion they can be exceedingly helpful. The problems arise if they are captured by an interested party, such as the pharmaceutical industry, just as clinical trials have been.

There is no reason why clinical trials should necessarily lead to a rigid standardization. After all, people do not respond to drugs the way automobiles respond to oil or to the tuning of their running parts. As discussed in chapter 3, the data from clinical trials of drugs like the antidepressants, where four of five people apparently responding to drug treatment would have responded if put on placebo, support the exercise of clinical discretion in the use of these drugs rather than a rigid standardization.

Furthermore, rather than leading to standardization, clinical trials might have been expected to lead to a democratization of practice. Medicine is far more specialized than it was in the 1960s and as such it might have been expected that we would question our doctors even less now than we did then, but the proliferation of controlled trials that have been published have provided results open to the public and, with the advent of the Internet, more accessible than in the past. From the 1960s on, patients with complaints from breast cancer to depression could face doctors proposing radical mastectomy or electroconvulsive therapy (ECT) and could talk data to them. No longer could a doctor tell a patient, "Come back and ask me that question when you've had medical training and several years of clinical practice." At least for a brief time, doctors were transformed from authorities into collaborators whose role was to review the evidence with their patients. The management of breast cancer and treatment with ECT gave rise in the 1960s and 1970s to the notion of informed consent,[7] as the results from breast cancer operations and ECT studies in the 1960s came into the public domain.

But where public data like this has democratized authority within medicine, the fact that the data on drugs and the full range of their effects is hidden has also led to a diminution of medical authority, replacing it with something closer to a healthcare totalitarianism. We can question our doctors now about drugs and their effects, but neither we nor they can readily find out what is going on. And against this background the set of guidances drawn up by experts that should enhance clinical practice has become a set of guidelines that have constrained practice, and, paradoxically, led to calls for increased standardization of practice as clinical outcomes fail to improve in response to the efforts of the guideline makers.

But it is another set of measurements that have invaded clinical practice and are leading to a further standardization of care that concern us here. These numbers come from the instruments used in trials, whether from blood tests for cholesterol, peak flow rates, or rating scale changes tracking our moods or sexual functioning. These measurements have been central to the running of modern clinical trials and there seems to be little awareness that taking these measurements out of context and importing them into clinical practice might create a host of unforeseen problems. The measurements have in fact taken on a life of their own.

THE SEDUCTIVE POWER OF SCALES

The seductive power of numbers can be seen by looking at the first measurement technology to have an impact on healthcare—the weighing scale. The earliest weighing scales began to appear in the 1870s.[8] Almost instantly people began weighing themselves and doctors began weighing patients. The new numbers persuaded doctors and the early insurance companies that a certain plumpness, which had formerly been seen as a sign of health, was actually a risk factor for future ill health. Physicians and insurers combined to extol the virtues of slimness. Within a remarkably brief period of time, European and American ideas of beauty also changed.[9] Gone was the appeal of a Rubenesque woman. Voluptuousness became passé, replaced by the slim flappers of the roaring twenties.

By the 1920s, public weighing scales, commonly with plates fastened to their front giving norms for weight by height, were a regular feature in drug stores or other retailers. Then, in the 1960s, small portable weighing scales that could be placed discretely in the bathroom appeared on the market and soon became a household staple.

In parallel with the sales of weighing scales, a new set of diseases began to gain attention and grow in frequency—the eating disorders.[10] Anorexia nervosa was first described in the 1870s. In the decades that followed, the new disorder seemed to become progressively more common and by the 1920s was occurring with noticeable frequency, though it is difficult to judge prevalence at the time with any certainty. The eating disorders exploded in the 1960s, spewing out variants such as bulimia nervosa, with estimates that up to a third of women might be affected. Curiously, these were Western diseases, not found in Asian or other populations. That eating disorders were apparently a Western phenomenon gave rise to questions about what it might be about the role of women in the West that would lead to problems like this. Was it wrong for women to work? Had they been abused in childhood? Were cultural expectations for women to be thin simply toxic?

There are biological, social, and psychological factors that contribute to eating disorders and that can help address such questions as why this syndrome primarily affects women rather than men. But the role measurement technology plays should also be considered. The weighing scale in this case offers possibilities to marry biological, social, and psychological inputs and expresses their result simply, concretely, and in a way that people can gauge from day to day, noting whether they are approaching or deviating from the goal they've set themselves. Without the weighing scale to organize these factors, it is hard to see how eating disorders could have mushroomed to affect 30 percent of Western populations.

It is tempting to relegate something as inert as the weighing scale to the margins of consideration. But its power as a behavioral reinforcer should not be underestimated. Stepping on the scales and finding the numbers are over a limit one thinks acceptable can be deeply unsettling. For anyone in training, falling outside a target on their stopwatch might be profoundly dispiriting to the point of abandoning the exercise, while shaving even single digits off a previous set of numbers can provide a huge incentive to keep going.

The example of eating disorders provides a dramatic metaphor for the problems of maintaining equilibrium once we position ourselves on a scale. In this case the numbers tantalize with seductive possibilities of control. Part of the problem is that numbers can trump non-numerical judgments, in the way a ringing telephone cuts across a live conversation we may be having. Unless we have great willpower, or wisdom, the only way to resist their lure may be to set up competing sets of numbers.

Similarly, as we have developed capacities to measure environmental radiation or chemicals, our difficulties with these hazards seem to increase rather than diminish. We need to be reminded that the rates of cancer from background radiation pose a lesser risk than being hit by a car crossing the street. Or that cabbages come with forty-seven natural pesticides in them, many of which would not get a license for use from regulators, but these are what give them their taste.

Or consider the lure of comparative measures in attempts to map and forecast economies. It is easy to produce figures from manufacturing industry and other areas of the economy and from this to construct indices of the Gross National Product (GNP), which people think is especially "good" if it appears to be growing from year to year. But presently scales like this one leave out such factors as the number of trees cut down, the amount of pollution generated, and changes in the quality of life of a nation's inhabitants—all areas that may critically affect our future well-being but can too easily be overlooked if attention is only paid to shifts in GNP numbers. Perversely as things are measured at present, an oil spill like that of the *Exxon Valdez* adds to measurable economic activity and increases GNP.

Our capacity to generate measures and scales in the health domain sets up formidable challenges that cannot readily be managed by just telling people to keep calm or be wise. Will we be helped or harmed by the increasing power of scanning technologies to pick up ever more subtle changes in breast tissue or thyroid gland configurations or prostate gland markers, for example? What will happen once we have technologies that can map out patterns of brain activation? We don't know. Will having wise heads at the medical helm be sufficient to stop us obsessing about the meaning of variations in our numbers?

One reason we can suspect wise heads at the helm will not be sufficient is that managing the numbers found in scales is not just a matter of advising people to put them in context. Like the brooms brought to unpredictable life in the Sorcerer's cave when in Disney's *Fantasia* the apprentice waves a magic wand, vivified by market forces the numbers can come to life. Scales set up markets. The numbers from weighing scales helped set up all sorts of markets in diets, health farms, and exercise equipment. Our performances as timed on stopwatches feed markets for sneakers, running gear, and lifestyle coaches. Our growing capacities to map individual variation from the genome to brain scanning will set up further markets for people wanting to minimize future risks for themselves or their children. Having identified a vulnerability in ourselves, we will all be in the market for a remedy.

RABBITS FROM HATS

The power that prompting concern in us about some measure of our apparent health can have in the development of new drug markets comes through dramatically in the cholesterol story. For fifty years it has been known that very high cholesterol levels and especially familial hypercholesterolemia, an uncommon genetic disorder that leads to high cholesterol levels, can be a risk factor for heart attacks. These are the people whose cholesterol levels really do count but these could often be picked up without a blood test by the old style clinical gaze alone—in people with this illness there are cholesterol deposits around the eyes.

In the early 1950s, the Framingham study, which followed 5,209 men and women from Framingham, Massachusetts, in an attempt to pinpoint the risk factors for heart attacks and strokes, identified the key risks as obesity, a history of heart attacks or other cardiovascular events, smoking, and a sedentary lifestyle.[11] Raised cholesterol was also a risk factor, but of much less importance; moreover, it was only a risk factor when one or more of these more serious risks were also present. The most important things, then, for people who have not already had a heart attack and even for those who have had a heart attack, are to reduce weight, get fit, and stop smoking rather than to measure their cholesterol levels. In fact most Western countries saw a 30 percent drop in cardiovascular mortality between the 1970s because of increased attention to smoking, diet, and fitness and the 1990s when the statin group of drugs became widely used to lower cholesterol levels. And aside from the selective use of statins after cardiovascular events, study data suggest that, if anything, there is an increase in mortality in people using statins who are not otherwise at risk of a cardiovascular event.[12]

While, therefore, there are some people, primarily in hospital care, who have already had a heart attack or stroke, who may be helped by cholesterol screening, widespread and indiscriminate cholesterol testing in society in general with the consequent treatment with statins that slightly elevated cholesterol readings almost inevitably lead to, may in fact lead to as much harm as good.

Since the development of the statins in the 1990s, pharmaceutical companies have put a premium on getting doctors to test for cholesterol and on prompting patients to find out about their cholesterol levels. Today, almost all adults in the United States, and increasingly people elsewhere, know their cholesterol levels. This campaign was facilitated by the fact that most routine blood tests that have been run since the 1980s have included those for cholesterol levels. As guidelines on cholesterol management began to recommend ever lower cholesterol levels, results that would not have been seen as problematic only a few years previously, began to trigger panic in doctors. In this way company marketing has effectively achieved the first case of mass screening for which informed consent was not sought.

While the cholesterol-lowering statins grew to become a $30 billion a year market in the late 1990s, it was also becoming clear that simply lowering cholesterol did not provide a person much benefit. Indeed, the drugs could be risky in their own right, and cholesterol itself, scientists were finding, was not without benefits. This however did not put a break on statin sales—the numbers were "refined." Popular articles and medical reports began to distinguish between high and low density cholesterol and their ratio to each other, as well as triglycerides and fatty acids (which are further lipids found in blood). Where we all might have had an average overall cholesterol level before, it was becoming increasingly unlikely that any of us would be absolutely "normal" on all these measures and could walk out of a doctor's office without being proffered a drug to match our numbers, even though the attention that cholesterol and other lipids now receive in medical encounters is out of all proportion to their clinical usefulness.[13]

Extrapolation from studies that demonstrated a benefit in men already ill to the rest of us has led to claims that "balancing" our lipids will reduce our future risk.[14] This is a completely mythical balancing, rather like remedying a supposed imbalance of neurotransmitters with antidepressants. Several studies have suggested there may be as much if not more benefit to be gained from adopting a Mediterranean diet, which is more likely to increase than reduce cholesterol levels.[15] For women in particular, the data suggests that attempting to reduce cholesterol levels may increase mortality.[16] Alarmingly women without coronary artery disease now constitute almost a quarter of those taking statins with almost 10 percent of women over the age of seventy being on statins.[17] More generally 40 percent of people taking a statin have no history of coronary artery disease.[18]

These developments have been driven by a series of studies designed to map out norms for cholesterol and lipid levels, the achievement of which would supposedly lead to minimal or no risk of cardiovascular events.[19] There is a set of cholesterol levels that is linked to almost no cardiovascular events—levels found in teenagers or people in their twenties. But these levels are linked to no cardiovascular events because cardiovascular events almost never happen at this age. There is thus no particular reason to believe that cholesterol levels in this range protect against strokes. Nevertheless, it is just these values that have been set up as the normal range for adults of every age. According to norms like these, 94 percent of New Zealand's population has elevations of their lipid levels that carry some risk.[20]

It is a clear contradiction to set up as a normative standard a level according to which 94 percent of a population is abnormal. These may be optimal cholesterol levels but they are not normal levels. This is akin to what happened with the advent of drugs like Viagra, when impotence was reconfigured as erectile dysfunction. Impotence had been a disorder of men who were completely or close to completely unable to function. But the marketers have progressively redefined the target so that now even twenty-year-olds, who from time to time have an erection that falls in any way short of full rigidity, are invited to think of themselves as having a condition that could benefit from treatment and are encouraged to see a pill as a way out of anxiety.

In the case of cholesterol, the context in which any discussion of cholesterol levels made sense—where patients had a history of heart attacks in their family, smoked, were obese, and were also hypertensive—was progressively stripped away, so that the clinical gaze now focuses on the numbers themselves and their deviation from norms, partly because here is an area where a drug can be prescribed and a doctor can document that something has been done.

Just being constantly reminded of our own numbers on a scale of cholesterol norms can seduce. Even someone like me who knows better, who knows that cholesterol levels are for the most part meaningless in terms of overall health, when faced with his own lipid numbers, if these are thought to be even marginally too high, is likely to be unnerved or perhaps challenged. "I know there's no real need to get this marginally elevated level down, but hey, let's see what I can do." Faced with an apparent deviation of our numbers from the norm, some of us can "feel" our arteries clog up on the spot and would find it almost impossible to do nothing.

Just as Sanjeebit Jachuk found his patients began suffering after a diagnosis of hypertension where they had been fine before (see chapter 3), so also many readers of this book would likely start to suffer from the effects they imagine excessive cholesterol brings if faced with their lipid levels. Once we only visited a doctor when we were suffering and we hoped to leave in a happier frame of mind about relief in the offing, often later grateful for an encouragement that we did not know at the time defied the numbers. Now we are much more likely to start suffering when some nonessential blood test, health program, or ad prompts us to visit a doctor, who is unlikely to counsel us to leave well enough alone.

At the epicenter of this are the companies who have cholesterol-lowering drugs to market. This is a market worth $35 billion per annum, with the best seller, Pfizer's Lipitor, making over $12 billion worth of sales in 2008. At the heart of the marketing of Lipitor have been a series of ads that have pulled no punches. One shows the soles of the feet of a corpse in the morgue, with a name tag on its left big toe, and a strap line on the side—Which would you rather have, a cholesterol test or a final exam? Another shows an open heart with its traceries of blood vessels and a strap line—Lipitor reduces risk of heart attacks by 36 percent. Behind claims like this, there is typically a study in which 3 percent of older men with a history of heart problems and other risk factors have a heart attack on placebo compared with 2 percent taking Lipitor or whichever drug—this is a 50 percent reduction in what is called relative risk in contrast to absolute risk. But even for consumers alert to this piece of trickery, there is nothing in the ad to let women or men with no history of heart problems know that these figures for risk reduction do not apply to them.

Pressure like this makes the idea of taking something that might lower lipids very seductive. So much so that even though using pills to lower cholesterol appears to increase mortality, the pill becomes a solution to the problem that attention to cholesterol levels has created. This follows the standard recipe for pulling a rabbit out of a hat—first put rabbit in hat.

A UNIVERSE TURNED RISKY

A remarkably similar dynamic has been playing out around another set of measurements. When I trained in the 1970s, osteoporosis was a rare disorder that involved an excessive thinning or weakening of bones, leading to an increased rate of fractures, which was diagnosed occasionally in older women who had unexpected fractures in response to minor traumas. It was also known that there was some loss of calcium in the bones of women after the menopause, but this was not seen as a particular problem.

In the 1970s with the marketing of hormone replacement therapy (HRT) for menopausal women the idea emerged that one of the benefits of treatment might be to keep women's bones young.[21] When in the 1980s, pharmaceutical sales of HRT fell following suggestions that it might lead to breast cancer, Wyeth, one of the primary makers of HRT, helped sponsor a more aggressive marketing of osteoporosis, and it began to be portrayed as a much more ominous disorder. This promotional campaign featuring a benefit of HRT to counter attention to possible risks turned around the sales of HRT.[22]

But osteoporosis only properly came into vogue after 1988 and the development of DXA (dual energy X-ray absorptiometry) scans. Using minimal radiation these low-cost machines measure bone density, something that had not been done before. In one sense the findings came as no surprise—there was variation around different sites in the body and in older women there was some thinning compared to women in their twenties. Across the lifespan, though, while women in their twenties have denser bones, they are perhaps the most abnormal: if we take both children, who have the thinnest bones, and older women into account, then bone densities as found in women in their twenties are far from being the norm for females.

DXA scans offered a golden opportunity to redefine osteoporosis, just as weighing scales did with refashioning standards of beauty. Women now were said to have the disease if their scans showed that bones in some part of their body had densities that were a standard amount less than the densities found in women in their twenties. All of a sudden one-third of postmenopausal women found themselves diseased.[23] A further large group of women—and their doctors—were faced with another problem. These were the women who fell in between the supposed optimal bone state of women in their twenties and the new diseased state. For women whose bones fell between these states a completely new condition was invented, osteopenia (literally, "less bone"). Women with osteopenia are at no increased risk of a fracture compared to their "normal" peers.

Two factors combined to ensure that the transformation in our perceptions to make room for this disorder would be particularly rapid.

One was that two companies, Merck and Procter and Gamble, were competing to be the market leader with products from a new drug group—the biphosphonates. Merck's Fosamax was up against Procter and Gamble's Actonel in a billion dollar battle. Both companies saw DXA scans as the way forward to increased sales and they competed to provide scanners for free to doctors—who of course could charge a fee for scanning.[24]

The biphosphonate drugs conveniently provided an answer to the image of bone thinning—offering, at least in popular understanding, to remineralize bones. Given to women with severe reductions in bone densities, the biphosphonates can reduce what are called fragility fractures—hairline fractures primarily of the vertebrae that are picked up on X-ray without the person ever being aware they have had anything wrong. However, there is no difference between those on the drug and those not in the number of women who present to their doctors with an obvious fracture. Somewhere between 80 and 90 percent of women to whom biphosphonates are now given are unlikely to get even the X-ray changes in the rate of hairline fractures, and in some of those with minimal reductions in bone densities the biphosphonates have been linked to increased rates of fractures of long bones such as the femur.[25] Aside from increased risks of fractures, up to one-third of women given biphosphonates will have significant gastric distress, a small number (1 in 10,000) will get osteonecrosis (bone death) of the jaw or other bones, and an unknown number will develop generalized pain syndromes, or eye problems including blindness, or cardiac problems that may increase the risk of a stroke.[26] The difficulty in knowing how many will suffer from these complications is that the company trial data is almost unbelievable—in the company trials that have been released the rates of gastric problems are the same on the active drug as for the placebo.

These risks might be worth running for those rare women who have a clinically established form of osteoporosis if there were good evidence that medication could help or help as much as getting fit. There is good evidence that factors such as levels of a person's physical fitness are better predictors of fractures than are bone densities, and good evidence that encouraging women to improve their fitness will reduce their fracture rates.[27] But fitness clinics don't distribute articles with the results of controlled trials demonstrating such benefits of good exercise, whereas doctors are bombarded with articles in which an artful use of statistics appears to confirm a benefit to drug treatment, and women are subjected to ubiquitous advertisements on the benefits of the drug.

And just as with the statins, for both doctor and patient prescribing a pill can seem easier than changing a lifestyle.

From the 1990s onward magazines for teenage girls began to feature discussions of osteoporosis. While none of these adolescents will have been the direct target of marketing by Merck and Procter and Gamble, still the change in culture these companies have created feeds through to all women, reinforcing the message in ads that are directly aimed at older women. Messages such as those in a Merck ad showing a very attractive woman apparently emerging from the bath, with a towel discreetly held to her upper chest but displaying enough of her body for the ad to be confident you will give a positive answer to its first question, "See how beautiful sixty can look?" This is followed by a further question, "See how invisible osteoporosis can be?" The sidebar then tells us that one in two women sixty and over have osteoporosis, and that while it may be invisible it leads on to broken bones and a dowager's hump. This Merck ad is not for Fosamax by name; instead it asks women to ask their doctor if a bone density test might be right for them.

The numbers that come from bone density scans and blood tests for cholesterol set up a new normality. If our numbers are abnormal, we almost immediately begin to feel at risk—dis-eased. And here we come to a key point. Whereas for centuries medicine had almost exclusively been about the treatment of diseases in the sense of biological disorders that posed an immediate threat to our lives, and still is in much of the world, Western medical practice now is increasingly about the management of risks—and this increasingly creates dis-ease.

When it came to treating diseases, epidemics aside, usually only a relatively small number of people had them. In the West much greater numbers are at risk as now defined. There are thousands of women with technical osteoporosis now for every one with clinical osteoporosis in the past, thousands with checklist depression now for every one with melancholia in the past, and entire populations with lipid abnormalities where hypercholesterolemia had been a rare disorder in the past.

In early twentieth century, we were rescued from the problems of a previous generation of celebrity drugs by the laboratory work of scientists and doctors from Robert Koch to Richard Cabot and others. Many physicians today remain confident that mapping of the human genome and other scientific developments will save us from the ravages of disease tomorrow. But there is a critical difference: the bacteriology of Koch alerted us to an external threat such as cholera, anthrax, or tuberculosis that we could mobilize against, whereas the mapping of the human genome promises to extend the riskiness of our universe. There are likely to be a much greater number of genetic markers for small degrees of risk than there will be genes for diseases. How do we mobilize against the uncertainties of the human body itself?

Furthermore, whereas the treatment of disease stops once the disease clears up, when it comes to managing risk, treatment potentially goes on forever. There is no natural endpoint except death itself. Where medicine once aimed at eliminating disease, now, for a pharmaceutical company, the trick is to persuade as many people as possible that they are at risk of a multitude of "diseases" and to convince doctors that these are all conditions that should be tested for and treated.

Insofar as being alive is risky, a health products market devoted to risk management has the potential to swallow up huge domains of our experience. Hitherto, sensibly or not so sensibly, we have often seen the risks in being alive in spiritual terms. But where before it was ascetics who attempted to control their bodies by fasting and punishment, now almost all ages and both sexes go to the same extremes in the name of health. Where once people in the West were said to have been born with an original stain, now we feel as though we have been born with a warranty—and if anything goes wrong we want to know who is to blame. Where once the focus was on living well in order to die well, now it is more likely to be on living well in order not to die, or at least to put off its eventuality as long as possible. There is a potential here not just for a health market, but for an ersatz religious universe. And if you're a drug company executive, there's opportunity here to sell not just pills but something closer to a sacrament.

In previous times we passed on a culture to our children embodied in fairy tales, folklore about health, national myths, and religious precepts, in which the life's risks were put in a larger context of meaning. Now an increasing part of what is transmitted centers on personal health for its own sake: figures for sugar and lipid levels, as increasing numbers of our children have diabetes or other dangerous metabolic states, or figures for peak respiratory flows as increasing numbers of young people have asthma, or statistics on some chemical imbalance as increasing numbers are being treated for ADHD, depression, or anxiety. Not only is such a culture two-dimensional, it changes the very nature of human experience.

MEASURING DIS-EASE

The new focus on blood sugars, blood lipids, bone density, and the like has transformed the encounters between doctors and patients. But the change has not come simply from blood tests and other obvious measurements. It has also come from the use made of scales developed to measure aspects of behavior. These rating scales were needed in trials of antidepressants, tranquilizers, analgesics, hypnotics, drugs for sexual dysfunction, and other drugs used to modify behavior, for the same reasons as cholesterol levels are needed in statin trials and DXA scans in biphosphonate trials. In lieu of evidence that patients get up from their beds and walk, feel better again, and return to work, these rating scales produce numbers that go in the right direction on treatment and can be held up as evidence that the treatments are working.

Rating scales consist of a series of items that physicians enquire about and then score the responses. In the case of depression, these typically included sleep, appetite, energy and interest levels, suicidality, feelings of guilt, and agitation. One of the very first of these scales was the Hamilton Depression Rating Scale (HDRS), published in 1960.[28] Although notionally credited to Max Hamilton, the scale was put together by Geigy to use in clinical trials of imipramine, their new antidepressant.

Many clinicians were initially skeptical of the merits of what appeared to be a basic checklist, not unlike the checklists in magazines, that the office receptionist could be easily trained to administer. Far from arguing against this clinical gripe, Hamilton apparently believed the main merit of the scale was that it facilitated the conduct of drug trials. Using the scale appeared to show imipramine and similar drugs, which increased appetite and sleep, worked compared to placebo. Clinicians could see there was a benefit with their own eyes, but rather than leave the matter to clinical judgment, the scale offered an apparently objective measure of effectiveness. But Hamilton was also aware that the wider use of such checklists might induce a substantial change in culture: "It may be that we are witnessing a change as revolutionary as was the introduction of standardization and mass production in manufacture. Both have their positive and negative sides."[29]

Forty years later, there are few clinicians who can remember that even Hamilton thought that checklists such as these were an abstraction from the richness of clinical reality. The rating scales that were initially validated by clinical judgment are now being increasingly imported into clinical practice to invalidate clinical judgment, apparently in the belief that reducing variability in the clinical encounter will make that encounter more "scientific." Whatever the merits of using a scale in a trial, it would not have made sense to Hamilton to approach every depressed patient the same way. Clinical encounters that use a rating scale will resemble each other much more than encounters with physicians where no rating scale is used. This might sound momentarily appealing—but clinical encounters based on a rating scale will also be difficult to distinguish from encounters with a receptionist trained to administer the scale, and this is not what we want from a doctor. We want the experience and discretion that goes with a clinical training rather than an encounter that ultimately could be delivered by computer.

Primary care physicians prescribe the greatest amount of psychotropic drugs these days and they are increasingly encouraged to administer depression or other behavioral rating scales when seeing patients. Many of the guidelines for prenatal care now advocate using anxiety and depression rating scales for all pregnant women. While this might pick up some women in need of treatment who would otherwise be missed, it will pick up a lot of women who aren't in fact depressed, but who because of temporary changes in sleep patterns or irritability may score in a zone of concern on rating scales one week but not the next. When the diagnosis is based on clinical judgment the estimate is that 3–4 percent of women may have a nervous disorder prenatally compared with estimates of 15–25 percent of women when the diagnosis is based simply on rating scale scores. These rating scale scores all too often translate into treatment, without further thought. As a result, the antidepressants have moved in less than ten years from being rarely used prenatally to being among the commonest drugs given in pregnancy—despite convincing evidence that they double the rate of birth defects and of miscarriages.[30]

Aware of this ambiguity in the value of rating scales—and the drug prescriptions that are likely to follow from their use—pharmaceutical companies now run symposia at major professional meetings aimed solely at introducing clinicians to rating scales. In the 1990s companies engaged in disease mongering by selling diseases such as social anxiety disorder or panic disorder in order to sell their drugs.[31] In the decade 2000–2010 what we might call measurement mongering has succeeded disease mongering as the key promotional instrument. Thus Pfizer at the 2007 American Psychiatric Association meeting, for example, supported a symposium entitled "From Clinical Skills to Clinical Scales: Practical Tools in the Management of Patients with Schizophrenia." The practical tools in question were rating scales whose items draw attention to ways in which the company's drug was superior to some others in the field. This is an ad in the form of a rating scale. It is just the same in its effects as makers of asthma drugs providing peak flow meters to doctors and Merck and Procter and Gamble providing DXA scanners, all the way back to the makers of antibiotics in the 1960s who provided thermometers to doctors.

Rating scales are not used just to sell diseases to doctors. Increasingly, companies disseminate rating scales directly to patient groups. Among the most strikingly successful maneuvers in this area has been to encourage patients with nervous problems to keep mood diaries. Getting patients to chart fluctuating emotional states has been a potent way to persuade both patients and their doctors that the patient has a bipolar disorder. In very short order, these methods have led to a boom in the diagnosis of bipolar disorder, with patients formerly seen as being depressed or anxious relabeled as bipolar and their treatment changed from one of the off-patent antidepressants to an on-patent mood stabilizer.

What has been lost since Hamilton's day is any sense that these rating scales are simply checklists. Far from being information rich, they are information poor. They may come with pompous, scientific-sounding names, but they have little more content than the checklists seen in periodicals like *Vogue* or *Esquire* that offer to map out aspects of our personal styles as lovers, socialites, or foodies. The main advantage likely to accrue from the use of these lists is to ensure that a number of questions that steer a doctor toward a particular prescription are checked off as asked. The allure to companies of these readymade questions in time-limited clinical exchanges is just this—these questions redefine clinical realities by pushing out what could be more probing and important questions that might lead away from drug treatments and toward efforts to modify lifestyles or change social situations. Increasingly, practice will be standardized—to the lowest common denominator.

When rating scales are imported into healthcare the clinical gaze risks being captured by those whose interests are served by the measurement technology. The rating scales add to company abilities to hypnotize clinicians and enfold them in a world defined by the marketing departments of pharmaceutical companies.

But it is not only the clinical gaze that is captured. The very nature of human experience can be redefined. Thus the creation of female sexual dysfunction (FSD) hinged on producing treatment changes on rating scales that include items such as clitoral numbness—because this is the kind of thing that can be tallied on a rating scale. Focusing on whether one's clitoris is numb or not, while making love, risks changing the entire experience of making love. It also creates a discontent, and perhaps focuses other discontents on this area, with a drug becoming the apparent answer to these discontents.[32]

The rating scale maps out the contours of this new condition. The measurement and disease mongering of FSD has led in recent years to women in their twenties with three young children who have lost interest in sex being encouraged to think they should have their testosterone levels checked rather than considering that their problems may stem from the circumstances in which they find themselves.[33] But aside from the women who may opt for low-dose testosterone as a result, the wider culture surrounding these issues has changed in ways that affect how all women perceive what is going on in them, in a manner analogous to the way the marketing of HRT up until recently persuaded a lot of women that being postmenopausal was to be diseased.

While rating scales, along with blood tests for cholesterol levels or bone scans for bone densities, do generate data, exclusive reliance on such data, an increasing temptation among harried doctors, leads to what I call informational reductionism. Critics have complained for decades about the biomedical reductionism that supposedly dehumanizes clinical exchanges. Reducing humans to their bodies—whether hormones or neurotransmitters or the mechanical actions of their heart—for these critics is not a fit way to treat people. But where an old-style medical encounter might lead to a focus on some important aspect of a patient's physical state, the upside of such reductionism has always been that the doctor might thereby pinpoint something that would help lift us out of some real disability or even save our life. In contrast, there is not a single benefit likely to accrue from this new informational reductionism whether embodied in lipid levels, bone density measurements, or rating scale scores—although the measurements are sold as empowering us.

In one sense measurements from mood scales to lipid levels involve new ways of looking at ourselves, and as such they can claim the mantle of scientific progress. But if they lead to overlooking context or other dimensions of an individual's functioning—dimensions that may not be open to measurement or that are simply not being measured—rather than being modestly scientific by measuring what we can and attending also to what we cannot measure, we risk being pseudoscientific. Scientific measurement and quantification succeed when they force us to look ever more closely at things while allowing us to see them in their wider contexts. By stripping away context, mindless measurement does exactly the opposite. This mindlessness is doing to medical practice something similar to what an exclusive focus on manufacturing goods driven by the target of increasing GNP is doing to the environment and the quality of life.

An older generation of clinicians would have readily made a case that even in the treatment of eating disorders weighing scales should rarely if ever be introduced. But where in the 1970s measurement technologies were considered by many an interference with clinical practice, today measurement management style is rapidly becoming the norm. Across medicine, clinicians are increasingly likely to feel uncomfortable at the prospect of encountering a patient without a battery of such technologies at the ready.

The diagnostic tests that have come into medicine since Richard Cabot's time are invaluable in some circumstances and no one would want to go back. Even the tests for bone densities or cholesterol levels and scales for aspects of behavior such as sexual functioning can be helpful. But doctors should also be able to encounter their patients as Alfred Worcester once did—person to person. The problem is that few doctors can now do this, raising the question as to whether the attempt to import into clinical care the measurement technologies needed for clinical trials, which are widely described as offering the gold standard of medical knowledge, is transforming medicine from a cottage practice into a scientific medicine or producing a golden sterility of the sort that once destroyed Midas.

The sterility of dumbed-down medicine comes through quite clearly in the case of the "operational criteria" that dominate mental healthcare. Against a background of competing views as to what constituted psychiatric disorders, in 1980 the American Psychiatric Association introduced operational criteria for its disorders into the new, third edition of its *Diagnostic and Statistical Manual (DSM-III)*.[34] From this point on, people would be said to have depression or schizophrenia or obsessive compulsive disorder if they had, say, five out of nine clinical features, or two features from column A and two from column B. The exercise was aimed at overcoming entrenched clinical biases that on the one hand saw psychiatric disorders as simply biological or on the other hand saw them as simply psychodynamic. But it was still assumed that the application of any checklist like this would require some exercise of clinical judgment so conditions such as pregnancy or influenza would be taken into account. But times have changed and a body representing both the American College of Obstetricians and American Psychiatric Association have recently suggested that 15 to 25 percent of expectant mothers may be depressed—on the basis of surveys in which women tick boxes on checklists of "depressive" symptoms.[35] These checked boxes have made antidepressants among the most commonly prescribed drugs in pregnancy.

In the wake of *DSM-III*'s publication, awareness of the criteria proposed for various disorders grew worldwide. The development of the Internet, which allowed criteria to be posted online, fostered a dramatic increase in measurement mongering to people wondering whether they met criteria for ADHD, Asperger's syndrome, PTSD, or a host of other disorders. In the extreme I have had people with successful careers in the public domain come to me after finding on the Internet that they seemed to meet criteria for Asperger's syndrome or other serious behavioral disturbances, when by virtue of their successful careers they could not have such a serious condition. Worse again, having taken the matter to mental health professionals, they found the professionals quite accepting that if they met criteria for ADHD and Asperger's syndrome they therefore had these disorders.

What is happening in the case of operational criteria is comparable to what clinicians now do faced with evidence from blood lipid levels or DXA scans—they agree the patients meet criteria for conditions for which treatments could be given. Where once doctors might have told someone not to worry about a finding or used the test results to talk to a patient about diet and lifestyle, now they will more likely default to prescribing Lipitor or Fosamax, Paxil or Zyprexa.

Making *DSM*'s operational criteria available on the Internet at the click of a mouse creates consumers in just the way giving DXA scanners to doctors did. This dynamic, amplified by the advertisements of the pharmaceutical industry, underpins the mushrooming of a range of disorders from FSD to PTSD but in particular the huge surge in diagnoses of behavioral disorders in children from bipolar disorder to ADHD, autism, Asperger's disorder, or depression—disorders that seem to clamor for a pharmacological fix.

There is a difference between meeting criteria for a disorder and having the disorder, but it takes an act of judgment informed by a culture to make the right distinctions. Severe reductions in bone density are linked to fractures, severe depression to suicide, marital breakdown, and loss of employment, and markedly raised lipids against a background of other risk factors are linked to cardiovascular events, but the availability of operational criteria for behavioral disorders, scanners for bone density, and blood tests for cholesterol have led to a far greater rate of diagnosis of a range of conditions that are, in effect, Lipitor, Fosamax or Prozac deficiency disorders rather than traditional medical disorders that come with real risks that would make treatment appropriate. We have moved from what was medicine to a new variant of horoscopy.

Meeting criteria has set up a market where both patients and doctors can feel they are doing something and doing it well. The medical response might be quite different if these drugs were not available by prescription only. But increasingly the position of the doctor has come to resemble that of the car salesman who might point out the green credentials of a hybrid car if there is one in his range, but for whom there is no incentive to advise the customer against driving as much.

Just as car salesmen compartmentalize the selling of cars from issues of climate change, so healthcare professionals increasingly segment risks according to their specialty. Doctors prescribing statins to lower cholesterol are typically happy if the drugs they prescribe do this, even though clinical trials show an increase in overall mortality if the patients who get these drugs have no other significant risks for heart attacks. In just the same way clinical trials suggest that Dianette or Ro-accutane for acne, beta-blockers for hypertension, beta-agonists (reliever inhalers) for asthma, blood-sugar-lowering agents for diabetes, rimonabant for weight loss, and varenicline or buproprion for smoking cessation can all trigger death, suicidality, or psychosis, but if the problem falls outside the usual purview of the treating doctor it is likely to remain invisible.[36] Even though the labels of these drugs come with warnings about mortality or suicide or psychosis, it can prove very difficult to get doctors to recognize the dangers and difficult to rescue patients from their doctor in these cases. Overall, drug treatments given by doctors in hospital settings are now the fourth leading cause of death in hospital settings.[37]

Given that the vast majority of medication is now given outside of hospital settings where treatment is less supervised so that problems are less likely to be detected before it is too late, one wonders what contribution drugs might be making to deaths in community settings. Where monitored by organizations such as the Institute for Safe Medication Practices, there is a 5 to 10 percent rise per year in the overall numbers of deaths or serious adverse events reported to the FDA, a large proportion of which come from blockbuster medications such as the asthma drug Singulair that Jane, described at the start of the chapter, was put on, or the diabetes drug Avandia, the mood stabilizer Seroquel, or Champix used for smoking cessation.[38]

THE LURE OF QUALITY

The mechanization and automation of production that came with the development of industry in the nineteenth century required a standard-ization of both goods and labor. At a basic level, if a machine was to be broken down into its components, new parts had to fit together just as well. For mass-produced goods ultimately to be consumed in as large quantities as possible, they had to have maximum compatibility—televisions, computers, and other electrical goods have to come with standard outlets or wireless components so that they can communicate together. And following from that, work on assembly lines that arose to facilitate manufacture of components was itself broken down into discrete segments and standardized.

From the 1970s onward, what appeared to work for industry became a model for those charged with running a health service. Against this background professional discretion seemed to perpetuate a cottage industry model and medical exchanges to involve the type of produc-tion that prevailed before mass production. What had spared medicine in previous decades was the relatively small scale of its enterprise, with inherently unpredictable demand and uncertain outcomes. Leaving it to doctors didn't cost much.

But things had begun to change. It was widely assumed in the 1950s that the rising availability of new and effective treatments to eliminate infectious and other diseases would lead to falling health costs—as ill-health was eliminated. Countries such as Britain decided it made economic sense to provide free health care: sick and diseased people drag the economy down and returning them to productive status would surely aid the economy.

Reading the literature that began to emerge in the 1970s on health costs and the efficiency of health services, whether in private healthcare systems or in socialized medical systems, however, is to encounter an astonishment among analysts at the time that, far from falling, health-care costs had begun to escalate rapidly during the 1960s, leading by the end of the decade to the first calls for cost containment and for a focus on eliminating the inefficiencies that it was assumed lay behind the rising costs. It was this set of concerns that underpinned in part the initial call for evidence-based medicine that, described in chapter 3, emerged in the 1970s. In its first manifestation advocates stressed that claims of efficacy and cost effectiveness for many medical procedures, from screening tests to high-cost coronary care units, might not be supported by the evidence. Sticking to what had been proven to work would, it was claimed, make for efficiencies and lower costs. When treatments work this is indeed what happens. But if the bills for US healthcare costs have grown from little more than 1 percent in the early post-World War II years to 17 percent of Gross Domestic Product and are continuing to grow, something else is clearly going on.

We will pick up the political question below of whether these are issues best left to the market or whether this is a point at which the government should intervene, but stepping back from this larger framework, evidence-based medicine has offered a technical response that to some held out the hope of avoiding political choices. What could be wrong with attempting to bring clinical practice up to a common standard? What could be wrong with making it more effective? Or, in management language, what could be wrong with having a quality service?

In the 1960s, to talk about quality in medicine would have conjured up visions of medical encounters to which doctors not only brought great medical skills but also were able to subordinate the clinical gaze to a concern for the situation of the person. Encounters, in other words, in which doctors were seen to have descended from the pedestal from which they had previously operated and begun to collaborate with their patients, using the new forms of evidence as a resource to determine what medical treatment best suited their patient or where their patient might be best served by looking at aspects of their lifestyle.

But this is not what has happened. Instead of our increased abilities to treat and cure in conjunction with increased funds for healthcare leading to a more humane system, the word "quality" as applied to healthcare has come to have more of an industrial meaning. Elsewhere in industry, goods or services meet quality standards if they are predictably the same each time. From this point of view, McDonald's offers a quality hamburger—even if for hamburger connoisseurs it might rank among the worst possible hamburgers.

One way to get the appearance of quality outcomes of this sort is to become increasingly a risk management service rather than a service aimed at curing diseases or caring for those who have them. It is a great deal easier to get quality outcomes in the reduction of blood pressure or blood sugar or blood cholesterol levels than it is in the treatment of strokes or heart attacks. Sugar and lipid levels invariably drop with treatment. Because of this, for managers within health care, against a background of escalating health costs, it is all but impossible not to McDonaldize their services. But focusing on this kind of outcome is rather like focusing on the valeting of a car rather than on repairing any real problems it has.

A quarter of a century ago, basing his case on the growing clamor to contain costs and the increasing premium on standardization, Thomas Bittker, a forensic psychiatrist from Reno, predicted that these essentially industrial processes would be applied to healthcare organizations, even to psychiatry, which at the time must have looked as far removed from a "quality" organization in the industrial sense as it was possible to be.[39] He outlined a world in which clinical care would be restructured just as pharmaceutical companies had been restructured in the 1960s and 1970s and the rest of industry had been restructured half a century earlier. The clinical encounter would be disassembled into its component parts and reassembled in a way that would enable managers, who clearly cannot alter the course of disease, to get as close to industry-standard quality outcomes as they could while managing their physician resource.

Bittker's predictions have all come true. Doctors, from those offering primary care to those offering respirology and mental health care, particularly in the United States, now are expected to practice according to strictly defined, brief medication management sessions with patients. So much is this the case that it is not uncommon to find American lawyers in malpractice cases referring to doctors as pharmacologists rather than doctors. Combining brief visits, which offer little chance to find out much about the person attending, with a set of disorders with which many physicians fundamentally disagree and sets of algorithms that dictate treatments with drugs that many think may well be inferior to the treatments they would wish to give, is producing an ever more dispiriting situation for many doctors.[40]

The case of Dr. N, the primary care physician discussed in the introduction, who spent his entire clinical contact time filling out forms so that he failed to recognize his patient's double amputation, while extreme, typifies where much of clinical practice is heading. In 1984, the US Public Health Service set up the Preventive Task Force, a body established to recommend what screening tests and other procedures might be put in place in primary care to improve the health of the population.[41] If primary care doctors were to implement all the screening recommendations suggested by this task force, they would have no clinical time left for the complaints that brought patients to them seeking help.[42] This is a new medicine in which good medical care is increasingly at odds with the smooth distribution of health products, a situation in which doctors practicing good medicine risk dismissal.

Present day healthcare systems employ doctors, of course, but it cannot be certain that future systems will need to do so to the same extent. The kind of quality that can be achieved screening for and managing risk factors brings these medical services into the domain of commodities in a way that could not have been done with traditional medical care. In the current jargon, these interventions can increasingly be commoditized and, rather than delivered in clinics, they might be delivered in retail outlets such as supermarkets. Something similar can be done with many basic legal services, leading to a perception that the tide is going out on professionalism.[43]

In the case of many of these medical practices, furthermore, if the drugs work well and the basic need is to have them delivered according to guidelines and algorithms, the job is likely to be done not just less expensively but possibly with greater fidelity by nurses or others if given the legal authority to dispense medicines, as both nurses and psychologists have been doing in many settings in the United States and Europe.

That the work of physicians has seemed increasingly to have become something of a factory or office job, or that doctors may have to worry about job security for the first time, will not cut much mustard with anyone who has always had to work in a factory or office. But the problem for all of us now is that there are times when we do need to be treated for diseases and cared for rather than simply risk-managed.

BEYOND MEASUREMENT

Many observers of current practices of medical care, especially those who attempt to tackle the question of medicine's interface with the market, get dewy-eyed about the vocational aspects of healthcare. While the more hard-headed analysts point out that since antiquity doctors have charged for their services, that for long periods up to the nineteenth century physicians were often indistinguishable from charlatans and quacks, and that medical organizations have often operated more as quite ruthless trade associations than as scientific bodies concerned about the welfare of patients, caring has nevertheless been held to be a great part of the medical art. Although doctors make a living out of treating sickness, they are not ordinarily thought to exploit people who are ill and vulnerable.

This is beautifully caught in the following quote by James Spence, in his day one of Europe's leading pediatricians, from a book published posthumously in 1960: "The real work of a doctor is not an affair of health centers, or laboratories, or hospital beds. Techniques have their place in Medicine, but they are not Medicine. The essential unit of medical practice is the occasion when, in the intimacy of the consulting room or sick room, a person who is ill, or believes himself to be ill, seeks the advice of a doctor whom he trusts. This is a consultation, and all else in Medicine derives from it."[44]

There is a difference between medicine of this kind, which still persists to some extent when we are very ill and in isolated pockets of practice, and the healthcare which offers us almost no time or opportunity to consult but which will screen, recall, educate, and sometimes coerce us into treatments, sometimes simply so that our "carers" can hit their targets. On one side is a healthcare in which patients unknowingly are helping doctors rather than being helped; on the other side is a form of practice that is beyond measurement.

The problem does not lie in our new technologies of curing. Penicillin and insulin allow much more effective caring than was possible before. But these drugs arose as part of a kind of medicine different from the statins for cholesterol lowering, biphosphonates for osteoporosis, or antidepressants. When doctors gave penicillin to patients they were in almost all cases helping their patients. When patients take a statin or a biphosphonate, they are in many cases, perhaps a majority of cases, helping their doctors, a drug company, or a government agency rather than themselves. Giving statins and biphosphonates routinely appears to be part of traditional medicine, but in fact these treatments are more closely linked to an approach now most commonly termed chronic disease management or preventive medicine. This approach emerged in the 1980s and led, for instance, to the establishment of the Preventive Task Force noted above. The initial impetus to this approach came from prior successes in the 1950s and 1960s screening for and eliminating infections through vaccination and other programs. A growing awareness of the role of raised blood pressure and diabetes in leading to deaths from heart attacks or strokes, as a result of reviews such as the Framingham study, appeared to provide comparable targets for screening.

There are solid economic arguments for a preventive approach to medicine. In the eighteenth century, France and Britain, wary about each other and about Germany, mapped out their citizenry and in so doing learned about links between environments and diseases, and how national productivity or defense might hinge as much on proper sanitation and the quality of food supplies as on industrial innovation. As James Lind remarked in the mid-eighteenth century, the British navy was losing more men to scurvy than to any hostile engagements with her enemies.[45] Florence Nightingale produced figures to show that more soldiers were dying in hospitals than on the battlefield in the Crimean War and went on to create modern nursing in response.[46] And Rudolf Virchow, a key person in the creation of both modern laboratory medicine and of the notion that citizens have a democratic right to health, went so far as to suggest that "medicine as social science and politics is nothing more than medicine on a grand scale."[47] Since then historical investigations have made it clear that poxes and pestilences have done more to bring down empires and economies than wars or failures in the marketplace.[48]

So what could be wrong with mass screening for cholesterol levels, mapping bone densities, and administering rating scales for undetected mood disorders? The first problem is that almost as soon as it appeared pharmaceutical companies realized that preventive medicine or chronic disease management offered the perfect cover for their marketing. Far better for companies to market a treatment doled out over decades than a brief course of antibiotics that saves a life. In the 1960s, when challenged by Senator Kefauver at the congressional hearings on the pharmaceutical industry about the high cost of their drugs, Francis Brown, the president of Schering Plough, responded "Senator, we can't put two sick people in every bed where there is only one person sick."[49] In the 1980s chronic disease management opened for industry a route to putting multiple diseases within the one patient, effectively having several different people being treated in the one body.

The second problem is that company marketing distributes the instruments that screen for what they want screened for while efforts by doctors or others to screen for more important risk factors are marginalized. In this way companies invert the hierarchy of risk. Where the advice should be "stop smoking and lose weight," it becomes "take a statin." There is little or no research on what it might be about our diets or lifestyles or environments that is leading to a surge in asthma diagnoses—the pressure is not there to research a disease that is not ordinarily fatal and for which the drugs available are so lucrative—Advair alone, the inhaler that Jane (described at the start of the chapter) was put on, is worth $8 billion per year to Glaxo-SmithKline, while the Singulair she also took is worth $5 billion to Merck despite the fact that the published studies show a minimal benefit for this treatment.

A third problem is that while there may have been a cost in terms of injuries from the vaccines and other treatments necessary to eliminate polio and other medical scourges, the benefits overwhelmingly outweighed the costs, but this is not often the case for the statins, biphosphonates, hypoglycemic agents for diabetes, beta-agonists or combined beta-agonists and steroids for asthma, or antidepressants, especially when all these drugs are given in primary care as they have to be to become blockbusters.

When it comes to managing risk factors or chronic treatment, medical discretion is called for, but such discretion is regarded as suspect by those who frame guidelines for diseases. To managers, permitting discretion appears to be a recipe to return medical practice to the cottage industry era. It is, moreover, difficult to exercise discretion when healthcare systems have been redesigned so that a doctor rarely sees the same patient on consecutive occasions or knows much about their family or circumstances.

Right through to the 1960s medicine remained a rather pure market catering to our needs to have cures to life-threatening diseases. But just as satisfying our basic needs for industrial goods half a century earlier led modern companies to focus then on marketing and the creation of ever-larger consumer demand, our liberation from servitude to many diseases laid the basis for a creation in both doctors and patients of medical wants that has underpinned the marketing of conditions such as osteoporosis, raised cholesterol levels, and a range of behavioral disorders from female sexual dysfunction to ADHD.

It also laid the basis for the emergence of the medical consumer, who would shop not just for drugs but also for services, especially services whose specification includes not only an adherence to guidelines but friendliness and the appearances of concern for the consumer. For advocates of free markets it was just this kind of consumer who would drive healthcare costs down.

But while a market of consumers of this sort can readily be envisaged for enhancement technologies from designer vaginas to optimal cholesterol levels and is perhaps the only way to handle these healthcare products, real disease is not something we consume. Like death, albeit slower, it consumes us. It may transform our identities irreversibly, in a way that no subsequent purchases can undo. We make our accommodations with disease as best we can, and since the time of Philippe Pinel that accommodation has involved a medical realization that sometimes the greatest wisdom is to do nothing other than have the medical team and the patient endure together.

Companies, however, have been so successful at restructuring the market in terms of the wants of both doctors, the primary consumers of blockbuster drugs, and patients, who are corralled by direct-to-consumer ads to seek out these treatments, that few medical or patient consumers now understand no. And this new consumer-driven market has all but swept away traditional medicine.

Is there any alternative to the health products market that appears to have replaced what once was medicine? To see where medicine might go instead, let us look at another set of productive relationships: the caring a parent, often in tandem with a whole village, gives a child that helps to produce a person. Caring of this sort remains in touch with the child's zone of proximal development so that they get the right challenges, opportunities, protections, and discipline at the right time. The right caring by a teacher or school similarly helps children develop. Caring of this sort is not at odds with technologies—mothers and teachers will want their children to have computers at an appropriate stage of development and make use of other tools of culture. It is a people, rather than raw material or technology, that ultimately forms the bedrock of an economy, especially a knowledge-based economy. It involves discretion—although this discretion is rapidly being eroded by increasing regulations about schooling requirements. These are areas, furthermore, where most of us want to limit the intrusions of both the market and the state.

This is very close to the kind of caring once found in the best of medicine, as exemplified by James Spence or Alfred Worcester—often delivered now as much by a multidisciplinary team as by an individual and increasingly dependent on cooperation between doctor and patient. Medical care of this kind is productive of people, and of human dignity—or as much dignity as a disease will allow. This caring will readily embrace the appropriate technologies, from insulin to surgery, in order to get the best possible outcome for the person. The focus on real disease that comes with such caring relegates consumption to a secondary role. No pharmaceutical company is ever likely to provide a scanner, meter, or rating scale for medical care that focuses on the person rather than a disease.

What is at issue can be illustrated by considering a doctor's role as the gateway to sick leave and disability payments. One of the most striking lessons doctors learned in World War II was that soldiers due to go on leave would often fail to report serious illness, while others with no prospects of leave became strikingly ill. The doctor was the passport out of active service, if he could be fooled into thinking you were ill. These insights were brought back from war by a generation of physicians who were more sensitive, accordingly, to the ways in which we might all be trying to escape from the prison of our circumstances—an element present in many consultations that cannot readily be measured but which may lead all of us to play along with suggestions that we have disorders like osteoporosis or mild asthma in need of management with the latest drug.

But it was only some doctors who had learned these lessons—not health economists or health planners or even all doctors, which may explain what happened next. The discovery of penicillin and streptomycin in the 1940s eliminated tertiary syphilis and tuberculosis and with these diseases the costs linked to the occupancy of thousands of beds. These cures returned thousands of people to able-bodied and productive status, thereby increasing the wealth of the nation. Further breakthroughs in the 1950s with the first treatments for asthma, first oral antidiabetic agents, first antihypertensives, first antipsychotics and antidepressants, should, if used judiciously, have increased national productivity by many multiples of what the treatments might have cost, but instead sickness rates and disability payments began to skyrocket and the costs of healthcare grew faster in the United States than elsewhere, growing from $100 per person per annum in 1950 ($500 per annum in today's prices) to $7,681 per person per annum in 2008.[50]

There was an increase in productivity but much less than in other countries. Where US medicine led the world in the 1960s, in 2000 the World Health Organization ranked the United States 72nd on what it termed health system attainment and performance and 24th from among 191 countries worldwide in terms of overall health, as measured by indices such as infant mortality and life expectancy,[51] while in 2008 the Commonwealth Fund ranked the United States last among developed countries in terms of quality of healthcare.[52]

One of the factors contributing to a comparative decline in American life expectancy rates is most visible among the elderly. Recent years have seen a startling rise in the extent of polypharmacy, where people are given several different drugs at the same time. It might not be so surprising to find that some people take both a treatment for asthma and for osteoporosis, but as Jane found when being treated for asthma alone few people end up with less than three different treatments. Similarly it is common in the mental health domain to find people on cocktails of four or more drugs rather than just an antidepressant. People with two conditions may be on seven to eight drugs. And ten drugs or more is fast becoming the norm for the elderly especially in the United States. But in this age group, in addition to the problems caused by each block-buster drug, there are the problems caused by the increased likelihood of interactions between them. In the elderly the rate of hospitalization due to adverse drug reactions is six times higher than in the young and rises sharply in proportion to the number of drugs being taken.[53]

It is almost impossible to get data linking polypharmacy to produc-tivity, because doctors simply do not collect it and companies have no incentive to look at it. Pharmaceutical companies have detailed data on what every doctor prescribes and use the data to spur their sales force on just like an athlete uses a stopwatch, but doctors only record and report one in a hundred of the deaths or serious injuries that happen on drugs. None of our measurements track people. Whether you think we are dealing with poisons to be used judiciously or fertilizers to be given out indiscriminately, few people can ingest ten or more chemicals given together without toxic effects—but we don't track this.

A recent report from the Congressional Budget Office identified the growth of prescription-only medicines and other high-tech medical developments as the greatest contributor to escalating costs of medical care in the United States.[54] But aside from the raw costs of drugs, phar-maceuticals contribute in many other ways to our rising health costs. If the increasing costs of drugs led to people being more productive this could be justified, but as we have seen repeatedly many of our more recent treatments if used injudiciously, as the clinical trials we have reviewed have shown, will injure and kill more than they save. Despite this evidence, the media hype surrounding new treatments raises expec-tations and leads people to seek medical care when they don't really need it. When companies manufacture new diseases (disease monger-ing) they also pull people into medical care who don't need it. In all these cases, as Sanjeebit Jachuk found back in the 1980s, a significant proportion of people will be made less healthy and less productive.

Finally, the drugs bring in their wake a fetish with measurement. In the face of ever-escalating costs doctors can only afford to do things that come with an evidence base demonstrating they "work." But here we run into a paradox. While the evidence from trials of many drugs, as discussed in chapter 3, shows that watchful waiting may help far more patients than intervening with an active drug, watchful waiting cannot be shown in its own right to "work." It can't be measured against anything. As a result, there is no longer any basis for medical discretion, no basis for a consultation. This is a world in which doctors are forced to adhere to guidelines and provide unambiguous benefits that can be demonstrated for instance when the figures on a peak flow meter go the right way. A world in which it only makes sense for insurance companies to reimburse for visible disorders of the type demonstrable on DXA scans or through blood cholesterol markers and for treatments that look good on company-run trials and sold on the promise that despite their cost doing what works will ultimately bring healthcare costs down.

In a world where measurement has such powerful effects, it seems more than ironic that measurements such as the ones cited for health-care costs and life expectancy have so little effect in galvanizing reform or seem only to demoralize us and perhaps inhibit our abilities to do anything. What is it that doctors and patients today are missing that might help them restore "care" to medicine, or what is it that they are up against that seems so difficult to grapple with?

7

The Eclipse of Care

Cora was eighteen and beautiful. Slim, with long blond hair, about average height. She had just finished high school, where she had been the homecoming queen. She was set to attend college, though she wasn't certain what direction to take there. She had a boyfriend but was worried he might want to leave her, while at the same time knowing her parents didn't approve of him.

At a rock festival with her boyfriend, she got lost and, trying to find him, had taken a fall and injured her arm. She was admitted to a local hospital for treatment and sent home from there. Several days later, in a state of perplexity she was brought to the psychiatric unit where I have inpatient beds.

Had she been traumatized or abused in some way? Had she been taking drugs and had a trip gone awry? Had her boyfriend left her? Her mental state was quite unstable, but despite having input from the many people involved in looking after someone in hospital I couldn't make a diagnosis I was happy with. Cora was not hearing voices, did not have delusional beliefs, and was not consistently depressed, elated, or anxious. But she was volatile. At times in the ensuing weeks, apparently improved, I gave her leave to go out with her parents, but she was typically brought back severely confused again—sometimes only minutes after having walked out through the hospital doors. At other times she was almost completely unresponsive and inaccessible. I could see no reason to give her an antidepressant or an antipsychotic. On occasion when she seemed particularly agitated I wrote her up for a minor tranquilizer—a benzodiazepine.

Finally after about six weeks she went on weekend leave with her parents, held steady on her own, and did not come back. I was happy to file her case as diagnosis unknown. I heard she was doing well at college and was still dating the same boyfriend.

I saw her again a year later—8 1/2 months pregnant. She was clearly too unwell to be managed at home. But where she had been mute and inaccessible previously, now she was overactive, manipulative, and attention-seeking while still seeming confused; her actions did not seem fully under her own control. She looked as though she might go into labor at any moment, so I held off medication.

After the birth, I sent her to a hospital that had a facility for new mothers and their babies. The psychiatric team that took over her care there, I learned, thought she had schizophrenia. She was put on regular antipsychotics but apparently was not making much progress and the baby was taken from her. Some months later, I heard she had been given weekend leave; one evening, having told her parents she was going out for a walk, she laid her neck on the track in the face of an oncoming express train.

Looking back at Cora's confusion, emotional lability, and switches between immobility and overactivity, I came to see that she had a text-book case of uncomplicated catatonia. Few readers of this book will know what catatonia is, as it has supposedly vanished, even though fifty years ago up to 15 percent of patients in asylums were estimated to suffer from it, and it was one of the most horrifying mental illnesses. While mental health professionals are aware catatonia is still listed in the *Diagnostic and Statistical Manual,* few would spot a case if faced with it.

If Cora had a rare condition that doctors do not now need to recognize, if she was the exception that proves the rule of medical progress, she would have been unfortunate. But in fact up to 10 percent of patients going through mental health units in the United States and indeed worldwide still have the features of catatonia—if these were looked for.[1] Sometimes the only condition they have is catatonia; other times catatonic features complicate another disorder and resolving the catatonia may make it easier to clear whatever other problem is present. But almost no one thinks of catatonia and so, like me, they miss the diagnosis. Cora was given antipsychotics, which are liable to make a catatonic syndrome worse. She died when a few days' of consistent treatment with a benzodiazepine would almost certainly have restored her to normal, making her death scandalous rather than accidental.

The benzodiazepines are a group of drugs that are no longer on patent, and thus no company has any incentive to help doctors see what might be in front of their eyes when it comes to a disease like catatonia. Instead, company exhortations are to attend to diseases for which on-patent drugs are designed, even if this means diseases conjured out of thin air—disease mongering—such as fibromyalgia to market on-patent medications such as Pfizer's Lyrica (pregabalin) or restless legs syndrome, a disorder conjured up as a target for GlaxoSmithKline's Requip (ropinirole).[2]

No one has any idea how many versions of Cora's story play out in daily clinical practice, the opportunity cost of disease mongering. These deaths are lost in the chatter about disorders that match up with on-patent drugs, invisible to doctors pleased with themselves for making a fashionable diagnosis like fibromyalgia and who, even in the face of treatment failure, will add ever more on-patent drugs to a patient's treatment regimen rather than go back to the drawing board and look more closely at the patient in front of them. Once upon a time the height of medical art lay in being able to go back and look at cases afresh and match the profile of symptoms against less fashionable or apparently uncommon disorders—no longer.[3]

But the outlines of an even more disturbing series of scandalous deaths have emerged from the pages of this book. Unlike catatonia, deaths in this case are from a disorder with no name. It is never recorded on death certificates as a cause of death even though we suspect that in hospital settings nearly two decades ago it was the fourth leading cause of death,[4] and reports to regulators of deaths from this cause increase annually.[5] It is almost certainly commoner now as drug prescriptions have escalated, and even commoner in community settings than in the hospital, but yet in an evidence-based medicine and guideline-driven era, there is no evidence base or guideline for its management.

If we are to cure this disease, we clearly need to name it. This is a disorder that was formerly sidelined as iatrogenic but if missing or corrupted data lie at the root of the problem, getting doctors to shoulder the blame—as iatrogenic suggests—no longer seems correct. A possible name is pharmakosis—a name that hints at some loss of insight.[6]

Here is where the interplay between cure and care, outlined in earlier chapters, comes into clearest focus. The critical test of medical care lies in how a doctor or medical system deals with the possibility that the latest treatment might be responsible for part of a patient's current problems—that the poison may actually be poisoning. Rather than care, for over a century we have had a default option to regard cures as an excellent form of care. But here is a disorder to cure, which offers no choice between cure and care—they are one and the same.

Thalidomide is the drug disaster that is classically seen as inaugurating our modern medical era but retrospectively it looks more like a bookend for an older style of medicine than representative of the problems that drug treatments and pharmaceutical companies now pose. Most of us, whether doctors or patients, likely think we can link problems as obvious as those caused by thalidomide to treatments we might have taken. But we are not faced with such obvious problems any more. The difficulties in grappling with what happens when treatments go wrong now come instead from the mechanisms put in place to ensure thalidomide could not happen again—these include controlled trials, a prescription-only status for drug treatments, and efforts to restrict drug use to traditional medical diseases. The story of tolbutamide, whose development paralleled that of thalidomide, brings out far better the difficulties we now face.

WHEN TREATMENT GOES WRONG

The discovery of insulin in 1922 is one of the most celebrated breakthroughs in medicine. A disease that came with sweet-smelling and frequent urine had been recognized in antiquity and had been named diabetes. It was occasionally possible to manage the disorder, which we now know is caused by a lack of insulin leading to raised blood sugars, for a time in older people by restricting sugar intake, but sweet-smelling urine heralded the end for most people. In childhood, the disease was even more malignant; for juvenile-onset diabetes, the discovery of insulin was the difference between life and death.

After 1924, the availability of insulin meant that a growing number of people could survive for decades longer than had been possible before that. Still, as those treated aged, a series of complications of living with diabetes became clear. The blood vessels of the eye might deteriorate, leading to blindness. Damage to the blood vessels or nerves to the pelvis brought about impotence. The nerves or bloods vessels to the legs might be compromised, leading to ulcers, possibly gangrene, and potentially amputation. The risk of heart attacks and strokes was increased.

It seemed reasonable at the time to think that these problems in part stemmed from the mismatch between naturally and artificially controlled blood sugars and in part from the fact that the insulin initially used was bovine or porcine rather than human insulin. But whatever the cause of such problems, people were alive who wouldn't have been alive and while they were alive the problems could be worked on. Perhaps improved preparations of insulin would reduce the risk of complications.

In an effort to improve the care of patients with diabetes, researchers renewed their focus on blood sugars and discovered that these vary substantially during the day in everyone, but especially in patients with diabetes. Might a tight control of blood sugar variability improve outcomes? Controlling blood sugars requires gadgets to read sugar levels and a range of insulin preparations. It also requires close cooperation between the medical team delivering care and the patient with the disease.

The teamwork that grew up around monitoring the hazards of diabetes and its treatment during the 1940s and 1950s became a byword for good medical care. Giving injections of insulin sounds simple, but there is a technique to giving the treatment subcutaneously. You need to learn what the symptoms of an overdose might be—slightly too much insulin risks reducing blood sugars to the point where the taker becomes confused or slips into a coma. Strategies have to be worked out to manage this hazard. The effort to balance the risks that come from allowing blood sugar levels to ride at too high a level and the risks inherent in reducing them too aggressively has to be incorporated into lives that need to be lived. A workman doing heavy labor will have to juggle things in a different way than a ghostwriter working by computer from home. Some people need gadgets to check their blood sugar levels, others seem able to read their bodies.[7]

Getting this right requires teamwork. The nurses of the diabetes team learn from Mr. X how he manages to slot the need for blood testing and injections into his schedule, while Ms. Y tells them of how she manages. They hear about how people juggle social situations, from business meals to outdoor activities with friends. And they pass these lessons on to new patients who have to be helped to handle the ramifications of a diabetes diagnosis at the right pace for them. If medical care is key to how well patients use the technologies available, and therefore how well they do, advance in technology is key to inching forward in treatment possibilities. Teamwork, in turn, helps make the best possible use of those new technologies—such as the new pills that were discovered in the 1950s that could, in tandem with insulin, better manage blood sugars.

While insulin mobilized all the best in medicine, it did not provide a good basis for business. Lilly attempted to wrest the American patent for insulin away from its discoverers—the University of Toronto—but failed.[8] But even had they succeeded, the commercial opportunities for an injection were limited, even though insulin was quickly used for all sorts of things other than just diabetes. The drug's appetite-increasing properties were put to use in rest cures aimed at "building people up" through a program of sleep and eating. In high doses insulin will induce a coma—the ultimate rest cure—and insulin-induced coma treatment was used to treat drug abuse and schizophrenia.[9] Despite all these uses, a pill would be far better for business than any injection because a much greater number of people have raised blood sugars (prediabetes) than have frank diabetes and this market would be easier to develop with a pill than with an injection.

The research that led to a pill that seemed promising stemmed from the first of modern medicine's magic bullets, the sulfanilamide antibiotics that were discovered in Germany just prior to the outbreak of World War II.[10] Building on these discoveries, French investigators soon developed a range of sulfa drugs, among which was one that lowered blood sugars. Despite the devastation of war, it was in fact a German company, Boehringer-Ingelheim, that in 1956 came up with the first oral blood-sugar-lowering drug (a hypoglycemic drug), carbutamide, and soon thereafter another—tolbutamide.

The Michigan-based Upjohn company bought the US rights for tolbutamide and began marketing it as Orinase in 1961. It effectively lowered blood sugar, but it turned out to be close to useless for the management of juvenile-onset diabetes. It would not replace insulin, then, but it might have a place in the treatment of patients who developed diabetes in their middle to older years who had been able to manage their condition by diet alone before they eventually graduated to insulin.

The availability of tolbutamide led to distinctions between type 1, or insulin-dependent diabetes, and type 2, or noninsulin-dependent diabetes. Where before there had been little emphasis on seeking out information on blood-sugar elevations, as few people wanted to know about diabetes until they had to, there was a new premium on detection. For people who had elevated levels of blood sugars but who were not overtly diabetic, dieting offered a means to help regulate their blood sugars, but this was hard work. Tolbutamide was an easier option. It even seemed possible that treating high blood sugars early might prevent people from developing diabetes. In addition, supplementing insulin with tolbutamide might minimize the requirement for insulin and offer better control of blood sugars, potentially reducing problems in the longer run.

In 1961 a long-term study by the National Institutes of Health (NIH) involving over a thousand patients began in which Upjohn's tolbutamide was compared to insulin, placebo, and an amphetamine derivative developed by Smith Kline & French, phentermine, which it was thought might help because it suppressed appetite and led to weight loss. In 1967, a problem came to light: more patients were dying on tolbutamide than on phentermine, insulin, or placebo. The result ran completely against expectation, as the trial protocol excluded anyone thought to be at risk of dying, and controlling blood sugars should have reduced the risk of complications.[11]

Had some of the treatment centers failed to adhere to the protocol or was there some other explanation of the findings? The investigators could find no explanation aside from some possible side effect of tolbutamide, and in 1969, the study was terminated so as not to put any patients on tolbutamide at further risk. The investigators consulted with Upjohn and the FDA, and an FDA meeting to discuss the study was organized for May 1970. The results of the study were not expected to be made public until an American Diabetics Association meeting the following month.

However, the study results appeared first in the business section of the *Washington Post,* just prior to the FDA meeting. The study, it seemed, had implications for the health of Upjohn that were of concern to many in the commercial sector. The first that many physicians knew of the issue was when anxious patients faced them in the clinic that day with the news. Close to a million people were on tolbutamide in the United States—a lot of anxious patients. This was not the way anyone was used to things happening in medicine.

Patients in many cases found that their doctors seemed personally offended, as if their judgments in putting the patient on this treatment were being questioned. But the doctors were stymied. Their patients didn't know what was going on, but neither did the doctors.[12] These doctors flooded the FDA with letters suggesting the bureaucrats had no idea how much distress this was causing patients. The FDA scrambled to respond but they too were faced with a novel situation. It had never been part of the FDA's brief to tell doctors how to practice medicine. They left the NIH academics to fight it out with academics recruited by or otherwise taking Upjohn's side.

Patients also sought out the FDA—asking the agency whether it was still safe to take tolbutamide. Some had worked out from the figures given in the media that over a decade tolbutamide may have killed more Americans than had then been killed in the Vietnam War. How could such a drug still be on the market? The FDA directed patients back to their doctor, still, the agency said, the person best placed to decide the right course of action for them.

The FDA was at pains to insist it was not involved in the practice of medicine and did not wish to subvert clinical judgment. As Senator Kefauver put it in the debate surrounding the 1962 Kefauver-Harris amendments to the FDA bill, introduced after the thalidomide crisis and aimed at controlling the pharmaceutical industry's inappropriate marketing of drugs, "It should be made very clear to Senators and to the country; this is not a Federal control bill. This is a Federal informa- tion bill. . . . I am not talking about regulating medicine between the physician and the patient."[13]

Many clinicians simply refused to believe the findings on tolbuta- mide. They were not used to having data trump their common sense. Perhaps there were more dead bodies in a trial of the drug, but these doctors had given tolbutamide to hundreds of patients, few if any of whom had dropped dead. Besides, how could trials like this take into account all the people whose lives must have been saved by having their blood sugars better controlled? It didn't make sense that a drug doing something so obviously right could be causing problems, no matter what a fancy controlled trial cooked up by some academics might have shown.

Upjohn moved quickly to mobilize a coalition of experts to cast doubt on the NIH research. These company-recruited academics pointed to a number of tolbutamide trials in which, they claimed, there had been no hint of a problem. While these trials were smaller, there were many trials on one side, with only one, albeit larger, trial pointing to a serious problem on the other. The insults began to fly between the academics, with one side accusing the other of being hysterical publicity seekers, attempting only to advance their careers, and the other pointing to the conflicts of interest stemming from participation in Upjohn-convened panels.[14] Tolbutamide remained on the market without warnings until the 1980s.

In the meantime, the availability of tolbutamide had put a new premium on detecting elevations of blood sugar. Because of this, when any of us have the most basic of blood screens, the results will include blood sugar levels. Studies of those results concluded that, as of 2008, 30 percent of Western populations have either diabetes or prediabetes. In the wake of such findings, majority medical opinion supported treatment for such patients as early as possible with the hypoglycemic successors to tolbutamide.[15]

A further National Institutes of Health trial, however, reported in 2008 that tight control of blood sugars with tolbutamide's hypoglycemic successors led in fact to a higher death rate than was found in patients whose blood sugar control was allowed to vary more.[16] By 2008 a series of blood-sugar-lowering drugs from Rezulin to Avandia either had to be withdrawn from the market or were required to carry warnings after evidence emerged that they too were linked to excess mortality. Nevertheless, the hypoglycemic market remains one of the blockbuster markets, in 2010, worth over $25 billion per annum and showing growth of 10 percent per annum. This has been a market in which the best teamwork and care in medicine has been harnessed to company sales, but if the data are to be believed, this teamwork is in fact now delivering at least some patients to an earlier death than they might have otherwise had.

The story of tolbutamide prefigures a series of crises that developed around Prozac in the 1990s and Vioxx in 2005. But in 1970, the issues were new for the regulators. Before the amendments to the US Food and Drugs Act triggered by thalidomide in 1962, such conflicts would have been straight contests between doctors and industry. It was in fact the number of doctors who spoke out, at a risk to their careers, that brought the problems with thalidomide originally to light. The public, however, attributed the discovery to the actions of the FDA and as a result for the first time saw in the FDA a third party whom they might turn to for help.

THE WIZARD OF OZ

When asked what a regulatory agency does, many involved in healthcare respond that agencies like the FDA, either in a commissioning capacity or in conjunction with universities, even if supported by pharmaceutical companies, are responsible for the clinical trials that bring drugs to market. In this view, the agency, directly or through independent investigators cooperating with them, designs the protocols for trials, arranges for the conduct of the research, collects, tabulates, and analyzes the data that academics then write up in articles that faithfully represent the data. These articles are peer-reviewed, and especially if outlining notable advances, they are likely to appear in the most distinguished journals, offering further assurance, so it is thought, of the validity of the data and the conclusions presented. It is also commonly assumed that the FDA in some way houses the raw data so that should a problem develop with a drug after marketing, someone independent of the pharmaceutical industry can consult the data and determine whether there is cause for concern. None of this is the case.

What most people think the FDA now does is very much what the American Medical Association used to do with all new drugs from the 1940s to the mid- 1950s but does not do now. Once the AMA stopped doing this, except in the increasingly rare instances, such as the NIH tolbutamide studies, in which the government or an independent institution decides to do a study itself, there is no independent research done on new drugs. When it comes to the study of drug treatments, the medical profession has been eclipsed. The public think the FDA has stepped into the breach but in fact pharmaceutical companies now control everything.

Companies decide which trials to conduct, which ones to make public, and what data to release. The trials are designed not only to gain regulatory approval but also to test for characteristics that fit company marketing requirements and may bear little relationship to what some of the drug's most telling effects are. Thus the "benefit" of SSRIs for premature ejaculation was so clear-cut that trials were almost unnecessary. In contrast, the effects of the drugs on mood were so weak that in the clinical trials of SSRIs as antidepressants, hundreds of patients were needed to come up with statistically significant results. Yet, the drugs were licensed for depression and have since been called antidepressants, while the effects on sexual functioning, if acknowledged at all, are labeled side effects. It is not the job of the FDA, or any regulator worldwide, to tell a company what its business should be.

Drug trials are increasingly conducted in settings and by notional investigators that suit company interests. When it came to testing antidepressants in children, the first wave of trials took place in North America, recruiting heavily among children in foster care, before a second wave moved to South Africa, Brazil, and elsewhere. It is not the job of the FDA, or any other regulator, to note this and wonder if trials done in circumstances such as these will produce results that should be allowed to dictate the treatment of the child across the road—or at least the regulators have not read their safety brief in this way.

In the case of tolbutamide, the study was run by the NIH, but now private companies known as clinical research organizations (CROs) run almost all trials. These trials may only have had ethics clearance from the CROs' own panels, and they may include nonexistent patients (one convenient aspect to these bogus patients, unlike those taking tolbutamide, is that they can't die). Also in contrast to the patients dying on tolbutamide, patients suffering adverse effects in company trials may be coded as dropouts for noncompliance rather than injured by treatment. Finally, in contrast to the tolbutamide trials, the publications stemming from company trials will likely be ghostwritten.

Of even greater importance is that in the case of tolbutamide, the investigators had the data, but today's investigators for statins, asthma drugs, hypoglycemics for diabetes, or antidepressants don't. The file of data from company trials of these drugs notionally goes to the FDA but the regulators in fact work from tables of the raw data already made up for them and company reports as to what the trials have shown. Furthermore, as of the 1990s, the FDA has been encouraged by both Congress and the executive branch of both Republican and Democratic administrations to see itself as a partner of industry; in this climate a zealous commitment to safety is not likely to be viewed with favor by their new partners.

There are no academics now who can speak out about a problem in the way the academics from NIH did in the case of tolbutamide. This shifts the burden to the FDA—but this agency is not equipped to be a scientific arbiter. The FDA acts essentially as an auditor for drug company data and no more. When the raw data are submitted to them, the agency typically samples the clinical records to determine whether they correspond with figures in various tables that have been constructed by the company.

FDA officials may analyze some of these tables themselves but usually will simply comment on the methods used by the company. If further analyses are deemed necessary, the company is asked to perform these. Should a problem arise with the drug after it has been approved for marketing, the FDA will typically write to the company and inquire what the company's database might reveal about the issue. They will ordinarily trust the report that is prepared by the company, despite a series of cases in which company reports have borne little relationship to the underlying raw data, as we shall see below.

The companies, not the regulators, write the labels and any warnings for the drug, though the FDA must approve them. There are a number of technical issues that are considered, such as the precise meanings the FDA has given to words like "rare" and "frequent." These have been tied down to rates that may be, for example, greater than 1 in 100 (frequent) or less than 1 in 10,000 (rare), and the FDA will ensure that such words are used in their technically correct fashion.

The FDA's role in a drug's regulation can be brought out by considering the agency's role in regulating a food like butter. While one officer in one part of the FDA may have to decide whether a drug can be labeled as a treatment for asthma or osteoporosis, another may be faced with a slab of yellow material a company wishes to label as butter. Is it butter or lard colored to look like butter? The regulator has a set of criteria for butter, dealing with what it should contain and what it cannot contain. If the yellow material meets the criteria, the regulator has no option but to let it on the market labeled as butter. In the case of butter or other foods words such as "organic," "fresh," and "local" are defined by the regulator, and the challenge for companies is often to find a way around the definitions in order to make use of these premium descriptive terms. It is not the job of the regulator to decide if this is good butter or not. Nor is it considered the job of the FDA to decide if butter is good for our health. Consumer agencies survey available butters to answer the first point, while medical associations or others in healthcare will issue guidance from time to time on whether we should be eating as much butter as we do.

But unlike butter, in the case of drugs FDA approval is now taken to mean that these treatments are good treatments and that treatment is good for you—with no consumer groups scrutinizing just how good these products are, and above all, no groups of physicians reviewing the issue of whether it is appropriate to be on as much treatment as we are.

There might be less cause for concern if the FDA were the type of investigative agency most people imagine must have been put in place following the thalidomide scandal or if it were the kind of agency that was in the business of ensuring our medicines get progressively better. When we go to sleep at night with a child in the next room on some new medication, we expect the treatment will be at least marginally better and safer than treatments we may have been prescribed when we were children. After all, the music system is so much more advanced than the one around when we were young and there is a computer now where there was once a typewriter. But this is not the case for many drug treatments. There is every chance our family members will be taking a drug, whether an antibiotic or antidepressant, that is less effective than the one we were treated with or a new drug whose hazards remain to be discovered. All that is in place between our children and possible disaster is a set of auditors whose job it is to tick the boxes.

It is in fact a lot harder for the FDA to audit the books of Pfizer, Lilly, or GlaxoSmithKline than it was for the Arthur Andersen firm to audit Enron. In financial circles it is recognized that after a period of time auditors come to see the world the way their clients do. As a result it is regarded as good practice for major corporations to change their auditors every five years. But there are no changes of auditors when it comes to pharmaceuticals.

When a plane falls out of the sky, the Aviation Safety Board audits what has gone wrong rather than the Federal Aviation Board, the agency responsible for letting a plane fly in the first instance. But when a problem blows up with a drug, it is often the same FDA officials who have made the decision to let the drug on the market who are now called upon to make a further set of judgments that may reflect badly on their original decision.

When the crisis blew up around drugs like tolbutamide in the 1970s, one of the few safeguards in place was that regulators worldwide were paid from the public purse. But things have changed. Britain was one of the first countries in the 1980s to switch to a system where industry paid to be regulated, and the regulator was encouraged to become a business selling "regulatory services" to the industry and promoting itself as one of the fastest licensing authorities in the world for new drugs.[17] The United States moved to a similar system in 1992, with the passage of a Prescription Drug User Fee Act (PDUFA) that allowed the FDA to collect a fee from industry based on marketing applications reviewed. The intention was, by employing more reviewers in order to speed up processing of industry applications, to get rid of the bureaucratic delay that, ironically, had been the FDA's only contribution to averting a thalidomide disaster.

A new emphasis on partnership has blurred the boundary between the FDA and industry. Since drugs began to be regulated in the United States in 1906 there has always been a revolving door between the regulatory agency and industry; senior figures in the regulatory apparatus found jobs in pharmaceutical companies or consulted for them after they left government, or employees from industry moved into senior regulatory positions. This was later true of the regulatory agencies that followed in Europe. This revolving door makes it difficult to know how independent our regulators are. If the regulator knew he could be scrutinized because the data from the clinical trials used to get drugs on the market were publicly available, this might not be a big issue, but the data are not available so none of us can assess how much the lure of a future job might bias a regulator to give a company favorable treatment.

Whatever shuttling between industry and the regulatory apparatus there has been, until the new emphasis on partnership between industry and regulator was put in place it would have been considered scandalous to find senior regulators sitting down with industry representatives, academics enmeshed in industry, and patient groups that had been sponsored by industry to issue a ghostwritten consensus statement advocating the detection and treatment of disorders in a manner that can only increase the sales of drugs.

Thus in 2005, Tom Laughren, head of the FDA section responsible for licensing drugs that act on the central nervous system (known as the CNS section), was a co-author on an article advocating the detection and treatment of mood disorders in those with other medical illnesses, and indeed giving consideration to prophylactic antidepressant treatment in those who might be put on other medical drugs at risk of triggering depression.[18] The article was in fact written by Scientific Therapeutics Information.

In 2003, Laughren was a participant in a "consensus conference" convened under the auspices of the American Academy of Child and Adolescent Psychiatry but organized by Best Practices, a marketing firm whose website states that "we bring together opinion leadership and direct services to the pharmaceutical and biotechnology industries."[19] Its services include "Consensus Development Conferences . . . in areas of clinical controversy." In this case the meeting was aimed at increasing the recognition and treatment of childhood bipolar disorder, a condition that few psychiatrists outside the United States believed existed.[20]

In 2007, Laughren was named as an "author" of an article promoting antipsychotic drug studies in children labeled with "Impulsive Aggression."[21] This article, like the others above, came out of a sponsored meeting; in this case by Abbott Pharmaceuticals, Bristol-Myers Squibb, GlaxoSmithKline, INC Research, Janssen, Johnson & Johnson, Eli Lilly, Novartis, Pfizer, Solvay, Annie E. Casey Foundation, Forest Research Institute, Jazz, Otsuka, and Sanofi Synthelabo.

In these cases, Laughren endorsed a treatment option when, in his FDA capacity, he might later be called on to adjudicate whether companies should have a license for marketing the use of antipsychotics for children who ostensibly have bipolar disorder or impulsive aggression disorder. There is no reason to believe that this quite extraordinary situation is anything other than standard behavior within the FDA now.

When we are ill, we are at our most vulnerable and need someone to look after us. Someone who ensures we get treatments that work, treatments that are as safe as they can be. For a century this figure, in the shape of doctors like Alfred Worcester and Richard Cabot, used to be our doctor. After the thalidomide tragedy in 1962 many of us also looked to the FDA as a guardian of our well-being, but if the regulator ever was a truly independent safeguard, the reality now is that he is more like a Wizard of Oz figure, pulling the strings of publicity rather than capable of making any meaningful changes—a figure who has made his accommodations with the witches of the East and North.

THE CUTTING EDGE OF CARING

In marked contrast to the increasingly cozy partnerships between regulators and industry in other countries of the world, there have been individuals within the FDA who in recent years have spoken out when they felt that critical health information was being suppressed or unnecessarily delayed. In 2004, David Graham from the FDA's safety department went public with news that as early as 2000 the scientific data had pointed to a seven-fold increase in the risk of a heart attack among people on Vioxx though the FDA were still refusing to require Merck to warn doctors and patients about this risk.[22] He estimated there might already have been thirty thousand unnecessary heart attacks that could be linked to Vioxx. Graham also pointed to the risks of death from asthma inhalers. Andy Mosholder, another FDA staffer, in 2004 similarly presented an analysis suggesting that the available company trials pointed to a risk of suicide from antidepressants. Both Graham and Mosholder were threatened and both needed support from the Whistleblowers Act. Terrible though such efforts to gag them are, it is unimaginable that anyone within the regulatory apparatus in Europe would step out of line in the way Graham or Mosholder did.

But why should a regulator have to lead the way? Drugs are available by prescription only in part so that doctors will sing out should there appear to be a problem. It's not the job of a regulator to go to the wall for patients—but it is close to the definition of good medical care for a doctor to do so. And even if all the doctors in a particular specialty have been cajoled by a pharmaceutical company's line or its perks, or fall short in their duty to provide safe care, still in the case of drugs such as Vioxx and Prozac the published data in major journals like the *Journal of the American Medical Association* and the *British Medical Journal* point to clear increases in risk that should have alerted the medical profession to look for problems. David Graham and Andy Mosholder were not dealing with confidential data that only the FDA had access to—they appealed to data that was within reach for thousands of doctors—but almost none spoke up.[23] Why not?

When doctors speak out about a treatment hazard, they often encounter antagonism from colleagues; the revelation is likely to be perceived as bad for medical business and to reflect badly on other doctors who have prescribed this treatment. This antagonism may be even more likely now as company marketing has become adept at ensuring that other doctors do not only see a product being attacked but see their own views being challenged. In addition, most doctors have accepted prescription privileges as a God-given right to a monopoly in drug treatments of people at their most desperate and most vulnerable and have divorced this right from a sense of duty to do something about the hazards of treatment. In this respect, doctors have become one more link in the drug distribution chain rather than the people who once took charge of medical treatments. Something quite extraordinary must have happened to produce such a change in the practice of medicine. The tolbutamide and, later, Prozac and Vioxx cases bring out what has changed.

Concerns that the blockbuster antidepressant Prozac might make people taking the drug suicidal broke in 1990, following the publication of a set of clinical cases in the *American Journal of Psychiatry,* as discussed in chapter 3.[24] As this article made clear, within days of starting Prozac some patients became more agitated and suicidal. The agitation got worse if the dose of the drug was increased. It cleared up if the treatment was stopped and reappeared if the treatment was restarted. While depression can cause suicidality, both the treating doctors and the affected patients identified the new state as quite different from their previous experience. In at least one case, the drug led to a completed suicide in a child being treated for anxiety. Finally, intervening with an antidote that blocked the effects of Prozac brought about an improvement. In this series of cases and in others published in the months that followed, according to the rules Robert Koch set out in the 1880s to determine when a bacterium or a drug might have brought about some effect (see chapter 3), there was a cast-iron argument that Prozac had caused the problem it stood accused of.

The main way hazards may be hidden right under the noses of doctors centers around Ronald Fisher's efforts in the 1930s to investigate whether fertilizers worked or not, as outlined in chapter 3. Fisher, quite arbitrarily, set up a standard—if on nineteen occasions out of twenty plants in a fertilized patch did better than those in an otherwise equal but nonfertilized patch, this was said to be statistically significant and the fertilizer could be said to be effective. If the result came out indicating that the fertilized patch did better only seventeen or eighteen times out of twenty, in Fisher's view, proper scientists should conclude they either had not designed the experiment correctly or they were dealing simply with the play of chance.

Soon after Fisher outlined his view of statistical significance, Jerzy Neyman, another early statistician, argued Fisher was throwing common sense out the window and offering a recipe for scientific sterility, not scientific progress. For most people, having a drug prove its worth in a study in which thousands of patients participate sounds more impressive than demonstrating a benefit in a handful of people. But as was discussed in chapter 3, the drug to go for is the one that consistently shows up as working in a small sample. Snake oil, which contains omega-3 and other fatty acids, could be shown to have statistically significant effects on depression rating scales or for pain relief purposes and possibly for some other conditions as well—provided several hundred patients are recruited to the trial. As Neyman was first to point out, we can be fooled by the fact that having hundreds of patients in a study can make a trivial finding statistically significant. Fooled to the extent that these hints of effectiveness can be sold by drug companies as convincing evidence their drug works and should all but be put in the drinking water.

Neyman's beef with Fisher becomes even clearer if we turn to drug hazards. To see this, let us move from fertilized fields to a hazard analogue, such as being faced with a loaded gun. If Fisher had said that it was only when there were bullets in nineteen chambers of a twenty-chambered gun that the gun could be said to be loaded this would make no sense to any of us. In the experiment that is real life, a lot of us wouldn't go near a gun with even one bullet in its twenty chambers. One bullet is significant enough for most of us. Fisher's approach makes sense in situations where skepticism is called for—as when faced with claims by a huckster or a company trying to make money out of a remedy for sick and vulnerable people. It might indeed be reasonable in this case to suspend skepticism if a treatment "worked" nineteen times out of twenty. But it makes no sense for doctors or patients to be skeptical when hazards are involved—only pharmaceutical companies have an interest in being skeptical about the existence of hazards.

But when it comes to drug hazards, pharmaceutical companies can now confidently bank on the medical community and the FDA following Fisher, not Neyman. The studies of Prozac, and later of other antidepressants, threw up double the number of suicidal acts than were found in patients on placebo, but the numbers involved were not statistically significant. Merck was happy to report over four times more heart attacks on Vioxx than on placebo, again because the numbers were not statistically significant. For Fisher, Merck, and Lilly, this essentially meant the suicides and heart attacks were not happening, whereas for Neyman the onus was on Merck and Lilly to show their gun wasn't loaded.

Following Fisher and the FDA, when it comes to a drug-induced injury, doctors now routinely line up to say the bullet through the head while on Zoloft or the heart attack while on Vioxx were just anecdotal events, and while anecdotes are regrettable, physicians have to deal in science, and if a finding is not statistically significant, the science doesn't support the existence of a risk. The doctors who line up in this way are not the rapidly vanishing doctors of yesteryear sticking to a regulatory line on things they know little or nothing about. Instead, they tend to be the most recently qualified doctors who, coached in the conventions of evidence-based medicine, are trained to follow Fisher and not Neyman when it comes to hazards.[25] In this respect, we are all at greater risk from tomorrow's doctors than from yesterday's.

These claims may seem incredible, so it is perhaps worth taking a little time to view the emperor from a few different angles before deciding whether he is really wearing any clothes or not. When the first concerns about Prozac made headlines in 1990 Lilly, understandably, rushed to defend their blockbuster. The company examined their clinical trials, which included over three thousand patients, for suicidal acts and published the results of their analysis in the *British Medical Journal,* claiming it showed no increase in risk on Prozac compared to placebo.[26] But smack in the middle of the article are the figures—six suicidal acts in 1,765 patients on Prozac versus one in 569 patients on placebo.

These figures indicate that while there is a chance there is no risk from Prozac, there is an equal chance that there is up to a sixteen-fold increase in the risk, and that the best guess is that there is roughly a doubling of risk on Prozac.[27] But according to Fisher's test there was no significant difference between placebo and Prozac on this score. The conclusion the company drew from this, fully endorsed by the *British Medical Journal* with no subsequent objections recorded from any of the 100,000 readers of the journal was that "data from these trials *do not show* that fluoxetine is associated with *an increased risk* of suicidal acts or emergence of substantial suicidal thoughts among depressed patients."[28] The six suicidal acts simply vanished.

A twelve-year-old schoolchild could have told the *British Medical Journal* that a doubling of risk is an increase. Lots of the one hundred thousand readers of the *British Medical Journal* work in fields that have nothing to do with the pharmaceutical industry. Even in areas of medicine working closely with that industry, many of the brightest and the best have no conflicts of interest, so missing this doubling of risk cannot be put down to conflict of interest. Missing the problem in this instance cannot be put down to lack of access to the data either—the doubling of risk that the company denied was hidden like a boat in a harbor by being put in one of the most widely read journals in the world. We seem to have entered an Alice in Wonderland world, in which things are whatever the Red Queen says they are.

Emboldened by the complete lack of objections to their depression paper, Lilly went on to analyze the suicidal acts from a series of trials they had done with Prozac in eating disorders. In these cases, any increase in risk could not be attributed to depression. Again there was an excess of suicidal acts on Prozac—a 1.4-fold increase in risk but because this increase was not deemed statistically significant, it too apparently didn't exist.[29]

When the FDA convened their public hearing in September 1991, there was room on the program for presentations from the public and for a presentation of the "science." In the three-minute slots they were given, many wives and mothers offered convincing testimony of how husbands and children had been prescribed the drug for anxiety, weight loss, or smoking cessation—conditions not linked to suicide—and, having apparently never been suicidal before, had gone on to commit suicide. FDA officials and experts present acknowledged that the testimonies were striking but made it clear they had to go by what the scientific data showed.[30]

The scientific data from their trials were presented by Lilly. None of the experts convened by the FDA, nor any of the regulatory officials speaking that day, nor any of those whose tales of horror were weighed on a scientific balance against the clinical trial data and found wanting appeared to notice that, actually, the trial data of increased suicides was entirely consistent with the personal tragedies.

But there is skullduggery to add to mystery here and a case for saying lack of access to the data also played a part in Lilly's getting away with their gamble. Unlike the readers of the *British Medical Journal,* the FDA had had a chance to see the real figures from the Prozac depression studies and plenty of opportunity to come to grips with the fact that there had in fact been NO suicidal acts on placebo—the real figures were six suicidal acts on Prozac versus zero on placebo. Technically, the risk on Prozac was infinitely greater than on placebo. Lilly had taken a suicide that had happened before the trial had started and filed it under the heading of placebo, in a manner that contravenes regulations and seems close to being fraudulent. These data are now in the public domain[31]—what is not public is any account from the FDA, or other regulators worldwide faced with the same data, as to why they chose to overlook this clearly inappropriate manipulation.

This single placebo suicide was very important to the company, and maybe to the FDA, because its addition to the calculation meant the increased risk on Prozac would not be statistically significant and if not statistically significant six suicidal acts on Prozac vanished. The company knew that medics across the board could be depended upon to agree with this view of significance.

Following Lilly's lead, GlaxoSmithKline in the case of Paxil and Pfizer in the case of Zoloft also took prestudy suicides and suicidal acts from Paxil and Zoloft trials, respectively—seven in the case of Paxil and three in the case of Zoloft—and dumped them into the placebo group, against regulatory rules. The FDA noted what was happening but did nothing, and again has offered no explanation since for their oversight.

Quite astonishingly, when the British regulator (the MHRA—Medicines and Healthcare products Regulatory Agency) caught up with this maneuver thirteen years later, in 2003, and asked GlaxoSmithKline for their Paxil suicide data, making it clear companies should not move prestudy suicides into the placebo group as they had been doing, GSK instead took suicides recorded after the trials of Paxil had concluded and coded them under placebo, even including in the placebo group a patient who had committed suicide after having started Prozac. The MHRA did not object.

When Vioxx ran into trouble with the FDA in the late 1990s, Merck did something similar. In a major trial comparing Vioxx to the older drug naproxen in the treatment of osteoarthritis (the VIGOR trial), the company reported seventeen heart attacks in 4,047 patients taking Vioxx versus four in 4,029 patients taking naproxen.[32] This more than fourfold increase in heart attacks could be made to vanish by breaking the patients up into groups and then reporting that when compared to naproxen, Vioxx did not increase the risk of a heart attack for patients without a previous history of cardiovascular disease. Creating groups such as those with previous history of cardiovascular disease and those without reduces the size of any one group compared to the overall group, thereby reducing the risk that a finding will be statistically significant.

In fact there had been three further heart attacks on Vioxx, making twenty in total; this only came to light when plaintiffs later took legal actions against Merck. The company had to make these three heart attacks disappear or they would have had to report that Vioxx significantly increased the risk of heart attack for all patients in the VIGOR trial, including those without previous cardiac problems.[33]

For most readers, the invented placebo suicides and suicidal acts in the Prozac, Paxil, and Zoloft trials and the three deleted heart attacks in the Vioxx trials are likely to seem to be the major issue. These manipulations are both a real problem and possibly a criminal offence, but they are a lesser problem than the invisibility of the seventeen Vioxx heart attacks and six Prozac suicidal acts. Lesser in the sense that companies only occasionally have to move a dead body or two from an inconvenient spot in the dataset to a less problematic one, but at the click of a statistical button they hide far more deaths in academic articles that remain permanently in full public view.

Explaining why Fisher's ideas have such traction within medicine is not easy. Regulators have followed this line because the definition of statistical significance offers them a rule of thumb, an almost mechanical procedure that takes the place of a judgment call. For pharmaceutical companies, the issue is simple; Fisher's ideas mean that positive effects in a minority of clinical trials can transform a weak and inessential drug into one apparently certified by science, while at the same time airbrushing its hazards out of existence.

But why do doctors follow this line? A number of medical academics have attempted to grapple with this, pointing out that current dependence on statistical significance testing has created a "junk epidemiology" in the domain of therapeutics. So Louis Lasagna, the first professor of clinical pharmacology in the United States, and later dean of medicine at Tufts University, who introduced randomized controlled trials into drug development, described the approach outlined above as "p-value madness" (to say something has a p-value less than 0.05 is another way to say a finding is statistically significant).[34] For Sandor Greenland, professor of epidemiology and statistics at UCLA, "statistical thinking [of this type] has produced a chronic psychosis"[35]—by which he means that researchers relying on Fisher's ideas have lost touch with reality. Ezra Hauer, a professor of civil engineering from the University of Toronto and authority on analyzing road traffic accidents, explains that "in this manner good data are drained of real content. The direction of the empirical conclusions is reversed and ordinary human and scientific reasoning is turned on its head."[36] For Charlie Poole, professor of statistics and epidemiology at the University of North Carolina, "Statistical significance should be abandoned immediately and universally."[37] Ironically when faced with this issue in 2011, with investors' dollars at stake, the US Supreme Court argued that statistical significance cannot be the arbiter of what an investor might deem a significant risk.[38] But patients it seems do not have the same rights as investors.

The differences between much of clinical practice and other branches of science were starkly framed by Kenneth Rothman, professor of epidemiology at Harvard and editor of the journal *Epidemiology*, in a note about submissions to the journal:

> When writing for *Epidemiology*, you can . . . enhance your prospects if you omit tests of statistical significance. . . . We would like to see the interpretation of a study based not on statistical significance, or lack of it, for one or more study variables, but rather a careful quantitative consideration of the data in the light of competing explanations. . . . Misleading signals occur when a trivial effect is found to be "significant," as often happens in large studies, or when a strong relation is found "non-significant," as often happens in small studies.[39]

Is Poole's term "junk epidemiology" too strong a term to use? Consider an analysis published in 2002 of the trials of Prozac, Paxil, Zoloft, Efexor, and other antidepressants submitted to the FDA by companies seeking to market their treatments for anxiety disorders.[40] To get into these studies patients had to be anxious and not depressed. The perception at the time was that anxiety had a minimal effect on the risk of suicide. Having combined the data for all these drugs, the authors announced a surprising finding, which the *American Journal of Psychiatry* was glad to accept. "We found that suicide risk among patients with anxiety disorders is higher than in the general population by a factor of 10 or more. Such a finding was unexpected. . . . The sample of patients selected was considered at minimal risk of suicide."[41] Nobody reading the *American Journal of Psychiatry* registered an objection to this conclusion, which was odd, given that there were eleven suicides in 12,914 anxious patients on active treatment compared with zero suicides in 3,875 patients taking placebo. The conclusion should have been that in this group of patients at minimal risk of suicide, the increased risk that came from antidepressants was more clearly visible than it had been in depression trials.

The same group of investigators looked at suicides and suicidal acts as reported in depression studies on the effects of the post-Prozac group of antidepressants, involving almost fifty thousand patients. The percentage of suicidal acts on antidepressants ranged from 0.15 to 0.20 percent, while on placebo it. was 0.10 percent. The findings were not considered statistically· significant, leading the authors to make the astounding statement that "*the only possible conclusion* supported by the present data is that prescription of SSRI antidepressants is not associated with a greater risk of completed suicide."[42]

In fact the situation was much worse. These investigators were not aware of ten suicides and suicidal acts miscoded by Glaxo and Pfizer under the heading of placebo. Taking these into account made the difference between antidepressants and placebo statistically significant, so that the only possible conclusion that the present data did *not* support was the conclusion that there was no increase in risk.

Where one might expect that evidence of only bare hints that a drug might work would not be sufficient to get a drug approved for market, while a doubling or tripling of a hazard on treatment would lead to warnings, this is not what happens. Where one might expect the burden of proving that black was really white would face companies rather than patients, it instead faces patients and any doctors who wish to look closely. This is the point where the world is turned upside down, where the baby is thrown out while the bathwater is carefully preserved.

Paul Anthony, speaking on behalf of the Pharmaceutical Manufacturers Association of America, makes the issues very clear:

> I want you to think about it [the issue of hazards] in terms of your reputation. It is really the reputation of a brand that is being signaled. Imagine . . . someone reporting that they had early information that you may be a child

molester. I know that sounds extreme but it is that type of thing. . . . It is just an allegation . . . [however] that is what people will remember, and that is the reason there is a lot of concern about presenting early signal information—when you don't really have any proof. It is very different than the kind of rigorous process we had in the past, where you had to do a trial and it had to be statistically significant before you presented that.[43]

One of the greatest ironies of our evidence-based medicine era is that, faced with evidence of an increased number of adverse events in clinical trial data for its drug, the ultimate company defense has been to fall back on anecdotes. The most astonishing example of this mode of defense followed concerns beginning in the mid- 1990s that the antipsychotic Zyprexa might cause diabetes. Faced with growing concerns, Lilly wheeled out a view from Henry Maudsley, who in 1879 had supposedly recognized an association between psychosis and diabetes.[44] Lilly authored or sponsored several series of articles that were liberally sprinkled with this quote as grounds to think it was schizophrenia after all, and not Zyprexa, that was causing the problem—with not a single published objection from the psychiatric profession in the United States or Europe.

Invoking Maudsley had an effect, perhaps because owing to an accident of history his name had ended up on Britain's most distinguished psychiatric research facility—the Maudsley Hospital. But in fact Maudsley disliked clinical practice and had very little experience with serious mental illness. He preferred writing. And the book in which a throwaway sentence about diabetes appears had been written when he was twenty-nine, so that even if he had been interested in patients he would not have had time to form a seasoned judgment about their condition, especially as patients with type-1 diabetes did not then live more than a few months from the onset of their illness, and type-2 diabetes was rare.

In North Wales, we had access to over three thousand consecutive admissions to the local asylum from 1875 to 1924, covering Maudsley's career. During this time over twelve hundred patients were admitted with a psychosis but not a single one had diabetes. We also identified every single one of the 396 patients with a psychosis who had presented for the first time to the modern services between 1994 and 2006—not a single one had type-2 diabetes. But the modern group, once on treatment with antipsychotic drugs, went on to develop diabetes at double the normally expected rate.[45] These figures show how ridiculous the Maudsley quote is, but for most doctors the anecdote, told repeatedly by a drug company, will continue to work.

FACTORY DOCTORS

In medicine up until the 1960s, if some doctor discovered a new disorder or described a body part, it was commonly named after him—so we have Bright's, Hashimoto's and Grave's diseases, Duchenne muscular dystrophy, Epstein-Barr virus, Nissl bodies, and Mullerian ducts.[46] It was the height of ambition for many male doctors to have their name linked in this way to a new observation or finding, and many of our most distinguished journals became well known because they published these new syndromes. Our brave new pharmaceutical era should be a golden one for doctors who have even a scrap of motivation in this direction.

Since the breakthrough with smoking and lung cancer, there is been a widespread recognition that many of our diseases are environmentally caused.[47] From chemicals in the air we breathe leading to respiratory disorders; to pesticides or other toxins leading to cancers, Parkinson's, and other neurological disorders; or aspects of the food we eat leading to cardiovascular disorders or gut cancers—across all these disorders lies the common factor of people ingesting some chemical or toxin.

But there is no other walk of life in which people ingest chemicals to the same extent, or in such concentrated forms, as happens among those treated in the modern practice of medicine. Unfortunate though it might be to put it in this way, medicine increasingly provides the perfect natural experiment to track the effects of poisons in the human body. Even if many of their colleagues disapproved, if the medical market were a free market working as Adam Smith described it, some doctors at least might be expected to hover around their patients like gulls around a trawler or robbers around a bank, because their career interests in reporting any new diseases and the concerns of patients at risk of suffering adverse reactions from treatment should coincide.

But this doesn't happen. It doesn't happen because companies rather than doctors run clinical trials. Moreover, companies sequester the data from those trials, so no one can use these data to determine what the hazards of treatment might be. Also, in their ghostwritten articles appearing in the very best journals, apparently authored by the most distinguished academics, companies have been able to interpret data pointing to marginal benefits from treatments as evidence that these treatments are remarkably effective, thus casting doubt on any remaining data that might point to the existence of hazards.

Locked into the distribution channel for prescription-only drugs, hemmed in by the science, doctors increasingly resemble the employees of the occupational health department of a factory that in the course of business exposes its workers to disability-inducing aerosols. These are doctors who are all too aware that their ongoing employment depends first on keeping mum about problems the workers may be having and second on being willing to recommend laying off workers at the first signs of any ill health—having persuaded them that they aren't fit for the job rather than conceding that job conditions might be the problem. The characteristic portrayal of a factory doctor like this, as opposed to the best of family doctors, lies precisely in the degree to which the one cares about patients and is prepared to speak out and the other can't.

The pressure on individual doctors in these situations can be forbidding, but we would still expect medical organizations to speak out about the hazards of treatment. Yet even after the FDA had finally conceded that antidepressants could cause suicide and required the drug companies involved to place warnings on their drugs to this effect, the American Psychiatric Association (APA) could still pose the question, "Do antidepressants increase the risk of suicide?" and answer it, "There is no evidence that antidepressants increase the risk of suicide,"[48] stating instead that "antidepressants save lives."[49]

At a time when healthcare is becoming standardized, when clinical prescribing is being constrained by guidelines, if drugs save lives, and hazards aren't worth mentioning, then why not let nurses—who are much less expensive—prescribe them? Nurses are much more likely to adhere to best practice, as embodied in guidelines. The APA statement amounts to a professional suicide note.

What does it take to back a profession into this kind of a corner? Some hints come from the kind of session held behind closed doors and without minutes that I was invited to attend in October 2005. It was convened by Britain's Royal College of Psychiatrists in the wake of the scandal over the suicide-inducing effects of antidepressants on children, to review whether the college needed more firewalls against pharmaceutical influence.[50] Most American medical associations have looked at their policies vis-à-vis industry in similar fashion in recent years.

The invited audience was small and included most of the officers of the college. The first half of the day was taken up by presentations about the pharmaceutical industry's view of its current position within the British economy—that half the day was handed over to industry was itself remarkable. These presentations claimed that the pharmaceutical industry was the largest funder of research in Britain, providing nearly

40 percent of all corporate monies in industrial research and development and 70 percent of Britain's medical research funding. Getting drug trials started in the UK was slow, however, we were told, and Britain was the most expensive place in Europe to do research. While the quality of research in Britain had been excellent, the rest of world was catching up, and clinical trials were moving to Russia, India, and China—a similar message to one delivered repeatedly to American academics for over a decade.[51]

There was a "we're all consenting adults" tone to the presentations. Company personnel made it clear that the pharmaceutical industry was a business whose bottom line was profit. The clinicians were told that if they had been to a sponsored meeting or seen a company representative they had worked with industry. And if they had read the scientific literature they would have been influenced by the pharmaceutical industry. The issue now, in the pharmaceutical industry's view, was how to put a framework in place to support the contribution industry could make to Britain's health and prosperity and enable medicine, the regulatory apparatus, and the pharmaceutical industry all to work in partnership.

The scandal of company suppression of clinical trial data showing that antidepressants made children suicidal had come to light the year before. Because of this, many of the clinicians present felt that however pharmaceutical companies dressed up their material, nothing about the claimed benefits to patients could be taken at face value. Some recognized the larger dilemma, namely, that we doctors were in the same business as the pharmaceutical industry. We never told patients when we felt industry's treatments weren't very good, because that would be saying that some of the treatments we were giving weren't very good. Were we professionals whose interests really diverge all that much from those of industry?

Industry was marketing drug solutions to medical problems—soon, how many among us physicians would know what a medical solution to a medical problem would look like or what our role vis-à-vis patients was other than to give drugs? Being told we should partner with the pharmaceutical industry was like telling a group of planners crafting a public transport policy that they had to partner with the automobile industry. Or someone charged with bringing peace that they had to partner with the arms industry.

Though the British rarely state anything plainly, these concerns among the attendees were expressed clearly enough. In response, industry took off its gloves. Padraig White, working for GlaxoSmithKline, told those assembled that current policies were in fact the result of the closest cooperation between industry and the most senior figures in British medicine. When it came to issues like our asking for the data from clinical trials, these notables would not be putting their knighthoods on the line to insist upon access to raw data from clinical trials. Within academic psychiatry alone, he went on, there were twenty-five senior figures in Britain each earning in excess of $200,000 a year out of links with industry, so academia was unlikely to side with their clinical colleagues. And finally, we clinicians all needed to note that 40 percent of British life insurance policies were invested in the pharmaceutical industry. Whether we liked it or not, we were shareholders in the industry, and rocking the boat would not be in our interest.

There was a time, not so long ago, when even senior figures from the pharmaceutical industry attending a meeting involving senior officers of a national medical association would have appeared grateful to be present and would have held their tongue when issues such as these were raised. But the balance of power and position had changed so much that a relatively junior official from the pharmaceutical industry felt able to tell a professional medical association to "Get real."

In such a world, what scope is there for professionalism? How can clinicians "get real"? A start might be to shift the focus represented by statements like the American Psychiatric Association's "antidepressants save lives" to something more in the spirit of "doctors can save lives." How would they do this? Well, if they have a good knowledge of the natural history of the conditions they treat and use agents of limited effectiveness and uncertain safety with care while enlisting their patients' support in monitoring the effects of any interventions, lives might then indeed be saved.

Industry monitors the prescribing habits of every doctor in the Western world. Data on who prescribes what is used by industry to shape tomorrow's sales pitch to produce an increase in prescriptions of their compounds or to determine why they are losing market share to one of their competitors.

In contrast, doctors record almost none of the problems that develop when they put patients on a drug. The FDA and other regulatory websites make it clear that doctors in the United States and Britain report only one in a hundred serious adverse events on drug treatment to the regulator. The postal service, in other words, does a vastly better job in tracking the fate of parcels than clinicians do in tracking their patients. Rather than becoming evidence-based, medicine is monitoring and quantifying exactly the wrong things. It quantifies hints that the latest snake oil has some benefits, helping drug companies smuggle their products through the regulations designed to prevent undue injuries to patients. But in the face of a growing series of premature deaths and other injuries induced by drug treatments, it does nothing.

THE RULE OF DOUBT

The question of whether Prozac was in fact causing serious problems unleashed on the FDA a set of public and media concerns to rival those that had broken around tolbutamide in 1970. In 1991 the agency organized public hearings on the issue, which gave rise to a dramatic clash between the personal histories of a range of patients and randomized trial data supplied by Lilly, the makers of Prozac. But in marked contrast to their handling of tolbutamide, the FDA introduced an extraordinary argument that would have brought howls of medical outrage in the 1970s but produced not a peep of protest in the 1990s.

If the FDA did the right thing and warned about risks, agency representatives argued, it might paradoxically increase the number of deaths. Even if some people became suicidal on Prozac, senior officials within the FDA and academics linked to Lilly claimed, their numbers would be smaller than the number of deaths likely to occur among people who because of the existence of a warning would be deterred from seeking treatment in the first place. Prominent warnings about risks of suicide, in other words, might lead to an increase in the number of deaths.[52]

There is an astonishing ethical calculus here. In the case of the antidepressants, even the FDA had doubts about whether the drugs worked. There was absolutely no evidence they reduce suicides—all the clinical trial evidence pointed to an increase in risk, so much so that the major companies were engaged in various subterfuges to minimize public attention on the problem.

Given the completely predictable vigor of pharmaceutical company marketing that has led doctors to switch patients to the latest branded drugs, such as from ibuprofen or naproxyn to Vioxx or from hypoglycemics such as metformin to Rezulin and Avandia almost from the day they are launched, not warning patients appropriately in these cases amounts to a covert vaccination program—we want to see as many people on these new drugs as possible. But unlike vaccination, as the use of blockbuster drugs has spread, whether for osteoporosis, lowering blood sugar, or mood stabilization, the human cost that clinical trials of these drugs point to is increasingly paid by people who do not stand to benefit.

When it comes to the injuries produced by other industrial products, it is now clear that companies have been quite prepared to sponsor studies designed to bring in results that cast doubt on claims that chemicals from vinyl chloride to lead pose any health risks. Recent legal actions involving Paxil and birth defects have unearthed documents suggesting that lawyers for GlaxoSmithKline have liaised with academics to generate studies that could in similar fashion be used to counter any claims that Paxil might cause birth defects.[53] This suggests that tactics honed in the battles over industrial pollution in the 1950s are being deployed within medicine today.

The most striking example of company willingness to put profits before all else came at the end of the 1960s, when in response to concerns about smoking and lung cancer, the tobacco companies sponsored a series of papers showing that from 1900 to 1960 respiratory and cardiac deaths fell and life expectancy rose in tandem with increased tobacco consumption. This use of apparently scientific data (but misleading analysis) was part of a campaign to sow doubt about a link between smoking and disease, caught exquisitely in company admissions that "doubt is our product."[54]

But the ultimate use of the "doubt is our product" strategy faces us now in the form of company arguments that doubt about a hazard means it can be disregarded. As long as the data do not point to a statistically significant increase in heart attacks on Vioxx or deaths on statins or biphosphonates, the companies argue that doubt remains, and while doubt remains the drug must be regarded as being, in effect, free of hazards. The FDA and most doctors join them in this argument—to add warnings would, according to the American Psychiatric Association, have "a chilling effect on appropriate prescribing for patients."[55]

A PREEMPTIVE STRIKE

When it comes to other chemicals and the problems they pose, no company can buy up all doctors and hence they have to cope with the abilities of doctors to spot new hazards and their preparedness to speak out about these hazards. But when it comes to drugs, the interests of doctors, regulators, and companies are now so closely allied that pharmaceutical companies have been able to deploy an extraordinary legal maneuver.

When in 1991 the FDA talked about the public health consequences of deterring patients from treatment with antidepressants, it was a view aired in the course of a public debate. It wasn't public policy. The regulators and drug companies were still notionally managing the labels on drugs rather than determining the treatment of patients. A few years later a case in Southern California, the Motus case, made it clear that efforts were underway to shift public policy in the direction of actively supporting treatment with drugs.

In early November 1998, Victor Motus, a prominent member of the Filipino community in Southern California, had a few nights of poor sleep. He owned an architectural firm, was president of the local school district board, and had just launched his campaign for a seat on the Cerritos city council. He was due to go to Washington to receive an award from President Clinton for work done for the local school. With his wife, Flora, he owned numerous rental properties, an antique store, and he held an 80 percent ownership interest in two restaurants. Even without all this, a few nights of poor sleep were hardly surprising in a fifty-one-year-old man.[56]

The only health problem Motus had was type 2 diabetes that he managed by a combination of diet and medication. When he developed problems sleeping, Flora made an appointment with a general practitioner, Dr. Trostler, on November 6, 1998 for her husband to obtain sleeping pills. During the visit, mention was made of financial problems with one of his restaurants, and even though there was no prior medical history to point to depression and little wrong clinically, educated by companies like Pfizer to think that sleep difficulties commonly pointed to a depressive disorder, in which case antidepressants would be a more appropriate treatment than hypnotics, Trostler gave Victor a sample pack of the antidepressant Zoloft—something unlikely to help his sleep. The Motuses were told that Zoloft might take several weeks to work.

Victor took Zoloft as instructed over the next six days. His family later said that for the first day he thought the drug was helping him. By the third day, he told his sister the drug didn't suit him, and his wife noticed he was pacing and sleeping even less at night. On the fourth day, he had become shaky. On the fifth day, his birthday, he told Flora "I don't feel like myself," "the drug is making me crazy," and "I want to kill myself." She urged him to continue taking the drug because the doctor had told them that it might not work for another week.

He was due to fly to Washington the next day, November 12, the sixth day of treatment. When his brother arrived to take him to the airport, Victor was not there. He was found in his car several blocks away, dead behind the wheel from a single gun shot to his head.

In 2001, Flora took legal action against the makers of Zoloft, alleging that Pfizer "negligently . . . failed to adequately warn the medical community, the general public and (her husband) . . . of the dangers, contraindications and side effects . . . of Zoloft." Malcolm Wheeler, the lead attorney for Pfizer, contacted the new chief counsel of the FDA, Daniel Troy. Troy had joined the Department of Justice the year before, from a legal office that had done over $358,000 worth of business with Pfizer that year. Troy filed an amicus brief in the Motus case. In order to file such a brief, he had to have clearance from the solicitor general in the George W. Bush government, Paul Clements, a former partner in King and Spalding, the main law firm representing GlaxoSmithKline, who were also faced with a series of suicide cases involving an antidepressant, in this instance Paxil.

Troy's brief argued that the California court had no jurisdiction in the case. The FDA is responsible for the labeling of drugs and if Pfizer had warned that the drug could cause people to become suicidal it would have broken the law. Troy was firing a shot across the court's bow to ensure it did not do anything that would "undermine the agency's authority to protect the public health."[57]

When considering warnings, according to Troy, the FDA has to take into account the risks posed by the untreated illness—depression. "Under-utilization of a drug based on dissemination of scientifically unsubstantiated warnings, so as to deprive patients of beneficial, possibly lifesaving treatment could well frustrate the purpose of federal regulation."[58]

This was an extraordinary and unprecedented move. This was not the conventional company argument that juries cannot possibly decide on the science of an issue such as whether a drug might cause suicide. Troy was arguing that a jury had no place in considering whether the FDA should have asked for warnings or not—and therefore the company could not be prosecuted provided it had followed the directives the FDA had given it, regardless of whatever effect the drug had or had not had on Victor Motus. This was even though, as federal law stands, companies are obliged to warn if there are hints of a problem—not just on the basis of proof of a problem.

The idea of using a federal agency to preempt legal action in a state court was Malcolm Wheeler's brainchild. He had used it first when defending the Honda Motor Company in a 1980 case in which a plaintiff argued the company should have installed airbags even though federal regulations didn't at the time require them.[59] This case went all the way to the Supreme Court who, noting that the car contained many other safety features such as seatbelts, sided with Honda.

In the case of cars and butter as outlined earlier, it is not the job of the regulator to even begin to think about whether people should be driving cars or using butter. In the Motus case, however, the Pfizer argument was that the FDA should be thinking not just about whether drugs would be used but also attempt to ensure that they would be used, and that in this light, warnings might put a chill on this use. This opens up an extraordinary vista—and certainly not the vista Senator Kefauver had in sight when sponsoring the 1962 amendments to the Food and Drugs Act.

When I turn the ignition key to start a car, wires have to connect to a starter motor and there has to be a flow of both oxygen and gasoline for the act of driving to become possible. For a physician to practice medicine, having a drug that works is helpful but often not essential. From time immemorial, and certainly as embodied in Pinel's famous aphorism about the art of medicine, good practice has been held to be much more likely where there is detailed knowledge about the hazards of any drug used. Semiautomatic prescribing has never been regarded as good practice.

In arguing about the merits of safety warnings, Wheeler and Troy portrayed the issue as being the equivalent of having airbags in a car, when in fact they were arguing against a need to have the ignition wires properly connected to the starter motor or letting people know that, in some instances, the ignition wires might default to the gas tank (an instance of immediate-onset side effects), or, in a case of later-onset adverse effects, faulty brake linings that would give way after six months. Safe starting connections and functioning brakes have never been optional extras to a car in the way airbags once were; they are integral to its basic operation.

Before there was a ruling on preemption in the Motus case, Pfizer in fact got the case thrown out, but on the basis of another astonishing defense—the prescription-only status of Zoloft that Senator Kefauver unwittingly cemented in place in 1962. In a pretrial deposition, Dr. Trostler testified that no matter what the warnings were on Zoloft, he would have gone ahead and prescribed the drug anyway. If a doctor testifies as Trostler did that he would have used the drug in a similar fashion whether there were warnings or not on it, any case against a pharmaceutical company on the basis of failure to warn about the risks of a drug that is available only by prescription collapses. The reason to make them available by prescription only was precisely this—to interpose a professional judgment between the patient and the pharmaceutical company. As a majority of his colleagues at the time also held the view that SSRIs posed no risk, Trostler was not at risk of a malpractice suit. Victor Motus, like almost everyone who dies unnecessarily on a prescription-only medicine, was the victim of a perpetrator-less crime.

The service that pharmaceutical companies get from primary care physicians or other medical doctors, in other words, goes well beyond what most industries get from their onsite doctors. Not only can companies typically depend on doctors not to rock the boat, but they can palm off any legal responsibility for injuries caused by exposure to chemicals onto the doctors who do the prescribing. Complain about or investigate a problem and the doctor knows he is in for a rough ride. But faced with a problem that turns up later, the company gets off scot-free because doctors refuse to accept that the chemicals have caused the problem.

DESCENT INTO THE UNDERWORLD

Before his doctor abandoned him, Victor Motus's case led to an unearthing of a series of documents about how Pfizer had transformed clinical trials into marketing exercises, recoded patient details where the original data were inconvenient, and planted ghostwritten articles in all major journals. By focusing attention on the role of ghostwriting and company manipulations of their data it set a template for later legal actions surrounding Vioxx and other drugs.

The Motus case also led directly to evidence of children becoming suicidal on Zoloft, ultimately triggering, in 2004, two further sets of public hearings on antidepressants and suicide in children. At the second of these FDA hearings, Tom Laughren, head of the Central Nervous System division at the FDA, presented the clinical trial data and the FDA's views of the data.

Members of the public were then given three-minute slots to present views—seventy-three of them. Among these, a series of doctors made presentations—almost all male and all warning against the issuing of warnings. These were intermingled with a series of mothers, a modern-day set of Demeters. Demeter was the Greek goddess of the Earth and of fertility whose daughter, Cora, was forcibly abducted and carried off to the underworld by Hades. Demeter protested to Zeus, who professed himself helpless, until Demeter threatened Earth with permanent winter. Zeus intervened and restored Cora to her mother as Persephone. Because Persephone had eaten some pomegranate seeds while in the underworld, however, she was obliged to return to Hades for the several months of winter each year.

These modern-day Demeters similarly aimed at shaming the heavens to take action. In a presentation with mythic resonance, in the 72nd slot Mathy Downing confronted Tom Laughren:

> On January 10th, 2004 our beautiful little girl, Candace, died by hanging four days after ingesting 100 mg of Zoloft. She was 12 years old. The autopsy report indicated that Zoloft was present in her system. We had no warning that this would happen. This was not a child who had ever been depressed or had suicidal ideation. She was a happy little girl and a friend to everyone. She had been prescribed Zoloft for generalized anxiety disorder, by a qualified child psychiatrist, which manifested in school anxiety. . . . She had the full support of a loving, caring, functional family and a nurturing school environment.
>
> Her death not only affected us but rocked our community. . . . When Candace died her school was closed for the day of her memorial service, a service that had to be held in the school gym in order to seat the thousand or so people who attended. How ironic, Dr. Laughren, that your family attended Candace's memorial service. Our daughters had been in class together since kindergarten. How devastating to us that your daughter will graduate from the school that they both attended for the past eight years and that Candace will never have the opportunity to do so.
>
> Candace's death was entirely avoidable, had we been given appropriate warnings and implications of the possible effects of Zoloft. It should have been our choice to make and not yours. We are not comforted by the insensitive comments of a corrupt and uncaring FDA or pharmaceutical benefactors such as Pfizer who sit in their ivory towers, passing judgments on the lives and deaths of so many innocent children. The blood of these children is on your hands. To continue to blame the victim rather than the drug is wrong. To make such blatant statements that depressed children run the risk of becoming suicidal does not fit the profile of our little girl.[60]

A few minutes earlier, Mary Ellen Winter had also confronted Laughren and the FDA about her twenty-three-year-old daughter, Beth, and brought a new player into the frame:

> Beth was looking forward to a career in communication and was experiencing some anxiety and having trouble sleeping when she consulted our family

physician. He prescribed Paxil and said she would start feeling better in two weeks. Seven days later Beth took her own life.

We, like most of you in this room, grew up with confidence in the strides made in medicine and accepted with faith antibiotics and vaccinations prescribed. We believed the FDA would always act to protect our family's well being. When my daughter went to our family GP last year, we trusted that our doctor was well educated and informed. We were wrong. We now know that pharmaceutical sales are a high stake business, driven to increase shareholder wealth. The consolidation of pharmaceutical companies like GlaxoSmithKline has resulted in increased sophistication in the quest to market and distribute pharmaceutical products. Priority has moved from health to profit. Not all doctors are equipped to understand the marketing targets they have become. The FDA has allowed our daughter to be the victim of a highly commercial enterprise that selectively releases clinical data to maximize sales efforts and seeks only to gain corporate profits. . . .

As residents of the State of New York, we thank our Attorney General, Elliot Spitzer, for addressing issues that the FDA has been unwilling to address. . . .[61]

A few weeks before, the attorney general's office in New York had opened a fraud action against GlaxoSmithKline. The brief had been prepared by the unlikeliest of heroines, Rose Firestein. Firestein was blind and in poor health, but she had a passionate concern for the abuse of children. She charged GlaxoSmithKline with fraudulent interference with the practice of medicine. The company had engineered sales of Paxil for use in treating children who were depressed through the publication of ghostwritten papers that had concealed the drug's hazards and portrayed the outcome of studies, like Study 329, as positive even though this and other clinical trials had failed to show the drug worked. Her trump card was the internal GlaxoSmithKline document I had made public at an FDA hearing on pediatric suicidality on antidepressants six months earlier that showed the company deliberately setting out to present the good bits of the evidence and suppress the rest, and to publish papers in influential journals that would lead doctors to prescribe a drug that the company had already internally recognized did not work.

When faced by GSK's lawyers with the argument Troy made in the Motus case, that the FDA's views preempted any views a state might have, Firestein responded that New York was not attempting to argue the toss with the FDA on the labeling of the drug. When it came to the practice of medicine in the state of New York, however, the state and not the FDA had primacy. GlaxoSmithKline settled, and as part of the settlement posted on their website details of all of their clinical trials.

Ultimately, Mary Ellen Winter, Mathy Downing, and others who testified played a part in forcing the FDA to bow and issue warnings that antidepressants might lead to suicide in children, warnings that were extended to adults in 2006. These mothers did not win because their pleas were impassioned. They won because the FDA, although still giving every sign of willingness to ignore the nineteenth bullet in the twenty-bullet gun barrel, faced with nineteen bullets there could see no way out of issuing warnings. The FDA have since gone further and issued suicide warnings for anticonvulsants and antipsychotics, as well as Champix and Zyban for smoking cessation, Roaccutane for acne, Tamiflu for flu, and Singulair for asthma, and have withdrawn from the market Rimonabant for weight loss and Cymbalta/Yentreve for urinary incontinence for this reason.

Legal actions against pharmaceutical companies are almost nonexistent outside the United States. In part this is because patients in Europe and other countries have universal healthcare and there is much less or no need to recover the costs of treatment for an injury from a pharmaceutical company. A great deal of what the world knows therefore about how pharmaceutical companies do business—how they market drugs, ghostwrite articles, ensure trials recruit just the right number of patients so that the results for serious hazards cannot become statistically significant—stems from legal actions in the United States.

The attempted preemptive strike engineered by Malcolm Wheeler and Dan Troy in the Motus case—that of claiming that federal regulatory agency statutes preempted any action, state or federal, against a pharmaceutical company—aimed at removing one of the few remaining impediments in the world to company abilities to do business. Although Pfizer won the Motus case by other means, other companies began to use preemption with increasing frequency, and success. A series of SSRI-induced suicides, Vioxx-induced heart attacks, and Avandia- and Rezulin-induced deaths were thrown out on this basis.

As the argument raised was legally unprecedented, it was taken all the way to the Supreme Court.[62] When preemption had first been raised in 1998, it had seemed inconceivable to most legal minds that such a defense might succeed as a matter of principle, but a decade of company arguments and lobbying had made a difference. In attempting to come to a resolution, the Supreme Court scheduled two cases. The first involved Pfizer's Rezulin, which had been approved in 1997 as a treatment to lower blood sugar and then withdrawn from the market in 2000 after being linked with an excess of deaths from liver failure. In this case in 2008, the nine justices tied 4 to 4, Chief Justice Rehnquist having recused himself on the basis that he held shares in Pfizer.[63]

A second case heard in October 2008 involved phenergan, a Wyeth drug, given for nausea, which when given by injection caused an arterial spasm that led to Diana Levine losing her right arm. At the heart of the case was the issue of whether this loss stemmed from a lack of warnings regarding its proper administration.[64] The issue was not whether Wyeth knew about the hazard, but rather whether the FDA had or had not specifically instructed the company to warn about the hazard and if not, whether this exculpated Wyeth—even if the company did know about the hazard. On March 4, 2009, the Court came to a 6–3 verdict against Wyeth and against preemption.[65]

For the moment therefore, the kind of documents on which Firestein based her case in New York may still occasionally come to light in actions taken by plaintiffs against drug companies. For the moment, companies remain somewhat limited in their abilities to interfere with the practice of medicine in whatever way they see fit. For the moment, the FDA has not unequivocally become the de facto regulator of medicine rather than just medicines.

As this was happening another drama was unfolding. As part of their settlement with New York State, GlaxoSmithKline agreed to post details of all their clinical trials. This sounds better than it is: the company only posted internal study reports, not the actual data. These differ little from ghostwritten articles. They do not let anyone establish, for instance, whether a dropout from a trial was really a dropout for noncompliance or whether the child had attempted to commit suicide.

But it is difficult to hide deaths. In 2007, Steve Nissen, a cardiologist at the Cleveland Clinic, combed through the data from trials on Avandia (rosiglitazone), GlaxoSmithKline's latest blockbuster, a successor to tolbutamide in the treatment of adult-onset diabetes, and found that, while no one trial of Avandia showed an excess of cardiac deaths, in all trials combined the drug was linked to a marked increase in such deaths.[66]

The Avandia story repeats all the elements of drug disasters from tolbutamide to Paxil. When first licensed by the FDA in 1999, there was no evidence that it saved lives, but influential academics lobbied regulators and other decision makers to ensure favorable treatment for this must-have drug. The American Diabetes Association came out strongly in favor of the drug even before it was approved.[67] Over the next five years, Avandia moved rapidly to blockbuster status despite warnings by the World Health Organization (WHO) in 2004 of an increased risk of death. Internal GlaxoSmithKline analyses also found increased—but nonsignificant—rates of cardiac events on Avandia in their clinical trials, but in public the company continued to argue that the drug was absolutely safe and sales continued to boom. In the face of Nissen's analysis, the company fast-tracked a major study of cardiac safety on the drug, the RECORD study, and published it claiming that it demonstrated that Avandia was safe.[68] Both the FDA and European regulators agreed. But mounting concerns led to hearings at the FDA, and further investigations by FDA staff, one of whom, Thomas Marciniak, found a pattern of concealment of serious events on Avandia in the RECORD study that echoed the hiding of deaths and other serious events on SSRIs and Vioxx.[69]

These events led a Senate committee to investigate GlaxoSmithKline and issue a damning report.[70] Legal cases have been instituted. These reveal extensive ghostwriting of the medical literature as part of the marketing of Avandia, comparable to that found in the marketing of Hormone Replacement Therapy (HRT)[71] or oral contraceptives such as Yaz. These cases reveal that the pattern of using evidence-based medicine to drive prescribing is now all but universal. Apparently rational prescribing in such circumstances is close to certain irrationality.

Zeus responded to Demeter that he was helpless to do anything about her daughter. Once, if our daughters were threatened by Hades, doctors from Philippe Pinel two centuries ago, to Alfred Worcester and Richard Cabot a century ago, and Dr. Lapin who looked after my father a quarter of a century ago, might have intervened on our behalf, but for the moment all we have standing between us and Hades is a small group, comprised of mothers and wives like Mathy Downing and Mary Ellen Winter and a dwindling number of Lapins, Worcesters, and Pinels. It is these who do the job of alerting us to the hazards of treatment, a job that one might have thought lay at the heart of good medical care. How long they can hold on before the Heavens answer is not clear.

8

Pharmageddon

Nothing more
But the sense
Of where we are

That seeks to find, to rescue
Love to the chill
Upper world, and to speak

A substantial language
Of Dignity
And of respect.

—George Oppen, "Orpheus"

Medicine as we have known it is at death's door. Real disease brings
the specter of death with it, and every medical journey to some extent
follows in the steps of Cora into the underworld, leaving Demeter to
implore heaven to restore her to some measure of life.

Over the last quarter of a century, what was medicine has increasingly turned into healthcare, part of a vast global market in health-
related products. Pharmaceuticals are exemplars of the goods in this
modern health products market, but entire services can be packaged
and managed as commodities, just as drugs are.

Only the market can guarantee efficient production, we're told, and we
must surrender to it. The industrialization and marketization of healthcare has entailed a gamut of changes similar to those that have been
seen in other industries. We see a standardization of care, with practices
geared to treating patients in the same way as a service station handles

a car that comes in for servicing—albeit with appropriate expressions of concern that wouldn't be necessary with a car. Meanwhile, the labor of taking risks in trials of new drugs has been outsourced to the Third World, Enron-scale scandals with drugs like Vioxx and Zyprexa have erupted, and to sell the products, healthcare advertisers now promise what automobile and shampoo advertisers have promised for years with purchase of their products—an enhanced life.

The corporate world of today's health services industry is a long way from the clinics in which nurses, doctors, and others working with those who are suffering try, often against the odds, to produce health. Ads for healthcare products that portray patients as vigorous and embracing life, as if drugs were just another set of consumer goods at the mall, conflict with the reality of diseases that shorten and compromise lives. People with diabetes are taught to prick the side of their fingers to get blood samples because the disease brings a risk of blindness and they may need the pulp of their fingers to remain touch-sensitive—good care does not deny these possibilities or put them in the small print of an advertisement. Medicine aims at a myriad of adjustments, with as much assistance as possible from technology, in order to cope with the frailties of the human body and mind; it aims at producing as much health as possible out of mankind's most debilitating afflictions.[1] This is quite a different project than the enhancements health products offer.

At the heart of medicine is an act of care by doctors who talk, look, listen, and do something for patients who come to a clinic acutely ill with an abdominal problem, a heart attack, or a broken limb, or drug-induced injury where every patient is different and care necessarily has to reflect this. While today's rhetoric is more and more about personalized medicine, the practice of dispensing health products has moved increasingly to standardized screenings for risk factors with treatments like the statins, or drugs for osteoporosis, nervous problems, or blood sugar control that clinical trials suggest in many cases are at least as likely to harm us as to help—a practice that is as far from caring as it is possible to get.

Generations of revolutionaries have talked about the alienation market forces and industrialization produce, the loss of jobs and skills, of values and ways of life, but many of us in the economically developed world have seen our material circumstances improve and have shrugged. Why should we expect anything less than comparable improvements in medical care—especially as we seem to hear of ever more medical breakthroughs in the media?

There are a few reasons why things are different now. One is that drugs and other services in the medical market physically act on the stuff of which we are made and may reconfigure us quite dramatically in ways we are not told about. Unlike short courses of antibiotics, which do not substantially change us, chronic courses of treatments aimed at managing risk factors do change us. Whether it be a cholesterol-lowering statin, an anti-inflammatory such as Celebrex, a treatment for osteoporosis such as Actonel, or a psychotropic cocktail, these drugs do not just have the action we are told about but often have much greater effects throughout the body than the one the company markets, potentially leading to an increased risk of dementia in the case of Vioxx and Celebrex, an enduring susceptibility to heart attacks in the case of Fosamax and Actonel, or changes in our ability to make love in the case of Paxil, Cymbalta, or Zoloft. Beyond these specific problems, the indiscriminate actions of many of these drugs on our physical constitution quite probably alter both our susceptibility to various diseases and our personalities too in subtle ways.

A second reason things are different now is that unlike other industrial processes, many of which have led to tangible benefits, the logic of healthcare marketing may block real benefits. Companies initially attempted to play down the evidence that ulcers were linked to a bacterium that could be eliminated, because this information wasn't good for business. They have similarly been extraordinarily successful at replacing older generations of antibiotics, psychotropic drugs, and anti-inflammatories with less effective and more hazardous agents such as Celebrex, Prozac, and Cipro. As a result some of us are now dying earlier than we should, and many more are suffering needlessly. By taking us away from productive work any premature deaths and incapacity come at a cost to the economy, and so it is in the interest of all of us to pay attention to the medical care each of us gets.

A third and perhaps most important reason is that these drugs also serve as a screen for a set of processes that act on us just as potently as the drugs themselves do. Companies take our inner aspirations and fears and mold a strategy designed to readjust our identities and get us to consume drugs more faithfully than we would do if we were living in a totalitarian regime and required to consume.[2] The changes in the way we live can be so mundane as to be almost invisible. Take the case of Josephine, a fit sixty-year-old who had been told she had osteopenia—a normal state for a woman of her age that comes with no risk of a fracture. But led to believe she has an illness, and put on

Actonel or Fosamax, she is now afraid to mow the lawn for fear of falling and breaking a hip—though mowing the lawn instead of taking the drugs is a better way of reducing her risk of a fracture. Josephine's sixties are being shaped in ways she could not easily guess by the patents on a group of drugs. Our very ideas of ourselves are now subject to change at intervals coinciding with the fall of off-patent and rise of newly patented compounds.

Macbeth's unmet desires for fame and power left him vulnerable to seduction by the witches. Many of us can live without fame and power, but we are almost all vulnerable to seductions that offer us freedom from disease, with possible enhancements of our potency or beauty. Just as reaching for what was on offer produced disaster for Macbeth, so also our reaching seems to have left us with potentially reduced life expectancies, a growing discontent with who we are, and an atrophied ability to care for others.

If we fall prey to the witches' seduction in the health domain, our abilities to resist the industrial processes now encroaching on teaching and farming and other domains are also likely to crumble. Ultimately even the rearing of children may be affected. The hour is already late; just as patients have been eliminated from medicine in favor of medical consumers, so teachers have been replaced by educators whose brief it is to make available a range of educational products to their clients rather than to try and foster the growth of a person. We may not be far from a time when, for the sake of ensuring quality upbringing, mothers (and fathers) will be encouraged to look after their young clients in standardized ways. If as a society we cannot care for patients, it is not clear that we can care for children or for the planet.

It doesn't have to be like this. Ironically, indeed tragically, our new medical systems now produce as many perverse outcomes as they do in part because of some mechanisms we have put in place that stem from our recognition of how central health is to everything that counts for us. Given this centrality, it seemed important to Senator Estes Kefauver to control the pharmaceutical industry, and he, on our behalf, attempted to do so by making new drugs available by prescription only and then only letting them on the market once they had been through controlled trials. These safeguards, which were designed to bolster the role of doctors and contain industry, have in industry's hand been turned to do just the opposite. Increasingly alienated, doctors are not the force they once were and it is very difficult to view them as a body likely to rise up and demand change.

If, however, there is a path down into Hades, there must also be a path up. And there is hope in the knowledge that life often teems even in the most inhospitable environments. The first step back is to decide what kind of society we want to live in, what kind of economy we want.

At present we are trained from infancy to believe that the key things we produce are cars, computers, pharmaceuticals, and other goods. No one would accept that these are the things we care about the most, but we have slipped into a de facto acceptance that these things have a primacy largely because they can be readily commodified and quantified. The problems with the kind of system we have ended up with become very clear when we find that the cleanup of an oil spill like the *Exxon Valdez,* because it leads to a quantifiable increase in the consumption of commodities, adds to our economic wealth. As the service sector of the economy has grown, we produce units of service rather than old-style goods and this is what Western economies now depend on to an ever greater extent.

When it comes to health and education, the dangers in this model become ever more apparent. Just as with the *Exxon Valdez* in measures of gross domestic product, so in health, the side effects of treatments are at present (a lawsuit or two aside) an unalloyed good for pharmaceutical companies. They tend to lead to treatment with ever more drugs to manage side-effect problems rather than to a reconsideration of the original treatment; for instance Avandia and Lipitor are given to manage the diabetes and raised cholesterol triggered by a guideline-mandated drug like Zyprexa rather than rejecting this newer drug and returning instead to older, off-patent, less expensive drugs that would be much less likely to cause these problems. Increasing rates of treatment-induced mortality so far have had little effect on these practices. Instead, we have increasing efforts to standardize treatment delivery through the development of guidelines, which happen to recommend the latest on-patent medications that in many cases clinical trials have suggested may increase rather than reduce mortality. In this way the side effects of our latest blockbuster drugs have become one of the primary drivers of health system growth.

Is there an alternative to these "diabolical" scenarios?

One option is to put a fostering of persons at the center of the economic (*oikos nomos*) stage. Just as in a home (*oikos*), it makes more sense to view our family or our people, rather than any provisions, the furnishings, or money salted away, as the ultimate source of our well-being, including our economic well-being. The trick will lie in redesigning the rules (*nomos*) of our collective home to reflect this. This would not mean turning our back on the production of goods. The problems we face do not come from technical advances—few among us would not welcome more effective treatments for dementia or cancer, and technical advances now seem a crucial component to saving life on the planet—the home of our homes.

The problems come from the social arrangements, the rules, through which at present all developments in health are filtered. It is these rules that give rise to our alienation and also increasingly block the emergence of the developments we need. Senator Kefauver adjusted the rules one way, perhaps the right way for his time, but in a manner that seems to be contributing to our problems now. Are there any adjustments that might steer medicine back toward what it could be and at the same time give us a glimpse of what a properly human economy (*oikumene*) might look like? There may be other steps to take, but following Kefauver we can look at company practices of sequestering clinical trial data that inhibit the ability of doctors to practice data-based medicine, the availability of medicines by prescription only, and the current patenting arrangements for drugs.

Reforms in these areas will require wisdom—having good intentions is not sufficient. Social arrangements have a great capacity to deliver exactly the opposite outcomes to those their proponents intended, as perhaps Kefauver's 1962 Act demonstrates better than anything else. But our intentions are also important. There must be some attempt to answer just what it is we want or need in order to determine whether our arrangements are likely to facilitate this or not. In the following pages I will review changes in terms of whether they are likely to foster an ability to care or not.

Our story will end on the wider shores of myth, where by myth I mean our more general orientation to the unknown. But it is in specific changes to the social arrangements that govern our way of life on the planet and vis-à-vis each other that the survival of medicine is likely to lie.

DATA-BASED MEDICINE

In the 1960s randomized controlled trials appeared to be an almost perfect way both to harness the benefits that industry could bring to the common good and to contain or even eliminate the evils of pharmaceutical marketing. In the 1990s, in response to growing commercial pressures on medicine, this medical turn to controlled trials evolved into a commitment to what came to be called evidence-based medicine. Far from resisting these moves that were meant to constrain it, industry embraced them, and from the 1990s has proselytized for evidence-based medicine. Few seem to have noticed the irony, and among those who do there is bewilderment as to how to manage this Hydra who grows new heads no matter what efforts are made to prune it back.

Medicine today has to be based on evidence—but what is evidence? Industry has masterfully exploited ambiguities in the word and, especially, a gap that lies between data—what actually happens to a patient—and the later construction of "evidence" as to what a drug does. Where doctors are faced with the word "evidence" they for the most part believe they are dealing with data-based medicine, and as long as they think this way industry can vigorously promote their version of what happened when drugs are given under the banner of "evidence"-based medicine.

There are several ways in which the data that should be at the heart of medical evidence are hidden by the pharmaceutical industry. First, there is a drug company's outright hiding of the data that is collected so that no one gets to see it. Second, the remaining data is disguised through certain kinds of statistical models and what comes out the far end is presented as "evidence," while the injuries that happen to you and me are degraded to the status of an anecdote. And finally companies have created a culture of data neglect, in which doctors have become blind to what is happening to the person in front of their eyes.

The issue of hiding data is not the scandal it should be in part because common perception is that drugs are made in company laboratories. This view misses something fundamental: companies make chemicals, but we are the laboratories in which modern drugs are made. Drugs are chemicals used for a social purpose—to treat conditions that we define as diseases. Drugs cannot come into being unless we as healthy volunteers and later as patients in clinical trials agree to take them to see what happens. Without our participation, there is no drug.

Our willingness to participate in these studies was borne out of a sense of civic duty in the 1950s. We participated on the understanding that taking risks might injure us but would benefit a community that included our friends, relatives, and children. We did so for free— in perhaps the greatest ever example of how a system geared around people rather than products can make much more economic sense. The system worked and extended the compass of human freedom from the many epidemics and other scourges to which our forefathers had been subject for millennia.

But the research in which we once participated has morphed from scientific studies whose data was in the public domain into company trials where the data has been sequestered. There are all sorts of protections now built into trials that weren't there in the 1950s—centering on informed consent about the possible benefits and side effects of treatment and suitable safeguards of anonymity. But we are never informed about and asked to consent to the sequestration of our data in company trials. We assume we are participating in science and that the data arising from the risks we take are available to scientists more generally, as they once were.

It would be an easy matter to remedy this—by ensuring that the consent forms for a trial tell us whether the company will sequester our data. Without this any participation in such studies is more likely to jeopardize the health and well-being of our friends, children, and communities than to widen the compass of freedom from disease because companies will parade clinical trials where injurious side effects are hidden, artfully coded, or simply eliminated as evidence that their drug could not have caused the injury, and if doctors or the courts believe them, any effort on our part to seek redress will fail at the first hurdle.

Evidence-based medicine as first conceived was a highly moral enterprise. It takes courage to subject all our preconceptions to testing, and then to treat the people who come to us for care on the basis of the data. But what passes for evidence-based medicine has now been subverted by companies into an exercise that skirts conflicting values by appealing to preselected "data" that are supposedly value neutral. We need to recover the perspective that science, far from being value free, values data and does so with a passion. "Controlled trials" that involve restricted access to data are not science, and following selected "data" can only diminish both the carers and the cared-for.

If all the data on the benefits and hazards of treatment were available, the exuberance that companies can engender by marketing agents of supposedly extraordinary efficacy and almost no risks would to some extent be curbed, and if curbed the vast profits that support the most sophisticated marketing on the planet, that conjures diseases out of vicissitudes and can reconfigure our very selves to suit its purposes, would in some measure be limited. If this happened clinical practice would have a better chance of returning to something closer to what it once was, when one person consulted another.

We might require companies to post all records from clinical trials, with suitable safeguards to protect individual patient identities, to an Internet site, before any analysis of the evidence was published. This would simply replicate for medicine the common scientific practice of journals like *Nature* or *Science* that require the relevant genetic sequence to be posted to the Internet before any claims are published.

But the simple idea of posting the data reveals a profound ambiguity in the notion of evidence-based medicine. While most people assume medicine has been data-based for the last twenty years or so, there are vanishingly few articles in journals or presentations at meetings—other than, ironically, some good case reports—that offer data. In the course of clinical trials things happen to patients, but these things are assembled and analyzed using models that come with assumptions including that if a finding is not statistically significant it essentially does not exist. It is the "results" of these analyses that are published—rather than any account of what in fact happened to patients. When it comes to results, he who controls the program giving rise to the results can control everything.[3]

When we have Pierre Touery drinking ten times the lethal dose of strychnine in front of our eyes and surviving because he had previously taken activated charcoal or when a child with bacterial endocarditis gets up off her deathbed and walks after being given penicillin, we have data-based medicine. When you are put on a statin, a biphosphonate, or a psychotropic drug because in some trial that has recruited hundreds or even thousands of subjects so that a finding on a blood test or rating scale that suits some company has become statistically significant, you are being subjected to results-based medicine rather than cared for with data-based medicine.

When it comes to the hazards of drugs as reported by their makers we are invariably dealing with results rather than data. Consider the following excerpt from the deposition of Ian Hudson, then head of Global Safety at GSK:

Q: Okay. So, your view is: It's simply impossible for SmithKline Beecham to decide whether Paxil did or did not contribute to the homicidal or suicidal behavior of any one given individual; is that your testimony?

A: We would certainly gather all the information, but on an individual case basis it would be impossible to decide whether paroxetine caused an event or not. . . . It is impossible, on an individual case basis, from individual reports, to assign causality especially in a very complicated area such as this. That's why, when we have issues, we review all the available data and make a determination, on the basis of all the available data, whether there is an issue or not.

Q: Okay. Do you believe that it is possible that Paxil has caused any person, worldwide, to commit an act of homicide or suicide?

A: I have seen no evidence to suggest that at all.[4]

Hudson is demonstrating the standard company approach to determining whether there is any link between an adverse effect and the company's drug. In brief, the company position is that unless an adverse event has been statistically significantly associated with the company's drug in a controlled trial, that event cannot be said to have been caused by the drug. And companies can ensure their drug *never causes anything* by making sure that trials are organized so that important adverse events cannot become statistically significant.

Taking this approach, even when faced with assessments by doctors or their own personnel that the company's drug has caused some problem, based perhaps on a temporal link between a Vioxx or a Paxil, say, and a side effect that emerges on treatment, clears when the treatment is stopped, and reappears when the treatment is restarted, the company will still not concede a link.

What, then, about the long list of side effects reported in ads for the drug or in the *Physicians' Desk Reference (PDR)*? The company view is that these have been reported but this is not the same thing as being caused. These reports are merely anecdotal unless or until they have occurred enough times in clinical trials to have their link to the drug come out as statistically significant. Drug company personnel will of course warn doctors about all proven hazards their treatment causes (conveniently, none as no trials are done to establish a linkage)—it would be inhuman to do otherwise in such a sensitive domain as medicine. But they will not, as they put it, spread rumors about their drug—that would be good neither for the company nor for the patient. In adhering to this kind of "science" company personnel—and doctors—have found a way to live with themselves that has echoes of a totalitarian regime where people have learned to live with themselves on the basis that they are obeying orders or keeping to the rule of law.

What these doctors miss is that companies are working from assumptions or results rather than from data. There may have been thousands of reports of a problem to the company as clinically significant as Pierre Touery's use of activated charcoal, but these never stand a chance of becoming statistically significant.

When John Snow, investigating the outbreak of cholera in London in 1856, found a cluster of deaths from the disease on Broad Street, he was not inhibited by considerations of statistical significance because this concept hadn't been invented. He was free to recognize a cluster. Clinical prudence dictated a course of action—remove the handle of the pump. Science mandates efforts to go behind the data in an attempt to establish what has given rise to the cluster. But if companies had controlled the pump and took an Ian Hudson approach, they would not countenance the removal of the handle or any investigation of what the mechanisms giving rise to the cluster might be—unless the findings were statistically significant, which in all likelihood at Broad Street they weren't.

This account of what happens when our deaths or injuries on treatment are hidden or disguised may also help explain why doctors neglect what is happening to the person in front of them—in a manner that seems close to the antithesis of what good care should be. Anything that happens to the patient in front of a doctor has been degraded to an anecdote rather than an event that the doctor needs to pay heed to. If the doctor, using standard methods to decide if treatment has caused a particular problem, attempts to report it to a journal, the report will be turned down on the basis that journals no longer take case reports. If the doctor tried to report it to either the company or the FDA, it disappears into a statistical black hole that can swallow thousands of such events without the slightest indigestion. In the case of Vioxx it is estimated that there were at least 30,000 heart attacks linked to this drug from the time clinical trials first showed an increase in risk to the point where it was conceded there might be a problem and Merck drew back from its marketing blitzkrieg.[5]

The result is that, astonishingly, in the midst of this emphasis on evidence, medicine is collecting even less evidence on those harmed by treatments than it has done in the past. Although we now have the ability to register all patients with particular diagnoses or patients receiving any drug and could track all outcomes and assemble the data on what actually happens when treatments are given, there is in fact a yawning hole—through which Cora and others in the prime of life are abducted by Hades. Those who love them, who are left behind, have a right to complain to Zeus that there has been a fundamental breach here in the contract between heaven and hell.

But in addition to frustrating the giving of decent and reliable medical care, the neglect of data on the problems treatment may cause is cutting off our ability to develop new drugs. The single most fruitful source for the discovery of new drugs continues to be observations that a drug given for one purpose in some cases is doing something else. It is perhaps no coincidence that as the possibility of reporting "adverse" events has dried up, with journals unwilling to take reports on unexpected outcomes in individual cases and companies hiding effects that do not fit with the business plan for a drug, so also drug discovery has dried to a trickle.

In response to questions as to whether major medical journals should insist on access to the raw data from controlled trials, the editorial staff of the *New England Journal of Medicine (NEJM)* said in April 2009 they do not see this happening in the near future—"that would be a large step outside our role"—while at the same time maintaining that the *NEJM* offers transparency.[6] As things stand we might all be safer if clinical trials were published in the *New York Times* rather than the *NEJM,* as the *Times* makes some effort to check the integrity of the primary sources for its stories, whereas the *NEJM* does nothing. When a *Times* story turns out to have been invented, as in the case some years ago of a series of articles written by Jayson Blair, it is national news, and the editor's job is on the line; not so when a drug trial such as Study 329 turns out to have been bogus.

Study 329 was the 1997 trial, discussed initially in chapter 4, in which Paxil was found to be no more effective yet more dangerous than placebo but from which GlaxoSmithKline (GSK) decided to select and publish the good bits, concealing the fact that six times more children became suicidal on Paxil than on placebo. The ghostwritten article was published in the most influential journal in child psychiatry, the *Journal of the American Association of Child and Adolescent Psychiatry,* whose editor at the time was Mina Dulcan. Dulcan had this to say in 2004 when interviewed by Shelley Jofre of the BBC after the history of the paper had become clear, and at a time when the paper was the basis of a fraud case taken by New York State against GSK:

> SJ: The interesting thing is that GlaxoSmithKline actually acknowledged internally three years before you even published Study 329 that it had failed to show that Paxil was better than placebo. They took a marketing decision to effectively pick out the best bits of the study and see if they could get it published.

> MD: That may be. That's not something that journals have any access to, that information.

> SJ: Do you have no regrets about publishing the study?

MD: I don't have any regrets about publishing at all. It generated all sorts of useful discussion, which is the purpose of a scholarly journal. The purpose of a scholarly journal is not to tell people what to do. The purpose of a scholarly journal is to put out the data. . . .

SJ: I can tell you that GlaxoSmithKline thought [publication] was fantastic and their sales reps were using your journal's name and influence to then say to doctors, here look, there's a published study, it works.

MD: Well, I think we all see salesmen of a whole variety of kinds, whether they are drug company salesmen or insurance salesmen and we certainly have no control over how they use something.

SJ: But, given what you know now about this drug and what it can do to children, don't you have any regrets that that published article was able to use your journal's good name to basically, as a cloak of respectability to say look, I have been in this journal. It must be true, look at the authors.

MD: I can't control the authors. No, I don't have regrets. . . . If someone misuses our journal we really have very little control over that. . . .

SJ: Are you aware that 329 was ghost written?

MD: I have no way of knowing that. It doesn't surprise me to know it happens, but we have no way of259 having that information.

SJ: Does it worry you, do you think it matters?

MD: Well, certainly if I were an author I would not put my name on anything that I didn't feel was accurate. I can't speak to what those authors, to the extent, how much they saw the data. Someone can write something and you may or may not agree with it. The fact that someone puts the words together may be a good thing or a bad thing depending on what the words are. . . .[7]

In contrast to what one imagines the position of the editor of the *New York Times* might be had they published Study 329, Mina Dulcan seems completely unfazed by her role in the publication of one of the most notorious studies of all time. At some point it is going to take a gutsy academic editor to risk being shut down by industry or the rest of us to consider whether we would be safer if publication of clinical trials happened in the *New York Times* and academic journals were reclassified as periodicals and academic meetings as trade fairs.

The response of many to these issues may be that we need a beefed-up FDA to police what is going on. We don't. It would do no harm to beef up, or exit, those in the FDA who are weak and bureaucratic. But the FDA's primary brief is to regulate the wording of advertisements rather than to care about patients. When these drugs were made available by prescription only it was because legislators thought to put them in the hands of an institution that looked a lot more powerful than the FDA and a lot more concerned about the welfare of patients—medical doctors. If medicine and its academics have been neutered, any other beefed-up agency or set of regulations can be too. Any regulations should follow from our values rather than substitute for them—and the values in this case are that if the data aren't available it's not science.

When it comes to the risks of treatment, the company trials that now dictate clinical practice are like the subprime mortgage market, in which risk was so cut up that all parties could act as though the hazards of lending had somehow vanished. By running small studies, the pharmaceutical industry has similarly cut up the appearance of risk to patients, using statistical significance to make these risks vanish. It then has come as a huge shock when large and independent studies show the risks to be alive and flourishing for Vioxx, Avandia, Advair, and other drugs. These shocks have been handled by denial.

Faced with these scenarios both doctors and patients cast around for a wizard for help but it has been as difficult to spot any influence for the good from the FDA as it was to spot any good from the financial regulators in the recent financial turmoil. In this case, doctors are the scarecrows, tin men, and lions who need to be told that they have the brains, hearts, and courage for the job. In the case of the FDA, we need a Dorothy to pull back the curtain and reveal the wizard as a simple auditor. But we have instead—to the benefit of no one except industry—drifted slowly into the position where professional bodies within medicine have turned to the FDA for a lead on the safety and efficacy of drugs where in the Kefauver hearings of 1962 it was envisaged that medicine would offer the FDA a lead. Given the failure of medicine to step up to the plate and the fact that the current regulations governing drugs have been in place for an extraordinary length of time—over fifty years, it is perhaps time to revisit what might be done.

PRESCRIPTION-ONLY STATUS

The problem within medicine, unlike the financial crisis, is not that we have abandoned regulations, but rather that the current regulations aren't working or are being manipulated to our disadvantage, in particular prescription-only regulations. Prescription-only status makes doctors, not patients, the primary consumers of our blockbuster drugs but this is a consumer group that in the 1950s effectively disbanded one of its only consumer bodies when the AMA stopped running its independent program of drug assessments. Medicine ever since has been like a frigate or tanker adrift on the high seas whose rudder is not functioning, a clear target for pirates.

Because doctors have always written prescriptions, and because today's doctors have only practiced in a prescription-only world, they think key medicines have always been available by prescription only. But prescription-only status is very recent, and just as with the French Revolution it may still be too early to judge all the consequences.

The initial prescription-only arrangements introduced in 1914 were a police function aimed at controlling the use of substances like heroin and cocaine. This seemed incompatible with the practice of medicine to many. We have since lost any perspective we once had that giving a doctor exclusive control over access to something as important as life-saving remedies might corrupt the doctor. The subsequent impetus to prescription-only status ironically first arose in the United States, the home of the free market, rather than in Europe or elsewhere. This restriction on the availability of drugs assumed that the doctors who prescribed medicines would be like Philippe Pinel in Paris two hundred years ago, Alfred Worcester a century ago in Massachusetts, or Nancy Olivieri in Toronto today (who lost her job after speaking out about the hazards of deferiprone as a treatment for thalassemia), doctors who were skeptical that all treatments were as beneficial as companies claimed and who were not afraid to speak out in defense of their patients.[8] If these hopes had been realized, we might not have the degradation of medical care we now have.

But these hopes have not been realized. Rather than a bulwark against industry, prescription-only privileges have become a bulwark for physicians against competitors in the health domain, like homeopaths, psychologists, nurses, and others—a "precious" just like the Ring of Power in *Lord of the Rings* to be guarded jealously. A ring that puts physicians directly in the gun sights of the most sophisticated marketing on the planet. All the while, doctors seem be shrinking as did Gollum, the figure in J.R.R. Tolkien's novel who, under the influence of the Ring, became a twisted shadow of what he should have been. Given this, it is unbelievable that there does not appear to be a single medical course anywhere that offers physicians any education on marketing. The only doctors who seem to know something about marketing are those who have worked in the pharmaceutical industry. In the *Lord of the Rings*, in true market style, it was ultimately the self-interest of Gollum that saved everyone else. But that was only a fable—and while saving us, Gollum's self-interest destroyed him.

If we are to continue with prescription-only status as we have it now, our safety depends critically on doctors stepping up to the plate. They need to report on hazards and need to find a way to ensure their reports aren't airbrushed out of existence. They need to insist on companies undertaking adequate studies of drugs. Moreover, if companies are to be allowed to market their drugs under the banner of science, doctors need to ensure that companies adhere to the norms of science and make the data from these studies available, or else they need to undertake the appropriate studies themselves. They do, after all, report on the hazards of over-the-counter medicines and, funded by federal monies, doctors have undertaken research on drugs like tobacco, aimed at nailing down its hazards. Prescription-only arrangements once seemed like a mechanism to enhance the ability of medicine to interrogate the companies producing these "ethical" drugs. If it has become instead a mechanism that neuters medicine, it is time for medicine to take stock and then take action.

There are alternate arrangements to the current ones. We could make new medicines available by prescription only for a limited period before a decision was made as to whether they could be sold over the counter, during which time doctors would work hard to establish all the hazards of the new drugs. Alternatively, rather than have all new drugs available by prescription only, we could opt to make just highly toxic drugs available indefinitely by prescription only. We might distinguish between drugs used for traditional medical purposes and drugs for something closer to lifestyle enhancement, with the first group being available by prescription only and the second not.

The SSRIs offer an instructive example of what happens when essentially the same drugs are available by prescription only and over the counter. The SSRIs are antihistamines that inhibit serotonin reuptake. Available by prescription only, one set of selective serotonin reuptake inhibitors lead to agitation and suicidality, while very similar SSRIs available over the counter for allergies have occasionally been linked to irritability but appear in general to cause fewer problems than their prescription-only cousins. In part the differences likely stem from the difficulties described in chapter 7 in the case of Victor Motus: it is not easy to stop a treatment that doesn't suit a particular patient when a doctor has told that patient they need to remain on the treatment for several weeks before it "works."

Doctors like Dr. Trostler, whom Victor Motus went to for help, have no training in the many things they do, aside from issuing a prescription for medication, that may enable or disable the people for whom they are trying to care from contributing to that care. They appear to have no feel for the fact that prescription-only arrangements put them in the position of a Roman emperor, with their patients in the role of tasters.

At a time when pregnant women have learned to shun over-the-counter drugs, even down to coffee, doctors have for over a decade dramatically increased their patients' prenatal consumption of SSRIs in the face of growing evidence these drugs double the rate of major birth defects and miscarriages. Drug companies like GlaxoSmithKline are aware that farmers have known for centuries to keep their herds out of fields in which the serotonin-reuptake-inhibiting St. John's wort grows as it leads to miscarriages, but these same drug companies have still manipulated doctors very successfully into herding women into the pastures in which their serotonin reuptake inhibitors grow.[9]

There are other benefits that might flow from lifting the prescription-only status of many drugs. The current arrangements constrain new drugs within a disease framework. If this were changed, a range of diseases from social phobia to osteopenia would vanish overnight. In the case of the antidepressants, for example, some that enhance appetite and sleep might be marketed as tonics rather than for depression. The SSRIs are more like St. John's wort and might be marketed similarly—for stress or burnout. At present, to get Prozac a person has to be labeled as suffering from depression or social phobia or obsessive-compulsive disorder first. If the drugs were marketed instead for stress or burnout there would be much less stigma in using them. In the case of the statins for cholesterol or biphosphonates for osteoporosis, the marketing would likely be aimed more for keeping arteries or bones young and not for supposed diseases. There might have been no fewer drugs sold but we would have fewer diseases. There would be a greater dividing line between medicine and daily life than there is now.

If many more drugs were available over the counter, company marketing would doubtless throw up a different set of abuses. It is doubtful, though, if the abuses could be any worse than the marketing of the proprietary panaceas that dominated the drug market in the late nineteenth and early twentieth centuries. But a century ago, when faced with these panaceas, there was a group of skeptics we could turn to—doctors. There are no skeptics now, and there need to be.

Where in the 1960s there was a gulf between the pharmaceutical and tobacco industries, partly owing to prescription-only arrangements, now it is increasingly difficult to distinguish between the two, except insofar as medicine supports one and not the other. If our current blockbusters were available over the counter, there is little doubt that the pharmaceutical industry would have marketed them as vigorously as the tobacco industry marketed cigarettes and likely caused as much damage with them as tobacco has. Would we be safer if our current blockbusters came with warnings that have the clarity of those found on tobacco products?

Abolishing prescription-only arrangements is a thought experiment. We have a tendency however to solve problems by opting for more rather than less regulation, and it is unlikely that this thought experiment is ever likely to be adopted. What we perhaps need to appreciate however is that these regulations are part of a growing apparatus within healthcare that Sam Sessions has referred to as a "Shadow Government."[10] Doctors are no longer free to follow the market for drugs on the basis of price or quality—they have to adhere to a variety of diktats in the form of guidelines and other instruments that have been fostered by companies. It is this range of instruments that pivot on the existence of prescription-only arrangements that effectively govern healthcare today. Whether in the United States or Europe, voices are increasingly raised against the involvement of government in healthcare—but when we look to Washington or other capitals for the culprits we are looking to the wrong place.

Another thought experiment might bring out what else could be done to make a prescription-only market work more efficiently than it does now.

RXISK.COM

In August 1973, a bank robbery at the Kreditbanken in Stockholm triggered a five-day siege with bank employees held hostage. After the siege ended, to the surprise of everyone many of the hostages, as if hypnotized, spoke well of their captors. "Stockholm syndrome" was born. Now recognized as common, the conditions that trigger this change in behavior seem to be isolation, a fear that your life is at risk, and kindness on the part of the hostage-takers.

Disease isolates us as profoundly as incarceration or anything else might. Our lives are at risk, and our doctors who control the exit to freedom are almost certain to be kind. But not a single doctor is trained to manage Stockholm syndrome, to suspect that our apparent insouciance or congenial conversation might conceal deep unhappiness with a proposed course of treatment or, even worse, alarm at new problems that have emerged on treatment.

From about the time of the 1973 Kreditbanken siege, doctors have become increasingly likely to suffer their own variant of Stockholm syndrome. If something goes wrong with a treatment a doctor gives, even though the label may concede that the drug can cause the problem, the makers of the drug and the doctor's colleagues will deny that it is likely to have done so in any particular case. Speaking up about a problem, once the material of medical advance, is now a recipe for professional suicide. A doctor attempting to rescue a patient is likely to be accused of being a persecutor who victimizes the patient by withholding effective treatment.

Offers to describe problems at professional meetings are turned down. Journals are ever less likely to accept publications outlining a new problem. Invitations to apply for better jobs, to attend conferences, or simply to go with colleagues to local eateries funded by drug companies are ever less likely to happen for doctors linked to adverse events. Those holding doctors hostage have been very kind indeed—there are ever fewer medical departments or medical conferences not awash with company support, when it comes to paying for meals with colleagues most doctors have forgotten what a credit card looks like, and of course in supplying drugs they supply the objects that make doctors desirable.

As a result bit by bit over the last forty years any of us seeking treatment have been disappearing in front of the eyes of our doctors, who in turn are increasingly inaudible and invisible to companies, academics, and regulators. A key component of the fog that envelopes both us and our doctors lies in the published trials that have hypnotized everyone. Individual observations, the logic goes, are unreliable, while trials supposedly offer reliable estimates about the consequences of treatment. When a doctor does report an adverse event to regulators, the report is invariably marked and filed as uncertain and unreliable information.

But we know that over 80 percent of the reports on the adverse consequences of treatment, dismissed as anecdotes, have turned out to be correct.[11] We also now know that close to 30 percent of the clinical trials that have been undertaken remain unreported, and that of the 50 percent that are reported almost all will be ghostwritten[12] and roughly

25 percent of the published trials altered to the extent that a negative result for a drug will have been transformed into evidence the drug works well and is safe.[13] In 100 percent of cases, the data from trials remain inaccessible to scrutiny. Given these facts it is not reasonable to suggest that the observations of doctors or patients are any less reliable than clinical trial evidence.

Reporting the adverse effects of treatments has always been a delicate thing for doctors, because it involves recognition that they may have harmed a patient they intended to help and also because drugs once seen as poisons are now seen as fertilizers necessary to our growth and well-being rather than risky. There is also no feedback to doctors after they make report that would incentivize them to report further—nothing that recognizes that what they have done could be beneficial.

As a result doctors now report fewer than 5 percent of serious adverse events on treatment. Faced with this lack of reporting, American and European regulators have allowed patients to report on the adverse effects of drugs. But the new systems put in place for online reporting by patients are not user friendly. Minimal information is sought rather than the greatest amount of and richest possible details. Other than for altruistic reasons, or out of anger, there is very little incentive for a patient to report.

Consider what could be done. Roughly 25 percent of serious events have not been reported before, but whether reporting on a new problem or a problem already featured on a drug's label or elsewhere in the world literature, there is still a matter of deciding when I turn blue on a drug known to cause some people to turn blue, if in fact my blue hue is linked to treatment. There are standard ways to check out the likelihood of a linkage by noting the time of onset of the problem, what happens if the drug is stopped or the dose reduced, what happens if the drug is reintroduced or the dose increased, whether I have ever had reactions like this before on another drug, and whether anything else makes a difference. This approach can also help us decide if a drug might be linked to a problem never before reported.

Imagine if on making a report you were taken through these questions and then issued with a letter from an expert website to take to your doctor outlining the suspected reaction and the factors that in your case might help you and your doctor decide if there is a link to treatment. Imagine that this letter also lays out a case to your doctor that in-person, professional observations as to whether your treatment was likely to be linked to the problem are at the moment much more credible than the clinical trial data, and then invites your doctor to supplement or take issue with your report.

A few days later on the basis of the best possible input from both your doctor and you, when the reaction is coded and the database to which you've reported can assess how many other reactions like this there have been, imagine both you and your doctor get letters letting you know that a thousand other people have reported a similar problem and a hundred other doctors have endorsed a link between treatment and the effect. If 80 percent of medical reporting is likely to be correct, there comes a point where, even if the clinical trial data says otherwise, it is just not reasonable to say the problem can't be happening in at least some people. This compilation of individual reports offers your doctor and you a variation on an age old strategy—if you're going to owe the bank money, it is best to owe so much the bank has a problem—in this case it will be regulators and companies who have the problem. Far from being inaudible you and your doctor have been handed a megaphone.

Now take one more step. Hundreds of billions of dollars have been pumped into genomic research but very few genes have been found for major illnesses based on studies that have recruited tens of thousands of patients. Researchers have found small genetic risks contributing to common diseases like diabetes, hypertension, or mood disorders but little else. However in the case of clearly described adverse reactions to drugs, studies may only need to recruit fifty to a hundred people to find a gene coding for the treatment-induced problem. This makes sense as treatment effects have to be mediated biologically and a striking reaction to a drug is much more likely to be mediated through a single protein than is a complex condition like diabetes.

Getting us and our doctors to report on effects and work together to clarify the nature of the problem—whether turning blue on treatment involves two different conditions with one being turning blue from the waist up and the other blue from the waist down—will set up exactly the kind of conditions that make it possible to detect genetic inputs to such treatment effects. An effect tied to a gene is very difficult to dismiss as an anecdote. Health providers, insurers, and investors won't dismiss them. These are genes, moreover, that will reduce rather than increase our health insurance premiums—they point to risks we can avoid rather than risks waiting to happen.

Genes are just a tip of an iceberg. They code for proteins that are part of a biological mechanism. Even without knowing the gene, clear descriptions of problems will in many cases enable physiologists, phar- macologists, and others to pinpoint the larger mechanism producing an outcome, making it possible to state that X causes Y—the cholera bacillus causes cholera or SSRIs can causally trigger a suicide.[14] It is in the laboratory rather than in a clinical trial we ultimately estab- lish causes—in Koch's laboratory rather than Snow's epidemiology. But where Snow saw his epidemiology as paving the way for a hunt for causes, the exclusive turn to clinical trials in medicine today stops doctors and others from any effort to hunt for the mechanisms that make sense of the trial data.

There are new forces, like the Internet, emerging that will either swing us back toward Koch or entrench a mindless turn to trials and guidelines. Seeking answers to health issues is now the second com- monest reason to access the web. Many companies are gearing up to create electronic medical records, into which many of these Internet sites feed—sites offering to tell us for instance whether problems have been reported on our treatment. But all of the sites we might visit are at present linked to evidence-based medicine and current guidelines. The promise of companies providing these new technologies to health- care organizations is that they will alert managers and doctors when prescribing if an electronic record strays from guidelines. This is sold as offering the organization a chance to ensure doctors give the best in medical care but in fact, unless medicine is driven by patients rather than guidelines, such electronic Big Brothers risk obliterating our indi- viduality comprehensively.

This top-down approach aims at replacing individual judgments with the wisdom of experts supposedly relying only on the best avail- able evidence. In contrast, the reporting model outlined above offers a bottom-up approach. It supplements the wisdom of experts with the wisdom of individual patients and doctors. This approach fits well with the ability of Google or social media like Facebook to track events.

If we are open to finding out what is really going on, we can get people not just to report events but to outline the impact of these events on their lives—the son who went off the rails on a stimulant and dropped out of college, the end of a marriage because of sexual dysfunction when taking an antihypertensive, the car crash because of temporary lack of coordination while on the heart drug amiodarone or many other drugs, the investigation for dementia because of cognitive difficulties on statins, the cost of a jail term following murder while on the smoking-cessation drug varenicline. We are aware these things can happen but have no idea how often they might be happening. We have no idea what the true costs of treatment might be, although we have hints that the cost of managing treatment-induced problems is more than the entire drugs budget.[15]

We are at a fateful moment. The Internet is awash with sites taking a top-down approach. None of these sites are ever likely to discover anything. Many of them are likely to aggravate our problems while promising to empower us. They coexist with and indeed all but entrench the greatest failure of the free market on the planet—no where else is there so much important data pertinent to economic well-being that remains uncollected and unused. A bottom-up approach in contrast would offer a market-based solution to a growing market failure and in so doing would wrest control away from the "shadow government"[16] that runs health care and would restore it to patients and doctors.

PATENTS ON DRUGS

When Senator Estes Kefauver attempted to come to grips with the pharmaceutical industry in the early 1960s, his bill ended up mandating randomized controlled trials without being aware he had done so, as one of his aides slipped these into the 1962 act. Kefauver maintained support for the prescription-only status of new drugs, despite expressing compelling doubts about arrangements in which one person orders what another will have to consume. But he couldn't muster the votes for the one thing he actively sought to change, the system of patenting drugs. Changing this system, he thought, was crucial to bringing down the prices of drugs.

The American—and now worldwide—system enables companies to take out product patents on drugs. A patent of this type offers companies a monopoly on a new drug for twenty years, effectively on a worldwide basis. We grant this privilege to companies in return for novel and truly beneficial compounds. But the system was put in place at a time when patents were restricted to a national territory and when the idea of a blockbuster drug was inconceivable.

The current arrangements have failed us—although they work wonderfully well for companies. They have failed in that companies are not producing novel drugs of the type we desperately need. We do not have the breakthroughs for cancers, dementia disorders, or for the neurological and rheumatoid conditions that still cripple and kill us—often from quite a young age.[17] In fact we now have a situation, brought about in part by product patents, where, in principle, it is not in the interest of companies to improve our therapies—certainly not to the extent that would eliminate disorders. Treatments that cure rather than maintain disorders risk leading to a fall in company revenues and, as the example of using antibiotics to cure ulcers shows, companies will make efforts to block the adoption of cures that appear on the horizon. Getting rid of the incentive to develop a blockbuster that product patents offer would reorient drug development back to what most people think both medicine and pharmaceutical companies are trying to do, which is to eliminate the scourge of disease.

Furthermore, the ability to have an exclusive patent on a drug creates conditions suitable to blockbuster marketing. As drugs have increased in celebrity status in the 1990s and 2000s, any independent assessments made of the therapeutic advantages offered by new drugs have consistently indicated that these have been minimal at best. Indeed, pharmaceutical companies now seem to be able to make blockbusters out of drugs that are virtual carbon copies of already available and cheaper drugs—Nexium out of Prilosec, Lexapro out of Celexa, Lyrica out of Neurontin. These are companies who are masters at generating and maintaining wants rather than companies who are any good at making drugs. Indian and Chinese pharmaceutical companies are today more innovative when it comes to producing novel and needed drugs than are the Western pharmaceutical manufacturers. As long as our companies can make their money from our wants there is no need for them to meet our needs.

It is far from clear that we need any patents on medicines. Asian companies have produced innovative compounds profitably without the protections of a product patent system. And as the makers of generic drugs show, a great deal of money can be made from drugs that are off-patent or sold over the counter. If patents are needed, one option is to reduce the length of protected time companies get for their patents—this was the option favored by Kefauver in 1962. Another option is to return to a system that offers patents on processes rather than products—a system that worked well in Germany for a century and led to the greatest rate of discovery of therapeutically useful drug treatments ever. If product patents are retained, at the very least we should insist on a return to the spirit of the law—namely that we, the community, will offer your company certain privileges in return for a genuine benefit.

Companies argue that the high cost of developing drugs, put at up to a billion dollars per drug, means they need the returns they get from the current system. But the greater part of these costs come from clinical trials that are in fact part of marketing and these costs escalate the weaker and less needed a drug is. The current patent system is central to both drug development costs and drug prices, and if we want to reduce drug prices the patent system has to change.

We have in fact engineered a lose-lose scenario. The current arrangements underpin the development of blockbusters that have become so important to the health of companies that they are prepared to conceal trials or adverse events that might pose problems for their marketing, ghostwrite such trials as are published, and aggressively counter attempts by doctors to describe problems that arise in the course of therapy. This is a situation that is as toxic to good medical care as it is possible to have.

THE FACTORIES OF POSTMODERNISM

In the 1990s a dispute blew up that has since been called the Science Wars.[18] At its most extreme, scientists who viewed the products of science as real were faced with radical skeptics, postmodernists from the humanities, who appeared to deny the reality of anything. Everything, including scientific articles, the postmodernists claimed, were just texts whose truth value was uncertain.

Postmodernism is linked to modern science. Once we in the West had seen God's revelation as coming in two books, the Bible and the Book of Nature. The rise of science led on to a radical or modernist doubt about the events portrayed in the text of the Bible. For a period, science remained immune to the crisis of belief in the biblical text, or indeed became a substitute for the lost certainties produced by viewing the Bible as simply a text. But as scientific advances began to show that older scientific "truths" were far from true, science itself faced a new radical doubt, postmodernism, that contested its claims to possess any revelation.

The response of science has been that any attempt to restructure science along postmodernist lines would produce a cargo cult. In the course of World War II, US Air Force planes flew into islands in the Pacific, disgorging all sorts of goods. Some of the islanders were so impressed by the appearance of these flying cornucopias that long after the US military left they maintained the runways and control huts, beside which they continued to fly the American flag, in the apparent belief that the right appearances would lead to the right results. These were the cargo cults. For scientists reality is not a text that can be read one way today and another tomorrow. The ultimate defense of science has been that its planes fly, whereas having postmodernists in a laboratory would reproduce the airstrips and the US flag—and leave us waiting forever for results.

The new drugs developed from the 1940s to the 1970s, based on breakthroughs in biology, pharmacology, and other medical sciences, meant the pharmaceutical industry of the time was about as far removed from a cargo cult as it was possible to be. In the face of such advances there was very little place for radical doubt. The first darkening of the medical horizon came in the 1960s with concerns about the emergence of a technological society, concerns that were applied to medicine by Ivan Illich in the 1970s. Illich's critique of medicalization came at a time when many had sensed the first intimations that not all was well with medicine.[19] The criticism at the time was directed at medicine itself, an apparently all-powerful institution, increasingly arrogating to itself the right to pronounce on life, death, and disability—not at industry.

Illich's critique crystallized battle lines already emerging between a medical sciences camp and a social sciences camp over "the medical gaze," discussed in chapter 6. For one side this gaze was good, for the other it was dehumanizing. Some critics saw an overlap between scientists, physicians, and capitalism on the one side, and social scientists and socialism on the other. The degree of identification here is not important and it varied widely. But the key point is that there was an opposition, issues were contested, and the debate was open to a wider public. At its extreme it spawned an antipsychiatry that contested the legitimacy of any mental illnesses. Three decades on, debate has all but ceased.

The turn to quantification in medicine has transformed social scientists, medical anthropologists, and others into Stepford handmaidens of the establishment who embrace the New Biology. A medico-pharmaceutical complex has triumphed; everyone seemingly accepts that it would be irrational to do anything but act in accordance with the "evidence." Any sustained attempt to critique current trends is now likely to be dismissed as not evidence-based or as an advocacy of postmodernism that denies the reality of disease or scientific progress—in just the way that critics of psychoanalysis were once deemed ipso facto to have an unresolved neurosis.

But, while we now have in branches of medicine the appearances of science—controlled trials, a relentless quantification, and a sometimes stupefying recourse to statistics—the health care planes aren't flying any more, in the United States especially. In fact quite the opposite, over the past two decades the figures for life expectancy in developed countries show the United States falling progressively behind other developed countries, despite spending more money on healthcare than any other nation on earth—falling behind as well in terms of any ability to care, as the expectation that we will be rescued by magic has led us to neglect many of the caring skills we had.[20]

Meanwhile, the marketing departments of pharmaceutical companies are the postmodernists par excellence. They rewrite the text that is the human body from year to year with afflictions such as osteopenia, erectile dysfunction, and pediatric bipolar disorder that appear out of nowhere, creations of ghostwriters who practice to deceive.

Take Donna, for example. In marketing Zyprexa for bipolar disorder, in 2002, Lilly produced Donna, "a single mom, in her mid-30s appearing in your office in drab clothing and seeming somewhat ill at ease. Her chief complaint is 'I feel so anxious and irritable lately.' Today she says she has been sleeping more than usual and has trouble concentrating at work and at home. However, several appointments earlier she was talkative, elated, and reported little need for sleep. You have treated her with various medications including antidepressants with little success. . . . You will be able to assure Donna that Zyprexa is safe and that it will help relieve the symptoms she is struggling with."[21]

In the 1960s and 1970s Donna would have been seen as anxious, a poster case for treatment with Valium. In the 1990s, presenting with the same symptoms, she would have been seen as depressed, and in need of treatment with Prozac. Neither neuroscience nor any aspect of clinical science had moved forward by 2002 in a manner that might justify rediagnosing Donna as bipolar. But this doesn't stop companies who are quite happy to read the vast majority of our problems one way today and quite another tomorrow.

And when it comes to the hazards of Zyprexa Donna may suffer from, just as with the hazards of the Lipitor she may have to take because Zyprexa has raised her cholesterol levels, or the Celebrex she may be on because of arthritis linked to Zyprexa-induced weight gain, or the Avandia she needs because Zyprexa has caused diabetes, Donna and her doctor will find themselves up against a radical skepticism. When it comes to the hazards of a pharmaceutical company's drug, the rules of science do not apply and causality, it seems, can never be proven. A more succinct definition of the arch-skepticism of postmodernism cannot be found than the phrase "doubt is our product."

Almost the only critique left in town is limited to attributing all our problems to conflict of interest—the reason things are going wrong is that companies can hire academics to proselytize on their behalf. Somewhat ironically the champion of this charge has been a Republican senator, Chuck Grassley, rather than anyone from academia or the "left."[22] While Grassley has been nothing if not magnificently persistent in pursuing academics with links to pharmaceutical companies, forcing a number of eminent figures[23] to resign from their university posts, and in proposing a Sunshine Act,[24] his activism risks creating the impression that our problems stem primarily from a few rotten apples in the academic barrel rather than from anything more deep-seated. This is postmodernism for the twenty-first century—the text gets written according to the interests of the piper who pays the tune.

This superficial conflict-of-interest critique helps industry by focusing attention away from their unwillingness to allow access to the data. It is ignorant of the history of science, forgetting that John Snow's case for removing the handle on the Broad Street Pump was only aired because it was in the interest of the owners of local abattoirs and other businesses who were being blamed for the cholera epidemic to provide a platform for these views that supported them.[25] It appears to imply that the State rather than private companies will need to run clinical trials or fund the academics who will present the results of these trials but this forgets that the specter of conflict of interest in science was first raised by another Republican—Dwight Eisenhower—concerned that public funding of research might lead to a military-industrial complex: "In holding scientific research and discovery in respect, as we should, we must also be alert to the equal and opposite danger that public policy itself could become the captive of a scientific and technological elite."[26] If there is no access to the data, it is immaterial if the funding for science comes from private or public sources.

Eisenhower caught a glimpse of a world in which both the market and science might become forces for alienation rather than liberation. We have arrived there. This is a failure of historic proportions—seen rarely before except in the former Soviet Union. In the face of this failure, some belated critiques of practices such as ghostwriting or concerns about conflict of interest are profoundly inadequate.

In the face of the industrial postmodernism we see today, we need to recapture the ability to say that an increase in mortality is an increase in mortality and blockbuster drugs cause adverse events. We need to be able to recognize that little that glistens with statistical significance is therapeutic gold, and refuse to allow companies, their experts, and regulators to stand common sense on its head. Speaking out would be a way for doctors and scientists to demonstrate the "right stuff." In addition to helping remedy our current difficulties, doing so might engage a wider public in the task of making real progress possible, rather than have us lulled into quiescence by fantasies of progress.

We need our media studies and other university departments to deconstruct industry rhetoric. But we also need to recover a belief in real progress and a faith in the biological sciences that would explain what lies behind the correlations thrown up by controlled trials. At present, in part because it suits industry, doctors are being taught that the controlled trials of evidence-based medicine are the answer to medicine's problems rather than being taught that they are a first step on the road to an answer—just as John Snow's isolation of the Broad Street Pump as a source of the cholera epidemic in London in 1856 was the first step on the road to an answer rather than itself the answer. It was Robert Koch's discovery of bacteria rather than Snow's researches that explained the cluster of events in Broad Street. Koch's work opened the way to a raft of inputs from the laboratory sciences into medical care that flourished in the work of clinicians like Richard Cabot a few years later.

THE FUTURE OF MEDICAL CARE

The juxtaposition of markets and health produces shudders, jolts, and every so often quakes as the tectonic plates of production, efficiency, equity, and choice collide. Americans embrace markets because they want choice—they don't want to be dictated to. Europeans have steered away from markets in medicine, seeing both equity and strength in the musketeer's one for all and all for one.

James Lind opened his treatise on scurvy in 1753 with the statement that "armies have been supposed to lose more of their men by sickness, than by the sword." Perhaps aware that empires and economies have been more likely to be destroyed by plagues and pestilences than by losses on the battlefield, Europeans have placed greater emphasis on ensuring the production of health by making it free and if necessary compulsory.[27] But the development in our day of biological interventions, from cosmetic surgery to risk management medicines, that have the appearance of medical treatments but far from enhancing productivity and well-being almost certainly reduce it, parasitize universal health care to the point where it may not survive. No one would ever have thought to include the proprietary medicines of the nineteenth century in a universal health care system, but this is close to what is happening now. And as a consequence, universal healthcare is also today under threat in Europe, where healthcare costs are rapidly rising toward American levels.

Americans meanwhile have seen the market deliver extraordinary developments in technology. They have seen transformations in living standards happening globally, and they believe that to some extent these developments have hinged on responses to consumer demand. Even within the health domain, consumer demand, for better or worse, has led to rapid developments in, for instance, cosmetic surgery. Pharmaceutical company executives lead the queue to say that if the same forces were unleashed more widely within the rest of medicine, we would solve all our healthcare problems.[28]

If, as commonly believed, both markets and science deliver progress, it seems inconceivable to many that the domain in which markets and science interact to the greatest extent would be one characterized by decline rather than progress. But when it comes to pharmaceuticals, because of prescription-only arrangements, the current operation of patent laws, the sequestration of trial data, the ease with which medical experts can be seduced by junk epidemiology, and the extent to which bad data has driven out good data, this is not a market that can respond to patient pressure. It is a market where patient pressure is perverted by pharmaceutical marketing campaigns, where outcomes can get worse with no apparent consumer (medical) concern, a market in which the mental sets of consumers (doctors) have been captured so that it is difficult for them to conceive of alternatives to those being sold to them, a market in which there is almost no possibility of discrepant data emerging to trigger a thought that might be unwelcome to a pharmaceutical company, a rigged market that operates in terms of five-year plans. Indeed, it is a polity, rather than a market, that in its control of information is perhaps best described as totalitarian.

Hitherto one of the major selling points of the Western way of doing things has not been the availability of consumer products such as Levi jeans so much as progress in health—our children have been less likely to die in infancy or childhood, our men and women less likely to succumb to a crabbed age and more likely to live beyond the traditional three-score and ten years. But there is a growing disenchantment with the Western way of doing things. And there is a growing likelihood that we in the West will be regarded as the new barbarians as we feed antipsychotic drugs to infants and envisage children as young as eight years old being put on drugs like the statins. Even though we have an increasing number of hospitals that look more like hotels, complete with gourmet meals and the latest online entertainment, there will be many who view these as the products of a healthcare system that is losing sight of some of the most precious things about being human, a system in which values are becoming valueless, a system in which ticking boxes is more important than trust in people, a system that, as a result, is losing its abilities to heal.

After Cora descended into Hades, in the face of Demeter's insistence, Zeus buckled and she returned as Persephone, bringing life back to the planet with her. After a wondrous period of time in the middle of the twentieth century when we combined to force open the gates of Hades and rescue children who might otherwise have died, today's Demeters find themselves faced with pharmaceutical companies adept at using a mother's wish to get the best possible treatment for her family, including the child in her womb, to expand their markets. In a tale of almost mythic resonance in its own right, Estes Kefauver, using the example of children deformed by thalidomide, attempted to restore wonder and force Hades back but ended up being outflanked. If with Demeter we hold that care of the sort outlined in these pages is the heartbeat of our world, we need to take up Kefauver's cause and see it through. Whether that heart continues to beat is up to each of us.

Notes

INTRODUCTION

1. Joseph T. Freeman, *Dr. Alfred J. Worcester: Early exponent of modern geriatrics*, Bulletin NY Academy of Medicine 64, 246–251 (1988).

2. Derek Kerr, *Alfred Worcester: A pioneer in palliative care*, American Journal of Hospice and Palliative Care, May, 13–36 (1992).

3. Charles Crenner, *Private Practice. The Early Twentieth-Century Medical Office of Dr. Richard Cabot* (Baltimore: Johns Hopkins University Press, 2006).

4. Ivan Illich, *Medical Nemesis: The Limits of Medicine* (London: Calder and Boyars, 1975).

5. http://www.socialaudit.org.uk/6070225.htm (accessed Feb. 27, 2007); on this Social Audit website, the section entitled "No Cards Please", announces the retirement of Charles Medawar and introduces the notion of Pharmageddon.

6. Charles Medawar, Graham Dukes, Tim Reed, Andrew Herxheimer, and David Healy, "Pharmageddon," http://www.socialaudit.org.uk/60700716 .htm#Pharmageddon (accessed July 30, 2007).

7. Jason Lazarou, Bruce H. Pomeranz, and Paul N. Corey, *Incidence of adverse drug reactions in hospitalized patients: A meta-analysis of prospective studies*, JAMA 279, 1200–1205 (1998).

8. John Abramson, *Overdosed America: The Broken Promise of American Medicine* (New York: Harper Perennial, 2004).

9. Jerome Kassirer, *On the Take* (New York: Oxford University Press, 2006); Marcia Angell, *The Truth about the Drug Companies* (New York: Random House, 2006); Merrill Goozner, *The $800 Million Pill* (Berkeley: University of California Press, 2004); Sheldon Krimsky, *Science in the Private Interest* (Lanham, MD: Rowman and Littlefield, 2004); Ray Moynihan and Alan Cassels, *Selling Sickness* (New York: Nation Books, 2005); Jeremy Greene, *Prescribing by Numbers* (Baltimore: Johns Hopkins University Press, 2007);

Alicia Mundy, *Dispensing with the Truth* (New York: St. Martin's Press, 2003); Abramson, *Overdosed America*; Melody Petersen, *Our Daily Meds* (New York: Farrar, Straus and Giroux, 2008); Alison Bass, *Side Effects* (Chapel Hill, NC: Algonquin, 2008).

10. Hank McKinnell, *A Call to Action* (New York: McGraw Hill, 2005).

11. Daniel Callahan and Angela A. Wasunna, *Medicine and the Market: Equity v. Choice.* (Baltimore: Johns Hopkins University Press, 2006).

12. Philippe Pinel (1809), *Traité médico-philosophique sur l'aliénation mentale*, in *Treatise on Mental Alienation*, trans. Gordon Hickish, David Healy, and Louis Charland, xiii (Chichester: John Wiley and Sons, 2009).

13. Kalman Applbaum, "Marketing Global Healthcare: The Practices of Big Pharma," *Socialist Register*, http://www.mcareol.com/mcolfree/mcolfre1/visiongain/blockbuster.htm (accessed June 17, 2008).

14. Spending on pharmaceutical drugs is listed at several locations on the IMS Health website; see http://www.imshealth.com (accessed June 28, 2008).

15. http://www.imshealth.com/deployfiles/imshealth/Global/Content/StaticFile/Top_ Line_Data/Global_Top_15_Therapy_Classes.pdf (accessed May 1, 2011).

CHAPTER 1

1. Alfred Worcester, *Past and present methods in the practice of medicine,* Boston Medical and Surgical Journal 166, 159–164 (1912).

2. Worcester, *Past and present methods in the practice of medicine.*

3. Arthur Kleinman, *The Illness Narratives* (New York: Basic Books, 1988).

4. Michael Oldani, *Filling Scripts: A Multi-Sited Ethnography of Pharmaceuticals Sales Practices, Psychiatric Prescribing, and Phamily Life in North America* (PhD dissertation, Princeton University, 2006).

5. http://www.decodog.com/invent/psychological1.html (accessed Oct. 27, 2009); available from the author.

6. http://www.fiercepharma.com/special-reports/pfizer-top-13-advertising-budgets (accessed Oct. 10, 2010).

7. Hank McKinnell, *A Call to Action* (New York: McGraw Hill, 2005).

8. Charles C. Mann and Mark L. Plummer, *The Aspirin Wars* (New York: Alfred A. Knopf, 1991).

9. Kalman Applbaum, *The Marketing Era* (New York: Routledge, 2004).

10. Applbaum, *The Marketing Era.* See also Kalman Applbaum, *Pharmaceutical marketing and the invention of the medical consumer,* PLoS Medicine 3, e189 (2006).

11. Joseph Liebenau, Medical Science and Medical Industry (Basingstoke: Macmillan Press, 1987).

12. James H. Young, *The Medical Messiahs: The Social History of Health Quackery in Twentieth-Century America* (Princeton: Princeton University Press, 1992).

13. Liebenau, *Medical Science and Medical Industry.*

14. Claude C. Hopkins, "My Life in Advertising" (1927), cited in James H. Young, *The Medical Messiahs: The Social History of Health Quackery in Twentieth-Century America*, 21 (Princeton: Princeton University Press, 1992).

15. British Medical Association, *Secret Remedies* (London: British Medical Association, 1909).

16. Charles E. Rosenberg, "The Therapeutic Revolution: Medicine, Meaning and Social Change in Nineteenth-Century America," in *The Therapeutic Revolution*, ed. M.J. Vogel and C.E. Rosenberg, 3–25 (Philadelphia: University of Pennsylvania Press, 1979).

17. British Medical Association, *Secret Remedies*.

18. Cited in BMJ 328:137 (2004), doi:10.1136/bmj.328.7452.1371.

19. Liebenau, *Medical Science and Medical Industry*; P.J. Hilts, *Protecting America's Health: The FDA, Business and One Hundred Years of Regulation* (New York: Alfred A. Knopf, 2003).

20. Edward S. Shorter, "Primary Care," in *The Cambridge Illustrated History of Medicine*, ed. Roy Porter (Cambridge: Cambridge University Press, 1996).

21. Mann and Plummer, *Aspirin Wars*.

22. Giulio Mandich, *Venetian patents (1450–1550)*, Journal of the Patent Office Society 30, 177 (1948); Frank D. Prager, *The early growth and influence of intellectual property*, Journal of the Patent Office Society 34, 106–140 (1952).

23. Christine MacLeod, *Inventing the Industrial Revolution. The English Patent System, 1660–1800* (Cambridge: Cambridge University Press, 1988); see Section 6, An Act concerning Monopolies and Dispensations with Penal Laws, and the Forfeitures thereof (better known as the Statute of Monopolies).

24. Peter Drahos and John Braithwaite, *Information Feudalism: Who Owns the Knowledge Economy?* (London: Earthscan, 2002).

25. Jean-Paul Gaudilliere, *How pharmaceuticals became patentable: The production and appropriation of drugs in the twentieth century*, History and Technology 24, 99–106 (2008); Maurice Cassier, *Brevets pharmaceutiques et sante publique en France*, Enterprise et histoire 36, 29–47 (2004).

26. Intriguingly, they also argued that patenting would confer state approval on certain drugs, offering their manufacturers a commercial advantage that could lead to injuries if the true hazards of the new drugs had not been fully recognized.

27. Michael Bliss, *The Discovery of Insulin* (Toronto: McClelland and Stewart, 1982).

28. http://en.wikipedia.org/wiki/Jonas_Salk.

29. David Healy, *The Antidepressant Era*, chap. 2 (Cambridge, MA: Harvard University Press, 1998).

30. Drahos and Braithwaite, *Information Feudalism*. The outlines of this agreement appear to have been formulated within Pfizer in the 1980s. It took a decade to make its way into international trade agreements.

31. India adopted a patent law in sync with Western laws in 2005 but before that the TRIPS agreement, which had significant input from Western pharmaceutical companies, came into being in 1995.

32. A new molecule should not come from an already patented class of drugs, except when this particular compound from within that class can be shown to

do something that other molecules in the class don't do. For example, a minor variation on the 1940s drug promazine, an antihistamine, made by adding a single chlorine ion, in 1950 produced a quite differently acting drug, chlorpromazine, the first of the antipsychotics. Another minor variation of promazine produced imipramine, the first of the antidepressants, and after that a series of other compounds were constructed that in addition to treating mental illness, by virtue of their different biological actions, opened mechanisms of the brain up to fresh investigation.

33. US Patent No. 5,229,382, filed on May 22, 1992 (a continuation of an application filed on April 23, 1991). European patent, EP-A- 0,454,436, filed on April 24, 1991.

34. At the point the parent was being patented, these isomers will have been declared and activity usually assigned to one of them.

35. David Healy, *Let Them Eat Prozac* (New York: New York University Press, 2004).

36. David Healy, "From Mania to Bipolar Disorder," in *Bipolar Disorder*, ed. Y. Latham and M. Maj (Chichester: John Wiley and Sons, 2009).

37. http://www.cafepress.com/bipolartshirts (accessed Sept. 1, 2007).

38. *Staying Well . . . with Bipolar Disorder*, Relapse Prevention Booklet (produced in association with the Manic-Depressive Fellowship sponsored by Eli Lilly and Company, 2005), 17.

39. Shankar Vedantam, "Suicide risk tests for teens debated," *Washington Post*, June 16, 2006; Shankar Vedantam, "The depressionist," *Washington Post*, May 26, 2009.

40. David Sheahan, "Angles on panic," in *The Psychopharmacologists*, ed. David Healy, 3, 479–504 (London: Arnold, 2000).

41. See Cora's story, chap. 7.

42. Thomas Hage, *The Demon under the Microscope* (New York: Harmony Books, 2006).

43. Richard Harris, *The Real Voice* (New York: Macmillan Press, 1964), 13.

44. Harris, *Real Voice*, 89.

45. Cited in Harris, *Real Voice*, 86.

46. Harris, *Real Voice*.

47. Cited in Harris, *Real Voice*, 76.

48. Harris, *Real Voice*, 47.

CHAPTER 2

1. Alexis Jetter, "Pregnant pause," *Vogue*, May 2009, 144–146

2. American Medical Association, *Nostrums and Quackery* (Washington, DC: American Medical Association Press, 1912).

3. Steven R. Belenko, *Drugs and Drug Policy in America* (Westport: Greenwood Press, 2000); David F. Musto, *The American Disease: Origins of Narcotic Control* (New York: Oxford University Press, 1987); Steven B. Karch, *A Brief History of Cocaine* (Boca Raton, FL: CRC Press, 1998).

4. Leo Meyler, *Side Effects of Drugs* (New York: Elsevier, 1952).

5. Philip Knightley, Harold Evans, E. Potter, and M. Wallace, *Suffer the Children: The Story of Thalidomide* (London: Andrew Deutsch, 1979).

6. Peter Temin, *Taking Your Medicine: Drug Regulation in the United States* (Cambridge, MA: Harvard University Press, 1980).

7. Louis Lasagna, *Congress, the FDA and new drug development: Before and after 1962*, Perspectives in Biology and Medicine 32, 322–343 (1989).

8. C. Robin Ganellin, "Cimetidine," in *Chronicles of Drug Discovery*, ed. Jasjit S. Bindra and Daniel Lednicer, 1–37 (New York: John Wiley and Sons, 1990).

9. Matthew Lynn, *The Billion-Dollar Battle: Merck v Glaxo* (London: Mandarin, 1991).

10. Barry J. Marshall (ed.), *Helicobacter Pioneers* (Carlton South: Blackwell, 2002).

11. Leigh Thompson, memo, Exhibit 98 in Forsyth v. Eli Lilly (Feb. 7, 1990).

12. Zyprexa Product Team Off-Site. Zyprexa: MultiDistrict Litigation 1596, Document ZY201548768 (July 25, 2001).

13. Gary D. Tollefson, Zyprexa Product Team: 4 Column Summary. Zyprexa: MultiDistrict Litigation 1596, Document ZY200270343 *(*1997); available on http://www.furiousseasons.com/zyprexa.docs (accessed Feb. 10, 2007).

14. Christoph U. Correll et al., *Cardiometabolic risk of second-generation antipsychotic medications during first-time use in children and adolescents*, JAMA 302, 1765–1773 (2009); Christopher K. Varley and Jon McClellan, *Implications of marked weight gain associated with atypical antipsychotic medications in children and adolescents*, JAMA 302, 1811–1812 (2009).

15. Terence Young, *Death by Prescription* (Toronto: Key Porter Books, 2001).

16. Lynn, *The Billion-Dollar Battle*, 18.

17. http://www.mcareol.com/mcolfree/mcolfre1/visiongain/blockbuster.htm (accessed June 17, 2008).

18. Lilly documents, *Cross-Brand Segmentation*. Zyprexa: MultiDistrict Litigation 1596, Document ZY200085380 and Document ZY200083203 (2000); available on http://www.furiousseasons.com/zyprexa.docs (accessed Feb. 10, 2007).

19. Lilly documents, *Cross-Brand Segmentation*. Zyprexa: MultiDistrict Litigation 1596, Document ZY200085380 and Document ZY200083203 (2000); available on http://www.furiousseasons.com/zyprexa.docs (accessed Feb. 10, 2007).

20. Lynn, *The Billion-Dollar Battle*, 19.

21. Edward Shorter, *From Paralysis to Fatigue: A History of Psychosomatic Illness in the Modern Era*, 311–313 (New York: Free Press, 1992).

22. Francoise Simon and Philip Kotler, *Building Global Biobrands*, 147 (New York: Free Press, 2003).

23. Julie M. Donohue, Merisa Cavasco, and Meredith B. Rosenthal, *A decade of direct-to-consumer advertising of prescription drugs*, New England Journal of Medicine 357, 673–681 (1991).

24. Pfizer's Lyrica emerged for fibromyalgia at this point.

25. Glen Spielmans, *Duloxetine does not relieve painful physical symptoms in depression: A meta-analysis*, Psychotherapy and Psychosomatics 77, 12–16 (2008).

26. George Ashcroft, "The receptor enters psychiatry," in *The Psychopharmacologists*, ed. David Healy, 3, 189–200 (London: Arnold, 2000).

27. Jeremy Greene, *Prescribing by Numbers* (Baltimore: Johns Hopkins University Press, 2007).

28. Steven Woloshin and Lisa M. Schwartz, *Giving legs to restless legs: A case study of how the media makes people sick*, PLoS Medicine 3, 170–174 (2006), doi:10.1371/journal.pmed.0030170. Just as GERD has been extended to infantile colic, so has restless legs to what used to be called growing pains in children, who accordingly now are likely to be treated with dopamine agonists—drugs that come with a risk of cardiovascular collapse and death.

29. Peter Kramer, *Listening to Prozac* (New York: Viking Press, 1993).

30. E. Fuller Torrey, *The going rate on shrinks: Big pharma and the buying of psychiatry*, The American Prospect, 15–16 (July 2002).

31. Daniel Bell, *The cultural contradictions of capitalism* (New York: Basic Books, 1995); Thomas Franks, *Commodify your Dissent* (New York: Norton, 1999); Joseph Heath and Andrew Potter, *The Rebel Sell: How the Counterculture Became Consumer Culture* (Chichester: Capstone, 2005).

32. Dora B. Weiner, *The Citizen-Patient in Revolutionary and Imperial Paris* (Baltimore: Johns Hopkins University Press, 2002).

33. Laurie Garrett, *Betrayal of Trust: The Collapse of Global Public Health* (New York: Hyperion, 2000).

34. Merrill Goozner, *The $800 Million Pill* (Berkeley: University of California Press, 2004).

35. British Medical Association, *Secret Remedies* (London: British Medical Association, 1909).

36. L. Kilker v. SmithKline Beecham d/b/a GlaxoSmithKline, First Judicial District of Pennsylvania, Civil Trial Division no. 1813 (Sept. 3, 2009).

37. John H. Coverdale, Laurence B. McCullagh, and Frank A. Chervenak, *The ethics of randomized placebo controlled trials of antidepressants with pregnancy women: A systematic review*, Obstetrics and Gynecology 112, 1361–1368 (2008); Anne Drapkin Lyerly et al., *Risk and pregnant body*, Hastings Center Report 39, 34–42 (2009) ; David Healy, Derelie Mangin, and Barbara Mintzes, *The ethics of randomized placebo controlled trials of antidepressants with pregnant women*, International Journal of Risk and Safety in Medicine 22, 1–10 (2010), doi:10.3233/JRS-2010–0487.

CHAPTER 3

1. Jason Dana and George Loewenstein, *A social science perspective on gifts to physicians from industry*, JAMA 290: 2, 252–255 (2003).

2. Michael A. Steinman, Michael G. Shlipak, and Steven J. McPhee, *Of principles and pens: Attitudes of medicine house staff toward pharmaceutical industry promotions*, American Journal of Medicine, 110, 551–557 (2001).

3. Meredith Wadman, *The senator's sleuth*, Nature 461, 330–33 (Sept. 17, 2009).

4. James Lind, *A Treatise of the Scurvy* (1752; Edinburgh: Edinburgh University Press, 1953), 145.

5. Philippe Pinel, *Traité médico-philosophique sur la manie* (1800), trans. D. Davis (London: Cadell and Davies, 1806).

6. Philippe Pinel, *Traité médico-philosophique sur l'aliénation mentale* (1809), trans. Gordon Hickish, David Healy, and Louis C. Charland (Chichester: John Wiley and Sons, 2009).

7. Pierre C.A. Louis, cited in A.M. Lilienfeld, *Ceteribus paribus: The evolution of the clinical trial*, Bulletin of the History of Medicine 56, 1–18, 6 (1982).

8. Pierre C.A. Louis, cited in M.D. Rawlins, *Development of a rational practice of therapeutics*, BMJ 301, 729–733 (1990).

9. L.M. Lawson (1849), cited in Charles E. Rosenberg, "The therapeutic revolution: Medicine, meaning and social change in nineteenth-century America," in *The Therapeutic Revolution*, ed. M.J. Vogel and C.E. Rosenberg, 20 (Philadelphia: University of Pennsylvania Press, 1979).

10. Rabies turned out to be caused by a virus rather than a bacterium.

11. Roy Porter, *The Greatest Benefit to Mankind* (London: Fontana Press, 1999).

12. Martha Marquardt, *Paul Ehrlich* (New York: Henry Schumann, 1951).

13. Paul De Kruif, *Microbe Hunters* (New York: Harcourt, 1926).

14. Sandra Hempel, *The Strange Case of the Broad Street Pump: John Snow and the Mystery of Cholera* (Berkeley: University of California Press, 2009).

15. Lawrence Altman, *Who Goes First? The Story of Self-Experimentation in Medicine* (New York: Random House, 1987).

16. Sanjeebit J. Jachuk, H. Brierley, S. Jachuk and P.M. Willcox, *The effect of hypotensive drugs on the quality of life*, Journal of the Royal College of General Practitioners 32, 103–105 (1982).

17. Ronald Fisher, *The Design of Experiments* (Edinburgh: Oliver and Boyd, 1935).

18. Steven T. Ziliak and Deirdre N. McCloskey, *The Cult of Statistical Significance: How the Standard Error Cost Us Jobs, Justice and Lives* (Ann Arbor: University of Michigan Press, 2008).

19. A phrase widely attributed to Charlie Poole.

20. Gordon C. Smith and Jill P. Pell, *Parachute use to prevent death and major trauma related to gravitational challenge*, BMJ 327, 1459–1461 (2003).

21. Thomas Hager, *The Demon under the Microscope* (New York: Harmony Books, 2006).

22. Philip J. Deveraux and the POISE Study Group, *Effects of extended release metoprolol succinate in patients undergoing non-cardiac surgery (POISE trial): A randomized controlled trial*, Lancet 371 (2008), doi:10.1016/S0140-6736(08) 60601-7.

23. Marc A. Pfeffer, Emmanuel A. Burdmann, Chao-Yin Chen et al., *A trial of darbepoetin alfa in type 2 diabetes and chronic kidney disease and anemia*, NEJM 361 (2009), doi:10.1056/NEJMoa0907845; Philip A. Marsden, *Treat-*

ment of anemia in chronic kidney disease: Strategies based on evidence, NEJM 361 (2009), doi:10.1056/NEJMe0909664.

24. Bruce M. Psaty and Richard A. Kronmal, *Reporting mortality findings in trials of rofecoxib forAlzheimer disease or cognitive impairment*, JAMA 299, 1813–1817 (2008).

25. Harry Collins and Trevor Pinch, *Dr. Golem. How to Think about Medicine* (Chicago: University of Chicago Press 2005).

26. Mary Robertson and Michael Trimble, *Major tranquilizers used as antidepressants*, J Affective Disorders 4, 173–193 (1982).

27. David Healy, *Let Them Eat Prozac* (New York: New York University Press, 2004).

28. The data for this figure stem from the FDA's review of antidepressants drugs. M. Stone and L. Jones, Clinical Review (2006), 31; http://www.fda.gov/ohrms/dockets/ac/06/briefing/2006-4272b1-index.htm.

29. Neither the data nor the arguments here apply to severe cases of depression in secondary care, melancholia for instance. This works to the advantage of companies, who can portray the much smaller placebo response in melancholia as good evidence that antidepressants do in fact work.

30. David Healy, *The assessment of outcome in depression: Measures of social functioning*, Reviews in Contemporary Pharmacotherapy 11, 295–301 (2000).

31. Daniel Kahnemann, Paul Slovic, and Amos Tversky, *Judgment under Uncertainty: Heuristics and Biases* (Cambridge: Cambridge University Press, 1982).

32. ALLHAT (The antihypertensive and lipid-lowering treatment to prevent heart attack trial), *Major outcomes in high-risk hypertensive patients randomized to angiotensin-converting enzyme inhibitor or calcium channel blocker vs. diuretic*, JAMA 288, 2981–2997 (2002).

33. Healy, *Let Them Eat Prozac*.

34. Joseph F. Wernicke et al., *Low-dose fluoxetine therapy for depression*, Psychopharmacology Bulletin 24, 183–188 (1988).

35. Jean Thuillier, *Ten Years that Changed the Face of Mental Illness*, trans. Gordon Hickish (London: Martin Dunitz, 1999).

36. David J. Osborn et al., *Relative risk of cardiovascular and cancer mortality in people with serious mental illness from the United Kingdom's General Practice Research Database*, Archives of General Psychiatry 64, 1123–1131 (2007); Sukanta Saha, David Chant, and John McGrath, *A systematic review of mortality in schizophrenia*, Archives of General Psychiatry 64, 1123–1131 (2007).

37. Archibald Cochrane, *Effectiveness and Efficiency* (London: Nuffield Provincial Hospitals' Trust, 1972).

38. "Percentage of practice that is evidence based" (Sheffield University website): http://www.shef.ac.uk/scharr/ir/percent/html (accessed Oct. 30, 2009).

39. Iain Chalmers, Kay Dickerson, and Thomas C. Chalmers, *Getting to grips with Archie Cochrane's Agenda*, BMJ 305, 786–788 (1992).

40. David L. Sackett, Brian R. Haynes, Gordon Guyatt, and Peter Tugwell, *Clinical Epidemiology: A Basic Science for Clinical Medicine* (Boston: Little

Brown, 1985); David L. Sackett and William M. Rosenberg, *The need for evidence-based medicine*, Journal of the Royal Society of Medicine 88, 620–624 (1995).

41. David Healy and Marie Savage, *Reserpine exhumed*, British Journal of Psychiatry 172, 376–378 (1998).

42. David L. Davies and Michael Shepherd, *Reserpine in the treatment of anxious and depressed patients*, Lancet 117–121 (1955).

43. Michael Shepherd, "Psychopharmacology: Specific and non-specific," in *The Psychopharmacologists*, ed. David Healy, 2, 237–257 (London: Arnold, 1998).

44. F. Horace Smirk and E. Garth McQueen, *Comparison of rescinamine and reserpine as hypotensive agents*, Lancet 115–116 (1955); Douglas C. Wallace, *Treatment of hypertension. Hypotensive drugs and mental changes*, Lancet 116–117 (1955).

45. Martin H. Teicher, Carol Glod, and Jonathan O. Cole, *Emergence of intense suicidal preoccupation during fluoxetine treatment*, American Journal of Psychiatry 147, 207–210 (1990).

46. Charles Medawar and Anita Hardon, *Medicines Out of Control?* (Amsterdam: Aksant, 2004).

47. Austin Bradford Hill, *Reflections on the controlled trial*, Annals of the Rheumatic Diseases 25, 107–113 (1966).

CHAPTER 4

1. These include commercial/financial, legal, and patent departments, as well as the relatively separate manufacturing operations.

2. CenterWatch, *State of the Clinical Trials Industry* (Boston: CenterWatch, 2009).

3. Kurt Eichenwald and Gina Kolata, "A doctor's drug studies turn into fraud," *New York Times*, May 17, 1999; Steve Stecklow and Laura Johannes, "Questions arise on new drug testing. drug makers relied on clinical researchers who now await trial," *Wall Street Journal*, Aug. 15, 1997; Carl Elliott, "Guinea pigging. Healthy human subjects for drug safety trials are in demand. But is it a living?" *New Yorker*, 36–41, Jan. 7, 2008.

4. E-mail from Ian Barton to Richard Eastell and Aubrey Blumsohn, cc M. Royer, April 24, 2003.

5. Aubrey Blumsohn, *Authorship, ghost-science, access to data and control of the pharmaceutical scientific literature—who stands behind the word?* American Association for the Advancement of Science Professional Ethics Reports 19 (Summer 2006), http://www.aaas.org/ssp/sfr1/per/per46.pdf.

6. Claire Dyer, *Aubrey Blumsohn: Academic who took on industry*, BMJ 340, 22–23 (2010).

7. Rather than break the law, companies use strategies such as distinguishing between parent and local companies or company-initiated and investigator-initiated studies—conveniently some of the most awkward results may lie in studies that can be defined as other than company studies.

8. Names include Alliance, Adis Communications, Alpha-Plus, Axis Healthcare Communications, ClinResearch, Complete Healthcare Communications, Current Medical Directions, Envision Pharma, Evolution Medical Communications, Excerpta Medica, Gardiner-Caldwell, GYMR, HealthCare Project Management, Heron Evidence Development, IntraMed, Lowe Fusion Healthcare, MedBio Publications, Medical Writes, MSource Medical Development, Pacific Communications, Pharmanet, Ruder Finn, Scientific Therapeutics Information, Synapse Medical Communications, Thompson Scientific Connections, Watermeadow Medical, and Wolters Kluwer Health.

9. WPP stands for Wire and Plastics Products PLC. But it has moved so far from its original business, to being the largest advertising agency in the world, that it is only called WPP today.

10. From GYMR website (accessed Feb. 25, 2004).

11. David Healy, *Let Them Eat Prozac* (New York: New York University Press, 2004).

12. There are recognized quality measures for reporting the results of RCTs including, for instance, specifying the randomization procedures and the primary endpoints of the original trial protocol. In blind assessments of the reports of trials run by industry compared to independent studies, those done by industry rate higher. When it comes to box ticking, medical writers are specialists in the exercise where academics are not.

13. Bruce M. Psaty and Richard A. Kronmal, *Reporting mortality findings in trials of rofecoxib for Alzheimer disease or cognitive impairment*, JAMA 299, 1813–1817 (2008).

14. Catherine DeAngelis and Phil B. Fontanarosa, *Impugning the integrity of medical science: The adverse effects of industry influence*, JAMA 299, 1833–1836 (2008).

15. See http://www.healyprozac.com for the entire document.

16. Armen Keteyian, "Suicide epidemic among veterans," *CBS News Investigates*, Nov. 13, 2007, http://www.cbsnews.com/stories/2007/11/13/cbsnews_investigates/main3496471.shtml. A CBS news investigation uncovers a suicide rate for veterans twice that of other Americans.

17. See http://www.healthyskepticism.org/presentations/2007/Study329.ppt (accessed Sept. 1, 2010).

18. Jon Jureidini, Leemon B. McHenry, and Peter R. Mansfield, *Clinical trials and drug promotion: Selective reporting of Study 329*, International Journal of Risk and Safety in Medicine 20, 73–81 (2009).

19. Alison Bass, *Side Effects* (Chapel Hill, NC: Algonquin Books, 2008).

20. Martin D. Keller, Neal D. Ryan, and Michael Strober et al., *Efficacy of paroxetine in the treatment of adolescent major depression: A randomized, controlled trial*, Journal of the American Academy of Child and Adolescent Psychiatry 40, 762–772 (2001).

21. See http://www.healthyskepticism.org/presentations/2007/Study329.ppt.

22. E-mail from Sally Laden to Daniel Burnham re Par 222 manuscript, Dec. 14, 2000.

23. Louis Sulman, *Certain conditions in which a volatile vasoconstrictor has proved of particular value—A preliminary report*, Medical Times 63, 374–375 (1935).

24. Nicholas Rasmussen, *On Speed: The Many Lives of Amphetamine* (New York: New York University Press, 2008).

25. Rasmussen, *On Speed*.

26. Rasmussen, *On Speed*.

27. Soma Weiss, *Chemical structure: biological action: therapeutic effect*, NEJM 220, 906–911 (1939).

28. Rasmussen, *On Speed*.

29. Louis Lasagna, "Back to the future: Evaluation and drug development 1948–1998," in *The Psychopharmacologists*, ed. David Healy, 2, 135–166 (London: Arnold, 1998).

30. Sandra Hempel, *The Strange Case of the Broad Street Pump: John Snow and the Mystery of Cholera* (Berkeley: University of California Press, 2009).

31. Robert Whitaker, *Anatomy of an Epidemic* (New York: Crown Publishers, 2010).

32. David Michaels, *Doubt Is Their Product* (New York: Oxford University Press, 2008).

33. Michaels, *Doubt Is Their Product*.

34. James Turk and Jon Thompson, *Universities at Risk: How Politics, Special Interests and Corporatization Threaten Academic Integrity* (Toronto: Lorimer Press, 2008).

35. Jason Lazarou, Bruce H. Pomeranz, and Paul N. Corey, *Incidence of adverse drug reactions in hospitalized patients: A meta-analysis of prospective studies*, JAMA 279, 1200–1205 (1998).

36. Charles M. Beasley et al., *Fluoxetine and suicide: A meta-analysis of controlled trials of treatment for depression*, BMJ 303, 685–692 (1991).

37. Ian Oswald, Letter, BMJ 303, 1058 (1991).

38. All correspondence is available on http://www.healyprozac.com.

39. M.N. Graham Dukes and Barbara Schwartz, *Responsibility for Drug-Induced Injury* (New York: Elsevier, 1988).

40. David Healy, Guest Editorial: *A Failure to Warn*, International Journal of Risk and Safety in Medicine 12, 151–156 (1999).

41. David Healy, *Emergence of antidepressant-induced suicidality*, Primary Care Psychiatry 6, 23–28 (2000).

42. Carl Elliott, Introduction, in *Prozac as a Way of Life*, ed. Carl Elliott and Tod Chambers (Durham, NC: Duke University Press, 2004). The original articles were P. Kramer, *The valorization of sadness: Alienation and melancholic temperament*, Hastings Center Report 30, 13–19 (2000); C. Elliott, *Pursued by happiness and beaten senseless: Prozac and the American Dream*, Hastings Center Report 30, 7–12 (2000); D. DeGrazia, *Prozac, enhancement and self-creation*, Hastings Center Report 30, 34–40 (2000); J.C. Edwards, *Passion, activity and "the care of the self,"* Hastings Center Report 30, 31–33 (2000); D. Healy, *Good science or good business?* Hastings Center Report 30, 19–22 (2000).

43. Cited in Elliott, Introduction, in *Prozac as a Way of Life*.

44. David Healy and Dinah Cattell, *The Interface between authorship, industry and science in the domain of therapeutics*, British Journal of Psychiatry 182, 22–27 (2003).

45. Aubrey Blumsohn, http://scientific-misconduct.blogspot.com(accessed Sept. 25, 2006).

46. The full letter read: "The report by the pharmaceutical industry was replete with exhortations that we should recognise the partnership industry have with academia. But it is difficult to know what kind of partnership you can have with an organisation that breaches the fundamental norms of science and threatens to sue those who point this out. Readers should be in little doubt that THES, the Lancet and BMJ soft-pedal on publication of issues like this on the counsel of their lawyers. At a recent Royal College meeting on conflict of interest, when College members expressed concern about industry suppression of data among other things, an industry spokesperson asked those assembled how Britain's leaders in that particular academic field, the 25 professors who, over and above their salaries, earned more than £150,000 per annum from links to industry, would view proposals to control conflict of interest. He also invited the College to take into account the fact that 40% of life assurance policies were invested in pharmaceutical shares and that anything that hurt industry would be bad for doctors. Where once medicine and the pharmaceutical industry were beating a way upstream in efforts to remedy some of humanity's real afflictions, industry turned into the current some years ago, dragging medicine back with it. In the process patients have been deserted in favour of a far greater number of consumers who could be super-sized on drugs they don't need for conditions like osteoporosis—if only the 'science' can be used to scare people into consuming. This new pharmaceutical industry would no more welcome a real partnership with science than would the fast-food or tobacco industries."

47. Jon Jureidini, Leemon B. McHenry, and Peter R. Mansfield, *Clinical trials and drug promotion: Selective reporting of Study 329*, International Journal of Risk and Safety in Medicine 20, 73–81 (2009). See also Melanie Newman, *The rules of retraction*, BMJ 341, 1246–1248 (2010).

48. David Healy, *Did regulators fail over selective serotonin reuptake inhibitors?* BMJ 333, 92–95 (2006).

49. Catherine De Angelis, *The influence of money on medical science*, JAMA 296, 996–998 (2006).

50. Cathryn Clary, *Zoloft: Publications Steering Committee Update* (July 27, 2000); document made available in Szybinski Case, available from the author.

51. David Healy and Dinah Cattell, *The Interface between authorship, industry and science in the domain of therapeutics*, British Journal of Psychiatry 182, 22–27 (2003).

52. L. Duggan et al., *Olanzapine for schizophrenia*, Cochrane Database of Systematic Reviews Issue 2 (2005), art. no.: CD001359, doi:10.1002/14651858 .CD001359.pub2.

53. Clary, *Zoloft: Publications Steering Committee Update*.

54. American College of Neuropsychopharmacology, *Preliminary report of the task force on SSRIs and suicidal behavior in youth*, Neuropsychopharmacology 31, 473–492 (2006).

55. Gary D. Tollefson et al., *Absence of a relationship between adverse events and suicidality during pharmacotherapy for depression*, Journal of Clinical Psychopharmacology 14, 163–169 (1994); Andrew Leon et al., *Prospective study of fluoxetine treatment and suicidal behavior in affectively ill subjects*, American Journal of Psychiatry 156, 195–201 (1999); Charles B. Nemeroff, Michael T. Compton, and Joseph Berger, *The depressed and suicidal patient: Assessment and treatment*, Annals of the New York Academy of Science 932, 1–23 (2001).

56. Kimberly A. Yonkers et al., *The management of depression during pregnancy: A report from the American Psychiatric Association and the American College of Obstetricians and Gynecologists*, General Hospital Psychiatry 31, 403–413 (2009).

57. Herschel S. Jick, James A. Kaye, and Susan Jick, *Antidepressants and the risk of suicidal behaviors*, JAMA 292, 338–342 (2004).

58. Charles M. Beasley et al., *Fluoxetine and suicide: A meta-analysis of controlled trials of treatment for depression*, BMJ 303, 685–692 (1991).

59. Robert D. Gibbons et al., *The relationship between antidepressant prescription rates and rate of early adolescent suicide*, American Journal of Psychiatry 163, 1898–1904 (2006).

60. Gardner Harris, "Senator Grassley seeks financial details from medical groups," *New York Times*, Dec. 7, 2009, http://www.nytimes.com/2009/12/07/health/policy/07grassley.html.

61. Duff Wilson, "Medical Schools quizzed on ghostwriting," *New York Times*, Nov. 17, 2009, http://www.nytimes.com/2009/11/18/business/18ghost.html.

62. Meredith Wadman, *The senator's sleuth*, Nature 461, 330–334 (2009).

63. http://www.gsk-clinicalstudyregister.com (accessed Oct. 23, 2009).

CHAPTER 5

1. Deborah Cohen, *Complications: Tracking down the data on oseltamivir*, BMJ 339, 1342–1347 (2009); Peter Doshi, *Neuraminidase inhibitors: The story behind the Cochrane review*, BMJ 339, 1348–1351 (2009).

2. Fiona Godlee, *We want raw data now*, BMJ 339, 1319 (2009).

3. Andrew Mosholder, *Review and evaluation of clinical data, application NDA # 20–272 (11th May 1993)*, cited in Robert Whitaker, *Mad in America* (Boston: Perseus Publishing, 2001).

4. David Healy, *The Creation of Psychopharmacology* (Cambridge, MA: Harvard University Press, 2002).

5. Richard Harris, *The Real Voice* (New York: Macmillan, 1964).

6. Robert Rosenheck et al., *Effectiveness and cost of olanzapine and haloperidol in the treatment of schizophrenia: A randomised controlled trial*, JAMA 290, 2693–2702 (2003); Jeffrey A. Lieberman et al., *Effectiveness of antipsychotic drugs in patients with chronic schizophrenia*, NEJM 353, 1209–1223 (2005); Peter B. Jones et al., *Randomized controlled trial of the effect on quality of life of second vs first generation antipsychotic drugs in schizophrenia*, Archives of General Psychiatry 63, 1079–1087 (2006).

7. Trevor A. Sheldon and George D. Smith, *Consensus conferences as drug promotion*, Lancet 341, 100–102 (1993).

8. J.F. Guest, W.M. Hart, R.F. Cookson, and E. Lindstrom, *Pharmacoeconomic evaluation of long-term treatment with risperidone for patients with chronic schizophrenia*, British Journal of Medical Economics 10, 59–67 (1996).

9. Stephen Almond and Orla O'Donnell, *The cost-effectiveness of olanzapine compared to haloperidol in the treatment of schizophrenia in the UK*. Final report prepared for Lilly Industries, Personal Social Services Research Unit, University of Canterbury (1996), PharmacoEconomics 17, 383–389 (2000).

10. Ann Mortimer et al., *Consensus statement on schizophrenia standards in care for maintenance therapy and poorly responding/treatment intolerant patients*, CINP meeting. International Journal of Neuropsychopharmacology 1, Abstracts Supplement (1998).

11. David Healy, *Psychopharmacology and the ethics of resource allocation*, British Journal of Psychiatry 162, 23-29 (1993).

12. Donald Eccleston, *The economic evaluation of antidepressant drug therapy*, British Journal of Psychiatry 163, Supplement 20 (1993).

13. Ffion Johnstone, Ian Rickard, and David Healy, *The costs of psychotropic medication*, British Journal of Psychiatry 167, 112–113 (1995).

14. See Dwight McKee and Allen Jones v. Henry Hart, Sydni Guido, Wesley Rish, Albert Masland, James Sheehan, and Daniel P. Sattele, CIVIL ACTION No. 4: CV-02–1910, in US District Court for the Middle District of Pennsylvania; M. Petersen, "Making drugs, shaping the rules: Big Pharma is eager to help states set medication guidelines," New York Times, Feb. 1, 2004, sec. 3:1, 10.

15. Timothy Kendall, Linsey McGoey, and Emily Jackson, *If NICE was in the USA*, Lancet, doi:10.10116/5c E (2009); Fiona Godlee, *NICE at 10*, BMJ 338, 344 (2009).

16. Carroll W. Hughes et al., *The Texas children's medication algorithm project: Report of the Texas consensus conference panel on medication treatment of childhood major depressive disorder*, Journal of the American Academy of Child and Adolescent Psychiatry 38, 1442–1454 (1999).

17. States that adopted the guidelines include Pennsylvania, California, Colorado, Nevada, Illinois, Kentucky, New Mexico, New York, Ohio, South Carolina, Maryland, Missouri, and Washington DC; in some cases, jurisdictions within these states adopted the guidelines.

18. Rob Waters, "Medicating Aliah," *Mother Jones*, May/June 2005, 50–55.

19. Duff Wilson, "Poor children likelier to get antipsychotics," *New York Times*, Dec. 12, 2009, http://www.nytimes.com/2009/12/12/health/12medicaid.html?_r=2&scp=1&sq=antipsychotics&st=cse.

20. National Institute for Health and Clinical Excellence (NICE), *Guidance on the use of newer (atypical) antipsychotic drugs for the treatment of schizophrenia*, Technology Appraisal Guidance 43 (June 2002), available at http://www.nice.org.uk.

21. L. Duggan et al., Olanzapine for schizophrenia, Cochrane Database of Systematic Reviews Issue 2, Art. No.: CD001359 (2005), doi:10.1002/14651858.CD001359.pub2.

22. David Healy et al., *Lifetime suicide rates in treated schizophrenia: 1875–1924 and 1994–1998 cohorts compared*, British Journal of Psychiatry 188, 223–228 (2006).

23. Joanna Le Noury et al., *The incidence and prevalence of diabetes in patients with serious mental illness in North West Wales: Two cohorts 1875–1924 and 1994–2006 compared.* BMC Psychiatry 8, 67 (2008), doi:10.1186/1471-244X-8-67.

24. This statement is based on my access to the data submitted to the Canadian regulator as part of a legal action on the patenting of Zyprexa.

25. This is based on conversations with some of those involved in the process.

26. Jeffrey A. Lieberman et al., *Effectiveness of antipsychotic drugs in patients with chronic schizophrenia*, NEJM 353, 1209–1223 (2005); Peter B. Jones et al., *Randomized controlled trial of the effect on quality of life of second vs first generation antipsychotic drugs in schizophrenia*, Archives of General Psychiatry 63, 1079–1087 (2006).

27. David Healy and David Nutt, *British Association for Psychopharmacology consensus on statement on childhood and learning disabilities psychopharmacology*, Journal of Psychopharmacology 11, 291–294 (1997).

28. Carroll W. Hughes et al., *The Texas children's medication algorithm project: Report of the Texas consensus conference panel on medication treatment of childhood major depressive disorder*, Journal of the American Academy of Child and Adolescent Psychiatry 38, 1442–1454 (1999).

29. "Depression: 3 million kids suffer from it. What you can do," *Newsweek*, Oct. 7, 2002, 52–61.

30. Vera H. Sharav, *The impact of FDA modernization act on the recruitment of children for research*, Ethical Human Sciences and Services 5, 83–108 (2003).

31. Martin D. Keller et al., *Efficacy of paroxetine in the treatment of adolescent major depression: A randomized, controlled trial*, Journal of the American Academy for Child and Adolescent Psychiatry 40, 762–772 (2001).

32. Kendall, McGoey, and Jackson, *If NICE was in the USA.*

33. Graham J. Emslie et al., *A double-blind, randomized placebo-controlled trial of fluoxetine in depressed children and adolescents*, Archives of General Psychiatry 54, 1031–1037 (1997). The internal FDA medical review of the trial makes it clear it was a negative study.

34. Graham J. Emslie et al., *Fluoxetine for acute treatment in children and adolescents: A placebo-controlled randomized clinical trial*, Journal of the American Academy of Child and Adolescent Psychiatry 41, 1205–1215 (2002). It is common in clinical trials to stop previous treatments and to put everyone on placebo for a week or two before starting the trial proper. This is called either the washout or the placebo run-in period, and its stated purpose is to wash out any prior drug treatments. It is common to exclude patients responding to placebo during this period.

35. David J. Carpenter et al., *Safety of Paroxetine in the Treatment of Children and Adolescents with OCD*, Abstract 58, presented at the 40th annual NCDEU meeting (2001); Daniel A. Geller et al., *Efficacy and Safety of Paroxetine in Pediatric OCD: Results of a Double-Blind Placebo Controlled Trial,*

presented at the 42nd Annual NCDEU Meeting, Session III–16 (2002) (also presented at the APA annual meeting, Philadelphia, May 2002, NR 349); Karen D. Wagner et al., *Safety and Tolerability of Paroxetine in Children and Adolescents: Pooled Results from Four Multi-center Placebo-Controlled Trials,* presented at the 42nd Annual NCDEU Meeting, Session II–61 (2002).

36. Karen D. Wagner et al., *Efficacy of sertraline in the treatment of children and adolescents with major depressive disorder: Two randomized controlled trials,* JAMA 290, 1033–1041(2003).

37. Wagner et al., *Efficacy of sertraline in the treatment of children and adolescents with major depressive disorder.*

38. Central Medical Affairs Team, *Seroxat. Adolescent Depression. Position Piece on the Phase 111 studies,* Oct. 1998, SmithKline Beecham Confidential Document, available from the author. This is also available on the Canadian Medical Association Journal website. W. Kondro, *Drug company experts advised staff to withhold data about SSRI use in children,* Canadian Medical Association Journal 170, 783 (2004), http://www.healthyskepticism.org/files/docs/gsk/paroxetine/study329/19981014PositionPiece.pdf.

39. This statement is based on my knowledge of what trials had been undertaken from scrutiny of company databases and the FDA's published statements about the trials that had been submitted to them.

40. Editorial: *Depressing research,* Lancet 363, 1335 (2004).

41. This is based on conversations with the key players in NICE at this time.

42. Anyone involved in framing guidelines is now involved in business and their judgments can have far-reaching financial consequences, as the money involved in the patent extensions for the SSRIs demonstrates. The story of another SSRI given to children may make this clear. Celexa (citalopram) was discovered by the Danish company Lundbeck and marketed by Forrest Laboratories in the United States. In 1996, Lundbeck started a trial of Celexa in children that wasn't published until 2006. In 2002, Forrest ran another study of Celexa in children in the United States. As the controversy surrounding antidepressants for children grew, Forrest personnel made presentations of their "data" for Celexa, which appeared to show it worked and was free of risks. A ghostwritten report on the results of the second study was published in June 2004; see Karen D. Wagner et al., *A randomized placebo-controlled trial of citalopram for the treatment of major depression in children and adolescents,* American Journal of Psychiatry 161, 1079–1083 (2004). There was no mention in all this of the earlier, unpublished Lundbeck study in which Celexa had failed to beat placebo and in which the rate of suicidality on Celexa was dramatically higher than on placebo (A.L. Von Knorring et al., *A randomized, double-blind, placebo-controlled study of citalopram in adolescents with major depressive disorder,* Journal of Clinical Psychopharmacology 26, 311–315 (2006). To the stock market analysts reviewing company share prices, Celexa looked good compared to the other drugs, which were running into trouble at the time. The Teamsters Union invested pension funds in the stock, while company board members sold stock and made money. As news of the earlier study spread, however, the value of Forrest's stock dropped. The Teamsters Union then took a securities action that resulted in a $65 million settlement in their favor (B.

Maier and B. Carey, "Drug maker accused of fraud," *New York Times*, Feb. 25, 2009, http://www.nytimes.com/2009/02/26/business/26drug.html?_r=3&ref =health). There is clearly a lot more at stake in these exercises than there ever had been in traditional medical trials.

43. Melanie Newman, *The rules of retraction*, BMJ 341, 1246–1248 (2010).

44. Erick H. Turner et al., *Selective publication of antidepressant trials and its influence on apparent efficacy*, NEJM 358, 252–260 (2008).

45. Jean Delay and Pierre Deniker, *38 Cas de psychoses traitées par la cure prolongée et continue de 4560 RP*, C.R. Congrès Méd Alién Neurol France 50, 497–502 (1952).

46. National Institute for Health and Clinical Excellence (NICE), *Bipolar disorder: Clinical Guideline 38* (2006), available at http://www.nice .org.uk.

47. Sumant Khanna et al., *Risperidone in the treatment of acute mania: Double-blind, placebo-controlled study*, British Journal of Psychiatry 187, 229–234 (2005).

48. Sandhya Srinivasan et al., *Trial of risperidone in India—concerns*, British Journal of Psychiatry 188, 489–492 (2006).

49. There are two versions of the guideline. A longer technical version makes it clear childhood bipolar disorder should not be diagnosed unless children meet the criteria for the adult form of the illness; the shorter version does not mention this. The shorter version is the one that has been disseminated.

50. http://www.best-practice.net (accessed Jan. 4, 2010).

51. In the case of overactive bladder, in clinical trials patients on anticholinergic drugs like Detrusitol used in instances of what once was called urge incontinence go to the toilet one less time in forty-eight hours. Renaming the condition as overactive bladder increased the numbers of patients from twelve to thirty million in the United States with trials showing the same minimal benefit—but substantial side effects.

52. P. Colbrook, *Can you ignore guidelines?* BMJ Careers, 143–144 (April 9, 2005).

53. Tim Croudace et al., *Impact of the ICD-10 primary health care (PHC) diagnostic and management guidelines for mental disorders on detection and outcome in primary care: Cluster randomized controlled trial*, British Journal of Psychiatry 182, 20–30 (2003); Peter Tyrer, Michael King, and J. Fluxman, *Treatment of common mental disorders in general practice: Are current guidelines useless?* British Journal of Psychiatry 183, 78 (2003).

54. Edward Evarts, "A discussion of the relevance of effects of drugs on animal behavior to the possible effects of drugs on psychopathological processes in man." in *Psychopharmacology: Problems in Evaluation*, ed. Jonathan O. Cole and Ralph W. Gerard, 284–306, esp. 302 (Washington, DC: National Academy of Sciences/National Research Council, 1959).

55. David Healy et al., *Psychiatric bed utilisation: 1896 and 1996 compared*, Psychological Medicine 31, 779–790 (2001).

56. Healy et al., *Lifetime suicide rates in treated schizophrenia*.

57. Le Noury et al., *Incidence and prevalence of diabetes in patients with serious mental illness in North West Wales*.

58. Craig W. Colton and Ronald W. Manderscheid, *Congruencies in increased mortality rates, years of potential life lost, and causes of death among public mental health clients in eight states*, Preventing Chronic Disease, 3:2 (2006), http://www.cdc.gov/pcd/issues/2006/apr/05_0180.htm.

59. Urban Osby et al., *Time trends in schizophrenia mortality in Stockholm County, Sweden: A cohort study*, BMJ 321, 483–484 (2000).

60. Matti Joukamaa, Markku Heliovaara, and Paul Knekt et al., *Schizophrenia, neuroleptic medication and mortality*, British Journal of Psychiatry 188, 122–127 (2006); David J. Osborn et al., *Relative risk of cardiovascular and cancer mortality in people with serious mental illness from the United Kingdom's General Practice Research Database*, Archives of General Psychiatry 64, 242–249 (2007); Suhanta Saha, David Chant, and John McGrath, *A systematic review of mortality in schizophrenia*, Archives of General Psychiatry 64, 1123–1131 (2007).

61. J.J.P. Kastelein et al., *Simvastatin with or without Ezetimibe in familial hypercholesterolemia*, NEJM 358, 1431–1443 (2008). Pfizer's torcetrapib was billed as doing the same, while still in development, but this development was ultimately stopped owing to a greater mortality in patients given torcetrapib; P.J. Barter et al., *Effects of Torcetrapib in patients at high risk for coronary events*, NEJM 357, 2109–2122 (2007).

62. Writing Group for the Women's Health Initiative Investigators, *Risks and benefits of estrogen plus progestin in healthy postmenopausal women: Principal results from the women's health initiative randomized controlled trial*, JAMA 288, 321–333 (2002).

63. ONTARGET, *Telmisartan, Ramipril, or both in patients at high risk for vascular events*, NEJM 358, 1547–1559 (2008).

64. Steven E. Nissen and Kathy Wolski, *Effect of Rosiglitazone on the risk of myocardial infarction and death from cardiovascular causes*, NEJM 356, 2457–2471 (2007).

65. Committee on Finance, US Senate, *Staff Report on GlaxoSmithKline and the Diabetes Drug Avandia* (2010), http://finance.senate.gov/press/Gpress/2010/prg022010a.pdf.

66. Craig J. Currie et al., *Survival as a function of HbA1c in people with type 2 diabetes: A retrospective cohort study*, Lancet (2010), doi:10.1016/S0140-6736(09)61969-3; Advance Collaborative Group, *Intensive blood glucose control and vascular outcomes in patients with type 2 diabetes*, NEJM 358, 2560–2572 (2008); Action to Control Cardiovascular Risk in Diabetes Study Group, *Effects of intensive glucose lowering in type 2 diabetes*, NEJM 358, 2545–2559 (2008).

67. Karen Davis et al., *Mirror, Mirror on the Wall: An International Update on the Comparative Performance of American Health Care* (Washington, DC: Commonwealth Fund, 2007), http://www.commonwealthfund.org/Content/Publications/Fund-Reports/2007/May; John Abramson, *Overdosed America* (New York: Harper Perennial, 2005).

68. American Academy of Pediatrics, "New AAP Policy on Lipid Screening and Heart Health in Children," http://www.aap.org/advocacy/releases/july08lipidscreening.htm (accessed Dec. 15, 2009).

69. Thomas Jefferson, Peter Doshi, Matthew Thompson, and Carl Heneghan, *Ensuring safe and effective drugs: who can do what it takes?* BMJ 342, 148–151 (2011).

70. Doron Garfinkel, Sarah Zur-Gil, and Joshua Ben-Israel, *The war against polypharmacy: A new cost-effective geriatric-palliative approach for improving drug therapy in disabled elderly people,* Israel Medical Association Journal 9, 430–434 (2007); Doron Garfinkel and Derelie Mangin, *Feasibility study of a systematic approach for discontinuation of multiple medications in older adults,* Archives of International Medicine 170, 1648–1654 (2010).

CHAPTER 6

1. Since then the FDA has added warning labels to Singulair indicating that it may cause depression and suicidality.

2. Neil Pearce, *Adverse Reaction: The Fenoterol Story* (Aukland: Auckland University Press, 2007).

3. For example, diacetyl put in processed foods as a butter flavoring leads to a bronchiolitis—referred to as popcorn lung.

4. Walter O. Spitzer et al., *The use of beta agonists and the risk of death and near death from asthma,* NEJM 326, 501–506 (1992); Shelley Salpeter, Nicholas S. Buckley, Thomas M. Ormiston, and Edwin Salpeter, *Meta-analysis: Effect of long-acting beta agonist on severe asthma exacerbations and asthma related deaths,* Annals of Internal Medicine 144, 904–912 (2006).

5. John Berger, *A Lucky Man* (Harmondsworth, UK: Penguin Books, 1973); M. Winckler, *The Case of Doctor Sachs* (New York: Seven Stories Press, 1998).

6. Steven Timmermans and Marc Berg, *The Gold Standard: The Challenge of Evidence Based Medicine and Standardization in Health Care* (Philadelphia: Temple University Press, 2003).

7. Edward Shorter and David Healy, *Shock Therapy* (New Brunswick, NJ: Rutgers University Press, 2008).

8. Hillel Schwartz, *Never Satisfied: A Cultural History of Diets, Fantasies and Fat* (New York: The Free Press, 1986).

9. Schwartz, *Never Satisfied.*

10. It is, however, difficult to know with any certainty what the prevalence of anorexia nervosa was before the 1960s. Whatever the prevalence of the disorder in some absolute sense, the number of patients accessing services for treatment was minimal compared with what came later. At one point in the 1970s and 1980s, almost all heads of psychiatric departments in London were eating- disorder researchers.

11. T.R. Dawber, G.F. Meadors, and F.E. Moore, National Heart Institute, National Institutes of Health, Public Health Service, and Federal Security Agency, Washington, DC, *Epidemiological Approaches to Heart Disease: The Framingham Study,* Presented at a Joint Session of the Epidemiology, Health Officers, Medical Care, and Statistics Sections of the American Public Health Association at the 78th Annual Meeting in St. Louis, MO, Nov. 3, 1950.

12. Theodore Eisenberg and Martin T. Wells, *Statins and adverse cardiovascular events in moderate-risk females: A statistical and legal analysis with impli-*

cations for FDA pre-emption, Journal of Empirical Legal Studies 5, 507–550 (2008).

13. In men who have had a previous cardiovascular event, lowering cholesterol levels with drugs appears to reduce their risk of dying from a further cardiovascular event. Yet even in this case, it is now clear that the statin group of drugs have anti-inflammatory properties, just like aspirin, which also reduces the risk of a further heart attack, and it may be their benefits stem from this effect rather than any action on cholesterol. These drugs act on a range of systems around the body, and it may turn out that in some cases the statins can be helpful for other reasons, but despite the vast sales of these drugs today and the numbers of people taking them, there has been almost no research looking beyond blood cholesterol levels—almost certainly because this could spoil a good marketing story.

14. John Abramson, *Overdosed America: The Broken Promise of American Medicine* (New York: Harper Perennial, 2004).

15. Ramon Estruch et al., *Effects of a Mediterranean-style diet on cardiovascular risk factors: A randomized trial,* Annals of Internal Medicine 146, 1–11 (2006).

16. Isabelle Savoie and Arminee Kazanjian, *Utilization of lipid-lowering drugs in men and women: A reflection of the research evidence,* Journal of Clinical Epidemiology 55, 97–98 (2002); Peter S. Sever et al., *Prevention of coronary and stroke events with atorvastatin in hypertensive patients who have average or lower than average cholesterol concentrations in the Anglo-Scandinavian Cardiac Outcomes Trial—Lipid lowering arm (ASCOT-LLA),* Lancet 361, 1149–1155 (2003).

17. Savoie and Kazanjian, *Utilization of lipid-lowering drugs in men and women.*

18. Colette B. Raymond et al., *Population-based analysis of statin utilization in British Columbia,* Clinical Therapeutics 29, 2107–2115 (2007).

19. Dudley Gentles et al., *Serum lipid levels for a multicultural population in Auckland, New Zealand,* New Zealand Medical Journal 120, 1–12 (2008).

20. Gentles et al., *Serum lipid levels for a multicultural population in Auckland, New Zealand.*

21. Robert A. Wilson, *Feminine Forever* (New York: M. Evans, 1966).

22. Gillian Sansom, *The Myth of Osteoporosis* (Ann Arbor, MI: Century Publications, 2003); Elaine S. Berman, *Too Little Bone: The Medicalization of Osteoporosis,* Journal of Women's Health and Law 1, 257–277 (1999).

23. K. Bassett, "On trying to stop the measurement of bone density to sell drugs," in *Tales from the Other Drug Wars,* ed. M.L. Barer et al. (Vancouver: Centre for Health Services and Policy Research, 2000).

24. http://www.npr.org/templates/story/story.php?storyId = 121609815.

25. Tamir Ali and Roger H. Jay, *Spontaneous femoral shaft fracture after long-term alendronate,* Age and Ageing 38, 625–626 (2009).

26. E.E. Roughead, K. McGeehan, and G.P. Sayer, *Biphosphonate use and subsequent prescription of acid suppressants,* British Journal of Clinical Pharmacology 57, 813–816 (2004); Redonda G. Miller et al., *Incidence of gastro-*

intestinal events among biphosphonate patients in an observational setting, American Journal of Managed Care 10, 207–215 (2004).

27. J.J. Wolff et al., *The effect of exercise training programs on bone mass: A meta-analysis of published controlled trials in pre and post-menopausal women,* Osteoporosis International 9, 1–12 (1999).

28. Max Hamilton, *A rating scale for depression,* Journal of Neurology, Neurosurgery and Psychiatry 23, 56–62 (1960).

29. Max Hamilton, "Rating Scales in Depression," in *Depressive Illness, Diagnosis, Assessment, Treatment,* ed. P. Kielholz, 100–108 (Berne: Hanns Huber Publishers, 1972).

30. David Healy, Derelie Mangin, and Barbara Mintzes, *The ethics of controlled trials in prenatal depression,* International Journal of Risk and Safety in Medicine 22, 1–10 (2010), doi:10.3233/JRS-2010-048.

31. Ray Moynihan and David Henry, *The fight against disease mongering: Generating knowledge for action,* Public Library of Science Medicine 3 (2006). All articles in this issue of the journal were on disease mongering.

32. Leonore Tiefer, *Female sexual dysfunction: A case study of disease mongering and activist resistance,* Public Library of Science Medicine 3, e178 (2006), doi:10.1371/journalpmed.0030178.

33. Jennifer Berman and Laura Berman, *For Women Only* (New York: Henry Holt, 2001).

34. *Diagnostic and Statistical Manual, Third Edition* (Washington, DC: American Psychiatric Association, 1980).

35. Kimberly A. Yonkers et al., *The management of depression during pregnancy: A report from the American Psychiatric Association and American College of Obstetricians and Gynecologists,* General Hospital Psychiatry 31, 403–413 (2009).

36. Now these drugs all carry warnings on their labels about the risk of suicide.

37. Jason Lazarou, Bruce H. Pomeranz, and Paul N. Corey, *Incidence of adverse drug reactions in hospitalized patients: A meta-analysis of prospective studies,* JAMA 279, 1200–1205 (1998).

38. The Institute for Safe Medication Practices, QuarterWatch 1–3 (2009), http://www.ismp.org/QuarterWatch/2009Q3.pd.

39. Thomas E. Bittker, *The industrialization of American psychiatry,* American Journal of Psychiatry 142, 149–154 (1985).

40. Philip M. Sinaikin, *Categorical diagnosis and a poetics of obligation: An ethical commentary on psychiatric diagnosis and treatment,* Ethical Human Sciences and Services 5, 141–148 (2003); Philip M. Sinaikin, *Coping with the medical model in clinical practice or "How I learned to stop worrying and love DSM,"* Journal of Critical Psychology, Counselling and Psychotherapy, 204–213 (2004).

41. http://www.ahrq.gov/clinic/USpstfab.htm.

42. Kimberly S. Yarnall, Kathryn I. Pollak, and Truls Ostbye, *Primary care: Is there enough time for prevention?* American Journal of Public Health 93, 635–641 (2003).

43. Larry Eliot and Daniel Atkinson, *The Gods That Failed: How Blind Faith in the Markets Has Cost Us Our Future* (London: Bodley Head, 2008).

44. James Spence, *The Purpose and Practice of Medicine* (Oxford: Oxford University Press, 1960).

45. James Lind, *A Treatise of the Scurvy* (1752; Edinburgh: Edinburgh University Press, 1953).

46. Mark Bostridge, *Florence Nightingale* (Harmondsworth, UK: Penguin Books, 2009).

47. L.J. Rather, *Collected Essays on Public Health and Epidemiology of Rudolf Virchow* (New York: Science History Publications, 1985).

48. Kenneth F. Kiple, *Plagues, Pox and Pestilence: Disease in History* (London: Weidenfeld and Nicolson, 1997).

49. Richard Harris, *The Real Voice* (New York: Macmillan Press, 1964), 64.

50. Eric Kimbuende, Usha Ranji, Janet Lundy, and Alina Salganicoff, *US Health Care Costs* (2010), http://www.kaiseredu.org/topics_im.asp?imID= 1&parentID=61&id=358 (accessed May 6, 2011); David Leonhardt, "The choice: A longer life or more stuff," *New York Times*, Sept. 27, 2006, http:// www.nytimes.com/2006/09/27/business/27leonhardt.html (accessed May 9, 2011).

51. The World Health Organization's ranking of the world's health systems, http://www.photius.com/rankings/who_world_health_ranks.html.

52. Bob Roehr, *Healthcare in the US ranks lowest among developed countries*, BMJ 337, 889 (2008).

53. Nananda Col, James E. Fanale, and Penelope Kronholm, *The role of medication noncompliance and adverse drug reactions in hospitalizations of the elderly*, Archives of Internal Medicine 150, 841–845 (1990).

54. US Congress, Congressional Budget Office, *Technological Change and the Growth of Health Care Spending* (Jan. 2008).

CHAPTER 7

1. Padmaja Chalassani, David Healy, Richard Morriss, *Presentation and frequency of catatonia in new admissions to two acute psychiatric admission units in India and Wales*, Psychological Medicine 35, 1667–1675 (2005).

2. Ray Moynihan and David Henry, *Disease Mongering is now part of the global health debate*, PLoS Medicine (2008), doi:10.1371/journal .pmed.0050106; Steven Woloshin and Lisa Schwartz, *Giving legs to Restless Legs. A case study of how the media makes people sick*, PLoS Medicine (2006), doi:10.1371/journal.pmed.0030170.

3. Jerome Groopman, *How Doctors Think* (New York: Norton, 2007).

4. Jason Lazarou, Bruce Pomeranz, and Paul Corey, *Incidence of adverse drug reactions in hospitalized patients: A meta-analysis of prospective studies*, JAMA 279, 1200–1205 (1998).

5. The Institute for Safe Medication Practices, QuarterWatch 1–3 (2009), http://www.ismp.org/QuarterWatch/2009Q3.pd.

6. Other options include pharmakosepsis, pharmacoscotoma, pharmacotoxicity, pharmakonosis.

7. Annemarie Mol, *The Logic of Care* (London: Routledge, 2008).

8. Michael Bliss, *The Discovery of Insulin* (Toronto: McClelland and Stewart, 1982).

9. Edward Shorter and David Healy, *Shock Therapy* (New Brunswick, NJ: Rutgers University Press, 2008).

10. Thomas Hager, *The Demon under the Microscope* (New York: Harmony Books, 2006).

11. Jeremy A. Greene, *Prescribing by Numbers: Drugs and the Definition of Disease* (Baltimore: Johns Hopkins University Press, 2007).

12. Greene, *Prescribing by Numbers*.

13. Louis Lasagna, *Congress, the FDA, and new drug development: Before and after 1962*, Perspectives in Biology and Medicine 32, 322–343 (1989).

14. Greene, *Prescribing by Numbers*.

15. http://www.aace.com/meetings/consensus/hyperglycemia/hyperglycemia .pdf.

16. Action to Control Cardiovascular Risk in Diabetes (ACCORD), *Effects of intensive glucose lowering in type 2 diabetes*, NEJM 358, 2545–2559 (2008).

17. John Abrahams, *Science, Politics and the Pharmaceutical Industry* (London: UCL and St. Martin's Press, 1995).

18. Dwight L. Evans et al., *Mood disorders in the medically ill: Scientific review and recommendations*, Biological Psychiatry 58, 175–189 (2005).

19. "Best Practice: Translating Scientific Discovery into CNS Therapeutic Advantage," http://www.best-practice.net (accessed June 6, 2008).

20. Gabrielle A. Carlson et al., *Methodological issues and controversies in clinical trials with child and adolescent patients with bipolar disorder: Report of a consensus conference*, Journal of Child and Adolescent Psychopharmacology 13, 13–27 (2003).

21. Peter S. Jensen et al., *Consensus report on impulsive aggression as a symptom across diagnostic categories in child psychiatry: Implications for medication studies*, Journal of the American Academy of Child and Adolescent Psychiatry 6, 309–322 (2007).

22. Testimony of David J. Graham MD, MPH, to Congress, Nov. 18, 2004, http://www.consumersunion.org/pub/core_health_care/001651.html.

23. Joseph S. Ross et al., *Pooled analysis of rofecoxib placebo-controlled clinical trial data: Lessons for postmarketing pharmaceutical surveillance*, Archives of Internal Medicine 169, 1976–1984 (2009).

24. Martin H. Teicher, Carol Glod, and Jonathan O. Cole, *Emergence of intense suicidal preoccupation during fluoxetine treatment*, American Journal of Psychiatry 147, 207–210 (1990).

25. David Healy, *The antidepressant tale: Figures signifying nothing?* Advances in Psychiatric Treatment 12, 320–328 (2006).

26. Charles M. Beasley et al., *Fluoxetine and suicide: A meta-analysis of controlled trials of treatment for depression*, BMJ 303, 685–692 (1991).

27. Using these data the relative risk for suicidal acts is 1.9 times greater on Prozac than placebo, with a 95 percent confidence interval from 0.2 to 16. This means while there is a chance that there is no increase in risk, the likeliest

guess from these data is that the increase in risk is 1.9 fold, but the data also show it could be a 16-fold greater risk.

28. Beasley et al., *Fluoxetine and suicide*; emphasis added by the author.

29. David E. Wheadon et al., *Lack of an association between fluoxetine and suicidality in bulimia nervosa*, Journal of Clinical Psychiatry 53, 235–241 (1992).

30. Food and Drug Administration, Psychopharmacological Drugs Advisory Committee, 34th Meeting, Sept. 20, 1991.

31. David Healy, *Did regulators fail over selective serotonin reuptake inhibitors?* BMJ 333, 92–95 (2006).

32. Carol Bombardier et al., VIGOR Study Group, *Comparison of upper gastrointestinal toxicity of rofecoxib and naproxen in patients with rheumatoid arthritis*, NEJM 343, 1520–1528 (2000).

33. David Armstrong, "Bitter Pill: How the New England Journal missed warning signs on Vioxx. Medical weekly waited years to report flaws in article that praised pain drug," *Wall Street Journal*, May 15, 2006.

34. Louis Lasagna, "Back to the future: Evaluation and drug development 1956 to 1996," in *The Psychopharmacologists*, ed. David Healy, 2 (London: Arnold, 1998).

35. Sandor Greenland, *Bayesian perspectives for epidemiological research*, International Journal of Epidemiology 35, 777–778 (2006).

36. Ezra Hauer, *The harm done by tests of significance*, Accident Analysis and Prevention 36, 495–500 (2004).

37. Charles Poole, *Why published epidemiology is really junk science*, Congress of Epidemiology, Toronto, June 13, 2001.

38. US Supreme Court, Matrixx Initiatives Inc. et al. v. Siracusano et al., No. 09–1156, decided March 22, 2011, 563 US.

39. Kenneth J. Rothman, *Writing for Epidemiology*, Epidemiology 9, 333–337 (1998).

40. Arif Khan et al., *Suicide risk in patients with anxiety disorders; A meta-analysis of the FDA database*, Journal of Affective Disorders 68, 183–190 (2002).

41. Khan et al., *Suicide risk in patients with anxiety disorders*.

42. Arif Khan et al., *Suicide rates in clinical trials of SSRIs, other antidepressants and placebo: Analysis of FDA reports*, American Journal of Psychiatry 160, 790–792 (2003).

43. Paul Anthony, *FDA "Drug Watch" early warnings will have lasting negative effect, PhRMA says*, The Pink Sheet, no. 001, June 2005.

44. Chris Bushe and Richard Holt, *Prevalence of diabetes and impaired glucose tolerance in patients with schizophrenia*, British Journal of Psychiatry (Supplement 47) 184, s67–71 (2004). This entire issue of the journal was a supplement paid for by Lilly. Several if not all articles will have been authored by company personnel. The other main British journal dealing with psychotropic drugs (Journal of Psychopharmacology) also included a Lilly-sponsored symposium shortly afterward. These supplements are worth a lot of money to journals and are often not peer-reviewed. The Maudsley quote appears in several of the articles in these two supplements.

45. Joanna Le Noury et al., *The incidence and prevalence of diabetes in patients with serious mental illness in North West Wales: Two cohorts 1875–1924 and 1994–2006 compared*, BMC Psychiatry 8, 67 (2004), doi:10.1186/1471-244X-8-67.

46. Barry G. Firkin and J.A. Whitworth, *Dictionary of Medical Eponyms* (Carnforth, UK: Parthenon Publishing, 1987). This volume, ironically in this context, was made available to British doctors as an educational gift from Glaxo.

47. David Michaels, *Doubt Is Their Product* (New York: Oxford University Press, 2008).

48. Parents Med Guide, *The use of medication in treating childhood and adolescent depression: Information for patients and families*, prepared by the American Psychiatric Association and American Academy of Child and Adolescent Psychiatry (2005), http://www.ParentsMedGuide.org (accessed Feb. 1, 2005).

49. American Psychiatric Association, "APA responds to FDA's new warning on antidepressants," news release, Oct. 15, 2004, http://www.psych.org/news_room/press_releases/04-55apaonfdablackboxwarning.pdf.

50. The session was convened on October 10—the 43rd anniversary of Kefauver's bill.

51. David Sheahan, "Angles on panic," in *The Psychopharmacologists*, ed. David Healy, 3, 479–504 (London: Arnold, 2000).

52. Food and Drug Administration, Psychopharmacological Drugs Advisory Committee, 34th Meeting, Sept. 20, 1991.

53. Lyam Kilker and Michelle David v. SmithKline Beecham, First Judicial District of Pennsylvania, Civil Trial Division 1813 (Sept. 2009).

54. The Tobacco Institute Inc., *Tobacco and the Health of the Nation* (San Francisco: Legacy of Tobacco Documents Library, UCSF, 1969), http://legacy.library.ucsf.edu/cgi/getdoc?tid=dxb34foo&fmt=pdf&ref=results. In a quite comparable fashion, pharmaceutical companies have promoted a series of studies that apparently showed declining suicide rates in line with rising antidepressant sales during the 1990s. For a list of such studies see Goran Isacsson et al., *Decrease in suicides among the individuals treated with antidepressants: A controlled study of antidepressants in suicide, Sweden 1995–2005*, Acta Psychiatrica Scandinavia 120, 37–44 (2009). This was most probably explained by factors like declining autopsy rates in the 1990s—a large number of suicides are only diagnosed at autopsy; see Svein Reseland et al., *National suicide rates 1961–2003: Further analysis of Nordic data for suicide, autopsies and ill-defined death rates*, Psychotherapy and Psychosomatics 77, 78–82 (2008).

55. American Psychiatric Association, "APA responds to FDA's new warning on antidepressants," news release, Oct. 15, 2004, http://www.psych.org/news_room/press_releases/04-55apaonfdablackboxwarning.pdf.

56. US District Court for the Central District of California, Flora Motus v. Pfizer Inc. (Roerig Division), CV 00-298, Nov. 11, 1999.

57. US Court of Appeal of the Ninth Circuit, Motus F v. Pfizer Inc. (Roerig Division), No 02-55372, 02-55498, Amicus Brief D Troy et al., Sept. 3, 2002.

58. US Court of Appeal of the Ninth Circuit, Motus F v. Pfizer Inc. (Roerig Division), No 02–55372, 02–55498, Amicus Brief D Troy et al., Sept. 3, 2002.

59. Montag v. Honda Motor Co., 75 F. 3d 1414, Jan. 22, 1996, http://www.appellate.net/briefs/geieramicus.pdf.

60. Joint Meeting of the CDER Psychopharmacologic Drugs Advisory committee and the FDA Pediatric Advisory Committee, Bethesda, Sept.ember 13, 2004, 435.

61. Joint Meeting of the CDER Psychopharmacologic Drugs Advisory committee and the FDA Pediatric Advisory Committee, Bethesda, Sept. 13, 2004, 332.

62. Greg D. Curfman, Stephen Morrissey, and Jeffrey Drazen, *Why doctors should worry about pre-emption,* NEJM 359, 1–3 (2009).

63. Warner-Lambert v. Kent Supreme court docket 06–1498. See www.scotuswiki.com/index.php?title=Warner-Lambert v. Kent.

64. Wyeth v. Diana Levine. In US Supreme Court, No. 06–1249 Citations 555 US 555,

65. "Supreme Court rules against Wyeth in liability case," Reuters, March 4, 2009, http://www.reuters.com/article/domesticNews/idUSTRE5233VS20090304.

66. Clifford J. Rosen, *The Rosiglitazone story: Lessons from an FDA advisory committee,* NEJM 357, 844–846 (2007), 1056/nejmp078167; Steven Nissen and Kathy Wolski, *Effect of rosiglitazone on the risk of myocardial infarction and death from cardiovascular causes,* NEJM 356, 2457–2471 (2007).

67. Deborah Cohen, *Rosiglitazone: What went wrong?* BMJ 341, 530–534, c4848 (2010).

68. Philip D. Home et al., *Rosiglitazone evaluated for cardiovascular outcomes in oral agent combination therapy for type 2 diabetes (RECORD): A multicentre, randomised, open-label trial,* Lancet 373, 2125–2135 (2009).

69. Cohen, *Rosiglitazone: What went wrong?*

70. US Senate, Committee on Finance, *Staff report on GlaxoSmithKline and the diabetes drug Avandia* (2010), http://finance.senate.gov/newsroom/chairman/release/?id = bc56b552-efc5-4706-968d-f7032d5cd2e4.

71. Adrienne Fugh-Berman et al., *Promotional tone in reviews of menopausal hormone therapy after the women's health initiative: An analysis of published articles,* Public Library of Science Medicine 8, e1000425 (2011).

CHAPTER 8

1. Annemarie Mol, *The Logic of Care* (London: Routledge, 2008).

2. Samuel Sessions and Alan Detsky, *The "Shadow Government" in Health Care,* JAMA 304, 2742–2743 (2010).

3. This is similar to the use of intelligence tests for political purposes in 1920s as outlined by Steven J. Gould. *The Mismeasure of Man* (Harmondsworth, UK: Penguin Books, 1980).

4. Deposition of Ian Hudson in Tobin v. SmithKline Beecham, Dec. 15, 2000, 30–33 (Harlow, UK).

5. Joseph S. Ross et al., *Pooled analysis of rofecoxib placebo-controlled clinical trial data: Lessons for postmarketing pharmaceutical surveillance*, Archives of Internal Medicine 169, 1976–1984 (2009).

6. Philip Fine, *Make Big Pharma provide their raw data*, University World News, Jan. 18, 2009, http://www.universityworldnews.com/article .php?story=20090115191615198.

7. Transcript from BBC Panorama program "Secrets of the Drugs Trials," Jan. 29, 2007, news.bbc.co.uk//1/hi/programmes/panorama/6317137 .stm.

8. Jon Thompson, Patricia Baird, and Jocelyn Downie, *The Olivieri Report* (Toronto: Lorimer, 2001).

9. David Healy, Derelie Mangin, and Barbara Mintzes, *The ethics of controlled trials in prenatal depression*, International Journal of Risk and Safety in Medicine 22, 1–10 (2010), doi:10.3233/JRS-2010-048.

10. Sessions and Detsky, *"Shadow Government" in Health Care*.

11. Geoffrey Venning, *Validity of anecdotal reports of suspected adverse drug reactions: The problem of false alarms*, BMJ 284, 249–253 (1982).

12. David Healy and Dinah Cattell, *The Interface between authorship, industry and science in the domain of therapeutics*, British Journal of Psychiatry 182, 22–27 (2003).

13. Erick H. Turner et al., *Selective publication of antidepressant trials and its influence on apparent efficacy*, NEJM 358, 252–260 (2008).

14. Gonzalo Laje et al., *Genetic markers of suicidal ideation emerging during citalopram treatment of major depression*, American Journal of Psychiatry 164, 1530–1538 (2007).

15. R. Bordet et al., *Analysis of the direct cost of adverse drug reactions in hospitalised patients*, European Journal of Clinical Pharmacology, 56, 935–941 (2001), doi:10.1007/s002280000260.

16. Sessions and Detsky, *"Shadow Government" in Health Care*.

17. Richard J. Wurtman and R.L. Bettiker, *The slowing of treatment discovery, 1965–1995*, Nature Medicine 1, 1122–1125 (1995).

18. Paul R. Gross and Norman Levitt, *Higher Superstition: The academic left and its quarrel with science* (Baltimore: Johns Hopkins University Press, 1994).

19. Ivan Illich, *Limits to Medicine (Medical Nemesis)* (Harmondsworth, UK: Penguin Books, 1976).

20. John Abramson, *Overdosed America: The Broken Promise of American Medicine* (New York: Harper Perennial, 2005).

21. Zyprexa: Primary Care Sales Force Resource Guide, Zyprexa MDL 1596, Plaintiffs' Exhibit 01926 (2002), 7.

22. Gardiner Harris, "Senator Grassley seeks financial details from medical groups," *New York Times*, Dec. 7, 2009, http://www.nytimes.com/2009/12/07/ health/policy/07grassley.html.

23. Emory University's Charles Nemeroff, Stanford's Alan Schatzberg, and Brown's Martin Keller—the "author" of Study 329.

24. Meredith Wadman, *The senator's sleuth*, Nature 461, 330–334 (Sept. 17, 2009).

25. Sandra Hempel, *The Strange Case of the Broad Street Pump: John Snow and the Mystery of Cholera* (Berkeley: University of California Press, 2009).

26. Dwight D. Eisenhower, Military industrial complex speech (1961), http://www.cnn.com/SPECIALS/cold.war/episodes/12/documents/eisenhower.speech (accessed April 21, 2002).

27. Kenneth Kiple, *Plagues, Pox and Pestilence* (London: Weidenfield and Nicholson, 1997).

28. Hank McKinnell, *A Call to Action* (New York: McGraw Hill, 2005).

Index

TEXT
10/12 Sabon

DISPLAY
Din

COMPOSITOR
Toppan Best-set Premedia Limited